The Film Researcher's Handbook

The Film Researcher's Handbook is a comprehensive reference guide to international film and video libraries, archives and collections. The *Handbook* will enable researchers to select footage sources by subject and location in North and South America, Asia, Australasia and Africa.

Features of the *Handbook* include:

* a guide to the perils and pitfalls of footage research

* information on fees, rights, copyright legislation and contracts

* a glossary of key terms in film research

* over 200 sources listed alphabetically both by country and by subject

* each entry gives details of opening hours, contact information, subjects and format of material held and research procedure.

Jenny Morgan is an experienced film researcher.

The Film Researcher's Handbook

A guide to sources in
North America, South America,
Asia, Australasia and Africa

Compiled by Jenny Morgan

A BLUEPRINT BOOK
published by Routledge
London and New York

First published 1996
by Routledge
11 New Fetter Lane, London EC4P 4EE

Simultaneously published in the USA and Canada
by Routledge
29 West 35th Street, New York, NY 10001

Routledge is an International Thomson Publishing company

© 1996 Compiled by Jenny Morgan

Typeset by Unwin Brothers Ltd, Woking, Surrey
Printed and bound in Great Britain by TJ Press (Padstow) Ltd, Padstow, Cornwall

British Library Cataloguing in Publication Data

A catalogue record for this book is available from the British Library

Library of Congress Cataloging in Publication Data

A catalogue record for this book has been requested

ISBN 0–415–15123–6

CONTENTS

ACKNOWLEDGEMENTS

The Film Researcher's Handbook compiled by Jenny Morgan.

Jenny would like to thank Helen Bennett and the Clipshop staff in helping with the compilation of this book.
  The publisher would like to thank Terry Moore and Helen Woodhall for the time they put into contacting archives.

Introduction

The Film Researcher's Handbook is a guide to sources of film and video-tape material in Africa, Asia, Australasia, North America and South America. The book has been compiled with the film researcher in mind, providing a good point to start research from in each country covered. The sources listed have all supplied, either directly or via agents, the information listed. Each source is actively selling film and/or videotape material. Research services without any material to sell have not been included. Most of the major collections in each country are listed along with some interesting and more obscure sources. Details of how to view the material, which formats are held, opening times, etc. will also be of great assistance.

   A film researcher's job is to provide illustrative material for a production, for example, a feature film clip to demonstrate an artiste's work, a period shot of a particular place to set the scene for a drama, or a modern stock shot of an aircraft taking off, etc. The variety of requests are endless. It is a job where you can never be completely confident that you will find the required material and often the simplest sounding clips turn out to be the most difficult to find. Having found some suitable material a film researcher then has to fulfil the technical requirements of his or her production so that the correct video or film format is ordered. Also to be negotiated are the relevant copyright fees depending on the intended audience of the finished production. There may be underlying rights to clear that the source may not have included in the copyright fees, for example, payments to actors or musicians appearing in the clip. A film researcher therefore needs good technical knowledge, to be able to negotiate fees, to be meticulous in finding potential problem areas, for example, rights that will be difficult to clear, to have a good artistic eye for selecting material and to be a tenacious researcher.

How to use this book

The book is divided into three main sections. The first is arranged by country within which companies (libraries, archives, etc.) are listed alphabetically. Each entry within this section is identified by an entry number. The second section lists companies by subject area. If an unlikely source holds material on a certain country, e.g. Villon Films in Canada has material on Cuba and Africa, then that has been included as a subject entry; otherwise it is sensible to assume that a library with location material has a good stock of material relating to its own country or immediate surroundings. The third section contains a listing of national archives.

   The index is also divided into three sections, one to identify sources holding specific subject material, another to list companies alphabetically by name and the last listing companies alphabetically within each country.

Details included in a typical entry

Entry number
This is the reference number given to each entry in the section listed by country.

Company name
This is the given name of the company including any well-known abbreviation.

Subjects
This is a summary of subject material including key words as listed in the subject index.

Contact details
Address, telephone, fax, telex and contact name(s) if given.

Description
A more detailed guide to the footage held with any relevant dates or titles of collections. It also includes information such as whether the library details are computerized, whether the rate cards, catalogues, promotional videos are available or if foreign languages (other than the native language) are spoken. Omission of any details means either the information was not received or the negative should be assumed.

Opening hours
When to contact the office (in local time).

Library components
What material is the footage held on? If film, what gauge: 16mm, 35mm or other? If video, what format: 1", D2, etc.? What line standard is the original: NTSC (National Television Standards Committee), PAL (Phase Alteration Line), or SECAM (Sequential Colour with Memory)? Libraries will often have a variety of formats but the original (master) material from which copies will be made is the most important factor.

Research
Is research always undertaken by staff or can an outside researcher visit the premises? Is an appointment necessary?

Procedure
How are enquiries dealt with? Can material be assembled on, for example, a VHS to view before selection or does it have to be viewed on the premises? Also shown is the average length of time it takes to gain access to the master material from which your copy will be made.

Foreign offices
Does the library have representatives or offices in other countries? If it does the parent company and country are indicated in the detailed description.

Film research guidelines

If embarking on film research without prior experience it is necessary to have an understanding of the likely obstacles you may encounter to ensure you do not commit your production to unforeseen costs or make

rash promises of exciting but unclearable material to enthusiastic producers or directors.

Glossary

Like most professions film research has its own commonly used terms.
These refer mainly to the technical aspects of the job. A list of these
terms and their meanings is included to help you communicate more suc-
cessfully with a library.

Actuality Material recorded at an actual event without any acting or
reconstruction.

Analogue An old method of recording. A linear recording medium still
used in news and some regional areas. Fast being replaced by digital
Beta.

Answer print *see* **Film.**

Archive An archive is dedicated to acquiring, assessing, preserving,
cataloguing and classifying film, video and documents/memorabilia relating to the film and television industry.

Broadcast standard The standard to which broadcasters and producers have to conform regarding their film/video material in order to com-
ply with the regulatory body governing the transmission of programmes.

Clearances Usually refer to the permissions needed in order to clear
the copyright of films, programmes, videos, stills, sound and documents
to be reused in another production.

Clip An extract from a completed programme or production.

Comopt *see* **Film.**

Cue sheet Usually refers to the music content of a production, giving
details of composer, publisher, musicians, title of track, etc.

Digital A high quality numerical recording offering no generation loss,
non-destructive and facilitating easy editing.

Dope sheet A form on which a cameraman records the day's shooting,
giving details of the scenes shot, the good and bad takes, etc.

Dupe Duplicate copy of a piece of material.

ENG (Electronic News Gathering) Essentially a lightweight camera orig-
inally developed for covering the news but now used for documentaries,
fly on the wall and corporate videos/films.

Film Describing a flexible material or 'base' which supports the photo-
graphic image. This may be **nitrate**, a highly unstable material which de-
teriorates with age – used mainly for 35mm before 1951 – or **safety
film**, such as acetate or polyester, etc. (always used for 16mm and
8mm). This base is then coated with an emulsion. The **gauge** refers to
the width of the film: 16mm, 35mm, 70mm, 8mm, Super 8mm, etc. A
negative is the master film put directly into the camera, which when

processed produces a negative image from which **positive** prints can then be made. A work print or slash print is normally made from the negative and used to make a trial edit producing a cutting copy, which is used as a guide to cut the negative. From the cut negative an **answer print** is made to assess the grading problems (colour matching, light and shade, etc.), then a show print or transmission print is produced taking any grading alterations into consideration. Another type of film made is **reversal**. This is a master film stock which is placed directly in the camera but which produces a positive image – used largely in the news and documentary area in the 1960s, 1970s and early 1980s prior to the emergence of **ENG**. Other types of prints used in the duplication of film at the intermediate stage (i.e. not used for final showing but to make duplicates from) are fine grain – a type of emulsion with very small silver particles producing a high quality intermediate – print, and lavender print, a 35mm stock usually made from the fine grain negative printed onto a blue positive print stock (hence the name lavender from the colour). It is used as a second master copy. Sound can be recorded on a magnetic or optical track that is separate or combined with the film. Commag refers to a film that has a magnetic strip along one edge onto which the sound is recorded. **Comopt** refers to an optical sound track printed onto the film.

Footage   A length of film expressed in feet. Often used in a general way to refer to film or video material.

fps   (frames per second). This indicates the number of frames that pass through the gate of a camera or a projector in one second. Cinema projection is usually 24 fps and television is 25 fps. The old silent films ran at a rate of anything from 18 to 21 fps so when run on modern equipment you get the funny fast walks.

FX   Abbreviation of 'effects' usually meaning sound effects, but, is also used in scripts to indicate a need for lively shots to spice up the action.

Gauge   *see* **Film.**

Line standard   The number of lines made by a signal travelling across the television screen to make up one video frame or picture. Early television used 405 lines. In the UK we now use 625 lines (or PAL – Phase Alteration Line). In the USA 525 lines (or NTSC – National Television Standards Committee) are used. In France 625 lines (or SECAM – Sequential Colour with Memory) are used.

m & e track   A music and effects track that is separate from the actual sound recorded when a film or video recording was made.

Master   The best available material from which copies can be made, not necessarily the original negative or video onto which the image was first recorded, often an intermediate or sub-master stage.

Material   General term used to describe film or video recordings.

Mute   Material that has no sound recorded onto it and probably has no sound available separately to synchronise with it; *see also* **Silent**.

Negative   *see* **Film.**

Newsreel   Any coverage, hourly, daily, weekly, of current events of political, economic and social significance, but particularly refers to the weekly news films shown in cinemas before television was widely available.

Nitrate *see* **Film.**

Original   The original film or video material onto which the pictures were first recorded and from which copies were made.

Out-takes   Rejected material not included in the final production, also know as a **Trim.**

P as B, P as C, P as T   (Programme as broadcast, programme as completed, programme as televised). Various names given to the information sheet, usually completed by a production assistant after a production, containing details of actors, royalties, locations, footage, music, etc.

Residuals   The payments writers, musicians, actors and performers require for their involvement in the reuse of a programme that they have participated in, whether it is an extract or a complete programme.

Reversal *see* **Film.**

Safety film *see* **Film.**

Silent   A film with no sound track where the picture area extends from sprocket to sprocket on the stock, not to be confused with a mute print, which has a blank sound track area and can be married up to a separate sound track.

Steenbeck   Registered trade name but often used as a generic term for a flat-bed viewing and editing table. Less likely to damage the film than projection and therefore used in archives. Other types are Prevost, Moviola, etc.

Stock shot   A sequence of film or video that could be reused in another context.

TX   Abbreviation for transmission (TXd = transmitted).

Trim *see* **Out-takes.**

UDC   (Universal Decimal Classification). A system used by film and television libraries to classify their film and television acquisitions.

Videocassette   Usually used to denote non-broadcast quality videotape of varying lengths which is housed in a plastic cassette. Generally used for viewing, for example, VHS and U-matic lowband.

Videotape   Magnetic tape used for the recording of pictures and sound which does not require laboratory processing. The various formats generally refer to the width of the tape: 2", 1", 3/4", 1/2", except in the case of the newer formats. D2 is a signal recorded in a digital or numerical expression onto the tape.

Viewing copy   Generally used to describe a copy of a film or videotape that can be viewed without interference to a master.

Researching libraries

There is no one system used by all libraries. They range from the very simple card index (or just one person's memory, particularly with private collectors) to complex computer systems. Each system has its limitations and inconveniences, although generally a computerized system does enable researchers to test their own word search ideas quickly rather than spending a long time with cross-referenced cards and massive number extensions or scanning barely viewable, randomly photographed microfiche. Once found you have to be able to understand the layout of the information to know whether the material is actually usable or (as with many archives) merely kept for posterity, the master being too fragile to copy. To this end many libraries prefer to do their own research, or only allow access to a researcher who has experience of their system. This can be frustrating when you feel sure material exists but that your contact is not searching hard enough. A persuasive but polite, amiable manner is therefore one of a film researcher's most valuable assets.

Fees

Fees can be charged from the moment a library starts looking for material for you and may vary dramatically. Different names apply to the fees you will come across; here are some of them –

Research fees   Charged if a library researches for you or sometimes if you have access to the library yourself. Extra charges can also be made for photocopies or print-outs. There is often a minimum fee so it's worth making up a full list rather than adding items one at a time.

Viewing fees   Charged for looking at the material either on the premises or if it is sent out for you to see. This could also be called a loan fee if the film or cassette needs to be returned.

Handling costs   Charged for physically getting the material out from storage, or sending it to a facility house. A minimum cost is usually incurred for up to, say, 5 items, so bear this in mind and make up a full order.

Technical costs   These are extremely variable and it is important to know exactly what you require before making costly mistakes. Technical work is normally undertaken at an approved facility house or laboratory so don't expect to be able to borrow master material and use your own discounted place. This is where some libraries make their money so make sure you get a quote before committing yourself to the order. You need to establish on what material the master exists or whether there is any choice, for example, there may be a video master you can use instead of having to use the film negative (this can be a better choice in terms of cost and quality, particularly if the video copy was made before the negative was sent out repeatedly and possibly damaged). Some master material may be totally unsuitable for your purposes, particularly if you have very high quality requirements, for example, film copies of videos are rarely acceptable and video converted from NTSC to PAL can be very disappointing. If a library has both PAL and NTSC copies of a piece of film make sure they were both made from a telecine transfer and that one tape is not a conversion of the other. Expect minimum charges for machine time – that is, the record and playback machines, plus time for the loading of each different spool. Additional expense may arise when selecting rare footage that is being preserved, from an archive. In this case you are expected to fund the making of a sub-master from which your copy will be made. The archive will keep this for itself or ostensibly for the benefit of any future (usually unlikely) customers.

Transport fees   Charged to cover the transport of the material to and from the library. Check if the library has a van service (particularly if you can wait a little longer for your material) since this prevents expensive charges for dispatch riders collecting material from outside storage, etc. Postal services are cheaper and can be very efficient, whereas courier and freight services are more costly and not necessarily quicker. Make sure you are given a choice of delivery both between the library and facility house and to you.

Licence fees/royalties   This is possibly the most complex and difficult area of all. Licence fees or royalties are fees payable to the copyright holder (or agent on his or her behalf) giving you the right to incorporate the material in your own production. The usage is normally limited to the specific production, so you cannot edit it into any future projects without prior permission. When editing has finished you are required to submit a royalty declaration to the library concerned giving the exact amount of footage used in the final cut. Some libraries will ask to see a finished copy of the production to check this and/or ask for the unused material or video sub-master to be given back to prevent further usage. Production staff are never very good at supplying this information so, consequently, most libraries charge a minimum royalty fee regardless of use so there is some return for their efforts. It is important to make clear what you want to use the footage for before ordering it. If there is only a small chance that your finished production will be sold to other territories, it is better to go back at a later date and pay for the additional rights. If, however, you have pre-sold the production and need, for example, world multimedia rights, you can benefit by paying 'up front' for these, usually getting a better deal than clearing each individual territory and medium. The clearing of rights has become extremely complicated. Some libraries publish voluminous rate cards to try to cover every option. Others do not print their rates at all, preferring to deal with each case individually. The main categories are –

   Television   Standard (regional or network); Non-standard (cable or satellite); Television commercials

   Non-Broadcast   Corporate (exhibitions, in-house usage, training); Education, schools usage (also known as non-theatric/non-paying audiences); Trapped audiences (oil rigs, aircraft)

   Theatrical   Cinema (feature and short films); Cinema commercials

   Pop promos   Normally covers usage in any medium/category

   Home video   Videograms (cassettes, disks, etc. private home use only)

   Multimedia   Normally a buy-out to include any kind of usage

   CDI/CDROM   Use of footage within computer programs (such a new area that many libraries aren't confident enough to sell for this usage at all); it would not be included in the above multimedia category.

The above categories can then be combined with various territories, or groups of territories, for example –

Single country (but not USA)

Regional

Scandinavia only

Europe only

Australasia only

USA only

World excluding or including USA

Then there is the question of how many transmissions/showings are needed and over what period of time (licence period). If you don't want a restriction on this you can pay for multiple transmissions and can have an indefinite licence period (perpetuity). The possibilities are endless and being continually asked for different quotes for different options is probably the least appealing side of both the librarians and film researcher's job.

Different rates can be applied by libraries depending on the exclusivity of their material. Sometimes you may have to pay a usage fee to the supplier of the material as well as to the copyright holder. This is often the case with public archives.

Underlying rights

When incorporating library material into a production you must always have the relevant permission(s) or right(s) to do so. In the simplest case, for example, using mute stock shot material, the only rights you will have to consider are those of the copyright owner (usually the source or represented by the source). However, if using programme extracts, sports material, feature film extracts, commercials, some news material or outtakes you could come across a multitude of different people and organizations you have to clear. These are referred to as underlying rights, being additional to the copyright clearance. This is a matter of examining the material carefully and taking advice from the source. For example, in an extract from a comedy programme you may have to clear the comedians (anybody in shot, whether speaking or not), script writers, possibly the producer, musicians and a composer. To some extent the clearances are also dependent on the use you want to put the footage to, for example, you may want to use some sports material featuring a particular athlete in a commercial you are making. This would be impossible unless you have already engaged the services of the personality in the promotion; you may be advertising a product that they would never endorse, or they may already have arrangements to promote a rival product. Another difficult situation is when the extract is used in a derogatory manner, e.g. use of a film clip to demonstrate a particularly poor bit of acting by an artist. In this circumstance to be able to produce a well-phrased, diplomatic letter explaining your intentions is essential. Different types of material have their own rules. Here are a few pointers –

Feature films In general you don't have to clear underlying rights unless an actor or producer has some control over the further use of a product, for example, Woody Allen usually does. A music declaration is always required; however, identifying incidental music in an extract can be difficult. You may also come across some television products made under a film agreement. In these cases you need advice from your source and must make sure you have a written understanding of the clearances you are required to make. Feature film extracts are strictly controlled, and by large, powerful organizations. Some flatly refuse to grant any rights and most charge enormous fees to discourage you.

The normal procedure is to contact the company's representative in your own country first (if there is one) and they will liaise with the head office for you. Clearances can take a long time so make sure you have at least four working weeks before needing the permission (i.e. your transmission date or filming date); penalty fees can be imposed for urgent clearances. An interview filmed with a star talking repeatedly about a particular film from which you are eventually refused to show clips can be a bit dull. Some companies will only license clips to the broadcaster and not the production company making the programme. In this case you would need to establish a contact name at your broadcasting company who will liaise with feature film companies for you. When contacting a feature film company you must supply the following information and preferably in writing –

1. The name, transmission date and nature of your programme – as a general rule only serious documentaries or industry related programmes will be given consideration
2. The title(s) and description of clip(s) you want to include
3. The context of use – to illustrate an interview, etc.
4. If you have any approval from the relevant star, agent, or producer, etc. it may help to support your case, so it is well worth including

News and current affairs Often this contains outside copyright material, for example, a foreign report from another TV station, amateur private footage, sports or entertainment footage. Some companies do not like their reporters to be used so if it is particularly necessary to your piece you may have seek their permission and possibly pay fees.

Animation/puppets With this kind of material you have to consider clearing the script writers, voices, music, and the puppeteers or animators.

Sports Sport is one of the most expensive areas you may encounter when dealing with clearances, unless you require a leisure or adventure type of sport. There are always federations, associations, committees to deal with – for example, the Football Association, the Olympic Committee, etc., and further usage is very tightly controlled. Some sources will carry out the clearances for you, but expect the fees to escalate considerably from their normal copyright charges.

Entertainment/comedy/performance material/drama In this area there are lots of clearances to consider, for example, dancers, choreographers, producers, comedians, musicians, conductors, writers, opera and recording companies, etc.

Out-takes/bloopers/funnies Called by a lot of different names, these are the clips that were made popular by programmes like 'It'll Be Alright On The Night', where artistes repeatedly get lines wrong, fall over, etc. This kind of material might have been transmitted (it happened during a live performance) or will have been edited out of a production. This can have a bearing on whether the clearances have to be separately negotiated or whether the clip is just seen to be an extract of a production (the fees for performers therefore coming under local union agreements and having predetermined rates). Actors making mistakes can sometimes be a sensitive area; again this is where letter-writing skills can greatly influence the recipient, the description of the clip being particularly important. It is not always easy to obtain such material; often specific programmes have contracts that provide them with exclusive access to clips, giving them the only copy. The producers of these programmes then will not sell those clips or divulge the sources that supplied them. Such programmes have arrangements with similar productions in other countries and circulate the clips only between themselves.

Commercials   This a short package containing all the performance clearance problems imaginable, artistes, musicians, writers, etc. In addition you are dealing with an advertised product so you will need approval from the manufacturer. If you are intending to use an archival commercial, i.e. one that is not currently being shown, you may find that the style no longer appeals or the agency that produced the commercial has no records of the participants.

Pop promos/publicity material   This refers to material used to accompany a band's current song or to advertise a new film or video release. This sort of material can be offered for use in a publicity context free of copyright clearance expenses but beware of the time limitations involved and the requirement to give sometimes very specific and long-winded credits. It is all very well if you have a daily magazine show, for example, and can promote a film or record at the relevant time, but don't expect to be given material free, cut it into a documentary and sell it six months later without attending to the normal clearance procedure. Pop promos and feature film clips can be very expensive to use after the promotional dates. With the different media outlets there are several opportunities to use material in a publicity context, for example, with a film there is the period of general release, the rental video release, the sell-through release and the transmission on television. Make sure your usage can be seen as promotional, however, or you will infringe the agreements between publicist and distributors.

Stills   Many productions contains stills, newspaper headlines, posters, etc. Do not assume you can automatically include them in your production and particularly not if you intend to 'lift' them from the extract for use later. If they are important to your production you will need to find out the copyright information and contact the relevant sources.

Fees payable   These depend on the age of the material and the various negotiated agreements with unions such as Equity, the Musicians' Union, the NUJ, and their counterparts in other countries. Some artistes however are not interested in the fees laid down by the unions and can demand any sum, so it is wise to investigate this before using the material and making assumptions. A lot of difficulties arise when you are clearing material for use in a relatively new medium, for example, home video or CDI. Contracts with artistes may not have included these possibilities at the time or these rights may have been bought out by another company or co-producer. Co-productions are a very obvious way of getting production money together so if you need world-wide clearance you may find you have to clear with a different company for each territory required.

Copyright legislation and implications

Copyright legislation differs from country to country and covers such things as assignments, licences, fair use, moral rights, performers' rights, secondary infringement, etc. In practice the film researcher needs a working knowledge of copyright law but relies on the legal profession for ultimate advice. Two concepts recur frequently –

Fair use/fair dealing   This refers to the provision under copyright law that enables a clip to be used without the permission of the copyright holder. The production must be newsworthy, educational or non-profit in nature. Correct acknowledgements must be displayed when using the material and you need to acquire an acceptable copy particularly if satisfying broadcast requirements. This is still an uncertain area and a good lawyer on the production is essential.

Public domain   The USA has this concept and will offer all kinds of material that doesn't require clearance other than paying the supplier. In the UK elements within a production are protected for differing lengths of time, i.e. a film may have been made over fifty years ago but it could have been based on a play protected until fifty years after the death of the author. You can also find that copyright to an archive film has been re-registered (particularly with the silent movies), a new sound track added and possibly the original negative restored. Sometimes you can get round this problem by finding an original version of the film, but again care has to be taken.

Contracts/licence agreements

It is always wise to obtain written permission to use extract material. Libraries usually have their own versions which vary in length and complexity enormously. Sometimes you are required to produce your own, which should be specially drawn up for your production by a lawyer. If a source will not sign your agreement (and lawyers can make them rather daunting) ensure you include the main elements in a letter to the source. As a guide, when composing a letter or looking though a contract before signature, make sure of the following –

1. The document clearly states that the licenser (copyright owner or library on behalf of) legally has the right to enter into an agreement with you.
2. The name of the contracting party or licensee (you) is clearly expressed and your production correctly referred to.
3. The material you are purchasing is detailed in such a way as to include everything you require. Sometimes you may be given a limit as to the length of extract you can use – make sure this is sufficient for your production and that it is not exceeded.
4. A statement covering who is responsible for any necessary clearances should be included. In practice this is nearly always the responsibility of the licensee, but, as you are relying on the source to supply the information, you could try to insert a line to the effect 'in accordance with the information supplied by licenser to licensee only and not further or otherwise'.
5. The licenser should undertake to provide you with a music cue sheet detailing the information to enable music clearances.
6. The contract should clearly state the rights you are purchasing – the media, territories, number of transmissions, etc. for the fee specified and over the term you require.
7. Check when the copyright fee is due or if any minimum charge is made regardless of use. The usage is in your control and nothing in the contract should make you legally obliged to include the material in your production.

8. Generally look out for clauses such as specific screen or verbal credits, the obligation to provide a copy of your production for the licenser to see, etc.

Researching in foreign archives

Detailed film research, like research of any kind, is a matter of dedication, leaving no stone unturned either at home or abroad. Anywhere can turn out to be a potential source of material, not just the libraries listed here. When contacting foreign sources you are obviously limited by language, differing terminologies, time zones, public holidays, etc. Added to this is the possibility and expense of viewing material before selection. It is important to find a good contact who you can communicate with. Try to establish before you go the exact procedure for researching, viewing and ordering, discovering any tedious but essential bureaucracy that has to be attended to. There would be no point in researching at the library and finding you have to wait several days or weeks for the material to appear from the vaults for viewing. This is where a fellow researcher's experience is invaluable. Try to talk to as many people as possible who might have been to or dealt with the library previously. Knowledge of your subject is important, particularly if this has to be communicated through an interpreter. Lateral thinking is an important skill in research and being able to acquaint another person with your project will enhance your chances of success.

Disclaimer

All reasonable measures have been taken to ensure the accuracy of the information in this publication, but we cannot accept responsibility for any errors or omissions therein or any liability resulting from any use or misuse of any such information or for any reliance placed thereupon.

Listing by country

Abu Dhabi

1 **NATIONAL LIBRARY - CULTURAL FOUNDATION**

Zaid the Second Street, Abu Dhabi 2380, Abu Dhabi

Subjects: National Archives.

Albania

2   **ARCHIVES D'ETAT DU FILM DE LA REPUBLIQUE D'ALBANIE**

Rue Aleksander Moisiu 76, Tirana, Albania
Ⓒ +355 42 327 33
Ⓕ +355 42 327 33

Subjects: National Archives.

Algeria

3 CENTRE DES ARCHIVES NATIONALES

B.P. 38 Birkhadem, Alger, Algeria
© +213 2 56 61 62
⚡ 62524

Subjects: National Archives.

Angola

4   CINEMATECA NACIONAL DE ANGOLA

Place Luther King 4, Luanda 3512, Angola
© +244 330918
⋏⋏ 3398 EDECINE AN

Subjects: National Archives.

Argentina

5 FOCUS STOCK FOTOGRAFICO / FABULOUS FOOTAGE

Avenue Santa Fe 3192 5 "A", Buenos Aires 1425, Argentina
© +54 1 822 5444
Ⓕ +54 1 821 6009

Subjects: Stock shots, locations, culture, industry, medicine, military, music, environmental, leisure, transport, natural history, space, trailers.

▦ Film; video (all film mastered onto tape).

Description: Complete contemporary film and videotape library with a vast range of quality images. Subject headings include agriculture, buildings, cities, countries, cultural activities, industry and business, landmarks, landscapes, medical, military, music, natural phenomena, news, period recreations, professions, rain forests, recreation, space, special effects, spectacles, sports, transportation, underwater, water and wildlife. They also hold special collections of Nazi propaganda footage, Russian history, Russian space program, B-movies and trailers. Computerized. Rate card and catalogue available. NB: Head office is in Toronto, Canada, details of Argentina office received from Canada only.

Foreign Offices: Argentina, Australia, Brazil, Canada, Chile, Germany, Indonesia, Japan, Malaysia, Philippines, Singapore, Spain, Mexico, USA.

6 FUNDACION CINEMATECA ARGENTINA

2nd Floor, Corrientes 2092, Buenos Aires 1045, Argentina
© +54 1 953 3755 / 7163
Ⓕ +54 1 951 8558

Contacts: Guillermo or Paulina Fernandez Jurade
Subjects: National Archives, feature films, documentaries, newsreels.

▦ 35mm, 16mm; video.

Research: Appointment necessary.

☺ Mon-Fri 10:00 to 17:00

Procedure: Problems at present with duplication of material.
Description: The library holds feature films, documentaries and newsreels. Not all copyrights are held.

7   IMAGE BANK / ARGENTINA

3rd Floor, Alsina 943, Buenos Aires 1088, Argentina
© +54 1 334 4099 / 1817
Ⓕ +54 1 334 4099 / 1817

Contacts: Mr Jorge Fisbein
Subjects: Stock shots, aerial photography, time-lapse, lifestyles, natural history, locations, sport.
All film and video formats and line standards held.
Research: By both staff and outside researchers. Appointment to visit.
Mon-Fri 09:00 to 17:00
Procedure: 3/4"/VHS (any line standard) for viewing. 24 hours for access to masters.
Description: Vast collection of stock material, contemporary and archival, acquired from Turner Broadcasting, Ocean Images, I.R.E., Pigeon Productions, MacGillivray Freeman Films, Dentsu Prox., McDonnell Douglas, Nature Conservancy, etc. Offices worldwide and major cities of North America - Chicago, Detroit, Mexico, Minneapolis, Atlanta, Dallas and Los Angeles. Computerized. English, French, Spanish, Italian, German and Greek spoken in the NEW YORK HEADQUARTERS.
Foreign Offices: Argentina, Brazil, Chile, Colombia, Australia, Canada, Hong Kong, Indonesia, Korea, Japan, Malaysia, Philippines, Singapore, Taiwan, Thailand, South Africa, UK, USA.

Australia

8 AUSTRALIAN BROADCASTING CORPORATION (ABC)

ABC TV Library Sales, GPO Box 9994, Sydney, NSW 2000, Australia
℡ +61 2 950 3269 / 3284
℻ +61 2 950 3277

Contacts: Cyrus Irani, Richard Carter
Subjects: Current affairs, stock shots, natural history, sport, lifestyles, locations.
🎞 16mm; Beta/Beta SP, 1", BVU, Umatic.
Research: By staff only. Clients may view in the office.
🕐 Mon-Fri 09:00 to 17:30
Procedure: VHS or Umatic viewing tapes supplied. 24 hours for access to masters.
Description: The ABC is the major government broadcaster holding Australian and international news and current affairs footage dating from 1960. They also hold a large stock footage library covering over 4000 subjects including a natural history collection, sport, lifestyle and location material. ABC are also agents for the Reuters/Visnews and Qantas libraries. Computerized. Rate card available. NB: ABC also have offices in Adelaide, Brisbane, Darwin, Melbourne, Perth and Hobart (Tasmania).

9 BEYOND INFORMATION SERVICES

Beyond 2000, 34 Hotham Parade, Artarmon, NSW 2064, Australia
℡ +61 2 438 5155
℻ +61 2 439 6549

Contacts: Lisa Savage, Annette Overton
Subjects: Medicine, science, environmental, landscapes.
🎞 Beta/Beta SP, 1", Umatic. PAL.
Research: By staff only.
🕐 Mon-Fri 09:00 to 17:30
Procedure: Viewing tapes assembled.
Description: An extensive collection of footage from internationally acclaimed science and technology series, Beyond 2000. Footage covers subjects shot worldwide and includes medical breakthroughs, laboratory work, people, robotics, Australiana, hi-tech gadgets, environment, international rural and city landscapes, wildlife, etc. Computerized. Rate card available. English and French spoken.

10   CENTRAL COAST MEDIA HOLDINGS (CCM GROUP)

1st Floor, 56 The Entrance Road, The Entrance, NSW 2261, Australia
© +61 43 331122
Ⓕ +61 43 341017

Contacts: Mark and Michelle Falzon
Subjects: Industry, natural history, aerial photography, lifestyles, landscapes.
🎞 16mm; Beta. PAL.
Research: By staff. Appointment to visit.
🕓 Mon-Fri 08:00 to 18:00
Procedure: Timecoded VHS available. Masters as reasonably required.
Description: Comprehensive range of Australian floral and landscape material on 16mm and Betacam plus a range of corporate industrial imagery. The collection specializes in central coast and New South Wales footage with aerial and lifestyle, etc. shots. Rate card and catalogue available.

11   CHANNEL 10 NEWS LIBRARY

P.O. Box 10, Sydney, NSW 2001, Australia
© +61 2 844 1363 / 2 844 1296
Ⓕ +61 2 281 6205

Contacts: Roz Hanratty
Subjects: Current affairs.
🎞 16mm; Beta/Beta SP. PAL.
Research: By staff. Appointment to visit.
🕓 7 days 09:00 to 19:00
Procedure: Viewing material on VHS or Betacam. 1-2 weeks for access to masters.
Description: The news library holds Australian news and current affairs footage owned by Channel 10 and dating from 1968 to the present day. Computerized. Rate card and catalogue available. English, French and Croatian spoken.

12   CVA FILM & TELEVISION

P.O. Box 25, West Perth, Western Australia 6872, Australia
℡ +61 9 481 6107
℻ +61 9 481 6107

Contacts: Sue Taylor, Derek Longhurst
Subjects: Mining, landscapes.
▦ 16mm; D2, 1", BVU, Umatic. PAL.
Research: By staff only.
☉ Mon-Fri 08:30 to 18:00
Procedure: PAL or NTSC VHS viewing cassettes. 1 week for access to masters.
Description: Extensive footage of different types of mining in Western Australia - particularly gold, iron ore and coal (underground and open cut). Various landscape shots of Perth and Western Australia. Computerized. German, French and Italian spoken.

13   DELTA PRODUCTIONS

P.O. Box 4836, Darwin, NT 0801, Australia
℡ +61 89 817435 / 817568
℻ +61 89 813213

Contacts: Bob West
Subjects: Historical archive, landscapes, tourism.
▦ BVU, Beta/Beta SP, SVHS. PAL.
Research: By staff. Appointment to visit.
☉ Mon-Fri 08:30 to 17:00
Procedure: Access to masters in 2-3 days.
Description: Main area covered is the Northern Territory of Australia with footage covering special events since 1982 and all major tourist locations and attractions. Delta also have some historical material dating from the 1920s to 1940s. Partly computerized.

14   FILM & TELEVISION INSTITUTE (WA)

92 Adelaide Street, Fremantle, Western Australia 6160, Australia
© +61 9 335 1055
Ⓕ +61 9 335 1283

Contacts: Rita Shanahan
Subjects: Film industry, television.
▦ Viewing material held on video only.
Research: By staff or outside researchers.
☉ Tues-Fri 12:00 to 17:30
Description: The Institute does not sell footage but has a small specialist collection of books, journals and videos on the subject areas of film and television available for research purposes. There is particular emphasis on technical and business matters. All copyrights reside with the individual filmmakers. Partly computerized.

15   FILM STOCK RESEARCH AUSTRALIA

64 Devonshire Street, Surry Hills, NSW 2010, Australia
© +61 2 281 1788
Ⓕ +61 2 281 1789

Contacts: Robert Johnson, Danny Younis
Subjects: Amateur films, documentaries.
▦ 16mm, 35mm; Beta SP, 1". PAL.
☉ 7 days 11:00 to 21:00 (except Mon 10:00 to 18:00)
Procedure: VHS viewing material. 48 hours for access to masters.
Description: Range of home movie material, news, nature, features and documentaries mainly pre 1970s. Partly computerized. Rate card available.

16 FILM WORLD

2 Whiting Street, P.O. Box 313, Artarmon, NSW 2064, Australia
© +61 2 438 1888
Ⓕ +61 2 439 8541

Contacts: Naomi Saville
Subjects: Newsreels, locations, natural history, lifestyles, tourism, travelogues.
🎞 Film; Beta/Beta SP, 1", D1. PAL and NTSC.
Research: By both staff and outside researchers. Appointment to visit.
☉ Mon-Fri 08:30 to 17:30
Procedure: VHS or Umatic viewing cassettes. 24 hours for access to masters.
Description: Over 3000 hours of footage covering archival news material, contemporary landscapes, wildlife and lifestyles. Film World are exclusive agents for the Cinesound and Movietone newsreel collection, Australian Tourist Commission, Queensland Tourist & Travel Corporation, Canadian company Fabulous Footage and many more. Computerized. Subject headings list and rate card available.

17   FILMSEARCH AUSTRALASIA

P.O. Box 46, Lindfield, NSW 2070, Australia
© +61 2 4162633
Ⓕ +61 2 4162554

Contacts: Chris Rowell
Subjects: Natural history, underwater photography, Asia.
▦ 16mm, 35mm; Beta SP, D2, 1". PAL.
Research: By both staff and outside researchers.
Appointment to visit.
🕓 Mon-Fri 09:00 to 17:00
Procedure: Timecoded PAL cassettes for viewing. 3 days for access to masters.
Description: Australian flora and fauna, underwater footage, some contemporary material and Asian footage.
Computerized. Rate card available.

18   HIPS FILM & VIDEO PRODUCTIONS

257 Coventry Street, South Melbourne, Victoria 3205, Australia
© +61 3 699 9427
Ⓕ +61 3 699 9392

Contacts: John Hipwell
Subjects: Energy conservation, industry.
▦ 16mm; Beta/Beta SP, Hi 8. PAL.
Research: By staff. Visits by appointment.
🕓 Mon-Fri 09:00 to 17:30
Procedure: Access to masters normally 48 hours.
Description: Productions deal with the subject of energy management and conservation showing several of the latest developments. Computerized. Rates on application.

19 HOLLYWOOD HOUSE VIDEO ARCHIVES / HOME ENTERTAINMENT HOLDINGS

Box 555, Bondi Beach, NSW 2026, Australia
ⓒ +61 2 365 1055
ⓕ +61 2 365 1577

Contacts: Joe Shellim
Subjects: Classic films, documentaries, music, space, film industry, animation, war, personalities, circus, natural history.
▦ Film; Beta, 1″, BVU, Umatic.
Research: By staff.
☉ Sun-Fri 10:00 to 19:00
Procedure: VHS viewing tape. Access to masters dependent on workload.
Description: Collection includes classic nostalgia movies complimented with interviews and rehearsals, behind-the-scenes, lost films, etc. Interviews with movie stars, candid films, footage of world leaders, space (NASA), music clips, nature and circus, cartoons, war and documentaries. Partly computerized. Rate card and catalogue available.

20   IMAGE BANK / AUSTRALIA

131 Blues Point, McMahons Point, Sydney, NSW 2060,
Australia
© +61 2 954 4255
Ⓕ +61 2 922 6373

Contacts: Ann Sidlow
Subjects: Stock shots, aerial photography, time-lapse,
lifestyles, natural history, locations, sport.
All film and video formats and line standards held.
Research: By both staff and outside researchers.
Appointment to visit.
🕐 Mon-Fri 09:00 to 17:00
Procedure: 3/4"/VHS (any line standard) for viewing. 24
hours for access to masters.
Description: Vast collection of stock material, contemporary
and archival, acquired from Turner Broadcasting, Ocean
Images, I.R.E., Pigeon Productions, MacGillivray Freeman
Films, Dentsu Prox., McDonnell Douglas, Nature
Conservancy, etc. Offices worldwide and major cities of
North America - Chicago, Detroit, Mexico, Minneapolis,
Atlanta, Dallas and Los Angeles. Computerized. English,
French, Spanish, Italian, German and Greek spoken in the
NEW YORK HEADQUARTERS. NB: also have an office in
Melbourne, Australia Tel: +61 3699 7833, Fax: 699 6777,
contact: Tracy Seymour.
Foreign Offices: Argentina, Brazil, Chile, Colombia, Australia,
Canada, Hong Kong, Indonesia, Korea, Japan, Malaysia,
Philippines, Singapore, Taiwan, Thailand, South Africa, UK,
USA.

21   M.C. STUART & ASSOCIATES (MSCAA)

88 Highett Street, Richmond, Victoria 3121, Australia
ⓒ +61 3 429 8666
ⓕ +61 3 429 1839

Contacts: Max Stuart, Paul Stuart
Subjects: Natural history, leisure, sport, music, culture, documentaries, animation, children's, feature films, entertainment.
🕓 Mon-Fri 07:00 to 19:00
Description: MSCAA represent some 40 Australian producers syndicating their programmes to many markets. The types of programmes handled include documentaries, children's programmes, cartoons, feature films, light entertainment, music (modern and classical), the Arts, Australian rules football and leisure sports. Computerized. Rate card and catalogue available. Italian and French spoken.
Foreign Offices: UK, France, Spain, Austria, Norway, Italy, Germany, Greece, Malaysia, Hong Kong, Japan, Canada, USA, Singapore, Sri Lanka, Turkey, Jordan, Thailand.

22   METRO TELEVISION VIDEO ARCHIVE

Paddington Town Hall, P.O. Box 299, Paddington, NSW 2021, Australia
ⓒ +61 2 361 5318
ⓕ +61 2 361 5320

Contacts: Helen Chapman, Peter Giles, Kate Ingham
Subjects: Documentaries, homosexuality, health, educational films.
▨ Videotape.
Research: By both staff and outside researchers.
Appointment to visit.
🕓 Mon-Fri 09:00 to 17:00
Procedure: Umatic, SVHS, VHS, Jsystem viewing tapes supplied.
Description: A wide and varied selection of independent and community produced material. Documentaries, short dramas, experimental pieces, conferences, seminars, community events and demonstrations. Copyrights held for some of the archive, currently in the process of negotiating with various organizations for copyrights going back over the last 20 years. Partly computerized. Catalogue available.

23   NATIONAL FILM AND SOUND ARCHIVE

G.P.O. Box 2002, McCoy Circuit, Acton, Canberra, ACT 2600, Australia
ⓒ +61 6 267 1711
Ⓕ +61 6 247 4651
⟋⟋ AA 61930

Subjects: National Archives.

24   NATIONAL LIBRARY OF AUSTRALIA

Film & Video Lending Service, Parkes Place, Canberra 2600, Australia
ⓒ +61 6 262 1361
Ⓕ +61 6 262 1634

Contacts: Reference Officer
Subjects: National Archives, educational films, documentaries, feature films, animation.
▦ 16mm; Umatic, VHS. PAL, some NTSC.
Research: Researchers can visit, appointments recommended not essential.
☉ Mon-Fri 09:00 to 16:30
Procedure: Free loan to institutes, businesses and groups. No masters held.
Description: Over 23 500 instructional and educational documentary titles held covering most subject areas. Also a film and TV study collection with feature films, short fiction, animation and experimental film and video. Computerized. Full catalogue available on microfiche and screen studies catalogue in print form.

25 NATURAL SYMPHONIES

4 George Street, Redfern, NSW 2016, Australia
ⓒ +61 2 318 1577 / 46 55 1800
ⓕ +61 2 318 1424 / 46 55 9434

Contacts: Neil O'Hare
Subjects: Underwater photography, natural history, culture, environmental.

Beta SP, D2, 1". PAL.

Research: By staff mainly. Visits by appointment.

Mon-Fri 09:00 to 17:00 (often contactable outside these times)

Procedure: Timecoded VHS or other formats available. 24 hours for access to masters.

Description: Shot in Australia and The South Pacific, the library ranges from aerial sequences to microscopic subjects including flora, fauna, marine life, tourist and research activities. All material is recorded on Betacam SP using BTS LDK 90 and 91 CCD cameras. Many of the sequences available are of animals, birds and locations that are extremely difficult to access and film owing to seasonal variations and remoteness. Material includes coral reefs, coral spawning, whales, dolphins and sea lions, Australian birds, animals, insects and reptiles, Australian environments and Aboriginal and islander culture. Computerized with database list on disk accessible by most word processors. Summary print outs and rate card available.

26   NOMAD FILMS INTERNATIONAL

Perth Business Centre, Stirling Street (P.O. Box 8240), Perth 6849, Australia
ⓒ +61 9 3881177
Ⓕ +61 9 3811122

Contacts: Doug Stanley and Kate Faulkner
Subjects: Natural history, medicine, science, lifestyles, locations, environmental, China, Jewish history, underwater photography.
▦ 16mm; Beta/Beta SP, D2, 1", Umatic. PAL and NTSC.
Research: By staff only.
🕓 Mon-Fri 08:30 to 18:30
Procedure: VHS or Umatic PAL/NTSC viewing copies. 3 days for access to masters.
Description: Enormous range of productions covering wildlife, medical and scientific topics with worldwide documentary series on people and places. Titles include The Intruders, A Walk in the Sea and Crocodiles - the deadly survivors (natural history), Land of the Dragon (Bhutan), Dream Merchants of Asia (Taiwan, India, Japan, Hong Kong), Journey to Hainan (China's most southerly province), Breakthroughs (science, medicine and technology), Eye in the Sky (satellite technology), Triumph of the Nomads (Aborigines) to name a few. Glossy brochures available for productions. Partly computerized.

27   NORMELLA PICTURES

P.O. Box 562, Toowong, Brisbane Q4066, Australia
ⓒ +61 7 3665172
Ⓕ +61 7 3667661

Contacts: Evan Ham
Subjects: Vietnam war, travelogues, culture.
▦ 16mm, 35mm; VHS. PAL.
Research: By staff and outside researchers under supervision.
🕓 Mon-Sat 08:00 to 17:00
Procedure: Viewing of workprints on premises or VHS. 48 hours for access to masters.
Description: 80 000 16mm feet of Vietnam and Cambodia footage dating from 1985 to 1993 covering a wide range of subjects (all on 16mm negative). 50 000 35mm feet of Vietnamese archive film of Indochina wars including Cambodia. 80 000 16mm feet of Northern Australia footage. Computerized. Rates negotiated on application. English and Vietnamese spoken.

28 OLIVER FILMS

508 City Road, South Melbourne, Victoria 3205, Australia
© +61 3 690 3300
Ⓕ +61 3 699 4640

Contacts: Frank Howson, Peter McBain
Subjects: Stock shots, natural history.
▦ 35mm.
Research: By staff only.
☉ Mon-Fri 09:00 to 18:00
Procedure: VHS viewing material can be supplied. Access to masters varies.
Description: Small but expanding collection of out-takes from feature films produced by Oliver Films. Stock footage of Melbourne and surrounding areas, also some Fiji jungle footage. Partly computerized. Catalogue and rate card available.

29 PARAMOUNT PICTURES / AUSTRALIA

Suite 3501, Level 35 Northpoint, 100 Miller Street, North Sydney, NSW 2060, Australia
© +61 2 922 2322
Ⓕ +61 2 955 6808

Contacts: Stephen Carey
Subjects: Feature films, television.
Procedure: All requests must be received in writing.
Description: Vast collection of feature films and TV series including The Accused, Breakfast at Tiffany's, Crocodile Dundee, Indiana Jones..., Top Gun, Witness, Cheers, Happy Days, Star Trek, etc. All requests must be in writing containing details of time required (standard use is not more than 2 minutes and not more than 2 seperate scenes), how and why of use, name and nature of project. Australia office deals with requests for Australia, New Zealand, all of the Far East except Japan, South Africa including Bophuthatswana and Namibia, and Bangladesh, India and Pakistan. See all entries for Paramount Pictures to check on territories covered by each office.
Foreign Offices: Australia, Canada, UK, USA.

30   REEFSCENES AUSTRALIA

P.O. Box 2427, Australia
ⓒ +61 77 214819
Ⓕ +61 77 713341

Contacts: Steve Gardner
Subjects: Underwater photography, natural history.
Beta SP, D2, Digital Beta, Hi 8. PAL.
Research: By staff only.
Mon-Fri 09:00 to 17:00
Procedure: Time coded VHS available. 48 hours for access to masters.
Description: Underwater, coral reef and marine related footage shot on Beta SP and Digital Betacam widescreen 16:9 format. Also natural history, underwater models and human related topics. Computerized. English, Pidgin and Norwegian spoken.

31   RONIN FILMS

P.O. Box 1005, Civic Square, ACT 2608, Australia
ⓒ +616 248 0851
Ⓕ +616 249 1640

Contacts: Michele Day, Maria Jacoveli, Carolyn Odgers
Subjects: Documentaries, educational films, Asian cinema, feature films.
16mm, 35mm; Beta/Beta SP, D2, 1″, Umatic. PAL and NTSC.
Research: By staff only.
Mon-Fri 09:00 to 17:00
Procedure: Preview material on video, mainly PAL, some on NTSC.
Description: Imported and Australian features and documentaries as well as video and non-theatrical titles. Partly computerized. Catalogue and rate card available.

32 SELECT EFFECTS – AUSTRALIA

11 Station Street, Naremburn, NSW 2065, Australia
ⓒ +61 2 437 5620
Ⓕ +61 2 901 4505

Contacts: Jill Freestone
Subjects: Special effects, computer imagery, time-lapse, animation.
▦ 16mm, 35mm; Beta SP. PAL.
Research: By outside researchers. Appointment to visit.
🕑 Mon-Fri 09:00 to 17:30
Procedure: VHS viewing tapes loaned. 1-2 hours for access to masters.
Description: Mainly computer generated effects but also time-lapse, animation and live action. Subjects covered include globes, fireworks, maps, grids, sport, health, entertainment, environment, music, space and hi-tech. This company represents US company Cascom International. Partly computerized. Catalogue showing a freeze frame of each effect in the library is available.
Foreign Offices: USA (Cascom International).

33 SPECIAL BROADCASTING SERVICE

Television Archives, Locked Bag 028, Artarmon, NSW 2064, Australia
ⓒ +61 02 430 2828
Ⓕ +61 02 430 3700

Contacts: Alex Surplice, Jenny Fuller
Subjects: Current affairs, sport, culture, racism.
▦ Film; videotape.
Research: By staff and outside researchers by appointment.
🕑 Mon-Fri 08:00 to 19:30
Description: The library holds all broadcast material purchased and produced by SBS-TV including news and current affairs plus subject areas - multiculturalism, world news, sport (particularly soccer), minority groups, etc. Partly computerized.

34 STORYTELLER PRODUCTIONS

11 Morrison Way, Willetton, WA 6155, Australia
ⓒ +61 9 354 2903
ⓕ +61 9 457 2583

Contacts: Mike Searle
Subjects: Natural history.
▦ Film; videotape.
Research: By both staff and outside researchers by appointment.
◷ Mon-Fri 09:00 to 17:00
Description: Large collection of natural history footage featuring endangered species from around the world. Rare animals such as Australia's rarest animal the western swamp tortoise. Whales, whale strandings, dolphins, aye aye, tigers, elephants, crickets, spiders, snails, bandicoots, etc. Also hold footage collections of USS Missouri, Australian Aboriginal Dancers and Spitfire Dig. Partly computerized.

Bangladesh

35 BANGLADESH FILM ARCHIVE

Block No. 3, Ganabhaban, Sher-e-Bangla Nagar, Dhaka
1207, Bangladesh
📞 +880 2 814816 / 323727

Subjects: National Archives.

Bermuda

36   BERMUDA GOVERNMENT ARCHIVES

30 Parliament Street, Hamilton HM12, Bermuda
Ⓒ +1 809 297 7833
Ⓕ +1 809 292 2349

Subjects: National Archives.

Bolivia

37 CINEMATECA BOLIVIANA

P.O. Box 9933, Pichincha Esq. Indaburo s/n, La Paz, Bolivia
© +591 1 325346
✁ 3288 CORMESA BV

Subjects: National Archives.

Botswana

38   BOTSWANA NATIONAL ARCHIVES AND RECORDS SERVICES

P.O. Box 239, Government Enclave - Khama Crescent/State Drive, Gaborone, Botswana
© +267 3601000
Ⓕ +267 313584
◰ 2994BD

Subjects: National Archives.

Brazil

39 ARQUIVO NACIONAL (AUDIOVISUAL AND CARTOGRAPHIC DIVISION)

Rua Azeredo Coutinho, 77/6 andar, Rio De Janeiro, RJ
20230, Brazil
© +55 21 252 2766
Ⓕ +55 21 232 8430
↗ 21 34103

Subjects: National Archives

40 IMAGE BANK / BRAZIL

433/5 Rua Visconde de Piraja, Rio de Janeiro 22410, Brazil
© +55 21 267 1643
Ⓕ +55 21 267 1890

Contacts: Jean-Claude Lozouet
Subjects: Stock shots, aerial photography, time-lapse,
lifestyles, natural history, locations, sport.
▦ All film and video formats and line standards held.
Research: By both staff and outside researchers.
Appointment to visit.
☉ Mon-Fri 09:00 to 17:00
Procedure: 3/4"/VHS (any line standard) for viewing. 24
hours for access to masters.
Description: Vast collection of stock material, contemporary
and archival, acquired from Turner Broadcasting, Ocean
Images, I.R.E., Pigeon Productions, MacGillivray Freeman
Films, Dentsu Prox., McDonnell Douglas, Nature
Conservancy, etc. Offices worldwide and major cities of
North America - Chicago, Detroit, Mexico, Minneapolis,
Atlanta, Dallas and Los Angeles. Computerized. English,
French, Spanish, Italian, German and Greek spoken in the
NEW YORK HEADQUARTERS. NB: Image Bank also have
offices in Porto Alegre, Brazil: Tel: (55 51) 337 1440/343
3023, Fax: (55 51) 343 3023, contact: Fernando Bueno and
in Sao Paulo, Brazil: Tel: (55 11) 852 3466, Fax: (55 11)
853 9064, contact: Jean Claude Lozouet.
Foreign Offices: Argentina, Brazil, Chile, Colombia, Australia,
Canada, Hong Kong, Indonesia, Korea, Japan, Malaysia,
Philippines, Singapore, Taiwan, Thailand, South Africa, UK,
USA.

41   NOVA IMAGENS / FABULOUS FOOTAGE

Rua Major Diogo 874, Sao Paulo 01324-000, Brazil
ⓒ +551 607 3456
Ⓕ +551 604 2709

Subjects: Stock shots, locations, culture, industry, medicine, military, music, environmental, leisure, transport, natural history, space, trailers.

▦ Film; video (all film mastered onto tape).

Description: Complete contemporary film and videotape library with a vast range of quality images. Subject headings include agriculture, buildings, cities, countries, cultural activities, industry and business, landmarks, landscapes, medical, military, music, natural phenomena, news, period recreations, professions, rain forests, recreation, space, special effects, spectacles, sports, transportation, underwater, water and wildlife. They also hold special collections of Nazi propaganda footage, Russian history, Russian space program, B-movies and trailers. Computerized. Rate card and catalogue available. NB: Head office is in Toronto, Canada, details of Brazil office received from Canada only.

Foreign Offices: Argentina, Australia, Brazil, Canada, Chile, Germany, Indonesia, Japan, Malaysia, Philippines, Singapore, Spain, Mexico, USA.

Brunei

42 RADIO TELEVISION BRUNEI

Bandar Seri, Bandar Seri Begawan 2042, Brunei
℄ +673 2 243111 Ext. 224
Ⓕ +673 2 227204
↗ BU2720 RTBPROG

Contacts: Mr. H.J.M.D. Salleh
Subjects: Drama, comedy, documentaries, children's.
▦ 16mm, 35mm; Video.
☉ Mon-Thur and Sat 07:45 to 12:15, 13:30 to 16:30
Procedure: Umatic and VHS viewing material in PAL and NTSC.
Description: Television output including full range of programmes and series. English and Malay spoken.

Brunei Darussalam

43   BRUNEI NATIONAL ARCHIVES

Brunei Museums, Ministry of Culture Youth and Sports,
Darussalam, Brunei Darussalam
© +673 2 244545/6
Ⓕ +673 2 44047
✍ BRUART 2655

Subjects: National Archives.

Canada

44 CANADIAN BROADCASTING CORPORATION (CBC)

Box 500, Station A, Toronto, Ontario M5W 1E1, Canada
© +1 416 205 7608
Ⓕ +1 416 205 6736

Contacts: Roy Harris
Subjects: Stock shots, natural history, locations, medicine, environmental.
▦ 16mm; Beta/Beta SP, 1", Umatic. NTSC.
Research: By staff only.
☻ Mon–Fri 08:30 to 17:30
Procedure: Timecoded cassettes made to order. 2–3 days for access to masters.
Description: CBC's archive contains a wide range of programme material including natural history and environmental footage, medical research, cities of the world, history, etc. from Arctic life to ancient Yemini ruins. Computerized. Rate card available.

45 CARLETON PRODUCTIONS

1500 Merivale Road, Ottawa, Ontario K2E 6Z5, Canada
© +1 613 224 1313 Ext. 330, 309
Ⓕ +1 613 224 9074

Contacts: Pat Billings, Randi Hansen, Dianne Van Velthoven, Mark Ross
Subjects: Locations, current affairs, sport.
▦ 3/4" master videotape.
Research: By staff.
☻ Mon–Fri 08:00 to 17:00
Description: Footage from across Canada (mostly from the capital area Ottawa), scenery, politics, special events and sports. Partly computerized (covering the last three years).

46   CHARLES CHAPLIN ENTERPRISES

318 Hillhurst Boulevard, Toronto, Ontario M6B 1N2, Canada
© +1 416 781 0131 / 2010
Ⓕ +1 416 366 6503

Contacts: Charles S. Chaplin
Subjects: Russia, documentaries, feature films, public domain.
▦ Various film formats. Can supply any video format on request.
Research: Visits by appointment only. Requests by fax or mail.
☉ 7 days 09:00 to 18:00
Procedure: NTSC (some PAL) videocassettes for viewing. 2 weeks for access to masters.
Description: Wide range of documentary and feature film productions, specializing in Russia and USA.

47   CINAR

1201 Rue St. Andre, Montreal, Quebec H2L 3S8, Canada
© +1 514 843 7070
Ⓕ +1 514 843 7080

Contacts: Suzan Ayscough
Subjects: Animation, feature films.
▦ 1″, Umatic. NTSC.
Research: Not a library service - make enquiries to Communications Dept.
☉ Mon-Fri 09:00 to 17:00
Procedure: VHS viewing tapes sent to clients.
Description: Cinar is a producer and distributor of family oriented live action and animation programmes. Cinar operates Crayon Animation, the largest animation studio in Eastern Canada plus a studio centre with a complete range of post production facilities. Partly computerized. Catalogue available. English and French spoken.

48 DOOMSDAY STUDIOS

212 James Street, Ottawa, Ontario K1R 5M7, Canada
ⓒ +1 613 230 9769
Ⓕ +1 613 230 6004

Contacts: Ramona Macdonald, Tony Kelleher
Subjects: Architecture, folklore, animation, feature films.
🎞 16mm, 35mm; 1″, Umatic. PAL and NTSC.
Research: By staff.
🕐 Mon-Fri 09:00 to 17:00
Procedure: Viewing material on 16mm or cassette.
Description: The library has a collection of Nova Scotia folk art including black and white footage of a folk festival in the 1970s. They also have Lithuanian folk art, experimental animation and various features. English, French, Spanish, German, Russian and Lithuanian spoken.

49 FABULOUS FOOTAGE

4th Floor, 19 Mercer Street, Toronto, Ontario M5V 1H2, Canada
ⓒ +1 416 591 6955
Ⓕ +1 416 591 1666

Contacts: Steve Race, Patricia Harvey, Rhonda Olson, Julie Kovacs
Subjects: Stock shots, locations, culture, industry, medicine, military, music, environmental, leisure, transport, natural history, space, trailers.
🎞 Film; video (all film mastered onto tape).
Research: By both staff and outside researchers.
🕐 Mon-Fri 09:00 to 21:00
Description: Complete contemporary film and videotape library with a vast range of quality images. Subject headings include agriculture, buildings, cities, countries, cultural activities, industry and business, landmarks, landscapes, medical, military, music, natural phenomena, news, period recreations, professions, rain forests, recreation, space, special effects, spectacles, sports, transportation, underwater, water and wildlife. They also hold special collections of Nazi propaganda footage, Russian history, Russian space program, B-movies and trailers. Computerized. Rate card and catalogue available. NB: This is the head office, there is also an office in Vancouver, Canada Tel: (604) 684 8484, Fax: (604) 681 3299.
Foreign Offices: Argentina, Australia, Brazil, Canada, Chile, Germany, Indonesia, Japan, Malaysia, Philippines, Singapore, Mexico, Spain, USA.

50 GREAT NORTH RELEASING

Suite 012, 11523-100 Avenue, Edmonton, Alberta T5K OJ8, Canada
© +1 403 482 2022
Ⓕ +1 403 482 3036

Contacts: Jim Fraser
Subjects: Documentaries, culture, lifestyles, science, sport.
16mm; Beta/Beta SP, 1", Umatic. PAL and NTSC.
Research: By staff only.
☺ Mon-Fri 09:00 to 17:00
Procedure: VHS viewing cassettes in PAL and NTSC. 2 weeks for access to masters.
Description: The library holds documentaries on aboriginal issues, vanishing lifestyles, human interest, science and sport. Rate card and catalogue available. English and French spoken.

51 IMAGE BANK / CANADA

Suite 307, 40 Eglinton East, Toronto, Ontario M4P 3A8, Canada
© +1 416 322 8840
Ⓕ +1 416 322 8855

Contacts: Laura and Andy Roeder
Subjects: Stock shots, aerial photography, time-lapse, lifestyles, natural history, locations, sport.
All film and video formats and line standards held.
Research: By both staff and outside researchers. Appointment to visit.
☺ Mon-Fri 09:00 to 17:00
Procedure: 3/4"/VHS (any line standard) for viewing. 24 hours for access to masters.
Description: Vast collection of stock material, contemporary and archival, acquired from Turner Broadcasting, Ocean Images, I.R.E., Pigeon Productions, MacGillivray Freeman Films, Dentsu Prox., McDonnell Douglas, Nature Conservancy, etc. Offices worldwide and major cities of North America - Chicago, Detroit, Mexico, Minneapolis, Atlanta, Dallas and Los Angeles. Computerized. English, French, Spanish, Italian, German and Greek spoken in the NEW YORK HEADQUARTERS. NB: Image Bank also have a Montreal office Tel: (514) 849 840, Fax: (514) 849 8055, contact: Ann Ross.
Foreign Offices: Argentina, Brazil, Chile, Colombia, Australia, Canada, Hong Kong, Indonesia, Korea, Japan, Malaysia, Philippines, Singapore, Taiwan, Thailand, South Africa, UK, USA.

52   IMAGES PIXART

1973 Falardeau, Montreal, Quebec H2K 2L9, Canada
ⓒ +1 514 521 8776
ⓕ +1 514 521 0541

Contacts: Emmanuelle de la Cressonniere
Subjects: Stock shots, environmental, culture, locations.
▦ Betacam.
Research: By staff. Appointment to visit.
☉ Mon-Fri 09:00 to 18:00
Description: Extensive collection of beauty shots of Canada
from coast to coast. Also stock footage covering ecological
and cultural issues in the province of Quebec for the last five
years. Computerized. Rate card available.

53   JACK CHISHOLM FILM PRODUCTIONS

Suite 50, 99 Atlantic Avenue, Toronto, Ontario M6K 3J8,
Canada
ⓒ +1 416 588 5200
ⓕ +1 416 588 5324

Contacts: Peter Robinson
Subjects: Stock shots, historical archive, locations,
time-lapse, current affairs, newsreels, natural history,
industry, science.
▦ 16mm, 35mm; Beta/Beta SP, 1", Umatic, SVHS, some
digital. NTSC.
Research: By staff only.
☉ Mon-Fri 09:00 to 17:30
Procedure: Umatic or VHS viewing copies. 24 hours for
access to masters.
Description: The stock footage library contains archive
material dating from 1896 up to present day. Subjects cover
major events around the world, wildlife, foreign locations,
industry and science as well as quality shots of clouds,
sunsets, time-lapse flowers, etc. The collection comprises of
10 000 hours of video footage and 4 million feet of film.
They hold 35mm neg of across Canada scenics plus the
Millenium television series. Computerized. Rate card
available. English and Italian spoken.

54 NATIONAL ARCHIVES OF CANADA

395 Wellington Street, Ottawa, Ontario K1A ON3, Canada
ⓒ +1 613 995 5138
ⓕ +1 613 995 6274

Subjects: National Archives, Canadian history.

Most film formats including 28mm. All video formats. NTSC.
Research: Visits by appointment, consultation prior to
viewing needed.

☉ Mon-Fri 08:30 to 16:45

Procedure: Viewing on premises only, SVHS, VHS and
Umatic available.

Description: The Archives hold materials on a large variety of
subjects related to Canadian history. Copyright or donor
restrictions may apply, information is supplied if known but
researchers have ultimate responsibility to search for
copyrights. Partly computerized. French and English spoken.

55 OASIS PICTURES

56 Shaftesbury Avenue, Toronto, Ontario M4T 1A3, Canada
ⓒ +1 416 925 4353
ⓕ +1 416 967 1292

Contacts: Valerie Cabrera, Peter Emerson
Subjects: Drama, comedy, science, exploration, Africa,
environmental, adventure sports, folklore, stunts.

16mm, 35mm; Beta/Beta SP, D2, 1", Umatic. PAL and
NTSC.
Research: Usually done by staff. Appointment recommended
to visit.

☉ Mon-Fri 09:00 to 18:00

Procedure: Viewing on VHS NTSC (some PAL available).
1-3 days for access to masters.

Description: The Oasis catalogue features a wide range of
comedy, family and action dramas plus documentaries with
subjects including exploration and adventure, gardening,
cottage living and its folklore, genetic engineering, fire
fighting, Africa, environmental change, stunt people, an
ancient aboriginal festival in South America, war reporters,
etc. Partly computerized. Catalogue available. English,
Spanish, Italian and French spoken.

56 PARAMOUNT PICTURES / CANADA

TV Division, 146 Bloor Street West, Toronto, Ontario M5S
1M4, Canada
ⓒ +1 416 969 9901
Ⓕ +1 416 922 4743

Contacts: Kevin Keeley
Subjects: Feature films, television.
Procedure: All requests must be received in writing.
Description: Vast collection of feature films and TV series
including The Accused, Breakfast at Tiffany's, Crocodile
Dundee, Indiana Jones..., Top Gun, Witness, Cheers, Happy
Days, Star Trek, etc. All requests must be in writing
containing details oftime required (standard use is not more
than 2 minutes and not more than 2 separate scenes), how
and why of use, name and nature of project. Canada office
deals with requests for Canada only. NB: The Europe office
based, in UK at 49 Charles Street, London W1X 7PA contact:
Julie Wineberg, Tel: (0171) 629 1150, Fax: (0171) 491
2086, handles requests for African countries not covered by
other offices, the Caribbean Islands and Japan. See all
entries for Paramount Pictures to check on territories
covered by each.
Foreign Offices: Australia, Canada, UK, USA.

57 QUALICUM FILM PRODUCTIONS

6340 Island Highway West, Qualicum Beach, BC V9K 2E5,
Canada
ⓒ +1 604 757 8390
Ⓕ +1 604 757 8844

Contacts: Dick Harvey
Subjects: Natural history, underwater photography, fishing.
▦ 16mm; Beta/Beta SP. NTSC.
Research: By both staff and outside researchers.
Appointment to visit.
◷ 7 days 08:00 to 18:00
Procedure: VHS or Umatic viewing cassettes. Same day for
access to masters.
Description: Qualicum specialize in nature and wildlife
photography, their particular interest over the last 30 years
being rivers. Material includes extensive footage of salmon
(migration, underwater, spawning, all species) also black
bears, eagles on rivers, ocean, underwater herring etc.

58 ROBERT BOCKING PRODUCTIONS

75 Hucknall Road, Downsview, Ontario M3J IWI, Canada
℡ +1 416 631 9845

Contacts: Robert Bocking
Subjects: Natural history, locations.
▦ Videotape.
🕑 Mon-Fri 09:00 to 17:00
Description: Nature footage and scenics from North
America, Costa Rica to the Arctic, Atlantic to the Pacific.
Partly computerized. Rate card and catalogue available.

59 SOCIETE RADIO-CANADA

1400 Boulevard Rene-Levesque Est, Montreal, Quebec H2L
2M2, Canada
℡ +1 514 597 7826
Ⓕ +1 514 597 7862

Contacts: Lucie Quenneville
Subjects: Current affairs, drama, environmental, stock shots.
Research: By staff. Appointment to visit.
🕑 Mon-Fri 09:00 to 17:00
Description: SRC television is the only national French
network in Canada. The library has a full range of material
dating from 1952 including current affairs, news, drama,
environmental programmes and stock shot footage. Partly
computerized. Rate card and brochure available.

60 VILLON FILMS

77 W 28 Avenue, Vancouver, BC V5Y 2K7, Canada
Ⓒ +1 604 879 6042
Ⓕ +1 604 879 6042

Contacts: Peter Davis
Subjects: Historical archive, documentaries, advertising, Africa, AIDS, apartheid, Cuba, culture, espionage, war.
Majority of material is 16mm. Some original video.
Research: Visits by appointment.
🕐 7 days, 24 hours
Procedure: Viewing of VHS and 16mm on premises, some video elsewhere.
Description: The collection comprises films made and collected by Peter including out-takes, commercials from the 1950s and 60s and valuable historical material. Subjects covered include Africa, AIDS, Rhodesia and Zimbabwe and especially South Africa 1900 to 1990; Catskills (Borscht Belt) 1900 to 1990; US covert activities, spies, the Cold War; D.H. Lawrence; Middle East late 1960s, 70s, 80s; US anti-war movement and counter culture 1960s and 70s; Britain early 1960s; World War II China; Native Americans (Crow and Navajo) 70s and 80s; Cuba 1960s. Partly computerized. Rates negotiable. English, French, Swedish and some Italian spoken.

Chile

61 BIBLIOTECA NACIONAL DE CHILE

Seccion Musica Y Medios Multiples, Avenida Libertador
Bernardo O'Higgins, Clasificador 1400, Santiago 651, Chile
Ⓕ +56 2 381975

Subjects: National Archives.

62 FOTOBANCO INTERNATIONAL / FABULOUS FOOTAGE

Andres de Fuenzalida 22, Off 1103, Providencia, Santiago,
Chile
Ⓒ +56 232 3417
Ⓕ +56 233 2366

Subjects: Stock shots, locations, culture, industry, medicine,
military, music, environmental, leisure, transport, natural
history, space, trailers.

Film; video (all film mastered onto tape).

Description: Complete contemporary film and videotape
library with a vast range of quality images. Subject headings
include agriculture, buildings, cities, countries, cultural
activities, industry and business, landmarks, landscapes,
medical, military, music, natural phenomena, news, period
recreations, professions, rain forests, recreation, space,
special effects, spectacles, sports, transportation,
underwater, water and wildlife. They also hold special
collections of Nazi propaganda footage, Russian history,
Russian space program, B-movies and trailers. Computerized.
Rate card and catalogue available. NB: Head office is in
Toronto, Canada, details of Chile office received from Canada
only.

Foreign Offices: Argentina, Australia, Brazil, Canada, Chile,
Germany, Indonesia, Japan, Malaysia, Philippines, Singapore,
Spain, Mexico, USA.

63 IMAGE BANK / CHILE

Calle Del Arzbispo, Providencia, Santiago, Chile
ⓒ +56 2 777 9662/1395
Ⓕ +56 2 737 9609/9071/0645

Contacts: Claudia Marchant
Subjects: Stock shots, aerial photography, time-lapse, lifestyles, natural history, locations, sport.
▦ All film and video formats and line standards held.
Research: By both staff and outside researchers. Appointment to visit.
🕒 Mon-Fri 09:00 to 17:00
Procedure: 3/4"/VHS (any line standard) for viewing. 24 hours for access to masters.
Description: Vast collection of stock material, contemporary and archival, acquired from Turner Broadcasting, Ocean Images, I.R.E., Pigeon Productions, MacGillivray Freeman Films, Dentsu Prox., McDonnell Douglas, Nature Conservancy, etc. Offices worldwide and major cities of North America - Chicago, Detroit, Mexico, Minneapolis, Atlanta, Dallas and Los Angeles. Computerized. English, French, Spanish, Italian, German and Greek spoken in the NEW YORK HEADQUARTERS.
Foreign Offices: Argentina, Brazil, Chile, Colombia, Australia, Canada, Hong Kong, Indonesia, Korea, Japan, Malaysia, Philippines, Singapore, Taiwan, Thailand, South Africa, UK, USA.

China, People's Republic of

64   CHINA RECORD CORPORATION

2 Fuxingmewai St., Beijing 100866, People's Republic of China
© +86 1 6092867
Ⓕ +86 1 3262693
⟋ 222309CRC CN

Subjects: National Archives.

Colombia

65 FUNDACION PATRIMONIO FILMICO COLOMBIANO

Carrera 13 # 13-24, Piso 9, Audiorio, Sante Fe De Bogota,
Colombia
© +57 1 2815241 / 2836496
Ⓕ +57 1 3421485

Contacts: Claudia Triana de Vargas, Jorge Nieto
Subjects: National Archives.
▥ Film; video. Original material.
Research: By outside researchers. Appointment necessary.
🕓 Mon-Fri 08:30 to 17:30
Procedure: Copyright needs to be checked prior to
duplication.
Description: The archive holds 120 000 reels of Colombian
newsreels, film and video productions. It also has 12 000
stills, press clippings and documents relating to Colombian
films and cinematography.

66 IMAGE BANK / COLOMBIA (ARCHIVO FOTOGRAFICO LTDA.)

Calle 82, No. 11-37 Of. 213, Bogota, Colombia
© +57 1 610 8020 / 8177
Ⓕ +57 1 610 8125

Contacts: Maria Victoria de Mazuera
Subjects: Stock shots, aerial photography, time-lapse,
lifestyles, natural history, locations, sport.
▥ All film and video formats and line standards held.
Research: By both staff and outside researchers.
Appointment to visit.
🕓 Mon-Fri 09:00 to 17:00
Procedure: 3/4"/VHS (any line standard) for viewing. 24
hours for access to masters.
Description: Vast collection of stock material, contemporary
and archival, acquired from Turner Broadcasting, Ocean
Images, I.R.E., Pigeon Productions, MacGillivray Freeman
Films, Dentsu Prox., McDonnell Douglas, Nature
Conservancy, etc. Offices worldwide and major cities of
North America - Chicago, Detroit, Mexico, Minneapolis,
Atlanta, Dallas and Los Angeles. Computerized. English,
French, Spanish, Italian, German and Greek spoken in the
NEW YORK HEADQUARTERS.
Foreign Offices: Argentina, Brazil, Chile, Colombia, Australia,
Canada, Hong Kong, Indonesia, Korea, Japan, Malaysia,
Philippines, Singapore, Taiwan, Thailand, South Africa, UK,
USA.

67   RCN TELEVISION DE COLOMBIA

Avenue de las Americas 65-82, Santafe de Bogota DC,
Colombia
© +57 1 290 6088 / 290 6614
(F) +57 1 260 0924

Contacts: Mauricio Calle, Maria Lucia Hernandez
Subjects: Drama.
Most video formats. NTSC.
Research: By both staff and outside researchers.
Appointment to visit.
Mon-Fri 08:30 to 18:30
Procedure: VHS viewing tapes. Access to masters variable.
Description: Television dramas and series including La Potra
Zaina, Azucar, La Cas del las dos Palmas, Maria, La
Voragine, La Otra Raya Del Tigre, Puerta Grande and
Inseperables. Brochures on productions available. English
spoken.

68   UNIVERSIDAD DE ANTIOQUIA

Escuela Interamericanan de Bibliotecologia - Biblioteca, Clle
67 No 53-108, Medellin A.A. 1307, Colombia
© +57 4 2630011 Ext.358 / 2634436
(F) +57 4 263 82 82

Subjects: National Archives.

Congo

69 BIBLIOTHEQUE NATIONALE DU CONGO

B.P. 1489, Brazzaville, Congo

Subjects: National Archives.

Costa Rica

70 DIRECCION GENERAL DEL ARCHIVO NATIONAL DE COSTA RICA

P.O. Box 10217-1000, Calle 7, avdas 4 y 6, San Jose, Costa Rica
Ⓒ +506 335754
Ⓕ +506 219129

Subjects: National Archives.

Cuba

71 CINEMATECA DE CUBA

Calle 23 No 155, 10300 La Habana 4, Cuba
© +53 7 3 4719 / 30 5041 to 45

Subjects: National Archives.

72 ICAIC

Calle 23, 1155 Vedado, Habana, Cuba
© +53 7 333862 / 34400 / 304666
Ⓕ +53 7 333032
⁘ 511419 ICAIC CU

Contacts: Leon Francisco, Rodriguez Antonio, Alfredo Calvino
Subjects: Historical archive, feature films, animation.
▦ 16mm, 35mm; Beta, Umatic. NTSC.
Research: By both staff and outside researchers.
☉ Mon-Fri 08:00 to 16:00
Procedure: VHS/Umatic/Betamax for viewing. Masters vary
- usually 1 week.
Description: Social, political and cultural footage from 1902
up to the present day with special emphasis on events from
1954 onwards. Features and short films covering all genres
and themes. Animation mainly for children. Partly
computerized. Rate card and catalogue available. English,
French and Russian spoken.

Ecuador

73 CINEMATECA NACIONAL DEL ECUADOR

P.O. Box 17 01 3520, Av 6 Diciembre 794 y Patria, Quito, Ecuador
ℭ +593 2 230 505

Subjects: National Archives.

Fiji

74   LIBRARY SERVICE OF FIJI

P.O. Box 2526, 162 Ratu Sukuna Road, Suva, Fiji
ⓒ +679 315344 / 315303
Ⓕ +679 303511

Subjects: National Archives.

Guinea, Republic of

75 ARCHIVES DE LA RADIO TELEVISION GUINEENNE

BP 391, Conakry, Guinea, Republic of
© +210 224 44 22 01 / 22 06
↗ 22341 RTG

Subjects: National Archives

Guinea-Bissau

76 INSTITUTO NACIONAL DE ESTUDOS E PESQUISAS (INEP)

Institut National des Etudes et des Recherches (INER), Complexo Escolar, 14 de Novembre Cobornel, P.O. Box 112, Bissau, Guinea-Bissau

© +245 252 21 13 01

Ⓕ +245 28 20

Subjects: National Archives.

Hong Kong

77 IMAGE BANK / HONG KONG

Suite A, 2nd Floor, Miami Mansion, 13-15 Cleveland Street,
Causeway Bay, Hong Kong
ⓒ +85 2 576 2022
Ⓕ +85 2 576 5990

Contacts: Bill Sargent
Subjects: Stock shots, aerial photography, time-lapse,
lifestyles, natural history, locations, sport.
All film and video formats and line standards held.
Research: By both staff and outside researchers.
Appointment to visit.
☉ Mon-Fri 09:00 to 17:00
Procedure: 3/4"/VHS (any line standard) for viewing. 24
hours for access to masters.
Description: Vast collection of stock material, contemporary
and archival, acquired from Turner Broadcasting, Ocean
Images, I.R.E., Pigeon Productions, MacGillivray Freeman
Films, Dentsu Prox., McDonnell Douglas, Nature
Conservancy, etc. Offices worldwide and major cities of
North America - Chicago, Detroit, Mexico, Minneapolis,
Atlanta, Dallas and Los Angeles. Computerized. English,
French, Spanish, Italian, German and Greek spoken in the
NEW YORK HEADQUARTERS.
Foreign Offices: Argentina, Brazil, Chile, Colombia, Australia,
Canada, Hong Kong, Indonesia, Korea, Japan, Malaysia,
Philippines, Singapore, Taiwan, Thailand, South Africa, UK,
USA.

78 TELEVISION BROADCASTS LTD. (TVB)

Videotape library / archive, Clearwater Bay Road, Kowloon,
Hong Kong
ⓒ +852 719 4828
Ⓕ +852 358 1337

Subjects: National Archives.

India

79 NATIONAL FILM ARCHIVE OF INDIA

Law College Road, Pune 411004, India
© +91 212 331559/338516/333649
✉ 145 7759 NFAI IN

Subjects: National Archives.

80 RAJSHRI PRODUCTIONS

Bhavana, 422 Veer Savarkar Road, Bombay 400025, India
© +91 22 4307688/4307626/4307802
Ⓕ +91 22 4229181

Contacts: K.K. Barjatya, P.K. Gupta
Subjects: Feature films, documentaries, Asian cinema.
▦ 35mm; Umatic, VHS. PAL.
Research: By staff only.
☉ Mon-Fri 10:00 to 17:30, plus half day on Saturday.
Procedure: Material supplied on VHS or 35mm print.
Description: Over 70 full length feature films in Hindi
language plus documentaries. English and Hindi spoken.

81 TIMES TELEVISION LIBRARY

The Time of India Building, 7 Bahadur Shah Zafar Marg, New
Dehli 110 002, India
© +91 11 3722094/3351606/3352087
Ⓕ +91 11 3715532/3715836
✉ 031-61337/38 INDIA IN

Contacts: Mr. Sanjay Sethi
Subjects: Drama, documentaries, industry, personalities,
cookery, music, fashion, sport, science, environmental,
culture.
▦ Most video formats. PAL.
Research: By both staff and outside researchers.
☉ 6 days, 10:00 to 17:00
Procedure: Viewing on VHS. 1-2 hours for access to BVU
and Beta masters.
Description: Times Television was formed in 1986 and has
produced and marketed a large range of programmes
covering subjects relating to India including social issues,
economy, business and industry, film industry awards,
fashion, personalities, cuisine of Eastern and Western India,
beauty contests, sport, science and the environment. They
also hold various drama serials plus a few pop concerts
including Bryan Adams and Jethro Tull. Partly computerized.
English and Hindi spoken.
Foreign Offices: UK.

Indonesia

82 IMAGE BANK / INDONESIA (CREATIVE RESOURCES)

J1 Pejuangan, No. 1, Blok B3, Jakarta 11520, Indonesia
ⓒ +66 21 548 7309
Ⓕ +66 21 548 5746

Contacts: Julie Dharmasurya
Subjects: Stock shots, aerial photography, time-lapse,
lifestyles, natural history, locations, sport.
▦ All film and video formats and line standards held.
Research: By both staff and outside researchers.
Appointment to visit.
☉ Mon–Fri 09:00 to 17:00
Procedure: 3/4″/VHS (any line standard) for viewing. 24
hours for access to masters.
Description: Vast collection of stock material, contemporary
and archival, acquired from Turner Broadcasting, Ocean
Images, I.R.E., Pigeon Productions, MacGillivray Freeman
Films, Dentsu Prox., McDonnell Douglas, Nature
Conservancy, etc. Offices worldwide and major cities of
North America – Chicago, Detroit, Mexico, Minneapolis,
Atlanta, Dallas and Los Angeles. Computerized. English,
French, Spanish, Italian, German and Greek spoken in the
NEW YORK HEADQUARTERS.
Foreign Offices: Argentina, Brazil, Chile, Colombia, Australia,
Canada, Hong Kong, Indonesia, Korea, Japan, Malaysia,
Philippines, Singapore, Taiwan, Thailand, South Africa, UK,
USA.

83 NATIONAL ARCHIVES OF THE REPUBLIC OF INDONESIA

Jalan Ampera Raya, Cilandak Timur, Jakarta Selatan 12560,
Indonesia
ⓒ +62 21 7805851 to 5853
Ⓕ +62 21 7805812

Contacts: Mr. A.A.G. Putra
Subjects: National Archives.
▦ 16mm, 35mm. Negatives of photographs.
Research: Researchers can visit with an appointment.
☉ Mon–Fri 09:00 to 15:00
Procedure: Written request, copyright clearance and relevant
fees paid.
Description: The audio-visual collection was started in 1980
and comprises films, photographs and sound recordings the
majority of the collection being photographs. The archive is a
division of the Indonesian National Archives, the copyright
holders being the state or individual creators of the material.
Catalogue computerized.

84 P.T. KREASIVIDEO HEDKWARTER MAS / FABULOUS FOOTAGE

Block B20, JL. Widjaya II, Kebayoran Baru, Jakarta 12160, Indonesia
© +62 21 720 7688
Ⓕ +62 21 720 7660

Subjects: Stock shots, locations, culture, industry, medicine, military, music, environmental, leisure, transport, natural history, space, trailers.

▦ Film; video (all film mastered onto tape).

Description: Complete contemporary film and videotape library with a vast range of quality images. Subject headings include agriculture, buildings, cities, countries, cultural activities, industry and business, landmarks, landscapes, medical, military, music, natural phenomena, news, period recreations, professions, rain forests, recreation, space, special effects, spectacles, sports, transportation, underwater, water and wildlife. They also hold special collections of Nazi propaganda footage, Russian history, Russian space program, B-movies and trailers. Computerized. Rate card and catalogue available. NB: Head office is in Toronto, Canada. Details received from Singapore office only.

Foreign Offices: Argentina, Australia, Brazil, Canada, Chile, Germany, Indonesia, Japan, Malaysia, Philippines, Singapore, Spain, Mexico, USA.

Iran

85   NATIONAL FILM ARCHIVE OF IRAN

P.O. Box 5158, Baharestan Sq., Teheran 11365, Iran
© +98 21 3291583
Ⓕ +98 21 3117734
⤷ 215642 RECU IR

Contacts: Fereydoun Khameneipour
Subjects: National Archives.
▦ Film.
Research: Researchers welcome with an appointment.
☺ Sat-Tues 08:00 to 16:00, Wed 08:00 to 15:00
Procedure: Limited access to master copies.

Israel

86 ARGO FILMS

43 Ben Yehuda St, Tel Aviv 69010, Israel
© +972 3 5228251
Ⓕ +972 3 5246910

Subjects: Feature films, documentaries, children's.
🕐 Sun-Thur 09:00 to 16:00
Description: Approximately 40 hours of programmes
including feature films (contemporary Israel), documentaries
(Ethiopian women) and children's shows (live and puppets).

87 DOKO VIDEO

33 Hayetzira Street, Ramat Gan 52521, Israel
© +972 3 5753555
Ⓕ +972 3 5753189

Contacts: Mrs Taly Kaufman
Subjects: Documentaries, war, Jewish history, travelogues,
technology, educational films, social history, children's.
▦ 8mm; D2, BVU. All line standards available.
Research: By staff.
🕐 Sun-Thur 09:00 to 17:00
Procedure: VHS viewing copies supplied. 3-7 days for
access to masters.
Description: Doko Video have a wide range of programmes
available covering every aspect of Israel (history, religion,
ethnic and social life, etc.). Titles available are listed in their
catalogue under the following headings - battles for peace,
holocaust and revival, follow the sun, biblical landscapes,
innovative technology, Jerusalem, discovering the past, the
social scene and children's program. Hebrew, English and
French spoken.

88   ENERGY PRODUCTIONS ISRAEL / VISUAL ENERGY

5 Hashla Street, Tel Aviv 62283, Israel
ⓒ +972 3 544 5588
ⓕ +972 3 546 1679

Subjects: Americana, sport, time-lapse, macro photography, natural history, locations, fashion, culture, landscapes, lifestyles, special effects.

▦ 16mm, 35mm, 70mm; most video formats.

Research: By staff. Visits by appointment.

☉ Mon-Fri 09:00 to 18:00

Procedure: Viewing tapes assembled. Masters copied after selection.

Description: Energy Productions hold the Timescape Image Library a huge library of stock material encompassing sports, wildlife, landmarks, cities, seascapes, macro/micro photography, fashion, underwater, botany, computer imagery and daily life from around the world. Also available via this office is The Playboy Fashion Collection, Namco Computer Imagery, Warren Miller Films and Sports Library, Windham Hills Video and Film Library and Bob Landis Wildlife. Computerized. Rate card and brochure available.

Foreign Offices: France, Germany, Italy, Japan, Spain, Sweden, Turkey, Israel, UK, USA.

89   IMAGE BANK / ISRAEL (IMAGE MAR'OT LTD.)

10th Floor, 4 Koifman Street, Tel Aviv 68012, Israel
© +972 3 510 4382
Ⓕ +972 3 510 4386

Contacts: Ms Aviva Weinman
Subjects: Stock shots, aerial photography, time-lapse, lifestyles, natural history, locations, sport.

All film and video formats and line standards held.
Research: By both staff and outside researchers. Appointment to visit.

☺ Mon-Fri 09:00 to 17:00
Procedure: 3/4"/VHS (any line standard) for viewing. 24 hours for access to masters.
Description: Vast collection of stock material, contemporary and archival, acquired from Turner Broadcasting, Ocean Images, I.R.E., Pigeon Productions, MacGillivray Freeman Films, Dentsu Prox., McDonnell Douglas, Nature Conservancy, etc. Offices worldwide and major cities of North America - Chicago, Detroit, Mexico, Minneapolis, Atlanta, Dallas and Los Angeles. Computerized. English, French, Spanish, Italian, German and Greek spoken in the NEW YORK HEADQUARTERS.
Foreign Offices: Argentina, Brazil, Chile, Colombia, Australia, Canada, Hong Kong, Indonesia, Korea, Japan, Malaysia, Philippines, Singapore, Taiwan, Thailand, South Africa, UK, USA.

90   JEWISH NATIONAL AND UNIVERSITY LIBRARY

National Sound Archives, P.O. Box 34165, Jerusalem 91 341, Israel
© +972 2 584 651
Ⓕ +972 2 511 771
✑ +972 2 25367

Subjects: National Archives, Jewish history
☺ Sun-Thurs 09:00 to 16:00

91 SHOVAL FILM PRODUCTION

32 Alenby Street, Tel Aviv 63325, Israel
Ⓒ +972 3 5179288
Ⓕ +972 3 5179289

Contacts: Benni Shvily
Subjects: Documentaries, feature films, war.
🎞 16mm, 35mm; all video formats.
Research: By staff and outside researchers. Appointment to visit.
🕑 Sun–Thur 09:30 to 16:00
Procedure: Viewing material on any video format. 24 hours for access to masters.
Description: Documentary film of Israeli history and wars. 20 feature films containing well known Israeli songs as well as World War II footage, Nazis fighting against British troops, etc. English and Hebrew spoken.

92 STEVEN SPIELBERG JEWISH FILM ARCHIVE

Law Building, The Hebrew University of Jerusalem, Mount Scopus, Jerusalem 91905, Israel
Ⓒ +972 2 882513
Ⓕ +972 2 322545

Contacts: Marilyn Koolik
Subjects: National Archives, Jewish history, newsreels.
🎞 Film; videocassettes.
Research: By both staff and outside researchers. Visits by appointment.
🕑 Sun–Thur 09:00 to 17:00
Description: Founded in 1969 the Spielberg archive maintains and acquires film and video material relating to Jewish and Israeli subjects. Newsreels include the Agadati Collection (1932 to 1956), the Carmel newsreels shot by Natan Axelrod (1905 to 1987), the Carmel-Herzliya and Geva newsreels. Computerized. Rate card available.

93 UNITED STUDIOS OF ISRAEL

Kesem St. 8, Herzlia 46100, Israel
Ⓒ +972 52 550 151-7
Ⓕ +972 52 550 334

Contacts: Mirjana Gross
Subjects: Newsreels, documentaries, educational films, war, current affairs, culture.
▦ 35mm; BVU.
🕐 Sun-Thur 08:00 to 17:00
Description: Newsreels made in Israel from 1951 to 1971 covering events, wars, emigrations, new settlements and political life in the state. Documentary films on education, the army, water problems, Arab and Jewish life, etc. Brochure available. NB: Collections are also at the Spielberg Archive (Jerusalem) and the Harvard Judaica Department (Boston USA).

Jamaica

94   NATIONAL LIBRARY OF JAMAICA

Audio Visual Archive Department, Box 823, 12 East Street, Kingston, Jamaica
ⓒ +1 809 9220620
Ⓕ +1 809 9225567
⟋⟍ Cable NALIBJAM

Subjects: National Archives.

Japan

95 AD HOC / FABULOUS FOOTAGE

N.T. Building, 7th Floor, 15-8 Nakata 2, Chikusa-ku, Nagoya
464, Japan
ⓒ +81 52 732 7051
Ⓕ +81 52 732 7052

Subjects: Stock shots, locations, culture, industry, medicine,
military, music, environmental, leisure, transport, natural
history, space, trailers.

Film; video (all film mastered onto tape).

Description: Complete contemporary film and videotape
library with a vast range of quality images. Subject headings
include agriculture, buildings, cities, countries, cultural
activities, industry and business, landmarks, landscapes,
medical, military, music, natural phenomena, news, period
recreations, professions, rain forests, recreation, space,
special effects, spectacles, sports, transportation,
underwater, water and wildlife. They also hold special
collections of Nazi propaganda footage, Russian history,
Russian space program, B-movies and trailers. Computerized.
Rate card and catalogue available. NB: Head office is in
Toronto, Canada, details of Japan office received from
Canada only.

Foreign Offices: Argentina, Australia, Brazil, Canada, Chile,
Germany, Indonesia, Japan, Malaysia, Philippines, Singapore,
Spain, Mexico, USA.

96 ARCHIVE FILMS JAPAN

East Roppongi Building, 3-16-35 Roppongi, Minato-Ku, Tokyo
106 Japan
© +81 3 3589 7423 / 7424
Ⓕ +81 3 3589 7466

Contacts: Yumiko Lino, Kyoko Saito
Subjects: Historical archive; newsreels, Hollywood, classic
films, film industry, educational films.
36mm, 16mm; various video formats with matching
cassettes.
Research: By staff. Appointment to visit.
☉ Mon-Fri 09:00 to 18:00
Procedure: Viewing tapes assembled. 24-48 hours for
access to masters.
Description: Over 5000 hours of newsreels, silent films,
classic comedies, Hollywood features, historical dramas,
documentaries and educational films. Represent The March
of Time, The RKO Shorts Library, International Film
Foundation, TV House and Videowest. Computerized. Rate
card and catalogue available. English spoken. NB: Head
office in New York, USA.
Foreign Offices: USA, France, Germany, Italy, Japan,
Netherlands, Sweden, UK.

97 ENERGY PRODUCTIONS TOKYO / IMAGICA CORP.

2-14-1, Higashigotanda, Shingawa-ku, Tokyo 141, Japan
© +81 3 3280 7524
Ⓕ +81 3 3280 7519

Subjects: Americana, sport, time-lapse, macro photography,
natural history, locations, fashion, culture, lifestyles,
landscapes, special effects.
16mm, 35mm, 70mm; most video formats.
Research: By staff. Visits by appointment.
☉ Mon-Fri 09:00 to 18:00
Procedure: Viewing tapes assembled. Masters copied after
selection.
Description: Energy Productions hold the Timescape Image
Library, a huge library of stock material encompassing sports,
wildlife, landmarks, cities, seascapes, macro/micro
photography, fashion, underwater, botany, computer imagery
and daily life from around the world. Also available via the
US office is The Playboy Fashion Collection, Namco
Computer Imagery, Warren Miller Films and Sports Library,
Windham Hills Video and Film Library and Bob Landis
Wildlife. Computerized. Rate card and brochure available.
Foreign Offices: USA, France, Germany, Italy, Japan, Spain,
Sweden, Turkey, Israel, UK.

98 FRONT LINE

Suite 3 Senyo Building, 5th Floor, 3-1-9 Nakameguro,
Meguro-ku, Toyko 153, Japan
℡ +81 3 3760 6271
℻ +81 3 3760 6012

Contacts: Seiichi Sugiura
Subjects: Stock shots, aviation, locations, natural history,
industry, space, time-lapse, transport, environmental.
🕓 Mon-Fri 10:00 to 18:00
Procedure: Viewing tapes loaned. Masters copied after
selection.
Description: Agents for UK company Index Stock Shots, USA
company Opus Global and Canadian company Fabulous
Footage in Japan.

99 IMAGE BANK / JAPAN

Gin-Ni Building, 9F, 2-6-16 Ginza, Chuo-Ku, Tokyo 104,
Japan
℡ +81 3 3562 5566
℻ +81 3 3562 5789

Contacts: Mr Haga-san (Mr Shigemitsu Haga)
Subjects: Stock shots, aerial photography, time-lapse,
lifestyles, natural history, locations, sport.
🎞 All film and video formats and line standards held.
Research: By both staff and outside researchers.
Appointment to visit.
🕓 Mon-Fri 09:00 to 17:00
Procedure: 3/4"/VHS (any line standard) for viewing. 24
hours for access to masters.
Description: Vast collection of stock material, contemporary
and archival, acquired from Turner Broadcasting, Ocean
Images, I.R.E., Pigeon Productions, MacGillivray Freeman
Films, Dentsu Prox., McDonnell Douglas, Nature
Conservancy, etc. Offices worldwide and major cities of
North America - Chicago, Detroit, Mexico, Minneapolis,
Atlanta, Dallas and Los Angeles. Computerized. English,
French, Spanish, Italian, German and Greek spoken in the
NEW YORK HEADQUARTERS.
Foreign Offices: Argentina, Brazil, Chile, Colombia, Australia,
Canada, Hong Kong, Indonesia, Korea, Japan, Malaysia,
Philippines, Singapore, Taiwan, Thailand, South Africa, UK,
USA.

100   NATIONAL FILM CENTER, NATIONAL MUSEUM OF MODERN ART

Tokyo Film Center - Archive, 3-1-4 Takane, Sagamihara-Shi, Kanagawa, Ken 229, Japan
Ⓒ +81 3 427580128
Ⓕ +81 3 427574449

Subjects: National Archives.

101   NHK INTERNATIONAL

NHK
INTERNATIONAL

Room 582, NHK Broadcasting Center, 2-2-1 Jinnan, Shibuya-ku, Tokyo 150-01, Japan
Ⓒ +81 3 3481 1875
Ⓕ +81 3 3481 1877
↗ J34553 INTRENHK

Contacts: Akiko Numakami, Fumiko Chiba, Yoko Hagimoto
Subjects: Current affairs, documentaries, sport, Vietnam war, China, Nippon News.
Most film and video formats. NTSC.
Research: By staff only.
☺ Mon-Fri 10:00 to 18:00
Procedure: Viewing on any format. Average of 4 days for access to masters.
Description: The NHK archives contain news, documentary, sports, etc. footage which has been broadcast on NHK over the past 40 years. Also included is exclusive footage of the Vietnam war and China from their respective governments. NHK owns the copyright for the vast majority of the available footage including the rights to Nippon News coverage of WWII and can assist with third party rights. Computerized. Rate card and catalogue available. English and Japanese spoken.

102   TOKYOVISION

Room 302 Nagai Building, 4-4-11 Akasaka, Minato-Ku, Tokyo 107, Japan
℃ +81 3 3586 6139
Ⓕ +81 3 3586 6257

Contacts: Atsushi Takahashi
Subjects: Documentaries.
▥ Beta/Beta SP, D2, 1″, 8mm video. NTSC.
Research: By staff only.
☺ Mon–Fri 10:00 to 19:00
Procedure: Viewing copies on any format. 10 days for access to masters.
Description: Tokyovision hold documentaries covering a wide range of subjects. Partly computerized. English and Japanese spoken.

Jordan

103 UNIVERSITY OF JORDAN LIBRARY

Amman, Jordan
© +962 6 843555 Ext. 3135
Ⓕ +962 6 832318
✎ UNVJ. JO 21629

Subjects: National Archives.

Kenya

104 CAMERAPIX

P.O. Box 45048, Nairobi, Kenya
ⓒ +254 2 223511 / 334398
Ⓕ +254 2 217244
〽 22576

Contacts: Mohamed Amin, Salim Amin
Subjects: Current affairs, natural history, culture.
▦ Videotape.
Research: By staff.
☉ Mon-Fri 08:00 to 17:00
Description: News, current affairs, wildlife and culture of Africa contained on approximately 6000 master videotapes.

105 KENYA NATIONAL ARCHIVES

P.O. Box 49210, Moi Avenue, Nairobi, Kenya
ⓒ +254 2 228959/228020/226007

Contacts: Mr Musila Musembi, Mrs A. Akhaabi, Mr Koo Ombati
Subjects: National Archives, current affairs, culture
▦ Film; video.
Research: Researchers need to purchase a permit to gain access.
☉ Mon-Fri 08:00 to 16:30, Sat 08:00 to 14:00
Procedure: Permission needed from the Director, fees for labour and copies.
Description: This is a public archive - the department being under the control of the Ministry of Home Affairs and National Heritage. All manner of records from public offices are held including files, reports, microfilms, maps, books, films, video and audio tapes plus a few cultural items. It also holds material from private individuals and publishes guides of these. Copyright is held by the owners, not the archive. Partly computerized.
Foreign Offices: Kenyan missions in other countries represent them, particularly the Kenya High Commission in London.

Kiribati

106 KIRIBATI NATIONAL ARCHIVES

P.O. Box 6, Bairiki, Tarawa, Kiribati
Ⓒ +686 21337
Ⓕ +686 28222

Subjects: National Archives.

Korea

107 IMAGE BANK / KOREA

Room 401, Kum-Pung Building, 48-27 Jeo-Dong 2KA,
Chung-Ku Seoul, Korea
ⓒ +82 2 273 2792
ⓕ +82 2 277 7064

Contacts: Mr Dong Hoon Han
Subjects: Stock shots, aerial photography, time-lapse,
lifestyles, natural history, locations, sport.
All film and video formats and line standards held.
Research: By both staff and outside researchers.
Appointment to visit.
☉ Mon–Fri 09:00 to 17:00
Procedure: 3/4″/VHS (any line standard) for viewing. 24
hours for access to masters.
Description: Vast collection of stock material, contemporary
and archival, acquired from Turner Broadcasting, Ocean
Images, I.R.E., Pigeon Productions, MacGillivray Freeman
Films, Dentsu Prox., McDonnell Douglas, Nature
Conservancy, etc. Offices worldwide and major cities of
North America - Chicago, Detroit, Mexico, Minneapolis,
Atlanta, Dallas and Los Angeles. Computerized. English,
French, Spanish, Italian, German and Greek spoken in the
NEW YORK HEADQUARTERS.
Foreign Offices: Argentina, Brazil, Chile, Colombia, Australia,
Canada, Hong Kong, Indonesia, Korea, Japan, Malaysia,
Philippines, Singapore, Taiwan, Thailand, South Africa, UK,
USA.

108 KOREAN FILM ARCHIVE

Seocho P.O. Box 91,
700 Seocho-dong, Seocho-gu, Seoul 137-070, Korea
© +82 2 521 3147/9 521 2102/2
Ⓕ +82 2 582 6213
✍ ARTCNTR K29150

Contacts: Mr. Sul Gee-hwan, Mr. Park Jin-Seok, Mr. Yang Jae-young
Subjects: National Archives, feature films, documentaries
Film; video.
Research: Restricted access to public.
Mon-Fri 09:00 to 18:00, Sat 09:00 to 13:00
Procedure: Copyright permission required prior to duplication.
Description: The archive holds feature films, documentaries, screenplays, posters, photographs, slides and books. Copyright is held by outside producers who need to be contacted prior to duplication. The library is in the process of being computerized, a catalogue only being published occasionally.

Korea, Democratic People's Republic of

109 NATIONAL FILM ARCHIVE - DEMOCRATIC PEOPLE'S REPUBLIC OF KOREA

15 Sochangdong, Central District, Pyongyang, Democratic People's Republic of Korea
✆ +850 2 3 45 51
✉ 5345 NFA KP

Subjects: National Archives.

Kuwait

110 AL-NAZAER COMPANY

P.O. Box 6301, Hawally 32038, Kuwait
© +965 2658 500 (10 lines)
Ⓕ +965 262 55 21
✏ 46364 NAZAER KT

Contacts: Mr Yousuf Al Refai, Mr Ali Al Refai
Subjects: Drama, entertainment, animation, documentaries.
▦ Beta SP, 1″, Umatic. PAL.
Research: By staff and outside researchers. Appointment to visit.
🕓 Open every day except Friday 08:00 to 13:00, 16:00 to 20:00
Procedure: VHS viewing material. One week for access to masters.
Description: The collection contains Arabic drama, short plays, musicals, variety, animated cartoon and documentaries (Arabic and English versions). Computerized. Catalogue available. English and Arabic spoken.

Lesotho

111   LESOTHO GOVERNMENT ARCHIVES

Ministry of Tourism, Sports & Culture, P.O. Box 52, Maseru, Lesotho
✆ +266 323034

Subjects: National Archives.

Malawi

112 NATIONAL ARCHIVES OF MALAWI

P.O. Box 62, McLeod Road, Zomba, Malawi
© +265 522 922 / 184
Ⓕ +265 522 148-33

Contacts: C.B. Malunga, Mrs. L.C. Chiotha, D.D. Najira
Subjects: National Archives.
Film.
Research: Researchers welcomed.
☺ Mon-Fri 07:30 to 12:00, 13:00 to 17:00
Procedure: Not yet established.
Description: The film collection was inherited from the Department of Information, the archives being a legal deposit and research facility enforcing the Printed Publications Act. Material relating to the country available elsewhere has also been purchased or given. A card catalogue, periodical registers and lists exist but as yet the library is not computerized.

Malaysia

113 IMAGE BANK / MALAYSIA

55-2 Medan Setia 1, Plaza Damansara, Damansara Heights,
Kuala Lumpur 50490, Malaysia
ⓒ +60 3 254 7133
Ⓕ +60 3 256 1812

Contacts: Dattin Tessie Lim
Subjects: Stock shots, aerial photography, time-lapse,
lifestyles, natural history, locations, sport.
All film and video formats and line standards held.
Research: By both staff and outside researchers.
Appointment to visit.
Mon-Fri 09:00 to 17:00
Procedure: 3/4"/VHS (any line standard) for viewing. 24
hours for access to masters.
Description: Vast collection of stock material, contemporary
and archival, acquired from Turner Broadcasting, Ocean
Images, I.R.E., Pigeon Productions, MacGillivray Freeman
Films, Dentsu Prox., McDonnell Douglas, Nature
Conservancy, etc. Offices worldwide and major cities of
North America - Chicago, Detroit, Mexico, Minneapolis,
Atlanta, Dallas and Los Angeles. Computerized. English,
French, Spanish, Italian, German and Greek spoken in the
NEW YORK HEADQUARTERS.
Foreign Offices: Argentina, Brazil, Chile, Colombia, Australia,
Canada, Hong Kong, Indonesia, Korea, Japan, Malaysia,
Philippines, Singapore, Taiwan, Thailand, South Africa, UK,
USA.

114 IMAGES OF THE EAST

19B Jalan 20/14, Petaling Jaya Selangor 46300, Malaysia
ⓒ +60 03 776 7199
Ⓕ +60 03 776 4560

Contacts: Theresa Khoo
Subjects: Stock shots, aviation, locations, natural history,
industry, space, time-lapse, transport, environmental.
Beta SP, 1", Umatic. PAL.
Research: By staff. Visits by appointment.
Mon-Fri 08:30 to 17:45
Procedure: Viewing tapes loaned. Masters copied after
selection, 3-4 days for access.
Description: Agents for UK company Index Stock Shots and
German company Modern Video Library in Malaysia and
Singapore. The library holds an A-Z of subject categories
including landscape, destination and sports footage from
Malaysia. Partly computerized. Rate card available. English
spoken.

115 NATIONAL ARCHIVES OF MALAYSIA

Jalan Duta, Kuala Lumpur 50568, Malaysia
ⓒ +60 3 2562688
ⓕ +60 3 2555679

Subjects: National Archives.

116 SISTEM TELEVISYEN MALAYSIA BERHAD

Animated and Post Production Techniques SDN BHD, 3rd
Floor, Wisma Ali Bawal, 11A Jalan Tandang, 46050 Petaling
Jaya, Kuala Lumpur, Malaysia
ⓒ +60 3 7942225
ⓕ +60 3 7941259

Contacts: Mr Khairuddin Bin Othman
Subjects: Stock shots.
▦ Beta/Beta SP, 1″, Umatic. PAL and NTSC.
Research: By staff and outside researchers. Appointment to
visit.
🕑 Mon-Sat 09:00 to 17:00
Procedure: Viewing material supplied on video. Access to
masters variable.
Description: Full range of stock shot material with subjects
listed under A-Z in their catalogue. Footage reflects the
customs, people, locations, buildings, industry, historical
sites, etc. of Malaysia. Partly computerized. English and
Malay spoken.

117   VIDEO HEADQUARTERS (KL) / FABULOUS FOOTAGE

47 Medan Setia, Bukit Damansara, Kuala Lumpur, 50490
Malaysia
Ⓒ +60 3 254 7011
Ⓕ +60 3 254 6151

Subjects: Stock shots, locations, culture, industry, medicine,
military, music, environmental, leisure, transport, natural
history, space, trailers.

▦ Film; video (all film mastered onto tape).

Description: Complete contemporary film and videotape
library with a vast range of quality images. Subject headings
include agriculture, buildings, cities, countries, cultural
activities, industry and business, landmarks, landscapes,
medical, military, music, natural phenomena, news, period
recreations, professions, rain forests, recreation, space,
special effects, spectacles, sports, transportation,
underwater, water and wildlife. They also hold special
collections of Nazi propaganda footage, Russian history,
Russian space program, B-movies and trailers. Computerized.
Rate card and catalogue available. NB: Head office is in
Toronto, Canada. Details received from Singapore office only.
Foreign Offices: Argentina, Australia, Brazil, Canada, Chile,
Germany, Indonesia, Japan, Malaysia, Philippines, Singapore,
Spain, Mexico, USA.

Malta

118 PUBLIC BROADCASTING SERVICES

Video Archives Service, P.O. Box 82, Valletta CMR 01, Malta
ⓒ +356 225051 Ext. 327
ⓕ +356 241189
⤳ 1443 MW

Contacts: Emmanuel Zammit, Victor Wickman
Subjects: Current affairs.
▦ 16mm, 35mm; Beta/Beta SP, 1″, Umatic. PAL.
Research: By staff or outside researchers. Appointment to visit.
☉ Mon-Fri 08:00 to 16:00
Description: Local and foreign news collection dating back to 1962, also a range of local programmes. Catalogue and rate card available. English spoken.

Marshall Islands

119   MUSEUM OF THE MARSHALL ISLANDS

Alele Museum Library, P.O. Box 629, Majuro MH 96960,
Marshall Islands
ⓒ +692 625 3372
Ⓕ +692 625 3226

Contacts: Alfred Capella
Subjects: National Archives.
▦ Video.
Research: Appointment required in advance.
☉ Mon-Fri 10:00 to 12:00, 15:00 to 17:00
Procedure: Master copies available for a fee, notice required.
Description: The library holds computerized and microfilm
records relating to government archives including court
records. Video films are also held on Marshall Islands oral
traditions.

Mauritius

120 MAURITIUS BROADCASTING CORPORATION

1 Louis Pasteur Street, Forest Side, Mauritius
ⓒ +230 675001/2/3 6743743
Ⓕ +230 6757332
⚡ 4230 MAUBROD IW

Contacts: Anne Marie Ginette Fabre
Subjects: National Archives, current affairs, religion, documentaries, children's, music, personalities, sport.
🎞 16mm, 35mm; Beta/Beta SP, BVU, Umatic. PAL and SECAM.
Research: By staff. Outside researchers by appointment.
🕐 7 days 08:30 to 17:00
Procedure: Viewing on 16mm and video. 2 hours for access to masters.
Description: A wide range of programme material covering political, international and local events, religion, documentaries, television for children and teenagers, musicals, interviews and sports. English and French spoken.

Mexico

121   ARCHIVO GENERAL DE LA NACION

Eduardo Molina y Albaniles, Col. Penitenciaria Ampliacion,
Apartado Postal 1999, Mexico 1, D.F., Mexico D.F. 15350,
Mexico
ⓒ +52 5 7895915
Ⓕ +52 5 7895915

Subjects: National Archives

122   BANCO INTERNATIONAL DE FOTOGRAFIA (BIF) / FABULOUS FOOTAGE

Avenida 3, 24 esq. Calle 1, Col. San Pedro de los Pinos
03801, Mexico
ⓒ +525 277 0438
Ⓕ +525 277 7933

Subjects: Stock shots, locations, culture, industry, medicine,
military, music, environmental, leisure, transport, natural
history, space, trailers.

Film; video (all film mastered onto tape).

Description: Complete contemporary film and videotape
library with a vast range of quality images. Subject headings
include agriculture, buildings, cities, countries, cultural
activities, industry and business, landmarks, landscapes,
medical, military, music, natural phenomena, news, period
recreations, professions, rain forests, recreation, space,
special effects, spectacles, sports, transportation,
underwater, water and wildlife. They also hold special
collections of Nazi propaganda footage, Russian history,
Russian space program, B-movies and trailers. Computerized.
Rate card and catalogue available. NB: Head office is in
Toronto, Canada, details of Mexico office received from
Canada only.

Foreign Offices: Argentina, Australia, Brazil, Canada, Chile,
Germany, Indonesia, Japan, Malaysia, Philippines, Singapore,
Spain, Mexico, USA.

Namibia

123 NATIONAL ARCHIVES OF NAMIBIA

Private Bag 13250, 4 Luderitz Street, Windhoek 9000, Namibia

✆ +264 61 293387

Subjects: National Archives.

New Zealand

124 KIDS TV

P.O. Box 8148, Symonds Street, Auckland 3, New Zealand
ⓒ +64 09 357 0724
Ⓕ +64 09 358 4809

Contacts: David Stewart
Subjects: Children's, educational films.
▦ Beta/Beta SP, D2, 1″. PAL.
Research: By staff.
☉ Mon–Fri 08:00 to 18:00
Procedure: Timecoded VHS cassettes for viewing. Immediate access to masters.
Description: Programmes that target an age range from 1-19 years. Subjects covered are music, sports, current affairs and education for children and parents. Copyright owned by Kids TV. Computerized.

125 NEW ZEALAND FILM ARCHIVE

P.O. Box 11-449, First Floor, The Film Centre, Cnr. Cable Street & Jervois Quay, Wellington, New Zealand
ⓒ +64 4 3847647
Ⓕ +64 4 3829595

Contacts: Bronwyn Taylor (public programmes), Diane Pivac (documentation)
Subjects: National Archives, newsreels, documentaries, feature films, animation.
▦ Film; video.
Research: By appointment only.
☉ Mon–Fri 09:00 to 17:00
Procedure: Access to view is available. Master material not available.
Description: Held in the archive's collection are New Zealand and overseas films from 1897 to the present day, comprising fiction and feature films, shorts animated films, documentaries, newsreels, video and television programmes. A wide variety of promotional, critical and historical documentation and information is also held for New Zealand and overseas films. Copyright is not held by NZFA. Computerized. Rate card available.

126 NEW ZEALAND FILM COMMISSION

P.O. Box 11-546, Wellington, New Zealand
ⓒ +64 4 385 9754
ⓕ +64 4 384 9719
⟋ N2 30386

Contacts: Lindsay Shelton
Subjects: Documentaries, drama, feature films.
🎞 16mm, 35mm; all videotape formats.
Research: By both staff and outside researchers.
Appointment to visit.
🕓 Mon-Fri 09:00 to 17:00
Procedure: VHS normally supplied for viewing. 1 week for
access to masters.
Description: Documentaries, dramas and films featuring New
Zealand subjects, its people and various related topics. Partly
computerized.

127 NEW ZEALAND TELEVISION ARCHIVE

Television New Zealand, P.O. Box
3819, Auckland, New Zealand
ⓒ +64 9 375 0942
ⓕ +64 9 375 0872

Contacts: Jane Hiscotte, Alan Ferris
Subjects: Current affairs, newsreels, documentaries, natural
history, leisure, stock shots.
🎞 Film; videotape.
Research: By staff.
🕓 Mon-Fri 08:00 to 18:00
Procedure: Print outs available for each request.
Description: News, current affairs, stock shots and general
programming from New Zealand Television dating from 1960.
Newsreels and documentaries purchased from the National
Film Unit (1940 to 1965). The archive also specialize in
natural history footage, spectacular scenery and recreational
sports action. 80% computerized.

Nigeria

128 FEDERAL UNIVERSITY OF TECHNOLOGY, AKURE LIBRARY

P.M.B 704, Akure, Nigeria

Subjects: National Archives

Papua New Guinea

129 NATIONAL LIBRARY OF PAPUA NEW GUINEA

Film Library, P.O. Box 5770, Boroko, Papua New Guinea
© +675 256200
Ⓕ +675 25 1331
↗ NE 22234

Contacts: Neil Nicholls (National Librarian), Mary Warus (Film Librarian)
Subjects: National Archives.
▦ 16mm; VHS, Umatic.
Research: Written request required prior to access.
🕐 Mon-Fri 09:00 to 12:00, 13:00 to 16:00
Procedure: Copies not normally available, may be considered on request.
Description: The collection consists of materials relating to Papua New Guinea dating from the 1920s to the present day. It also keeps footage passed on from the Office of Information (established in August 1953 and abolished in December 1983). Two catalogues are presently available, one for the 16mm collection and another for the VHS collection.

Peru

130   NATIONAL ARCHIVES OF PERU

P.O. Box 3124, Manuel Cuadros s/n, Lima 100, Peru
© +51 14 275930

Subjects: National Archives.

Philippines

131 IMAGE BANK / PHILIPPINES

Rom 1014, Cityland, Tower II, Velero Street, Cor HV dela
Costa Street, Salacedo Village, Makati Metro Maila,
Philippines
© +63 2 894 2122
Ⓕ +63 2 813 8675

Contacts: Datin Tessie Lim
Subjects: Stock shots, aerial photography, time-lapse,
lifestyles, natural history, locations, sport.
▥ All film and video formats and line standards held.
Research: By both staff and outside researchers.
Appointment to visit.
◷ Mon-Fri 09:00 to 17:00
Procedure: 3/4"/VHS (any line standard) for viewing. 24
hours for access to masters.
Description: Vast collection of stock material, contemporary
and archival, acquired from Turner Broadcasting, Ocean
Images, I.R.E., Pigeon Productions, MacGillivray Freeman
Films, Dentsu Prox., McDonnell Douglas, Nature
Conservancy, etc. Offices worldwide and major cities of
North America - Chicago, Detroit, Mexico, Minneapolis,
Atlanta, Dallas and Los Angeles. Computerized. English,
French, Spanish, Italian, German and Greek spoken in the
NEW YORK HEADQUARTERS.
Foreign Offices: Argentina, Brazil, Chile, Colombia, Australia,
Canada, Hong Kong, Indonesia, Korea, Japan, Malaysia,
Philippines, Singapore, Taiwan, Thailand, South Africa, UK,
USA.

132 UNIVERSITY OF THE PHILIPPINES FILM CENTER ARCHIVES

P.O. Box 214, Magsaysay Avenue, Quezon City 1101,
Philippines
© +63 2 962722
Ⓕ +63 2 992863 / 986780
⋀ 63199 ETPIMO PN

Subjects: National Archives.

133   VHQ DIMENSIONS / FABULOUS FOOTAGE

Unit 601, One Corporate Plaza, Metro Manila 845-A,
Philippines
ⓒ +63 2 812 0241
ⓕ +63 2 812 6910

Subjects: Stock shots, locations, culture, industry, medicine,
military, music, environmental, leisure, transport, natural
history, space, trailers.

▦ Film; video (all film mastered onto tape).

Description: Complete contemporary film and videotape
library with a vast range of quality images. Subject headings
include agriculture, buildings, cities, countries, cultural
activities, industry and business, landmarks, landscapes,
medical, military, music, natural phenomena, news, period
recreations, professions, rain forests, recreation, space,
special effects, spectacles, sports, transportation,
underwater, water and wildlife. They also hold special
collections of Nazi propaganda footage, Russian history,
Russian space program, B-movies and trailers. Computerized.
Rate card and catalogue available. NB: Head office is in
Toronto, Canada. Details received from Singapore office only.

Foreign Offices: Argentina, Australia, Brazil, Canada, Chile,
Germany, Indonesia, Japan, Malaysia, Philippines, Singapore,
Spain, Mexico, USA.

Saudi Arabia

134 KING SAUD UNIVERSITY LIBRARIES

P.O. Box 22480, Dhiriyya, Riyadh 11495, Saudi Arabia
© +966 1 4676152
Ⓕ +966 1 4676162
✎ 401019 KSU SJ

Subjects: National Archives.

Seychelles, Republic of

135   NATIONAL ARCHIVES AND MUSEUMS - SEYCHELLES

P.O. Box 720, Victoria, Mahe, Republic of Seychelles

Subjects: National Archives.

136   SEYCHELLES BROADCASTING CORPORATION (SBC)

P.O. Box 321, Hermitage, Mahe, Republic of Seychelles
ⓒ +248 224161
Ⓕ +248 225641
✎ 2315

Contacts: Ibrahim Afif, Jean-Claude Matombe, Catherine Belmont
Subjects: Current affairs.
▦ BVU, Umatic. PAL.
Research: By staff only.
🕓 Mon–Fri 08:00 to 16:00
Procedure: Limited access to material.
Description: Footage relates mainly to news and current affairs of the Seychelles, copyright is held by them in most cases. The library was set up mainly to serve the needs of the SBC news and production teams. Partly computerized. English, French and Kreol spoken.

Singapore

137 IMAGE BANK / SINGAPORE (ASIA CREATIVE RESOURCES)

Suite 02-10 Beach Centre, 15 Beach Road, 0718, Singapore
ⓒ +65 338 3502/3
Ⓕ +65 338 0349

Contacts: Yvonne Tan
Subjects: Stock shots, aerial photography, time-lapse, lifestyles, natural history, locations, sport.
▦ All film and video formats and line standards held.
Research: By both staff and outside researchers. Appointment to visit.
🕓 Mon-Fri 09:00 to 17:00
Procedure: 3/4"/VHS (any line standard) for viewing. 24 hours for access to masters.
Description: Vast collection of stock material, contemporary and archival, acquired from Turner Broadcasting, Ocean Images, I.R.E., Pigeon Productions, MacGillivray Freeman Films, Dentsu Prox., McDonnell Douglas, Nature Conservancy, etc. Offices worldwide and major cities of North America - Chicago, Detroit, Mexico, Minneapolis, Atlanta, Dallas and Los Angeles. Computerized. English, French, Spanish, Italian, German and Greek spoken in the NEW YORK HEADQUARTERS.
Foreign Offices: Argentina, Brazil, Chile, Colombia, Australia, Canada, Hong Kong, Indonesia, Korea, Japan, Malaysia, Philippines, Singapore, Taiwan, Thailand, South Africa, UK, USA.

138 VIDEO HEADQUARTERS / FABULOUS FOOTAGE

40-41 Duxton Hill 0208, Singapore
© +65 732 8085
Ⓕ +65 733 0070

Contacts: Mavis Holborn
Subjects: Stock shots, locations, culture, industry, medicine, military, music, environmental, leisure, transport, natural history, space, trailers.

Film; video (all film mastered onto tape).
Research: By staff and outside researchers. Appointment to visit.

Mon-Fri 09:00 to 18:00
Procedure: Time-coded VHS/Umatic viewing copies. 3-5 days for access to masters.
Description: Complete contemporary film and videotape library with a vast range of quality images. Subject headings include agriculture, buildings, cities, countries, cultural activities, industry and business, landmarks, landscapes, medical, military, music, natural phenomena, news, period recreations, professions, rain forests, recreation, space, special effects, spectacles, sports, transportation, underwater, water and wildlife. They also hold special collections of Nazi propaganda footage, Russian history, Russian space program, B-movies and trailers. Computerized. Rate card and catalogue available. English and Mandarin spoken. NB: Head office is in Toronto, Canada.
Foreign Offices: Argentina, Australia, Brazil, Canada, Chile, Germany, Indonesia, Japan, Malaysia, Philippines, Singapore, Spain, Mexico, USA.

Solomon Islands

139 NATIONAL ARCHIVES OF SOLOMON ISLANDS

P.O. Box 780, Hibiscus Avenue, Honiara, Solomon Islands
© +677 21426
Ⓕ +677 21397
✐ HQ 66311

Subjects: National Archives.

South Africa

140   IMAGE BANK / SOUTH AFRICA

P.O. Box 783227, Sandton 2196, South Africa
ⓒ +27 11 883 7825/6
ⓕ +27 11 884 1581

Contacts: Laurence Hughes
Subjects: Stock shots, aerial photography, time-lapse,
lifestyles, natural history, locations, sport.
▦ All film and video formats and line standards held.
Research: By both staff and outside researchers.
Appointment to visit.
🕐 Mon-Fri 09:00 to 17:00
Procedure: 3/4"/VHS (any line standard) for viewing. 24
hours for access to masters.
Description: Vast collection of stock material, contemporary
and archival, acquired from Turner Broadcasting, Ocean
Images, I.R.E., Pigeon Productions, MacGillivray Freeman
Films, Dentsu Prox., McDonnell Douglas, Nature
Conservancy, etc. Offices worldwide and major cities of
North America - Chicago, Detroit, Mexico, Minneapolis,
Atlanta, Dallas and Los Angeles. Computerized. English,
French, Spanish, Italian, German and Greek spoken in the
NEW YORK HEADQUARTERS.
Foreign Offices: Argentina, Brazil, Chile, Colombia, Australia,
Canada, Hong Kong, Indonesia, Korea, Japan, Malaysia,
Philippines, Singapore, Taiwan, Thailand, South Africa, UK,
USA.

141   PAUL ZWICK PRODUCTIONS

P.O. Box 91134, Auckland Park 2006, South Africa
ⓒ +27 11 789 6390/1
ⓕ +27 11 789 6044

Contacts: Paul Zwick
Subjects: Natural history, locations.
▦ Beta/Beta SP. PAL.
Research: By staff. Visits by appointment.
🕐 Mon-Fri 08:30 to 18:00
Procedure: Timecoded VHS tapes compiled. 3 hours for
access to masters.
Description: Various wildlife scenes of southern African
game reserves, extensive footage of Indian Ocean islands -
Mauritius and Comores, also footage of major US cities -
New York, Las Vegas, San Francisco, etc. Computerized.
English, Afrikaans and Hungarian spoken.

142   SOUTH AFRICAN NATIONAL FILM VIDEO & SOUND ARCHIVES

Private Bag X236, 698 Churchstreet East, Arcadia Pretoria 0002, Pretoria 0001, South Africa
ⓒ +27 12 343 9767/8/9
ⓕ +27 12 344 5143

Contacts: Johan de Lange
Subjects: National Archives, South Africa, apartheid, arts.
▦ Most film formats; Beta/Beta SP, 1″, Umatic, VHS. PAL.
Research: Research by appointment only - not open on Fridays to public.
🕐 Mon-Fri 08:00 to 16:00
Procedure: Viewing on premises on all formats. 3 days for access to masters.
Description: The collection contains films, videos, gramophone records, CDs, audio cassettes and documentation all relating to South Africa. There is also an information centre on the arts. Copyrights all reside with the original owners of the material except for a few exceptional cases. Partly computerized. Catalogue available. English and Afrikaans spoken.

143   STOCK OPTIONS

P.O. Box 87622, Houghton 2041, South Africa
ⓒ +27 11 788 7248 / 880 1287
ⓕ +27 11 788 9996

Contacts: Margi Sheard, Sandee Daniell
Subjects: Natural history, travelogues, locations, anthropology, aerial photography.
▦ 16mm, 35mm; Beta SP, 1″, D1. PAL, some NTSC masters available.
Research: By both staff and outside researchers. Appointment to visit.
🕐 Mon-Fri 08:30 to 17:30 (contactable until 22:00 by telephone)
Procedure: Umatic/VHS for viewing. 2 hours for local access to masters.
Description: Stock Options have African wildlife material (16mm and Beta SP), African landscapes, seascapes including aerial footage (16mm and 35mm), ethnic tribes and customs and international travel footage (Beta SP). Computerized. Catalogue and rate card available.
Foreign Offices: Represented by Index Stock Shots in London, Energy Productions in Los Angeles and Film World Research in Sydney.

Sri Lanka

144   SRI LANKA NATIONAL LIBRARY SERVICES BOARD

National Library of Sri Lanka, P.O. Box 1764, 14
Independence Avenue, Colombo 07, Sri Lanka
ⓒ +94 1 698847 / 685199 / 685201
Ⓕ +94 1 685201

Contacts: Mr M.S.U. Amarasiri (Director)
Subjects: National Archives, science, social history
▦ Video.
Research: Researchers can visit.
☉ Tues-Sat 09:00 to 17:00
Procedure: Material seen on site only, cannot be loaned.
Description: The library holds material relating to social
sciences, humanities, science and technology, library and
information science, mass communications. Materials
comprise of books, periodicals, newspapers, micro-fiches,
microfilms, manuscripts, maps, computer discs, recordings
and video cassettes. Partly computerized.

Sudan

145   NATIONAL RECORDS OFFICE, THE

P.O. Box 1914 Khartoum, Al-Jumhuryyia Street, Khartoum,
Sudan
℗ +249 11 81995 / 84255
⁄⁄ Watjaiq - Khartoum

Subjects: National Archives

Syria

146 ASSAD NATIONAL LIBRARY

Omayyad Square, Damascas, Syria
ⓒ +963 11 3332883
Ⓕ +963 11 3320804
⤳ 419134

Contacts: Ghassan Lahham (Director)
Subjects: National Archives.
☉ Open 6 days (12 hours)
Procedure: Access to masters not yet permitted.
Description: The library holds copyright material from 1984
and is in the process of computerization.

---

147 SHAMRA for Production and Distribution

P.O. Box 149, Damascus, Syria
ⓒ +963 11 665601
Ⓕ +963 11 662812
⤳ 411404 SY

Contacts: Khaldoun Al Maleh
Subjects: Comedy, animation, drama.
▦ Beta/Beta SP, 1″, BVU, Umatic. PAL.
Research: Appointment to visit.
☉ Sat-Thurs 09:00 to 21:00
Description: Arab speaking comedies, television series and
plays. Also a collection of TV programmes and cartoon films
dubbed into Arabic - rights held for distribution to Arabic
speaking TV stations. Computerized. English spoken.
Foreign Offices: Greece.

Taiwan, Republic of China

148   IMAGE BANK / TAIWAN (HARVARD MANAGEMENT SERVICES)

9th Floor, 118 Nanking East Road, Sec. 5, Taipei 0718, Taiwan, Republic of China
℃ +886 2 769 1752/765 7364
Ⓕ +886 2 767 1661

Contacts: David Tsai
Subjects: Stock shots, aerial photography, time-lapse, lifestyles, natural history, locations, sport.
▦ All film and video formats and line standards held.
Research: By both staff and outside researchers. Appointment to visit.
☉ Mon-Fri 09:00 to 17:00
Procedure: 3/4"/VHS (any line standard) for viewing. 24 hours for access to masters.
Description: Vast collection of stock material, contemporary and archival, acquired from Turner Broadcasting, Ocean Images, I.R.E., Pigeon Productions, MacGillivray Freeman Films, Dentsu Prox., McDonnell Douglas, Nature Conservancy, etc. Offices worldwide and major cities of North America - Chicago, Detroit, Mexico, Minneapolis, Atlanta, Dallas and Los Angeles. Computerized. English, French, Spanish, Italian, German and Greek spoken in the NEW YORK HEADQUARTERS.
Foreign Offices: Argentina, Brazil, Chile, Colombia, Australia, Canada, Hong Kong, Indonesia, Korea, Japan, Malaysia, Philippines, Singapore, Taiwan, Thailand, South Africa, UK, USA

Tanzania

149 AUDIO VISUAL INSTITUTE, NATIONAL LIBRARY & ARCHIVE

P.O. Box 31519, Dar Es Salaam, Tanzania
℡ +255 51 72601/2/3/4

Contacts: M.I. Kange, Eva Sessoa
Subjects: National Archives, educational films, engineering, health, agriculture, tourism, current affairs.
▤ 16mm, 35mm.
Research: Permission and appointment needed prior to research.
🕐 Mon-Fri 07:30 to 15:30
Procedure: On request.
Description: Copyright to materials in the collection is owned by respective producers of films. The library is not computerized. A book catalogue is issued.

Thailand

150   IMAGE BANK / THAILAND

6th Floor, Apartment 92, 427 Silom Road (SOI Silom 7),
Bangrak, Bangkok 10500, Thailand
© +66 2 231 5518/9
Ⓕ +66 2 231 5786

Contacts: Ms. Yuwadee Jaiyen
Subjects: Stock shots, aerial photography, time-lapse,
lifestyles, natural history, locations, sport.
▦ All film and video formats and line standards held.
Research: By both staff and outside researchers.
Appointment to visit.
◷ Mon-Fri 09:00 to 17:00
Procedure: 3/4″/VHS (any line standard) for viewing. 24
hours for masters.
Description: Vast collection of stock material contemporary
and archival acquired from Turner Broadcasting, Ocean
Images, I.R.E., Pigeon Productions, MacGillivray Freeman
Films, Dentsu Prox., McDonnell Douglas, Nature Conservancy
etc. Offices worldwide and major cities of North America -
Chicago, Detroit, Mexico, Minneapolis, Atlanta, Dallas and
Los Angeles. Computerized. English, French, Spanish, Italian,
German and Greek spoken in the NEW YORK
HEADQUARTERS.
Foreign Offices: Argentina, Brazil, Chile, Colombia, Australia,
Canada, Hong Kong, Indonesia, Korea, Japan, Malaysia,
Philippines, Singapore, Taiwan, Thailand, South Africa, UK,
USA.

151   NATIONAL ARCHIVES OF THAILAND

Samsen Road, Bangkok 10300, Thailand
© +66 2 2823829
Ⓕ +66 2 2816947

Subjects: National Archives.

Tunisia

152   CENTRE DE DOCUMENTATION NATIONALE (CDN)

4 Rue Ibn Nadim, Cite Montplaisir - BP 350, Tunis 1002,
Tunisia
© +216 1 894 266
Ⓕ +266 1 792 241

Contacts: Abdelbaki Daly, Director General
Subjects: National Archives
Research: By staff only.
☺ Mon-Thurs 08:00 to 18:00, Fri and Sat 08:00 to 13:30
Description: The centre holds databases (biographies,
politics, French culture), 8000 monographs, 10 000
newspaper articles, 50 000 photographs, microfiche and
journals.

Turkey

153 BARLIK FILM

Ahududu CD. 32/3, Beyoglu, 80060 Istanbul, Turkey
© +90 1 212 2441542
Ⓕ +90 1 212 2510386

Contacts: Ali Barlik
Subjects: Feature films.
▦ 35mm; Beta/Beta SP, 1″, Umatic. PAL.
Research: Appointment to visit.
🕐 Mon-Fri 10:00 to 17:00
Procedure: Viewing material on VHS.
Description: A wide selection of Turkish made feature films.
Computerized. English and Turkish spoken.

154 ENERGY PRODUCTIONS ISTANBUL

Turkocagi Caddesi 4, Basin Sarayi Kat 4, Cagaloglu 34440
Istanbul, Turkey
© +90 1 212 511 87 37
Ⓕ +90 1 212 514 07 61

Subjects: Americana, sport, time-lapse, macro photography,
natural history, locations, fashion, culture, landscapes,
lifestyles, special effects.
▦ 16mm, 35mm, 70mm; most video formats.
Research: By staff. Visits by appointment.
🕐 Mon-Fri 09:00 to 18:00
Procedure: Viewing tapes assembled. Masters copied after
selection.
Description: Energy Productions hold the Timescape Image
Library, a huge library of stock material encompassing sports,
wildlife, landmarks, cities, seascapes, macro/micro
photography, fashion, underwater, botany, computer imagery
and daily life from around the world. Also available via this
office is The Playboy Fashion Collection, Namco Computer
Imagery, Warren Miller Films and Sports Library, Windham
Hills Video and Film Library and Bob Landis Wildlife.
Computerized. Rate card and brochure available.
Foreign Offices: France, Germany, Italy, Japan, Spain,
Sweden, Turkey, Israel, UK, USA.

155 IMAGE BANK / TURKEY (TRANSIMAJ MAR'OT LTD)

Ulusyolu Gundes Sitesi, Istanbul, Turkey
ⓒ +90 1 257 0327/8
Ⓕ +90 1 257 0328

Contacts: Dr Pinar Bakir
Subjects: Stock shots, aerial photography, time-lapse, lifestyles, natural history, locations, sport.
All film and video formats and line standards held.
Research: By both staff and outside researchers. Appointment to visit.
☉ Mon-Fri 09:00 to 17:00
Procedure: 3/4"/VHS (any line standard) for viewing. 24 hours for access to masters.
Description: Vast collection of stock material, contemporary and archival, acquired from Turner Broadcasting, Ocean Images, I.R.E., Pigeon Productions, MacGillivray Freeman Films, Dentsu Prox., McDonnell Douglas, Nature Conservancy, etc. Offices worldwide and major cities of North America - Chicago, Detroit, Mexico, Minneapolis, Atlanta, Dallas and Los Angeles. Computerized. English, French, Spanish, Italian, German and Greek spoken in the NEW YORK HEADQUARTERS.
Foreign Offices: Argentina, Brazil, Chile, Colombia, Australia, Canada, Hong Kong, Indonesia, Korea, Japan, Malaysia, Philippines, Singapore, Taiwan, Thailand, South Africa, UK, USA.

156 KILIC FILM

Yesilcam Sk., 26/2 Beyoglu, 80070 Istanbul, Turkey
ⓒ +90 1 212 245 1584 / 249 5804
Ⓕ +90 1 212 244 1612

Contacts: A. Erol Kilic
Subjects: Feature films.
35mm; Beta/Beta SP, Umatic. PAL.
Research: Viewing cassettes on Betamax and VHS.
☉ Mon-Fri 09:00 to 17:00
Description: Theatrical, video and TV films from all over the world. German, English and Turkish spoken.

157 TURKISH FILM AND TV INSTITUTE

80700 Kislaonu-Besiktas, Istanbul, Turkey
ⓒ +90 1 166 10 96
Ⓕ +90 1 167 65 99

Subjects: National Archives.

Uruguay

158 ARCHIVO NACIONAL DE LA IMAGEN - SODRE

Sarandi 430 1er piso, Casilla de Correo 1412, Montevideo
11.000, Uruguay
Ⓒ +598 2 955493
Ⓕ +598 2 963240
∿ UY 6553

Contacts: Juan Jose Mugni (Director), Graciela Dacosta
(Librarian)
Subjects: National Archives.
▦ Film; video
Research: Research by appointment only.
☺ Mon-Fri 10:00 to 16:00
Procedure: Access to masters not possible.
Description: The archive collects materials relating to cinema
including books, serials, brochures, press books and cuttings,
photographs, slides, films and videos. The collection is
available for study purposes only.

USA

159   ACTION SPORTS / SCOTT DITTRICH FILMS

P.O. Box 301, Malibu, CA 90265, USA
ⓒ +1 310 459 2526
Ⓕ +1 310 456 1743

Contacts: Patrick
Subjects: Adventure sports, leisure, locations.
Film.
Research: By both staff and outside researchers.
Appointment to visit.
☺ Mon-Fri 09:00 to 17:00
Description: Actions sports footage - surf, snow, waterskiing, mountain biking, kayak, skating, rollerblading, windsurfing, waves, snowboarding, etc. Also location shots such as sunsets, Los Angeles and tropical. Partly computerized. Rate card and catalogue available.

160   ACTION SPORTS ADVENTURE (ASA)

1926 Broadway, New York, NY 10023, USA
ⓒ +1 212 721 2800
Ⓕ +1 212 721 0191

Contacts: Rob Pavlin, Jill Schiffman
Subjects: Sport, Olympics, historical archive, leisure, natural history.
Various film and video formats/line standards available.
Research: By staff.
☺ Mon-Fri 09:30 to 18:30
Procedure: Time-coded VHS and 3/4" cassettes. 24 hours for access to masters.
Description: The library holds important historical collections of footage from the world's best known sports cinematographers and exclusively represents various sports leagues, teams and governing bodies. ASA are the official filmmakers and exclusive stock footage representatives for the US Soccer Federation. All major sports such as basketball, football, soccer, hockey, as well as Olympic disciplines, recreational and aesthetic sports are covered together with wildlife and nature footage. Computerized. Demo reel and promotional material available. English and Spanish spoken.

161   AIRLINE FILM & TV PROMOTIONS

13246 Weidner Street, Pacoima, CA 91331-2343, USA
℃ +1 818 899 1151
Ⓕ +1 818 896 5929

Contacts: Alf or Mikael Jacobsen
Subjects: Aviation, locations, leisure.
▦ 35mm.
Research: By staff. Visit by appointment.
☉ Mon- Fri 08:00 to 17:00
Description: Footage of commercial airlines - take-offs,
landings, in flight - worldwide. Establishing shots of many
capital cities. Sports and recreational activities. Rate card
available.

162   AL GIDDINGS – IMAGES UNLIMITED

8001 Capwell Drive, Oakland, CA 94621, USA
℃ +1 510 562 8000
Ⓕ +1 510 562 8001

Contacts: Terry Thompson
Subjects: Natural history, underwater photography,
environmental.
▦ 16mm, 35mm; most video formats. NTSC.
Research: By staff. Appointment to visit.
☉ Mon- Fri 09:00 to 17:00
Procedure: Umatic/VHS tapes compiled or view at studio.
1- 3 days for access to masters.
Description: Library of material made up from Al Giddings
undersea and nature adventure television specials. Images
range in diversity from whales and sharks to minute
creatures, and from polar regions to tropical islands. Scenics,
wildlife, nature and marine life from ocean floor to mountain
top, tropics, desert, north and south poles, kelp forests,
redwood forests, rainforest, storms, moons, divers,
shipwrecks, etc. New footage from an expedition to the
shipwrecked Titanic. Computerized. Brochure available.

163   A.M. STOCK EXCHANGE, THE

Suite 207, 4741 Laurel Cyn. Bl., N. Hollywood CA 91607, USA
ⓒ +1 818 762 7865
Ⓕ +1 818 762 7886

Contacts: Chris Angelich
Subjects: Stock shots, locations.
🎞 35mm, 16mm; 3/4" master videotape.
Research: By staff.
🕐 Mon-Fri 09:00 to 18:00
Description: Stock footage library with a wide variety of modern shots. They will also do custom stock shots for clients. Shots include skylines, buildings, schools, colleges, restaurants, houses, cities - Los Angeles, San Francisco, Palm Springs, New York, Washington DC, Philadelphia, Chicago, Detroit, Atlanta, etc. Computerized. Rate card available.

164   AMATEUR ATHLETIC FOUNDATION LIBRARY

2141 West Adams Boulevard, Los Angeles, CA 90018, USA
ⓒ +1 213 730 9696
Ⓕ +1 213 730 9637
✎ 9102 409848

Contacts: Shirley Ito, Michael Salmon
Subjects: Sport.
🎞 16mm, 35mm; 1", Umatic. NTSC and PAL.
Research: By both staff and outside researchers.
🕐 Mon-Fri 10:00 to 17:00
Procedure: Viewing copies usually VHS. 48 hours minimum for access to masters.
Description: The library specializes in sports material consisting of instructional, Olympic games and track and field footage. Copyright varies depending on the footage. Computerized. English and Spanish spoken.

165 AMAZING IMAGES

Suite 1581, 6671 Sunset Boulevard, Hollywood CA 90028, USA
℡ +1 213 962 1899
Ⓕ +1 213 962 1898

Contacts: Michael Peter Yakaitis
Subjects: Historical archive, newsreels, classic films, trailers, out-takes, personalities.
🎞 16mm, 35mm; video.
Research: By staff only.
🕐 Mon–Fri 09:30 to 18:00
Procedure: VHS or Umatic viewing copies. 24 hours for access to masters.
Description: The collection begins pre-1900 and includes old Hollywood stars of silent and sound motion pictures, locations around the globe, newsreels, historical events, world war, comedy, censorship, serial and weekly magazines, bloopers, Kodascopes, out-takes and film trailers. There is also a wide assortment of animal footage, celebrities and industrial material. Partly computerized. Rate card available.

166 AMERICAN MOTION PICTURES

2247 15th Avenue West, Seattle, WA 98119, USA
℡ +1 206 282 1776
Ⓕ +1 206 282 3535

Contacts: Jacki Artley
Subjects: Feature films, children's, entertainment.
🎞 Beta SP, D2, 1″. NTSC and PAL.
Research: By staff only.
🕐 Mon–Fri 08:30 to 17:00
Procedure: Viewing copies as required, normally VHS. 10 days for access to masters.
Description: American motion pictures hold children's entertainment, talkshows, features and full length movies. All copyright is held by them. English, German and French spoken.

167   ARCHIVE FILMS

530 West 25th Street, New York, NY 1001, USA
ⓒ +1 212 620 3955
ⓕ +1 212 645 2137

Contacts: Patrick Montgomery
Subjects: Historical archive, newsreels, Hollywood, classic films, film industry, educational films.
▦ 35mm, 16mm; various video formats with matching cassettes.
Research: By staff. Appointment to visit.
☾ Mon-Fri 09:00 to 18:00
Procedure: Viewing tapes assembled. 24-48 hours for access to masters.
Description: Over 5000 hours of newsreels, silent films, classic comedies, Hollywood features, historical dramas, documentaries and educational films. Represent The March of Time, The RKO Shorts Library, International Film Foundation, TV House and Videowest. Computerized. Rate card and catalogue available.
Foreign Offices: France, Germany, Italy, Japan, Netherlands, Sweden, UK, USA.

168   ARCTURUS MOTION PICTURES

65 Gray Cliff Road, Newton, MA 02159, USA
ⓒ +1 617 332 3802
ⓕ +1 617 332 3310

Contacts: David Breashears
Subjects: Himalayas, mountaineering, culture, religion, aerial photography.
▦ 16mm; 1″ with matching 3/4″ and VHS.
Research: By both staff and outside researchers. Appointment to visit.
☾ Mon-Fri 09:00 to 17:00
Procedure: All material on viewing cassettes. Copies from video masters.
Description: Collection specializes in the Himalayas with emphasis on the Mount Everest region. Extensive scenics and aerial shots of the area. Sherpa, Buddhist and Tibetan culture. Partly computerized. Rate card and catalogue available.

169   A.R.I.Q. FOOTAGE

One Main Street, East Hampton, New York 11964, USA
Ⓒ +1 516 329 9200
Ⓕ +1 516 329 9260

Contacts: Joe Lauro, Mart Heideman
Subjects: Historical archive, classic films, comedy, music, newsreels, industry, space.
Various film and video formats. All line standards available.
Research: By staff. Visits by appointment.
☾ Mon-Fri 09:00 to 17:30
Procedure: Viewing material on VHS and Umatic. 24 hours for access to masters.
Description: Footage covers 1895 to 1990 with a very strong historical archive. Universal newsreel (1929 to 1967), musical performance footage including Jazz, Blues, Country, Rock and Roll, Pop from 1910 to 1990, silent films, industrial footage, space program, life styles and a range of general subject. Computerized. Rate card available.

170   BIG FIGHTS, THE

9 East 40th Street, New York, NY 10016, USA
Ⓒ +1 212 532 1711
Ⓕ +1 212 889 1745

Contacts: Bill Cayton, Steve Lott
Subjects: Boxing, Olympics.
Film; videotape.
Research: By both staff and outside researchers. Appointment to visit.
☾ Mon-Fri 09:00 to 17:30
Description: Extensive archive of boxing and Olympics footage acquired over the last 25 years. Also pocket billiards and the complete Madison Square Garden sports events from 1901 to 1975. Footage is licensed to the trade only - TV companies, film companies, etc. Partly computerized. Catalogue available.

171   BROAD STREET PRODUCTIONS

10 West 19th Street, New York, NY 10011, USA
© +1 212 924 4700
Ⓕ +1 212 924 5085

Contacts: Jody Bergedick, David Fink
Subjects: Industry, skylines, business.
16mm. Most video formats. NTSC.
Research: By both staff and outside researchers.
Appointment to visit.
☉ Mon- Fri 09:00 to 18:00 (other days and hours on request)
Procedure: Timecoded VHS or Umatic viewing copies.
Access to masters within 24 hours.
Description: The collection contains material relating to
business and finance with footage of financial markets,
industrial processes, city skylines, hi-tech communications
imagery and business people in various situations. Partly
computerized. Catalogue and rate card available.

172   BUDGET FILMS STOCK FOOTAGE

4590 Santa Monica Blvd, Los Angeles, CA 90029, USA
© +1 213 660 0187
Ⓕ +1 213 660 5571

Contacts: Layne Murphy
Subjects: Historical archive, newsreels, documentaries.
Film; videotape.
Research: By staff. Visits by appointment.
☉ Mon- Fri 09:00 to 17:00
Description: Vintage footage dating from the 1890s through
to 1970s. The library contains theatrical, news, documentary
and experimental and television materials.

173   CABLE FILMS & VIDEO

Country Club Station, Kansas City, MO 64113, USA
© +1 913 362 2804
Ⓕ +1 913 341 7365

Contacts: Herbert Miller
Subjects: Classic films, comedy.
Film; 1", 3/4", VHS.
Research: By staff.
☉ Mon- Sat
Description: American and some foreign classic feature films
dating from 1915. The majority of the material comes from
the silent film era through to the 1930s and 40s. Excerpts
they are able to offer include Charlie Chaplin, Buster Keaton,
Douglas Fairbanks Snr. as well as It's A Wonderful Life and
Night Of The Living Dead. Catalogue available.

174 CAE-LINK CORPORATION

P.O. Box 1237, Binghamton, NY 13902-1237, USA
ℂ +1 607 721 5850
Ⓕ +1 607 721 5574

Contacts: Paul Redfern
Subjects: Aviation.
▦ Beta/Beta SP, D2. NTSC.
Research: Researchers can visit by appointment.
◷ Mon-Fri 09:00 to 17:00
Procedure: Time coded VHS for viewing. 48 hours or less for access to masters.
Description: Extensive footage of flight, air traffic control and medical simulators, also some aircraft footage.

175 CAMEO FILM LIBRARY

10620 Burbank Blvd, N. Hollywood, CA 91607, USA
ℂ +1 818 980 8700
Ⓕ +1 818 980 7113

Contacts: Marilyn Chielens, Steven Vrabel
Subjects: Stock shots, locations, aerial photography, aviation, military.
▦ 35mm.
Research: By staff only.
◷ Mon-Fri 08:30 to 17:30
Description: A wide variety of stock shots including worldwide establishing shots, military aircraft, period and contemporary military, aerial footage, sunrises and sunsets, etc. Rate card available.

176   CASCOM INTERNATIONAL

806 4th Avenue South, Nashville, TN 37210, USA
© +1 615 242 8900
Ⓕ +1 615 256 7890

Contacts: Victor Rumore
Subjects: Special effects, computer imagery, time-lapse, animation.
16mm, 35mm; Beta SP. PAL.
Research: By outside researchers. Appointment to visit.
Mon-Fri 09:00 to 17:30
Procedure: VHS viewing tapes loaned. 1-2 hours for access to masters.
Description: Mainly computer generated effects but also time-lapse, animation and live action. Subjects covered include globes, fireworks, maps, grids, sport, health, entertainment, environment, music, space and hi-tech. Catalogue showing a freeze frame of each effectin the library is available.
Foreign Offices: Australia (Select Effects).

177   CBS NEWS ARCHIVES

524 West 57th Street, New York, NY 10019, USA
© +1 212 975 2875
Ⓕ +1 212 975 5442

Contacts: Neil Waldman
Subjects: Current affairs.
Film and video formats.
Research: By both staff and outside researchers.
Mon-Fri 08:00 to 18:00
Procedure: Timecoded VHS/Umatic for viewing. 48 hours for access to masters.
Description: The CBS news archives contains thousands of miles of footage shot over more than 40 years - coverage that chronicles the vast body of worldwide and domestic news stories from CBS News. Constantly being updated. Partly computerized. Rate card and brochure available.

178   CINEMA NETWORK (CINENET)

Suite 111, 2235 First Street, Simi Valley CA 93065, USA
ⓒ +1 805 527 0093
ⓕ +1 805 527 0305

Contacts: Richard Spruiell, Jim Jarrard
Subjects: Stock shots, natural history, locations, sport, time-lapse, underwater photography.
🎞 35mm, 16mm; NTSC videotape.
Research: By staff. Appointment to visit.
Procedure: Viewing tapes compiled. Masters copied after payment received.
Description: Stock footage library with very comprehensive A-Z listing of subjects - almost every topic you can think of is covered in their brochure, they also undertake custom filming. Computerized on Cinemind software. Rate card and brochure available.

179   CNN LIBRARY TAPE SALES

4th Floor, One CNN Center, Atlanta GA 30303, USA
ⓒ +1 404 827 4262 / 1088
ⓕ +1 404 827 1840

Contacts: Ainie Hastings, Brian Fulford
Subjects: Current affairs.
🎞 Beta/Beta SP, 1", Umatic, VHS. NTSC.
Research: By staff only.
🕑 Mon-Fri 10:00 to 20:00
Procedure: Timecoded 3/4" for viewing. 5 days for access to masters.
Description: CNN national and international news coverage dating from 1980 to present day. Highlights include the Berlin Wall, Operation Desert Storm, Challenger explosion, Tiananmen Square, Military action and press conferences. Computerized.

180 COE FILM ASSOCIATES

65 East 96th Street, New York, NY 10128, USA
© +1 212 831 5355
© +1 212 996 6728

Contacts: Arlene Gross
Subjects: Natural history, locations, Americana, documentaries, drama.
🎞 16mm; Beta/Beta SP, 1", BVU, Umatic. PAL and NTSC.
Research: By staff only.
🕑 Mon-Fri 09:30 to 17:30
Procedure: Umatic/VHS NTSC or PAL loaned. 24 hours for access to masters.
Description: Footage derives from documentaries and dramas produced by Coe Film Associates and covers nature, wildlife, destinations, Americana and New York City. Computerized. English, Spanish and French spoken.

181 COLUMBIA PICTURES / COLUMBIA TRISTAR INTERNATIONAL

10202 West Washington Boulevard, Culver City, CA 90232, USA

Contacts: Vary depending on product and territory being requested.
Subjects: Feature films, television.
🕑 24 hour telephone information service.
Description: Columbia's library includes Laurence of Arabia, On the Waterfront, Tootsie, Close Encounters..., Ghostbusters, Dracula, Philadelphia, Days of our Lives, Bewitched, The Monkeys, Soap, Hart to Hart, etc. Clips are only likely to be agreed for industry related programmes with tight control kept on the classic films. Supply detailed information when submitting your request. Culver City office operate a 24 hour information line giving details required. Contact for feature film clip enquiries Tel: (310) 280 7306. Contact for television product Tel: (310) 280 7374. NB: French office deal with French speaking African territories and Turkey, Fax: (33 1) 44 40 63 01. UK office, Fax: (171) 528 8525, deals with Africa, Israel, Malta, Mauritius and the Seychelles.
Foreign Offices: France, UK, USA.

182 DARINO FILMS

222 Park Avenue South, New York, NY 10003, USA
© +1 212 228 4024
Ⓕ +1 212 473 7448

Contacts: Ed Darino
Subjects: Special effects, computer imagery, trailers, stock shots, environmental.
Research: By staff. Appointment to visit.
🕐 Mon-Fri 09:00 to 17:00
Description: Darino Films hold a library of special effects comprised of computer graphics and animated backgrounds. They also have The Producers Library of approximately 10 hours of stock footage, environmental, historic, nature, cities, etc. In addition they have the Hollywood Vaults collection of 2500 trailers. Computerized. Rate card and brochure available.

183 DICK WALLEN PRODUCTIONS

P.O. Box 2261, Escondido, CA 92033, USA
© +1 619 749 4406
Ⓕ +1 619 749 4408

Subjects: Motor racing.
Research: By staff. Visits by appointment.
🕐 Mon-Fri 09:00 to 18:00
Description: Motor racing stock footage library dating from 1959 through to 1988. Formula 1, Grand Prix, dirt track, Trans-am, Indy, motorcycle USA, etc.

184 DOWNTOWN COMMUNITY TELEVISION

87 Lafayette Street, New York, NY 10013, USA
© +1 212 966 4510
Ⓕ +1 212 219 0248

Contacts: Anita Tovich
Subjects: Current affairs, crime, civil rights, farming, immigration.
🎞 All material on video, various formats. NTSC.
Research: By staff. Appointment to visit.
🕐 Mon-Fri 10:00 to 18:00
Procedure: Viewing material supplied from in-house editing facilities.
Description: Footage covers international political issues in Asia, Central America and the former Soviet Union. Subjects include crime, labour issues, urban issues, farm problems, human interest and Asian-American immigrants. Computerized. Catalogue and rate card available. English, Spanish, Portuguese and French spoken.

185   EM GEE FILM LIBRARY

Suite 103, 6924 Canby Avenue, Reseda CA 91335, USA
ⓒ +1 818 881 8110
ⓕ +1 818 981 5506

Contacts: Murray Glass
Subjects: Public domain, classic films, feature films, comedy, documentaries, westerns, animation.
▦ All film formats; VHS, Umatic. NTSC.
Research: By both staff and outside researchers.
☉ Mon-Fri 08:30 to 17:00
Procedure: Viewing material on 16mm or VHS. 1 week for access to masters.
Description: Approximately 3000 titles in all genres - silent and sound, black and white and colour. Their speciality is in public domain material covering all subject areas including comedies, documentaries, westerns, animation and feature films. Partly computerized. Catalogue and rate card available.

186   ENERGY PRODUCTIONS' TIMESCAPE IMAGE LIBRARY

4th Floor, 12700 Ventura Boulevard, Studio City, CA 91604 USA
ⓒ +1 818 508 1444
ⓕ +1 818 508 1293

Contacts: Joan Sargent, Randy Gitsch
Subjects: Americana, sport, time-lapse, macro photography, natural history, locations, fashion, culture, landscapes, lifestyles, special effects.
▦ 16mm, 35mm, 70mm; most video formats.
Research: By staff. Visits by appointment.
☉ Mon-Fri 09.00 to 18.00
Procedure: Viewing tapes assembled. Masters copied after selection.
Description: Energy Productions hold the Timescape Image Library, a huge library of stock material encompassing sports, wildlife, landmarks, cities, seascapes, macro/micro photography, fashion, underwater, botany, computer imagery and daily life from around the world. Also available via this office is The Playboy Fashion Collection, Namco Computer Imagery, Warren Miller Films and Sports Library, Windham Hills Video and Film Library and Bob Landis Wildlife. Computerized. Rate card and brochure available. NB: Energy also have a New York office, Tel: (212) 686 4900, Fax: (212) 686 4998.Mon-Fri 09:00 to 18:00
Foreign Offices: France, Germany, Italy, Japan, Spain, Sweden, Turkey, Israel, UK, USA.

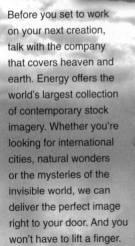

187   ESTUARY PRESS

Suite 279, 408 13th Street, Oakland CA 94612, USA
© +1 510 763 8204
℉ +1 510 763 8204

Contacts: Paul Richards
Subjects: Civil rights, protests, Vietnam War.
Research: By Paul Richards.
☺ No office hours. Contact anytime.
Procedure: VHS viewing tapes on request. Access to masters varies.
Description: The collection contains the films of Harvey Wilson Richards including 1960s Bay Area peace and civil rights protests, anti Vietnam War protests, California farm workers, forestry and logging. Mississippi civil rights movement 1963 and 1964. Catalogue available. English and Spanish spoken.

188   FABULOUS FOOTAGE BOSTON

Fabulous Footage Inc.
The complete stock film/video library.

37 Walnut Street, Wellesley, MA 02181, USA
© +1 617 237 6555
℉ +1 617 237 1556

Contacts: Steve Garson
Subjects: Stock shots, locations, culture, industry, medicine, military, music, environmental, leisure, transport, natural history, space, trailers.
▦ Film; video (all film mastered onto tape).
Research: By both staff and outside researchers.
☺ Mon–Fri 09:00 to 21:00
Description: Complete contemporary film and videotape library with a vast range of quality images. Subject headings include agriculture, buildings, cities, countries, cultural activities, industry and business, landmarks, landscapes, medical, military, music, natural phenomena, news, period recreations, professions, rain forests, recreation, space, special effects, spectacles, sports, transportation, underwater, water and wildlife. They also hold special collections of Nazi propaganda footage, Russian history, Russian space program, B-movies and trailers. Computerized. Rate card and catalogue available. NB: Head office is in Toronto, Canada. There is also an office in Hollywood, USA Tel: (213) 463 1153, Fax: (213) 463 1391.
Foreign Offices: Argentina, Australia, Brazil, Canada, Chile, Germany, Indonesia, Japan, Malaysia, Philippines, Singapore, Spain, Mexico, USA.

189   FILM & VIDEO STOCK SHOTS

Suite E, 10700 Ventura Boulevard, Studio City CA 91604,
USA
ⓒ +1 818 760 2098
Ⓕ +1 818 760 3294

Contacts: Stephanie Siebert, William Bolls
Subjects: Stock shots, current affairs, leisure, natural history,
time-lapse, locations, macro photography, animation, culture,
landscapes.
▦ Film; videotape.
Research: By staff. Appointment to visit.
☺ Mon-Fri 09:00 to 17:00
Description: Huge selection of both current and archival film
and videotape original images. Subjects include news events,
action sports, nature and wildlife, time-lapse cinematography,
landscapes and cityscapes, microscopy, cartoons, lifestyles
and travel footage. Next business day turnaround on master
footage orders and competitive rates. Computerized.
Brochure and rate card available.

190   FILM BANK STOCK FOOTAGE FILM & VIDEO LIBRARY

425 South Victory Boulevard, Burbank, CA 91502, USA
ⓒ +1 818 841 9176
Ⓕ +1 818 567 4235

Contacts: Paula Lumbard, Elizabeth Canelake
Subjects: News, space, special effects, science, sport,
medicine, time-lapse, aerial photography, natural history,
animation, locations, environmental.
▦ 16mm, 35mm; most video formats. NTSC masters.
Research: By staff only. Researchers occasionally visit for big
projects.
☺ Mon-Fri 09:00 to 17:00
Procedure: Umatics loaned or VHS assembled. 24 hours for
access to masters.
Description: Diverse collection of broadcast quality film and
video images aimed at supplying the full range of client
productions. Most subjects are covered in the library, the
latest new collections being world locations, children of the
world, environmental images (destruction, scientific and
beauty shots), History of Flight, more space and solar flares,
aerials across the US, agriculture and animals. Partly
computerized. Catalogue and rate card available.

191   FILM/AUDIO SERVICES

Suite 311, 430 West 14th Street, New York NY 10014, USA
© +1 212 645 2112
Ⓕ +1 212 255 4220

Contacts: Bob Summers, Mike Cocchi, Dean Cady
Subjects: Historical archive, travelogues, culture, educational films, industry, public domain.

▦ Most film and video formats. NTSC.

Research: By staff preferably. Appointment to visit.

☼ Mon-Fri 09:00 to 18:00 (or by appointment)

Procedure: Viewing material on VHS or 3/4" NTSC. 24 hours for access to masters.

Description: Worldwide travel footage dating from 1926 to 1980s; education and industrial films from the 1930s to 60s; historical actuality public domain material sourced from the National Archives and Library of Congress sold at less cost. Inexpensive and fast turnaround film to NTSC Beta SP and 1" tape in house. Partly computerized. Catalogue and rate card available. English and some Spanish spoken.

192   FILMS OF INDIA

P.O. Box 48303, Los Angeles, CA 90048, USA
© +1 213 383 9217

Contacts: Mr R.A. Bagai
Subjects: Asian cinema, dance, drama, documentaries, culture, religion.

▦ Film.

Research: By staff. Appointment to visit.

☼ Mon-Fri 09:30 to 17:30

Description: Feature films, shorts, drama, documentaries, religious films, etc. Ram Bagai also has extensive footage of Ghandi having acquired a large film library after his assassination. Brochure available.

193   FISH FILMS FOOTAGE WORLD

4548 Van Noord Avenue, Studio City, CA 91604-1013, USA
ⓒ +1 818 905 1071
ⓕ +1 818 905 0301

Contacts: David Fishbein
Subjects: Historical archive, stock shots, time-lapse, underwater photography, Americana, locations, leisure, comedy, transport, industry.
Research: By staff. Appointment to visit.
☺ Mon–Fri 09:00 to 17:00
Description: Vintage and contemporary footage covering all subject areas. Time-lapse, underwater, scenics, aerials, sports, specializing in lifestyles, comedy, historic events, transportation, Americana, educational, travel, industrial, public domain. Partly computerized. Rate card and brochure available.

194   FRANKLIN D. ROOSEVELT LIBRARY

511 Albany Post Road, Hyde Park, NY 12538, USA
ⓒ +1 914 229 8114
ⓕ +1 914 229 0872

Contacts: Mark Renovitch
Subjects: Historical archive, newsreels, amateur films.
▦ 16mm, 35mm.
Research: Limited research by staff. Appointment to visit advised.
☺ Mon–Fri 08:45 to 17:00
Procedure: Viewing material not supplied. 2 weeks for access to masters.
Description: The collection contains newsreels and home movie footage of Franklin and Eleanor D. Roosevelt. Some of the material is public domain but most is copyrighted by other institutions.

195   FRONTLINE VIDEO & FILM

243 12th Street, Del Mar, CA 92014, USA
ⓒ +1 619 481 5566
ⓕ +1 619 481 4189

Contacts: Ira Opper
Subjects: Adventure sports, surfing, leisure.
☺ Mon–Fri 09:00 to 17:00
Description: Stock footage library specializing in surfing (archive and contemporary), also have many action sports including bodyboarding, jet skiing, wavesailing, windsurfing, snowboarding, skiing, skateboarding, etc. Partly computerized. Rate card and brochure available.

196   GLOBAL VILLAGE STOCK FOOTAGE LIBRARY

1717 Darby Road, Sebastopol, CA 95472, USA
ⓒ +1 707 829 9542
ⓕ +1 707 829 9542

Contacts: Michael Heumann, Marcia Ludwig
Subjects: Travelogues, locations, culture, stock shots.
Beta/Beta SP, Umatic. NTSC.
Research: By staff on database - response by fax.
🕐 7 days 24 hours a day.
Procedure: Viewing on Umatic or VHS NTSC. 48 hours for access to masters.
Description: Global Village is a collection of video stock images gathered from around the world for the travel programmes distributed by International Video Network, Rand McNally Videos, Reader's Digest Videos and the Discovery Channel "World Away" series. They are also a clearing house and referral service for collections belonging to other producers and various public domain image libraries. Computerized database covering over 10 000 subjects available free plus rate card. English and German spoken.

197   HISTORIC THOROUGHBRED COLLECTIONS

35 Monterey Lane, Sierra Madre, CA 91024, USA
ⓒ +1 818 355 4361

Contacts: Joe Burnham, Thom Murray
Subjects: Horse racing.
16mm, 35mm; Beta/Beta SP, 1", Umatic. NTSC.
Research: Visits by appointment.
🕐 No formal hours. Answerphone service at all times.
Procedure: Timecoded cassettes available to serious customers.
Description: Collection specializes in US thoroughbred racing from 1930 to 1987 featuring famous horses such as Triple Crown winners. Establishing shots of most famous US tracks, for example Churchill Downs, Belmont, Saratoga, Santa Anita, Hollywood Park and Del Mar. Original material all film, colour since 1950s; much transferred to video. Partly computerized.

198 HOLLYWOOD FILM REGISTRY

6926 Melrose Avenue, Hollywood, CA 90038, USA
℮ +1 213 937 7067
Ⓕ +1 213 655 8889

Contacts: Dan Price
Subjects: Historical archive, stock shots, locations, personalities, Americana, documentaries, classic films, motor racing.
▦ 16mm, 35mm; most video formats.
Research: By both staff and outside researchers. Appointment to visit.
☺ Mon–Fri 10:30 to 17:30
Procedure: Viewing on VHS, Umatic, 35mm. 24 hours for access to masters.
Description: Encompasses 10 major collections. American Film Registry (from silent era on - institutional, travel, Imperial China...), Dennis Film Libraries (news, establishing shots, personalities, space...), Documentary Productions (Americana, motor sport), Keystone Collection (comedy), Paper Prints (1890s to 1910), Sand Castles (current establishing shots), Sandler Film Library (historical library used for stock by Hollywood producers since the 1930s), Slapstick & Gags (silent movies), Video & Film Stringers (current stock shots), Visual Dynamics (virtual encyclopaedic library up to the early 1970s). Partly computerized. Rate card available.

199 HOT SHOTS COOL CUTS

1926 Broadway, New York, NY 10023, USA
℮ +1 212 799 9100
Ⓕ +1 212 799 9258

Contacts: Andrew Conti
Subjects: Stock shots, historical archive, aviation.
▦ 35mm.
Research: By staff. Researchers can visit by appointment only.
☺ Mon–Fri 09:30 to 18:00
Procedure: VHS and Umatic viewing tapes (PAL and NTSC). 24 hours for access to masters.
Description: Hot Shots exclusively represent an international network of cinematographers with extensive contemporary and archival holdings covering all topics imaginable including the stock footage rights to the Pan Am film library and the Hearst Entertainments historical collection. Catalogue and rate card available. Computerized. English and Spanish spoken.

200   ICARUS FILMS INTERNATIONAL

153 Waverly Place, New York, NY 10014, USA
ⓒ +1 212 727 1711
ⓕ +1 212 989 7649

Contacts: Julie Goldman
Subjects: Current affairs, documentaries.
Description: 400 titles, mainly documentaries, on social and political themes.

201   IMAGE BANK / FILM DIVISION

4th Floor, 111 Fifth Avenue, New York NY 10003, USA
ⓒ +1 212 529 6700
ⓕ +1 212 529 8889

Contacts: Brian Mitchell
Subjects: Stock shots, aerial photography, time-lapse, lifestyles, natural history, locations, sport.
All film and video formats and line standards held.
Research: By both staff and outside researchers. Appointment to visit.
Mon-Fri 09:00 to 17:00
Procedure: 3/4"/VHS (any line standard) for viewing. 24 hours for access to masters.
Description: Vast collection of stock material, contemporary and archival, acquired from Turner Broadcasting, Ocean Images, I.R.E., Pigeon Productions, MacGillivray Freeman Films, Dentsu Prox., McDonnell Douglas, Nature Conservancy, etc. Offices worldwide and major cities of North America - Chicago, Detroit, Mexico, Minneapolis, Atlanta, Dallas and Los Angeles. Computerized. English, French, Spanish, Italian, German and Greek spoken in the NEW YORK HEADQUARTERS.
Foreign Offices: Argentina, Brazil, Chile, Colombia, Australia, Canada, Hong Kong, Indonesia, Korea, Japan, Malaysia, Philippines, Singapore, Taiwan, Thailand, South Africa, UK, USA.

202   IMAGEWAYS

Second Floor, 412 West 48th Street, New York NY 10036, USA
© +1 212 265 1287
Ⓕ +1 212 586 0339

Contacts: Adam Sargis, Kenneth Powell, Ray Sidwell
Subjects: Stock shots, newsreels, comedy, animation, classic films, documentaries, industry, educational films, television.
Film; 1" videotape with timecoded 3/4" cassettes.
Research: By staff. Appointment to visit.
Procedure: Timecoded cassette compiled. Masters copied after selection.
Description: Stock footage library with material dating from 1905 to present day. Footage comes from newsreels, silent films, cartoons, historical films, Hollywood features, documentaries, industrial films, educational films, television programmes and original shot material. Collection is approximately 70% colour and 30% black and white. Computerized. Rate card available. Minimum license fee charged on delivery of master material.

203   INTERNATIONAL AD CENTER, INTERNATIONAL AIR CHECK (IAC)

3261 N.E. 14th Avenue, Pompano Beach, Florida 33064, USA
© +1 305 785 6133
Ⓕ +1 305 941 2043

Contacts: Bill Klokow
Subjects: Advertising.
Beta/Beta SP, Umatic, VHS. NTSC.
Research: By both staff and outside researchers. Appointment to visit.
☉ Mon-Fri 09:00 to 18:00
Procedure: VHS viewing tapes supplied for a fee. 1-7 days for access to masters.
Description: IAC have an extensive collection of more than 400 000 commercials dating back to 1976. Each area is retrievable by brand or product category. Copyright clearance is necessary in only a few instances. Computerized. Promotional flyer and rate card available. English and Spanish spoken. NB: IAC also have a contact telephone number in New York (212) 246 1446.

204   INTERNATIONAL MEDIA RESOURCE EXCHANGE

124 Washington Place, New York, NY 10014, USA
ⓒ +1 212 463 0108
Ⓕ +1 212 243 3805

Contacts: Karen Ranucci
Subjects: Latin America, documentaries, animation, music.
🎞 Most video formats. NTSC.
Research: By both staff and outside researchers.
Appointment to visit.
🕓 Mon- Fri 10:00 to 17:00
Procedure: Viewing on Umatic, VHS, Betamax. 2 weeks for
access to masters, can rush.
Description: More than 500 films and videos of all genres
made by Latin Americans including short fiction, features,
documentaries, video art animations and music videos.
Computerized. English and Spanish spoken.

205   INTERNATIONAL VIDEO NETWORK (IVN)

Worldwide Stock Footage Library,
2242 Camino Ramon, San Ramon, CA 94583, USA
ⓒ +1 510 866 1344 Ext. 217
Ⓕ +1 510 866 0614

Subjects: Locations, travelogues, leisure.
🎞 16mm; 1", Beta SP with matching VHS.
Research: By staff only.
🕓 Mon- Fri 09:00 to 18:00
Procedure: Viewing tapes loaned. Masters copied after
selection.
Description: Over 100 hours of destination footage,
countries and cities all over the world. Also includes
adventure and sporting activities. Partly computerized. Rate
card and catalogue available.
Foreign Offices: UK.

206   IVY CLASSICS

725 Providence Road, Charlotte, NC 28207, USA
© +1 704 333 3991

Contacts: Joshua Tager
Subjects: Feature films, television.
▦ 16mm, 35mm; D2, 1", BVU, Umatic, VHS.
Research: Fee charged for research.
☉ Mon-Fri 09:30 to 17:30
Procedure: Film or VHS for viewing. 2 weeks for access to masters.
Description: Over 250 feature films dating from 1917 to 1985, over 400 filmed short subjects from 1927 to 1985 and over 100 filmed TV shows.

207   JOHN E. ALLEN

116 North Avenue, Park Ridge, NJ 07656, USA
© +1 201 391 3299
ⓕ +1 201 391 6335

Contacts: John E. Allen, Beverley Allen
Subjects: Historical archive, newsreels, war, Russia, industry, transport, classic films, educational films, travelogues.
▦ Mainly film; some video.
Research: By both staff and outside researchers.
☉ Mon-Fri 09:00 to 18:00
Description: Kinograms from 1915 to 1931. Telenews 1947 to 1953. World War I and II, Spanish American War, Mexican Revolution, Russian Revolution, Hungarian Revolution, Spanish Civil War, Korean War, etc. Industry 1910 to 1950s, transportation, educational, ethnographic, travel, nature, features 1905 to 1950s, stills, posters and lobby cards. Partly computerized. Rate card available.

208   JUDSON ROSEBUSH COMPANY

154 West 57th Street, New York, NY 10019-3321, USA
© +1 212 581 3000
ⓕ +1 212 757 8283

Contacts: Judson Rosebush, Kristine Watt
Subjects: Animation.
▦ Video and computer programmes.
Research: By both staff and outside researchers.
☉ Mon-Sat 08:00 to 20:00
Procedure: Viewing on CD-ROMs, MACs and video. 5 days for access to masters.
Description: The library specializes in computer animation dating from 1970 to 1990. Computerized. Catalogue and rate card available. English, Spanish and French spoken.

209   KESSER STOCK LIBRARY

21 SW 15 Road, Miami, Florida 33129, USA
© +1 305 358 7900
Ⓕ +1 305 358 2209

Contacts: Emily Wilson, Charles Carrubba
Subjects: Stock shots, locations, space, agriculture, leisure,
fishing, time-lapse, underwater photography, aviation.
Research: By staff.
🕑 Mon- Fri 09:00 to 17:00
Description: Range of archival and contemporary stock shot
material. Subjects include world destinations, wildlife,
sunsets, fireworks, horseracing, time-lapse and underwater
photography, agriculture, space, fishing, etc. Partly
computerized. Rate card and brochure available.

210   KING 5 TELEVISION

2814 Hocking Street, Placerville, CA 95667, USA
© +1 916 621 1771
Ⓕ +1 916 621 1771

Contacts: Michael Dennis
Subjects: Adventure sports.
🎞 Umatic, VHS. NTSC.
Research: By both staff and outside researchers.
Appointment to visit.
🕑 7 days 09:00 to 17:00
Procedure: Viewing on VHS or Umatic. 5 days for access to
masters.
Description: King 5 have the largest collection of whitewater
rafting footage in the US, shot from both the boat and shore
point of view. Most US and some foreign rivers are covered.
Computerized.

211   KPNX-TV

P.O. Box 711, Phoenix, Arizona 85001, USA
© +1 602 257 1212
Ⓕ +1 602 258 2439

Contacts: Steve Widmann
Subjects: Current affairs.
🎞 Videotape.
Research: By both staff and outside researchers.
Appointment to visit.
🕑 Mon- Fri 09:00 to 17:00
Procedure: Requests preferred in writing.
Description: KPNX-TV have a video tape news archive that
dates back to 1978. Footage also includes scenic Arizona
and related material. Partly computerized.

212   KSTP-TV NEWS LIBRARY

3415 University Avenue, St. Paul, MN 55114, USA
© +1 612 642 4443 / 4411
Ⓕ +1 612 642 4409

Contacts: Patty Johnson
Subjects: Current affairs.
Film; video.
Research: By staff only. Appointment to visit.
🕑 Mon-Fri 08:30 to 17:00
Description: KSTP-TV have archives holding film of news events dating from 1950 to 1975, and video from 1975 to the present day. Coverage includes events taking place in Minnesota and the surrounding area. Partly computerized.

213   LARRY DORN ASSOCIATES / WORLD BACKGROUNDS

Suite 306, 5820 Wilshire Boulevard, Los Angeles CA 90036, USA
© +1 213 935 6266
Ⓕ +1 213 935 9523

Contacts: Linda Dorn
Subjects: Stock shots, locations, Americana, aerial photography, underwater photography, aviation, transport, space.
35mm originals; 1" with matching 3/4" and VHS videotapes.
Research: By staff. Appointment to visit.
🕑 Mon-Fri 09:00 to 17:00
Procedure: Viewing tapes compiled. Masters copied on selection.
Description: Period and contemporary stock footage. European establishing shots, worldwide locations, Americana, scenics, aerials, various airlines and international airports, period wars, space, etc. Computerized. Rate card available.
Foreign Offices: France, Italy, UK.

214   LIBRARY OF CONGRESS - MOTION PICTURE & BROADCASTING DIVISION

10 First Street, S.E., Washington, DC, USA
© +1 202 707 5840
Ⓕ +1 202 707 2371

Subjects: National Archives.

215 MARINE GRAFICS

Box 2242, Chapel Hill, NC 27515, USA
© +1 919 362 8867
Ⓕ +1 919 362 8861

Contacts: Bill Lovin
Subjects: Underwater photography, environmental.
🎞 16mm neg with matching 1", original Beta SP and M2 (video NTSC).
Research: By staff.
Description: Underwater stock footage. Unusual marine life, behaviour, marine mammals, divers, shipwrecks, sharks, manta rays, dangerous marine life, scenics of the Caribbean and Pacific, beaches, ships, environmental damage, rainforest, Mayan ruins, Red Sea/Caribbean/South Pacific/Atlantic/Great Lakes/rivers. Rate card and brochure available. NB: Also represented by Energy Productions.
Foreign Offices: See Energy Productions listings.

216 MERKEL FILMS ACTION SPORTS LIBRARY

P.O. Box 722, Carpinteria, CA 93014, USA
© +1 805 648 6448
Ⓕ +1 805 644 4329

Contacts: Dan or Rita
Subjects: Adventure sports, leisure, sailing.
Research: By staff.
🕐 Mon-Fri 08:00 to 17:30
Procedure: Preview tapes compiled.
Description: Action sports including surfing, windsurfing, snowboarding, jet skiing, track field, ballooning, bungee jumping, tennis, water skiing, America's Cup sailing. Also tropical scenes, fish, dolphins and ocean waves. New footage is added about every two weeks. Computerized. Rate card available.

217   MOONLIGHT PRODUCTIONS

3361 Saint Michael Court, Palo Alto, CA 94306, USA
ⓒ +1 415 961 7440
Ⓕ +1 415 961 7440

Contacts: Dr. Lee Tepley
Subjects: Underwater photography, environmental.
16mm transferred to 1″ + timecoded cassettes; some original video.
Research: By staff. Appointment to visit.
Mon-Fri 09:00 to 17:30
Description: Collected over the last 30 years, an extensive library of all types of undersea life, especially whales, dolphins and other large marine mammals. Also material of undersea lava flows and pollution. Partly computerized. Rates negotiable. Stock footage list available.

218   MYSTIC SEAPORT MUSEUM

Film & Video Archives, 75 Greenmanville Avenue, P.O. Box 6000, Mystic, CT 06355-0990, USA
ⓒ +1 203 572 5379
Ⓕ +1 203 572 5328

Contacts: Suki Williams
Subjects: Maritime, sailing.
16mm; videotape. NTSC.
Research: By staff preferably - space limited.
Mon-Fri 09:00 to 17:00
Description: A collection of maritime images by both professionals and amateurs. Material includes square riggers, J boats, yachting, seafaring, ocean races, America's Cup races, shipbuilding and restoration. Whaling footage from 1917, New England lighthouses, recreational boating and other subjects of interest. The collection also includes many international ports and islands. Partly computerized. Catalogue of completed programmes available.

219   NATIONAL ARCHIVES AND RECORDS ADMINISTRATION

Motion Picture, Sound and Video Branch, Washington, DC 20408, USA
ⓒ +1 202 501 5446
Ⓕ +1 202 501 5778

Subjects: National Archives.

220 NATIONAL CENTER FOR FILM AND VIDEO PRESERVATION

The American Film Institute, P.O. Box 27999, 2021 North Western Avenue, Los Angeles, California 90027, USA
© +1 213 856 7637
Ⓕ +1 213 467 4578

Subjects: National Archives.

221 NBC NEWS ARCHIVES

30 Rockefeller Plaza, Room 902, New York, NY 10112, USA
© +1 212 664 3797
Ⓕ +1 212 957 8917

Contacts: Nancy Cole, Yuien Chin
Subjects: Current affairs, culture, religion, environmental, natural history, personalities, social history.
▦ 16mm, 35mm; most video formats. NTSC.
Research: By both staff and outside researchers. Appointment to visit.
☺ Mon-Fri 09:00 to 18:00
Procedure: Time-coded viewing material. Fast turnaround service.
Description: Over four decades of news events worldwide. The library covers social commentary, interviews, cultural, historical and religious programming, the environment, wildlife and stock shots for almost any subject imaginable. Computerized. Rate card available. Chinese and Spanish spoken.

222 NEW & UNIQUE VIDEOS

2336 Sumac Drive, San Diego, CA 92105, USA
© +1 619 282 6126
Ⓕ +1 619 283 8264

Contacts: Mark Schulze, Patricia Mooney
Subjects: Adventure sports, motor racing.
Research: By staff only.
☺ Mon-Fri 09:00 to 17:00
Procedure: VHS viewing (NTSC - PAL on request). 2-4 weeks for access to masters.
Description: Action sports, particularly mountain biking and motor sports. Also scenics predominantly from the American Southwest. Catalogue available.

223   NEW YORK ZOOLOGICAL SOCIETY

The Wildlife Conservation Society Office of Media Studies,
185th Street and Southern Blvd, Bronx, NY 10460, USA
© +1 718 220 5134
Ⓕ +1 718 220 7114

Contacts: Thomas Veltre
Subjects: Natural history, environmental, biology.
16mm, 35mm; most video formats. NTSC.
Research: Limited research by staff - $150 minimum for
VHS. Appointments.
Mon-Fri 10:00 to 17:00
Procedure: VHS tapes compiled dependent on workload. 2-3
days for access to masters.
Description: The collection is comprised of film shot at the
Bronx Zoo, NY aquarium and other NYZS facilities as well as
film from research expeditions sponsored by the society over
the last 80 years. Good close-ups of many rare species in
naturalistic settings, historical material on field research and
much good wildlife from East Africa in 1960s and 1970s.

224   NEWSREEL VIDEO SERVICE

7329 Donna Avenue, Reseda, CA 91335, USA
© +1 818 344 7107
Ⓕ +1 818 996 4856

Contacts: Lois Arnote
Subjects: Newsreels, current affairs, stunts, fires.
Videotape.
Research: By staff. Appointment to visit.
7 days 09:00 to 21:00
Description: News footage of LA gangs, LA riot footage
(approx. 10 hours), gang shootings in progress, SWAT teams,
FBI raids, movie celebrities, movie stunts and river rescues.
Newsreel also specialize in footage of fires, commercial
structure fires, house fires, car fires, bush fires, oil well fires
and high rise building fires - plenty of spectacular flames.
Computerized. Promotional video available.

225   NORTHSTAR PRODUCTIONS

3003 "O" Street NW, Washington DC 20007, USA
ⓒ +1 202 338 7337
ⓕ +1 202 337 4387

Contacts: Don North
Subjects: War, locations, industry, leisure.
▦ Videotape.
Research: By both staff and outside researchers.
Appointment to visit.
🕐 7 days
Description: Footage of various international war zones including Afghanistan (1987 combat), El Salvador (Guerilla war 1983 to 1990), Nicaragua, Middle East (Beirut siege 1982), Gulf War and rebuilding of Kuwait, Vietnam (1967 to 1990), Sarajevo. Also footage from Hong Kong, Austria, Prague, Washington DC, Estonia (Balkans independence movement), Finland (modern and World War II) etc. Partly computerized. Brochure available.

226   OPUS GLOBAL / THE ELECTRONIC LIBRARY

1133 N. Highland Avenue, Hollywood, CA 90038, USA
ⓒ +1 213 993 9888
ⓕ +1 213 993 9899

Contacts: Todd Stubner, Masih Madani
Subjects: Stock shots, time-lapse, feature films, advertising, newsreels.
▦ Most film and video formats. NTSC.
Research: By staff and outside researchers. Appointment to visit.
🕐 7 days 24 hours
Procedure: Viewing on VHS, Umatic, CD-ROM. Less than 24 hours for access to masters.
Description: Contemporary and archival collection ranging from material specially shot for stock footage (real time and time altered) and out-takes from productions to vintage newsreels, feature films and commercials. The electronic library contains more than two million scenes catalogued by a unique object and relational database. Queries can be made on the content of image, the patterns, colours, texture and shapes of image objects, related layout and position information as well as keywords. Images are available in all formats including MPEG and JPEG for use in all mediums including CD-ROM. Stills, sound effects and music are also supplied. Fully computerized. Rate card and catalogue available electronically.
Foreign Offices: Represented by Front Line in Japan.

227   ORIGINAL FILMVIDEO LIBRARY

P.O. Box 3457, Anaheim, CA 92803, USA
ⓒ +1 714 526 4392
Ⓕ +1 714 526 4392

Contacts: Ronnie L. James
Subjects: Classic films, advertising, trailers, television, animation.
▦ 16mm, 35mm.
Research: By staff only.
☉ Mon-Fri 10:00 to 16:00
Procedure: Viewing tapes available for small fee. All prints on site.

Description: Over 10 000 original rare 16mm and 35mm prints of vintage TV shows dating mainly from 1948 to 1970 and mostly produced by US companies. Many legendary talents rediscovered in forgotten or undocumented appearances on television, from Gloria Swanson to Richard Burton. Also thousands of TV commercials, movie preview trailers and other shorts. Transfers from prints can be made on site to VHS and Umatic via the Elmo TRV-16G system. Additionally there is an exhaustive reference library on TV and movies. Selective catalogue available, collection constantly being added to. Rates quoted based on title and use.

228   PARAMOUNT PICTURES

Clip Licensing Division, 5555 Melrose Avenue, Hollywood, CA 90038, USA
ⓒ +1 213 956 5184
Ⓕ +1 213 956 8319

Contacts: Larry McCallister
Subjects: Feature films, television.
Procedure: All requests must be received in writing.
Description: Vast collection of feature films and TV series including The Accused, Breakfast at Tiffany's, Crocodile Dundee, Indiana Jones..., Top Gun, Witness, Cheers, Happy Days, Star Trek, etc. All requests must be in writing containing details of time required (standard use is not more than 2 minutes and not more than 2 seperate scenes), how and why of use, name and nature of project. US office deals with all requests for US plus theatrical films/videos and festivals, also worldwide clearances if US is included. NB: For use within Central and South America contact the Latin America office at the same address: Susan Bender Tel: (213) 956 5410, Fax: (213) 956 3938. See all entries for Paramount Pictures to check on territories covered by each office
Foreign Offices: Australia, Canada, UK, USA.

229   PARAMOUNT PICTURES FILM LIBRARY

Hal Wallis Building, Room 108, 5555 Melrose Avenue,
Hollywood CA 90038, USA
(C) +1 213 956 5510
(F) +1 213 956 1833

Contacts: Pat Harris
Subjects: Stock shots, aerial photography, transport,
aviation, locations, building, skylines, out-takes.
35mm.
Research: By staff only (no charge made). Appointment to
visit.
Mon-Fri 09:00 to 18:00
Procedure: Film transferred to video at clients cost. 4-5
days for access to masters
Description: Out-takes and unused footage from
Paramount's features and television series spanning over 50
years. Over 9000 contemporary scenes catalogued in the
past year. Subjects vary from aerials of cities and
countrysides, stationary and moving process for cars, planes
and trains, buildings of every type, scenery to aviation,
amusements and skylines. Material is exclusively 35mm
including 3 strip technicolor. Rate card available.

230   PETRIFIED FILMS / THE IMAGE BANK

Room 204, 430 West 14th Street, New York NY 10014, USA
(C) +1 212 242 5461
(F) +1 212 691 8347

Contacts: Lori Cheatle, Rob Cates
Subjects: Historical archive, Hollywood, transport,
consumerism, Americana, industry, war, aviation, feature
film, out-takes.
35mm, 16mm; some on 1″, D2, 3/4″ with matching VHS.
Research: By staff. Visits by appointment.
Mon-Fri 09:30 to 18:00
Procedure: Viewing tapes assembled. Masters copied after
selection.
Description: Historical collection including pre-1951 Warner
Brothers stock and pre-1965 Columbia Pictures stock. A-Z of
subjects including action sequences, period recreations,
establishing shots, projection backgrounds, cityscapes and
worldwide locations. Industrial, military and aviation
collections. Car culture and 1950s daily life in the US.
Majority dates from 1920s to 1960s. Partly computerized.
Rate card and catalogue available.
Foreign Offices: Contact local Image Bank office.

231   PHOTO-CHUTING ENTERPRISES

12619 Manor Drive, Hawthorne, CA 90250-4313, USA
℗ +1 213 678 0163

Contacts: Jean Boenish
Subjects: Adventure sports.
16mm; 1", Umatic. PAL and NTSC.
Research: By staff only. Appointment to visit.
7 days answerphone service
Procedure: Viewing material on PAL or NTSC VHS.
Description: Footage covers the sports of parachuting, sky diving and BASE jumping. The collection is the work of free-fall cameraman and film maker Carl Boenish filmed between the early 1960s to 1984, it consists of classic free fall footage of sport parachuting from aircraft or fixed objects. English and some French spoken.

232   PLANET PICTURES

P.O. Box 65862, Los Angeles, CA 90065, USA
℗ +1 818 246 7700
℗ +1 818 240 8391

Contacts: Jenny Hayden
Subjects: Documentaries, medicine, health, educational films, natural history, time-lapse.
Time-lapse on film; mainly video.
Research: By both staff and outside researchers. Appointment to visit.
Mon–Fri 09:00 to 18:00
Description: Over 400 hours of footage and completed documentaries on a variety of subjects – medicine and health, high technology, workplace, nature, timelapse, wildlife, adventure, arts and entertainment and people. Computerized. Brochure available.

233   PORT AUTHORITY OF NEW YORK AND NEW JERSEY

1 World Trade Center, 86th North, New York NY 10048, USA
© +1 212 435 4707
Ⓕ +1 212 435 3523

Contacts: Bernard J. Shusman
Subjects: New York, buildings.
Beta SP. NTSC.
Research: By staff only.
Mon–Fri 08:00 to 16:00
Procedure: Timecoded VHS for viewing. 1 week for access to masters.
Description: New York City and New Jersey scenes - aerials and ground level. World Trade Center (including rebuilding after bomb blast), lower Manhattan area, New York airports and New York port. Partly computerized. Catalogue and rate card available. Some Spanish spoken.

234   PRODUCERS LIBRARY SERVICE

1051 N. Cole Avenue, Hollywood, CA 90038, USA
© +1 213 465 0572
Ⓕ +1 213 465 1671

Contacts: Jeffrey Goodman, Richard Scott
Subjects: Stock shots, documentaries, film industry.
Film; 200 videotape masters.
Research: By staff. Appointment to visit.
Mon–Fri 09:00 to 17:30
Description: Hollywood history from 1910, specializing in the golden age of Hollywood. Represent Orion Pictures and TV stock footage, ABC Circle Films and many footage collections of filmmakers. Mainly computerized. Rate card and brochure available.

235   PYRAMID FILM & VIDEO

2801 Colorado Avenue, Santa Monica, CA 90404, USA
© +1 310 828 7577
Ⓕ +1 310 453 9083

Contacts: Arthur C. Passante
Subjects: Documentaries, natural history, medicine, health, sport, arts, entertainment.
Research: By both staff and outside researchers. Appointment to visit.
☺ Mon–Fri 08:00 to 17:00
Procedure: VHS or 16mm for viewing. 1 week average for access to masters.
Description: Over 500 titles of speciality short films covering nature, medicine, health, sports/action, documentary, history, art, media studies and entertainment. Catalogue and rate card available.
Foreign Offices: 80 worldwide distributors but all stock footage licensing is handled by this office.

236   RICHTER PRODUCTIONS

33 West 42nd Street, New York, NY 10036, USA
© +1 212 947 1395
Ⓕ +1 212 643 1208

Contacts: Robert Richter, Madeline Solano
Subjects: Environmental, Africa, Asia, Latin America.
16mm; most video formats. PAL and NTSC.
Research: Both both staff and outside researchers.
☺ Mon–Fri 10:00 to 18:00
Procedure: Viewing material on VHS NTSC. 3 days for access to masters.
Description: The collection includes documentaries on environmental and social conditions mainly filmed in the developing world. Footage shows tropical rain forests and people of the forests in Asia, Africa and Latin America; also urban and rural scenes of people and living conditions in many developing world countries. Some restrictions on rights. Partly computerized. English, Spanish and some French spoken.

237 SACRAMENTO ARCHIVES & MUSEUM COLLECTION CENTER

55 Sequoia Pacific Boulevard, Sacramento, CA 95814, USA
℡ +1 916 264 7072

Contacts: Charlene G. Noyes
Subjects: Current affairs.
🎞 Film.
Research: By both staff and outside researchers.
Appointment to visit.
🕑 Thur-Fri 8:15 to 12:00, Wed-Fri 16:00 to 20:00
Description: Footage from local NBC affiliate, KCRA TV dating from 1959 to 1976. Includes events of local, regional, state and national significance broadcast on news.

238 SECOND LINE SEARCH

1926 Broadway, New York, NY 10023, USA
℡ +1 212 787 7500
🄵 +1 212 787 7636

Contacts: Susan Luchars, George Bartko
Subjects: Locations, historical archive, sport, natural history, aerial photography, time-lapse, Americana, out-takes, industry, lifestyles.
🎞 Variety of film and video formats.
Research: By staff.
🕑 Mon-Fri 09:30 to 18:00
Procedure: Umatic viewing cassettes (NTSC or PAL). 2-3 days for access to masters.
Description: A variety of material including scenics, archival footage, sports, wildlife, news, aerials, international locations, Americana, oddities/bloopers, industry, technology, lifestyle and time-lapse. Computerized. French, Spanish, Portuguese, Italian and German spoken.

239   SHERMAN GRINBERG FILM LIBRARIES

630 9th Avenue, New York, NY 10036, USA
ℂ +1 212 765 5170
Ⓕ +1 212 262 1532

Contacts: Nancy Casey, Bernard Chertok
Subjects: Current affairs, newsreels, advertising, stock shots.
16mm, 35mm; most video formats. NTSC.
Research: By both staff and outside researchers.
Appointment to visit.
☺ Mon-Fri 09:30 to 17:30
Procedure: Viewing as specified by client. 1-2 days for
access to masters.
Description: A comprehensive collection of news coverage of
the 20th Century, the library encorporates ABC Network
News, Pathe News and Paramount News. Also represented
are major libraries such as 20th Century Fox and HBO. Thirty
years of television commercials are also available. Sherman
Grinberg also have an office in Los Angeles at 1040 N.
McCadden Place Tel: (213) 464 7491, Fax: (213) 462 5352,
contacts: Bill Brewington, Linda Grinberg. Partly
computerized. Catalogue and rate card available.

240   SOURCE STOCK FOOTAGE LIBRARY, THE

738 N. Constitution Drive, Tuscon, Arizona 85748, USA
ℂ +1 602 298 4810
Ⓕ +1 602 290 8831

Contacts: John Willwater, Bill and Lynne Briggs
Subjects: Stock shots, natural history, industry, time-lapse,
locations, mining.
Research: By staff.
☺ Mon-Fri 08:00 to 17:00
Description: Scenics, time-lapse, clouds and suns, animals,
petrochemical and mining industrial, US and international
destinations, desert plants and animals, cowboys, Phoenix,
Tuscson, Alaskan wilderness and animals. Computerized.
Rate card and brochure available.

241   SPECTRAL COMMUNICATIONS

Suite 106, 178 S. Victory Boulevard, Burbank CA 91502, USA
© +1 818 840 0111
Ⓕ +1 818 840 0618

Contacts: Michael Povar
Subjects: Personalities.
▦ Various videotape formats. NTSC.
Research: By staff only. Appointment to visit.
🕐 Mon-Fri 09:00 to 17:00
Procedure: Umatic viewing material. 24 hours for access to masters.
Description: The collection consists of over 1000 celebrities at premieres and award shows previously used in documentaries. Also held is a selection of establishing shots of Southern California. Computerized. Catalogue and rate card available.

242   SPORTS CINEMATOGRAPHY GROUP

73 Market Street, Venice, CA 90291, USA
© +1 310 785 9100
Ⓕ +1 310 396 7423

Contacts: David Stoltz
Subjects: Sport, leisure, underwater photography, motor racing.
▦ Mainly film; some videotape.
Research: By staff. Appointment to visit.
🕐 Mon-Fri 09:00 to 18:00
Description: Contemporary high action sports footage including extensive coverage of skydiving, summer and winter mountain sports, water sports, motor racing, beach sports, etc. The library also has underwater and nature footage. Partly computerized. Rate card and brochure available.

243 STIMULUS / IMAGE RESEARCH

P.O. Box 170519, San Francisco, CA 94117, USA
© +1 415 558 8339
Ⓕ +1 415 864 3897

Contacts: Grant Johnson
Subjects: Computer imagery, special effects, space, landscapes, science, educational films.
Beta/Beta SP, Umatic. NTSC (also various formats of stills).
Research: By staff only.
Mon-Fri 09:00 to 17:00
Procedure: VHS viewing cassettes, NTSC. 3 days for access to masters.
Description: Stimulus are producers of scientific and educational video programming. Their stock collection includes Western US scenics, landscapes, geological and computer generated terrain imagery. Also held is aerial, satellite and computer terrain imagery of full US, some world and planetary locations. Partly computerized.

244 STOCK SHOTS

1085 Louise Avenue, San Jose, CA 95125, USA
© +1 408 971 1325
Ⓕ +1 408 723 3846

Contacts: Tom Mertens
Subjects: Transport, agriculture, locations, medicine, health.
20 000 feet of film; 500 hours of videotape.
Research: By staff.
Mon-Fri 10:00 to 16:00
Description: Silicon Valley, San Francisco aerials, rail transit, agriculture, Europe, Asian, Africa collection filmed 1945 to 1975. Also incorporates The Justin Byers Film Collection. Partly computerized. Rate card available.

245 STREAMLINE ARCHIVES

Suite 1314, 432 Park Avenue South, New York NY 10016, USA
© +1 212 696 2616
Ⓕ +1 212 696 0021

Contacts: Mark Trost
Subjects: Stock shots, newsreels, current affairs, classic films, feature films, educational, industry, sport, television, advertising, travelogues.
🎞 16mm, 35mm; most video formats. PAL, NTSC and SECAM.
Research: By staff only. Appointments for viewings.
🕐 Mon-Fri 09:30 to 19:30
Procedure: Viewing tapes assembled on VHS or Umatic. 24 hours for access to masters.
Description: Streamline's archives are being continually expanded including educational, government and industrial films, newsreels (from the turn of the century through to the early 1970s), silent comedies, television programmes and commercials, sports films, theatrical shorts, classic features and trailers as well as travel video and daily news footage (1986 to present) from Cablevision's award winning News 12 Long Island channel. Computerized. Rate card and catalogue available. English, Spanish and Japanese spoken.

246 STUART JEWELL PRODUCTIONS

2040 Garden Lane, Costa Mesa, CA 92627, USA
© +1 714 548 7234
Ⓕ +1 818 508 1293 (agents fax)

Contacts: Agent Energy Productions
Subjects: Documentaries, natural history, culture, locations, time-lapse, aerial photography, steam trains.
🎞 16mm, 35mm; Beta SP, D2 1", BVU. NTSC.
Description: Series of worldwide documentaries mostly natural history subjects - titles include Rolling to Guatemala, Following the Oregon Trail, Winter in Yellowstone, Teton and Mount. Rainer National Parks, The Great Aerial Odyssey, locations including Alaska, Hawaii, Borneo, Thailand, Africa, Egypt, India, Nepal plus steam trains in America, Canada, Australia and Guatemala. Partly computerized. NB: Represented by Energy Productions.
Foreign Offices: Contact local Energy Productions office.

247   TELECINE INTERNATIONAL PRODUCTIONS

P.O. Box 8426, Universal City, CA 91608, USA
© +1 818 889 8246
© +1 818 889 5605

Contacts: Nick Archer
Subjects: Stock shots, locations, transport, aviation, time-lapse, landscapes.
🎞 35mm.
Research: By both staff and outside researchers.
🕐 Mon–Fri 09:00 to 18:00
Procedure: Film/cassette viewing reels. Minimum royalty due for masters.
Description: Worldwide establishing shots, cityscapes and traffic from 1957 to present day, transportation, jets, buildings, scenics, moons, sunrises, suns, time-lapse clouds. Rate card and brochure available.

248   THOMAS HORTON ASSOCIATES

222 Sierra Road, Ojai, CA 93023, USA
© +1 805 646 7866

Contacts: Jean Garner
Subjects: Documentaries, adventure sports, exploration, natural history, underwater photography, Africa.
🎞 16mm, 35mm; most video formats. PAL and NTSC.
Research: By both staff and outside researchers. Appointment to visit.
🕐 Mon–Fri 08:00 to 18:00
Procedure: Viewing on NTSC Umatic or VHS. 3 days for access to masters.
Description: Series of documentaries titled Search For Adventure (over 39 one-hour programmes) including adventure sports, exploration, nature and underwater footage. The collection also includes 18 hours of 16mm footage shot in Spring 1993 of African animals and people in South and Central Africa. Catalogue and rate card available. Spanish, French and German spoken.

249   TIMESTEPS PRODUCTIONS

2 Glenside, W. Orange, NJ 07052, USA
℃ +1 201 669 1930
℉ +1 201 731 8546

Contacts: Marilyn Petrokobi
Subjects: Historical archive.
🎞 16mm original transferred to 1″ and Beta SP. NTSC.
Research: By staff only.
🕑 Mon–Fri 09:00 to 18:00
Procedure: Timecoded VHS (NTSC) for viewing. 3–4 days for access to masters.
Description: Historical archive with footage covering all subjects dating from 1895 to 1959. Computerized. Catalogue and rate card available.

250   TRAILERS ON TAPE

Suite 1, 1576 Fell Street, San Francisco CA 94117-2146, USA
℃ +1 415 921 8273 / 5449
℉ +1 415 921 8273

Contacts: Bill Longen, Stanton Schaffer
Subjects: Trailers.
🎞 16mm, 35mm; most video formats. NTSC.
Research: By staff only.
🕑 Mon–Sat 10:00 to 14:00
Procedure: Timecoded VHS available for fee. 48 hours for acess to masters.
Description: Over 6000 classic movie previews covering the 1920s through to the early 1970s. Partly computerized. Catalogue and rate card available.

251   TWENTIETH CENTURY FOX

2121 Avenue of the Stars, Los Angeles, CA 90067, USA
ⓒ +1 310 203 4613
ⓕ +1 310 203 4611

Contacts: Vary depending on requested material
Subjects: Feature films, television, animation.
Procedure: All requests must be in writing addressed to Los Angeles office.
Description: All clearances for Twentieth Century Fox product is handled in the Los Angeles office. Information required before contacting relevant person (by fax) is: name, address, telephone/fax of licensee; name and nature of programme; intended use of clip; title, description of scene and length of clip; media, territory, term and air dates required. For feature films, use of still photographs and audio bites contact: Rebecca Herrera, Fax: (310) 203 4118. For TV series (other than The Simpsons and Steven Bochco products) contact: Lisa Alcov or Laura Jenkins, Fax: (310) 203 1067. For The Simpsons and Bochco Shows contact: Suzanne Krajewki, Fax: (310) 277 9041.

252   UCLA FILM & TELEVISION ARCHIVE RESEARCH & STUDY CENTER

46 Powell Library, 405 Hilgard Avenue, Los Angeles, CA 90024-1517, USA
ⓒ +1 310 206 5388
ⓕ +1 310 206 5392

Subjects: Newsreels, current affairs.
Variety of film and video formats.
Research: Researchers can visit premises. Appointment necessary to view.
☺ Mon-Fri 08:30 to 17:00
Procedure: Viewing on VHS or 35mm.
Description: 200 000 film and television programmes and over 27 million feet of newsreel footage. The collection also includes news and public affairs programmes. Copyright is held for some items only. Computerized.

253   UNIVERSITY OF SOUTH CAROLINA NEWSFILM LIBRARY

Instructional Services Center, Columbia, South Carolina
29208, USA
© +1 803 777 6841
℉ +1 803 777 6841

Contacts: Andrew Murdoch, Don McCallister
Subjects: Newsreels, out-takes.
▦ 16mm, 35mm; most video formats. NTSC.
Research: Copies of story descriptions sent free.
Appointment to visit.
🕐 Mon–Fri 08:00 to 17:00
Procedure: Umatic or VHS timecoded viewing cassettes.
Masters vary.
Description: The University is in the process of receiving the
Movietone Newsreel collection from 20th Century Fox. At
present they have the out-takes from 1919 to 1934 plus the
newsreels and their associated out-takes from September
1942 to August 1944. They are also acquiring other film
collections, the most significant being the local TV news -
NBC affiliate WIS-TV, this footage dates from 1959 through
to the mid 1970s documenting many of the important events
and personalities in South Carolina during that time.
Computerized. Rate card available.

254   UNIVERSITY OF WASHINGTON PRESS

P.O. Box 50096, Seattle, WA 98145-5096, USA
© +1 206 543 4050
℉ +1 206 543 3932

Contacts: Jessica Lind, Bob Hutchins
Subjects: American Indians.
Research: No research. Preview copies on request.
🕐 Mon–Fri 08:30 to 17:00
Procedure: 30 day loan with credit card deposit. 3 days for
access to masters.
Description: Full collection of ethnomusicology filmed by R.
Garfias. The library specializes in native American Indians of
the early 20th Century and includes the titles In the Land of
the War Canoes (Edward S. Curtis) and Kwakiutl of British
Columbia (Franz Boas).

255   VIDEO TAPE LIBRARY

Suite 2, 1509 N. Crescent Heights Blvd, Los Angeles CA 90046, USA
© +1 213 656 4330
Ⓕ +1 213 656 8746

Contacts: Melody St. John, Peggy Shannon
Subjects: Stock shots, current affairs, newsreels, locations, beauty, comedy, classic films, sport, leisure, environmental, medicine, out-takes.

▦ 20% film; 80% video.

Research: By both staff and outside researchers.

☉ Mon–Fri 09:00 to 17:00

Procedure: 24 hour turnaround for research, preview and master footage.

Description: Enormous range of stock shot material ranging from archival footage (1898) to current news topics. Over 2 million shots on virtually every subject including locations, disasters, sports, medical, comedy, lifestyles, politics, time-lapse, film and television classics, newsreels from 1929 to 1967. Computerized. Rate card and brochure available.

256   VIDEO YESTERYEAR

Box C, Sandy Hook, CT 06482, USA
© +1 203 744 2476
Ⓕ +1 203 797 0819

Contacts: Jon Sonneborn
Subjects: Historical archive, classic films, television.

☉ Mon–Fri 08:00 to 17:00

Description: Large collection of vintage film and television clips. Catalogue available.

257   WGBH FILM & VIDEO RESOURCE CENTER

125 Wester Avenue, Boston, MA 02134, USA
© +1 617 492 3079
Ⓕ +1 617 783 4243
✍ 710 330 6887

Contacts: Vladimir Stefanovic, Patricia Barraza
Subjects: Documentaries, natural history, science, medicine, animation, aviation.
🎞 16mm, 35mm; Beta/Beta SP, D2, 1″, Umatic. NTSC.
Research: By staff only.
🕓 Mon-Fri 09:00 to 17:00
Procedure: Viewing on VHS or Umatic as requested. 3 days for access to masters.
Description: WGBH is one of the largest documentary producing stations in the US Public Broadcasting System, producing over 30% of prime time PBS programmes. Having been in existence since 1955 the extensive library holds material covering subjects such as nature, science, scenics, animation, wildlife, high tech, health/surgery and flight. The majority of copyright is held by WGBH. Partly computerized. Catalogue and rate card available. English, Spanish and Macedonian spoken.

258   WILLIAM G. BEAL

512 Franklin Avenue, Pittsburgh, PA 15221, USA
© +1 412 243 7020
Ⓕ +1 412 243 4520

Contacts: William G. Beal
Subjects: Documentaries, educational films, industry, medicine, sailing.
▦ 80% film; 20% videotape.
Research: By staff. Appointment to visit.
☉ Mon-Fri 09:00 to 17:00
Description: Footage from productions spanning the last 40 years. Productions made for clients in various industries including steel, glass, aluminum, ceramics, electronics, foundries, oil and gas and plastics. Documentaries made for hospitals, museums, colleges, universities and community organizations of all types. Special collection of tropical sailing subjects filmed in the Bahamas and Caribbean.

259   WORLDVIEW ENTERTAINMENT

6 East 39th Street, New York, NY 10016, USA
© +1 212 679 8230
Ⓕ +1 212 686 0801

Contacts: Sandra Birnhak, Marcy Stuzin
Subjects: Historical archive, classic films, newsreels.
▦ 16mm, 35mm; all video formats. NTSC.
Research: By staff only. Appointment to visit.
☉ Mon-Fri 09:30 to 18:00
Procedure: Umatic/VHS viewing tapes assembled.
Description: Large and comprehensive library of silent films. Archival and newsreel footage dating from the late 1890s to the 1950s. Mostly on card catalogue but in the process of computerization. Catalogue and rate card available.

260 WORLDWIDE TELEVISION NEWS (WTN)

1995 Broadway, New York, NY 10023, USA
℄ +1 212 362 4440
Ⓕ +1 212 496 1269
⟋ 237853

Contacts: Vincent O'Reilly, David Seevers
Subjects: Current affairs, newsreels, environmental, sport.
▦ 16mm; Beta/Beta SP, D2, BVU, Umatic. NTSC. PAL -
London office.
Research: By staff or outside researchers. Appointment to
visit.
🕑 Mon-Fri 09:00 to 19:00
Procedure: VHS dubb, other formats on request. 24 hours
for access to masters.
Description: Dating from 1963 and formerly known as
UPITN, WTN is the successor to the UPI-Movietonews
collection. The library consists of mainly domestic and
foreign news but also produces weekly features, an
entertainment and sports service, the Earthfile Environment
programme and Roving Report - a weekly service of five
in-depth reports. Copyright is held for most material, others
obtained on a case by case basis, restrictions may occur with
sports and entertainment footage. Computerized. Catalogue
of Roving Reports available plus rate card. English, Spanish
and French spoken.

261 WPA FILM LIBRARY

5525 W. 159th Street, Oak Forest, IL 60452, USA
℄ +1 708 535 1540
Ⓕ +1 708 535 1541

Contacts: Michael Mertz
Subjects: Historical archive, newsreels, industry, Americana,
music, transport, fashion, locations, natural history.
▦ 10 000 hours film; 2000 hours videotape.
Research: By both staff and outside researchers.
🕑 Mon-Fri 8:30 to 17:00
Description: Complete historical materials from 1896 to the
present day. Specialities include newsreels, Americana from
the 1940s and 50s, early rock and roll performances
(Hullabaloo in 1964/5, The Music Scene in 1969/70), UFOs,
automobiles, fashions, American Civil Rights, contemporary
geographic materials, nature and wildlife, American industry
collection from the 1940s to the present day. Also represent
British Pathe News for North America only. Partly
computerized. Rate card and brochure available.

262 ZIELINSKI PRODUCTIONS

Suite 80, 7850 Slater Avenue, Huntington Beach, CA 92647, USA
ⓒ +1 714 842 5050
ⓕ +1 714 842 5050

Contacts: Richard Zielinski
Subjects: Stock shots, sport, aerial photography, underwater photography.
8mm, 16mm; all video formats.
Research: By staff.
7 days, 24 hours
Procedure: Timecoded VHS (or as required) for viewing. Masters on-site.
Description: A collection of worldwide stock footage dating back 25 years including sports material (all levels), aerial and underwater photography, oldies, events, hi-tech, people, activities, equipment, etc. Will shoot original material if they don't have stock. Computerized. Rate card available.

Vietnam

263 VIETNAM FILM INSTITUTE

115 Ngoc Khanh Street, Hanoi, Vietnam
© +844 2 43451

Subjects: National Archives.

Zambia

264   MULTIMEDIA ZAMBIA AUDIO VISUALS ARCHIVE

P.O. Box 320199, Bishops Road, Kabulonga, Lusaka
101001, Zambia
ⓒ +260 1 264117
Ⓕ +260 1 264117
⚞ ZA 40340

Subjects: National Archives.

265   ZAMBIA NATIONAL BROADCASTING CORPORATION

Library Services, P.O. Box 50015, Lusaka, Zambia
ⓒ +260 1 252793
⚞ ZA 41221

Contacts: J.R. Chanda
Subjects: Current affairs, culture, music, drama, sport.
Film; videotape.
Research: By both staff and outside researchers. Requests in
writing.
🕐 Mon-Fri 08:00 to 17:30, Sat-Sun 08:00 to 13:00
Description: The political development of Zambia, economic
and business issues affecting the Zambian economy plus
traditional music, dance and locations. Drama from Zambia,
sport, etc. Also represent URTNA in Africa. Computerized.

Zimbabwe

266 NATIONAL ARCHIVES OF ZIMBABWE

Private Bag 7729 Causeway, Borrowdale Road, Gun Hill,
Harare, Zimbabwe
✆ +263 4 792741

Subjects: National Archives.

Listing by subject

Advertising

INTERNATIONAL AD CENTER, INTERNATIONAL AIR CHECK (IAC)

3261 N.E. 14th Avenue, Pompano Beach, Florida 33064, USA
© +1 305 785 6133
Ⓕ +1 305 941 2043

Contacts: Bill Klokow
Subjects: Advertising.
Beta/Beta SP, Umatic, VHS. NTSC.
Research: By both staff and outside researchers.
Appointment to visit.
Mon- Fri 09:00 to 18:00
Procedure: VHS viewing tapes supplied for a fee. 1- 7 days for access to masters.
Description: IAC have an extensive collection of more than 400 000 commercials dating back to 1976. Each area is retrievable by brand or product category. Copyright clearance is necessary in only a few instances. Computerized. Promotional flyer and rate card available. English and Spanish spoken. NB: IAC also have a contact telephone number in New York (212) 246 1446.

OPUS GLOBAL / THE ELECTRONIC LIBRARY

1133 N. Highland Avenue, Hollywood, CA 90038, USA
© +1 213 993 9888
Ⓕ +1 213 993 9899

Contacts: Todd Stubner, Masih Madani
Subjects: Stock shots, time-lapse, feature films, advertising, newsreels.
▦ Most film and video formats. NTSC.
Research: By staff and outside researchers. Appointment to visit.
◷ 7 days 24 hours
Procedure: Viewing on VHS, Umatic, CD-ROM. Less than 24 hours for access to masters.
Description: Contemporary and archival collection ranging from material specially shot for stock footage (real time and time altered) and out-takes from productions to vintage newsreels, feature films and commercials. The electronic library contains more than two million scenes catalogued by a unique object and relational database. Queries can be made on the content of image, the patterns, colours, texture and shapes of image objects, related layout and position information as well as keywords. Images are available in all formats including MPEG and JPEG for use in all mediums including CD-ROM. Stills, sound effects and music are also supplied. Fully computerized. Rate card and catalogue available electronically.
Foreign Offices: Represented by Front Line in Japan.

ORIGINAL FILMVIDEO LIBRARY

P.O. Box 3457, Anaheim, CA 92803, USA
© +1 714 526 4392
Ⓕ +1 714 526 4392

Contacts: Ronnie L. James
Subjects: Classic films, advertising, trailers, television, animation.
▦ 16mm, 35mm.
Research: By staff only.
🕐 Mon-Fri 10:00 to 16:00
Procedure: Viewing tapes available for small fee. All prints on site.
Description: Over 10 000 original rare 16mm and 35mm prints of vintage TV shows dating mainly from 1948 to 1970 and mostly produced by US companies. Many legendary talents rediscovered in forgotten or undocumented appearances on television, from Gloria Swanson to Richard Burton. Also thousands of TV commercials, movie preview trailers and other shorts. Transfers from prints can be made on site to VHS and Umatic via the Elmo TRV-16G system. Additionally there is an exhaustive reference library on TV and movies. Selective catalogue available, collection constantly being added to. Rates quoted based on title and use.

SHERMAN GRINBERG FILM LIBRARIES

630 9th Avenue, New York, NY 10036, USA
© +1 212 765 5170
Ⓕ +1 212 262 1532

Contacts: Nancy Casey, Bernard Chertok
Subjects: Current affairs, newsreels, advertising, stock shots.
▦ 16mm, 35mm; most video formats. NTSC.
Research: By both staff and outside researchers. Appointment to visit.
🕐 Mon-Fri 09:30 to 17:30
Procedure: Viewing as specified by client. 1-2 days for access to masters.
Description: A comprehensive collection of news coverage of the 20th Century, the library encorporates ABC Network News, Pathe News and Paramount News. Also represented are major libraries such as 20th Century Fox and HBO. Thirty years of television commercials are also available. Sherman Grinberg also have an office in Los Angeles at 1040 N. McCadden Place Tel: (213) 464 7491, Fax: (213) 462 5352, contacts: Bill Brewington, Linda Grinberg. Partly computerized. Catalogue and rate card available.

STREAMLINE ARCHIVES

Suite 1314, 432 Park Avenue South, New York NY 10016, USA
ⓒ +1 212 696 2616
ⓕ +1 212 696 0021

Contacts: Mark Trost
Subjects: Stock shots, newsreels, current affairs, classic films, feature films, educational, industry, sport, television, advertising, travelogues.
🎞 16mm, 35mm; most video formats. PAL, NTSC and SECAM.
Research: By staff only. Appointments for viewings.
🕐 Mon-Fri 09:30 to 19:30
Procedure: Viewing tapes assembled on VHS or Umatic. 24 hours for access to masters.
Description: Streamline's archives are being continually expanded including educational, government and industrial films, newsreels (from the turn of the century through to the early 1970s), silent comedies, television programmes and commercials, sports films, theatrical shorts, classic features and trailers as well as travel video and daily news footage (1986 to present) from Cablevision's award winning News 12 Long Island channel. Computerized. Rate card and catalogue available. English, Spanish and Japanese spoken.

VILLON FILMS

77 W 28 Avenue, Vancouver, BC V5Y 2K7, Canada
ⓒ +1 604 879 6042
ⓕ +1 604 879 6042

Contacts: Peter Davis
Subjects: Historical archive, documentaries, advertising, Africa, AIDS, apartheid, Cuba, culture, espionage, war.
🎞 Majority of material is 16mm. Some original video.
Research: Visits by appointment.
🕐 7 days, 24 hours
Procedure: Viewing of VHS and 16mm on premises, some video elsewhere.
Description: The collection comprises films made and collected by Peter including out-takes, commercials from the 1950s and 60s and valuable historical material. Subjects covered include Africa, AIDS, Rhodesia and Zimbabwe and especially South Africa 1900 to 1990; Catskills (Borscht Belt) 1900 to 1990; US covert activities, spies, the Cold War; D.H. Lawrence; Middle East late 1960s, 70s, 80s; US anti-war movement and counter culture 1960s and 70s; Britain early 1960s; World War II China; Native Americans (Crow and Navajo) 70s and 80s; Cuba 1960s. Partly computerized. Rates negotiable. English, French, Swedish and some Italian spoken.

Aerial photography

ARCTURUS MOTION PICTURES

65 Gray Cliff Road, Newton, MA 02159, USA
ℂ +1 617 332 3802
Ⓕ +1 617 332 3310

Contacts: David Breashears
Subjects: Himalayas, mountaineering, culture, religion, aerial
photography.
16mm; 1″ with matching 3/4″ and VHS.
Research: By both staff and outside researchers.
Appointment to visit.
Mon–Fri 09:00 to 17:00
Procedure: All material on viewing cassettes. Copies from
video masters.
Description: Collection specializes in the Himalayas with
emphasis on the Mount Everest region. Extensive scenics and
aerial shots of the area. Sherpa, Buddhist and Tibetan
culture. Partly computerized. Rate card and catalogue
available.

CAMEO FILM LIBRARY

10620 Burbank Blvd, N. Hollywood, CA 91607, USA
ℂ +1 818 980 8700
Ⓕ +1 818 980 7113

Contacts: Marilyn Chielens, Steven Vrabel
Subjects: Stock shots, locations, aerial photography, aviation,
military.
35mm.
Research: By staff only.
Mon–Fri 08:30 to 17:30
Description: A wide variety of stock shots including
worldwide establishing shots, military aircraft, period and
contemporary military, aerial footage, sunrises and sunsets,
etc. Rate card available.

CENTRAL COAST MEDIA HOLDINGS (CCM GROUP)

1st Floor, 56 The Entrance Road, The Entrance, NSW 2261,
Australia
ⓒ +61 43 331122
ⓕ +61 43 341017

Contacts: Mark and Michelle Falzon
Subjects: Industry, natural history, aerial photography,
lifestyles, landscapes.
🎞 16mm; Beta. PAL.
Research: By staff. Appointment to visit.
🕑 Mon-Fri 08:00 to 18:00
Procedure: Timecoded VHS available. Masters as reasonably
required.
Description: Comprehensive range of Australian floral and
landscape material on 16mm and Betacam plus a range of
corporate industrial imagery. The collection specializes in
central coast and New South Wales footage with aerial and
lifestyle, etc. shots. Rate card and catalogue available.

FILM BANK STOCK FOOTAGE FILM & VIDEO LIBRARY

425 South Victory Boulevard, Burbank, CA 91502, USA
ⓒ +1 818 841 9176
ⓕ +1 818 567 4235

Contacts: Paula Lumbard, Elizabeth Canelake
Subjects: News, space, special effects, science, sport,
medicine, time-lapse, aerial photography, natural history,
animation, locations, environmental.
🎞 16mm, 35mm; most video formats. NTSC masters.
Research: By staff only. Researchers occasionally visit for big
projects.
🕑 Mon-Fri 09:00 to 17:00
Procedure: Umatics loaned or VHS assembled. 24 hours for
access to masters.
Description: Diverse collection of broadcast quality film and
video images aimed at supplying the full range of client
productions. Most subjects are covered in the library, the
latest new collections being world locations, children of the
world, environmental images (destruction, scientific and
beauty shots), History of Flight, more space and solar flares,
aerials across the US, agriculture and animals. Partly
computerized. Catalogue and rate card available.

IMAGE BANK / FILM DIVISION

4th Floor, 111 Fifth Avenue, New York NY 10003, USA
© +1 212 529 6700
© +1 212 529 8889

Contacts: Brian Mitchell
Subjects: Stock shots, aerial photography, time-lapse, lifestyles, natural history, locations, sport.
All film and video formats and line standards held.
Research: By both staff and outside researchers. Appointment to visit.
Mon-Fri 09:00 to 17:00
Procedure: 3/4"/VHS (any line standard) for viewing. 24 hours for access to masters.
Description: Vast collection of stock material, contemporary and archival, acquired from Turner Broadcasting, Ocean Images, I.R.E., Pigeon Productions, MacGillivray Freeman Films, Dentsu Prox., McDonnell Douglas, Nature Conservancy, etc. Offices worldwide and major cities of North America - Chicago, Detroit, Mexico, Minneapolis, Atlanta, Dallas and Los Angeles. Computerized. English, French, Spanish, Italian, German and Greek spoken in the NEW YORK HEADQUARTERS.
Foreign Offices: Argentina, Brazil, Chile, Colombia, Australia, Canada, Hong Kong, Indonesia, Korea, Japan, Malaysia, Philippines, Singapore, Taiwan, Thailand, South Africa, UK, USA.

LARRY DORN ASSOCIATES / WORLD BACKGROUNDS

Suite 306, 5820 Wilshire Boulevard, Los Angeles CA 90036, USA
© +1 213 935 6266
© +1 213 935 9523

Contacts: Linda Dorn
Subjects: Stock shots, locations, Americana, aerial photography, underwater photography, aviation, transport, space.
35mm originals; 1" with matching 3/4" and VHS videotapes.
Research: By staff. Appointment to visit.
Mon-Fri 09:00 to 17:00
Procedure: Viewing tapes compiled. Masters copied on selection.
Description: Period and contemporary stock footage. European establishing shots, worldwide locations, Americana, scenics, aerials, various airlines and international airports, period wars, space, etc. Computerized. Rate card available.
Foreign Offices: France, Italy, UK.

PARAMOUNT PICTURES FILM LIBRARY

Hal Wallis Building, Room 108, 5555 Melrose Avenue,
Hollywood CA 90038, USA
ⓒ +1 213 956 5510
ⓕ +1 213 956 1833

Contacts: Pat Harris
Subjects: Stock shots, aerial photography, transport,
aviation, locations, building, skylines, out-takes.
🎞 35mm.
Research: By staff only (no charge made). Appointment to
visit.
🕑 Mon-Fri 09:00 to 18:00
Procedure: Film transferred to video at clients cost. 4-5
days for access to masters
Description: Out-takes and unused footage from
Paramount's features and television series spanning over 50
years. Over 9000 contemporary scenes catalogued in the
past year. Subjects vary from aerials of cities and
countrysides, stationary and moving process for cars, planes
and trains, buildings of every type, scenery to aviation,
amusements and skylines. Material is exclusively 35mm
including 3 strip technicolor. Rate card available.

SECOND LINE SEARCH

1926 Broadway, New York, NY 10023, USA
ⓒ +1 212 787 7500
ⓕ +1 212 787 7636

Contacts: Susan Luchars, George Bartko
Subjects: Locations, historical archive, sport, natural history,
aerial photography, time-lapse, Americana, out-takes,
industry, lifestyles.
🎞 Variety of film and video formats.
Research: By staff.
🕑 Mon-Fri 09:30 to 18:00
Procedure: Umatic viewing cassettes (NTSC or PAL). 2-3
days for access to masters.
Description: A variety of material including scenics, archival
footage, sports, wildlife, news, aerials, international locations,
Americana, oddities/bloopers, industry, technology, lifestyle
and time-lapse. Computerized. French, Spanish, Portuguese,
Italian and German spoken.

STOCK OPTIONS

P.O. Box 87622, Houghton 2041, South Africa
ⓒ +27 11 788 7248 / 880 1287
ⓕ +27 11 788 9996

Contacts: Margi Sheard, Sandee Daniell
Subjects: Natural history, travelogues, locations, anthropology, aerial photography.
▦ 16mm, 35mm; Beta SP, 1″, D1. PAL, some NTSC masters available.
Research: By both staff and outside researchers. Appointment to visit.
☻ Mon–Fri 08:30 to 17:30 (contactable until 22:00 by telephone)
Procedure: Umatic/VHS for viewing. 2 hours for local access to masters.
Description: Stock Options have African wildlife material (16mm and Beta SP), African landscapes, seascapes including aerial footage (16mm and 35mm), ethnic tribes and customs and international travel footage (Beta SP). Computerized. Catalogue and rate card available.
Foreign Offices: Represented by Index Stock Shots in London, Energy Productions in Los Angeles and Film World Research in Sydney.

STUART JEWELL PRODUCTIONS

2040 Garden Lane, Costa Mesa, CA 92627, USA
ⓒ +1 714 548 7234
ⓕ +1 818 508 1293 (agents fax)

Contacts: Agent Energy Productions
Subjects: Documentaries, natural history, culture, locations, time-lapse, aerial photography, steam trains.
▦ 16mm, 35mm; Beta SP, D2 1″, BVU. NTSC.
Description: Series of worldwide documentaries mostly natural history subjects - titles include Rolling to Guatemala, Following the Oregon Trail, Winter in Yellowstone, Teton and Mount. Rainer National Parks, The Great Aerial Odyssey, locations including Alaska, Hawaii, Borneo, Thailand, Africa, Egypt, India, Nepal plus steam trains in America, Canada, Australia and Guatemala. Partly computerized. NB: Represented by Energy Productions.
Foreign Offices: Contact local Energy Productions office.

ZIELINSKI PRODUCTIONS

Suite 80, 7850 Slater Avenue, Huntington Beach, CA 92647, USA
℡ +1 714 842 5050
Ⓕ +1 714 842 5050

Contacts: Richard Zielinski
Subjects: Stock shots, sport, aerial photography, underwater photography.
🎞 8mm, 16mm; all video formats.
Research: By staff.
🕑 7 days, 24 hours
Procedure: Timecoded VHS (or as required) for viewing. Masters on-site.
Description: A collection of worldwide stock footage dating back 25 years including sports material (all levels), aerial and underwater photography, oldies, events, hi-tech, people, activities, equipment, etc. Will shoot original material if they don't have stock. Computerized. Rate card available.

Agriculture

AUDIO VISUAL INSTITUTE, NATIONAL LIBRARY & ARCHIVE

P.O. Box 31519, Dar Es Salaam, Tanzania
℡ +255 51 72601/2/3/4

Contacts: M.I. Kange, Eva Sessoa
Subjects: National Archives, educational films, engineering, health, agriculture, tourism, current affairs.
🎞 16mm, 35mm.
Research: Permission and appointment needed prior to research.
🕐 Mon-Fri 07:30 to 15:30
Procedure: On request.
Description: Copyright to materials in the collection is owned by respective producers of films. The library is not computerized. A book catalogue is issued.

KESSER STOCK LIBRARY

21 SW 15 Road, Miami, Florida 33129, USA
℡ +1 305 358 7900
🖷 +1 305 358 2209

Contacts: Emily Wilson, Charles Carrubba
Subjects: Stock shots, locations, space, agriculture, leisure, fishing, time-lapse, underwater photography, aviation.
Research: By staff.
🕐 Mon-Fri 09:00 to 17:00
Description: Range of archival and contemporary stock shot material. Subjects include world destinations, wildlife, sunsets, fireworks, horseracing, time-lapse and underwater photography, agriculture, space, fishing, etc. Partly computerized. Rate card and brochure available.

STOCK SHOTS

1085 Louise Avenue, San Jose, CA 95125, USA
℡ +1 408 971 1325
🖷 +1 408 723 3846

Contacts: Tom Mertens
Subjects: Transport, agriculture, locations, medicine, health.
🎞 20 000 feet of film; 500 hours of videotape.
Research: By staff.
🕐 Mon-Fri 10:00 to 16:00
Description: Silicon Valley, San Francisco aerials, rail transit, agriculture, Europe, Asian, Africa collection filmed 1945 to 1975. Also incorporates The Justin Byers Film Collection. Partly computerized. Rate card available.

AIDS

VILLON FILMS

77 W 28 Avenue, Vancouver, BC V5Y 2K7, Canada
ⓒ +1 604 879 6042
Ⓕ +1 604 879 6042

Contacts: Peter Davis
Subjects: Historical archive, documentaries, advertising, Africa, AIDS, apartheid, Cuba, culture, espionage, war.
Majority of material is 16mm. Some original video.
Research: Visits by appointment.
7 days, 24 hours
Procedure: Viewing of VHS and 16mm on premises, some video elsewhere.
Description: The collection comprises films made and collected by Peter including out-takes, commercials from the 1950s and 60s and valuable historical material. Subjects covered include Africa, AIDS, Rhodesia and Zimbabwe and especially South Africa 1900 to 1990; Catskills (Borscht Belt) 1900 to 1990; US covert activities, spies, the Cold War; D.H. Lawrence; Middle East late 1960s, 70s, 80s; US anti-war movement and counter culture 1960s and 70s; Britain early 1960s; World War II China; Native Americans (Crow and Navajo) 70s and 80s; Cuba 1960s. Partly computerized. Rates negotiable. English, French, Swedish and some Italian spoken.

American Indians

UNIVERSITY OF WASHINGTON PRESS

P.O. Box 50096, Seattle, WA 98145-5096, USA
© +1 206 543 4050
Ⓕ +1 206 543 3932

Contacts: Jessica Lind, Bob Hutchins
Subjects: American Indians.
Research: No research. Preview copies on request.
☺ Mon-Fri 08:30 to 17:00
Procedure: 30 day loan with credit card deposit. 3 days for access to masters.
Description: Full collection of ethnomusicology filmed by R. Garfias. The library specializes in native American Indians of the early 20th Century and includes the titles In the Land of the War Canoes (Edward S. Curtis) and Kwakiutl of British Columbia (Franz Boas).

Animation

AL-NAZAER COMPANY

P.O. Box 6301, Hawally 32038, Kuwait
© +965 2658 500 (10 lines)
Ⓕ +965 262 55 21
✎ 46364 NAZAER KT

Contacts: Mr Yousuf Al Refai, Mr Ali Al Refai
Subjects: Drama, entertainment, animation, documentaries.
▦ Beta SP, 1″, Umatic. PAL.
Research: By staff and outside researchers. Appointment to visit.
☼ Open every day except Friday 08:00 to 13:00, 16:00 to 20:00
Procedure: VHS viewing material. One week for access to masters.
Description: The collection contains Arabic drama, short plays, musicals, variety, animated cartoon and documentaries (Arabic and English versions). Computerized. Catalogue available. English and Arabic spoken.

CASCOM INTERNATIONAL

806 4th Avenue South, Nashville, TN 37210, USA
© +1 615 242 8900
Ⓕ +1 615 256 7890

Contacts: Victor Rumore
Subjects: Special effects, computer imagery, time-lapse, animation.
▦ 16mm, 35mm; Beta SP. PAL.
Research: By outside researchers. Appointment to visit.
☼ Mon-Fri 09:00 to 17:30
Procedure: VHS viewing tapes loaned. 1-2 hours for access to masters.
Description: Mainly computer generated effects but also time-lapse, animation and live action. Subjects covered include globes, fireworks, maps, grids, sport, health, entertainment, environment, music, space and hi-tech. Catalogue showing a freeze frame of each effectin the library is available.
Foreign Offices: Australia (Select Effects).

CINAR

1201 Rue St. Andre, Montreal, Quebec H2L 3S8, Canada
℡ +1 514 843 7070
ℱ +1 514 843 7080

Contacts: Suzan Ayscough
Subjects: Animation, features films.
▦ 1″, Umatic. NTSC.
Research: Not a library service - make enquiries to
Communications Dept.
🕐 Mon-Fri 09:00 to 17:00
Procedure: VHS viewing tapes sent to clients.
Description: Cinar is a producer and distributor of family
oriented live action and animation programmes. Cinar
operates Crayon Animation, the largest animation studio in
Eastern Canada plus a studio centre with a complete range
of post production facilities. Partly computerized. Catalogue
available. English and French spoken.

DOOMSDAY STUDIOS

212 James Street, Ottawa, Ontario K1R 5M7, Canada
℡ +1 613 230 9769
ℱ +1 613 230 6004

Contacts: Ramona Macdonald, Tony Kelleher
Subjects: Architecture, folklore, animation, feature films.
▦ 16mm, 35mm; 1″, Umatic. PAL and NTSC.
Research: By staff.
🕐 Mon-Fri 09:00 to 17:00
Procedure: Viewing material on 16mm or cassette.
Description: The library has a collection of Nova Scotia folk
art including black and white footage of a folk festival in the
1970s. They also have Lithuanian folk art, experimental
animation and various features. English, French, Spanish,
German, Russian and Lithuanian spoken.

EM GEE FILM LIBRARY

Suite 103, 6924 Canby Avenue, Reseda CA 91335, USA
ⓒ +1 818 881 8110
ⓕ +1 818 981 5506

Contacts: Murray Glass
Subjects: Public domain, classic films, feature films, comedy, documentaries, westerns, animation.
All film formats; VHS, Umatic. NTSC.
Research: By both staff and outside researchers.
Mon-Fri 08:30 to 17:00
Procedure: Viewing material on 16mm or VHS. 1 week for access to masters.
Description: Approximately 3000 titles in all genres - silent and sound, black and white and colour. Their speciality is in public domain material covering all subject areas including comedies, documentaries, westerns, animation and feature films. Partly computerized. Catalogue and rate card available.

FILM & VIDEO STOCK SHOTS

Suite E, 10700 Ventura Boulevard, Studio City CA 91604, USA
ⓒ +1 818 760 2098
ⓕ +1 818 760 3294

Contacts: Stephanie Siebert, William Bolls
Subjects: Stock shots, current affairs, leisure, natural history, time-lapse, locations, macro photography, animation, culture, landscapes.
Film; videotape.
Research: By staff. Appointment to visit.
Mon-Fri 09:00 to 17:00
Description: Huge selection of both current and archival film and videotape original images. Subjects include news events, action sports, nature and wildlife, time-lapse cinematography, landscapes and cityscapes, microscopy, cartoons, lifestyles and travel footage. Next business day turnaround on master footage orders and competitive rates. Computerized. Brochure and rate card available.

FILM BANK STOCK FOOTAGE FILM & VIDEO LIBRARY

425 South Victory Boulevard, Burbank, CA 91502, USA
© +1 818 841 9176
℉ +1 818 567 4235

Contacts: Paula Lumbard, Elizabeth Canelake
Subjects: News, space, special effects, science, sport, medicine, time-lapse, aerial photography, natural history, animation, locations, environmental.
▦ 16mm, 35mm; most video formats. NTSC masters.
Research: By staff only. Researchers occasionally visit for big projects.
☉ Mon-Fri 09:00 to 17:00
Procedure: Umatics loaned or VHS assembled. 24 hours for access to masters.
Description: Diverse collection of broadcast quality film and video images aimed at supplying the full range of client productions. Most subjects are covered in the library, the latest new collections being world locations, children of the world, environmental images (destruction, scientific and beauty shots), History of Flight, more space and solar flares, aerials across the US, agriculture and animals. Partly computerized. Catalogue and rate card available.

HOLLYWOOD HOUSE VIDEO ARCHIVES / HOME ENTERTAINMENT HOLDINGS

Box 555, Bondi Beach, NSW 2026, Australia
© +61 2 365 1055
℉ +61 2 365 1577

Contacts: Joe Shellim
Subjects: Classic films, documentaries, music, space, film industry, animation, war, personalities, circus, natural history.
▦ Film; Beta, 1″, BVU, Umatic.
Research: By staff.
☉ Sun-Fri 10:00 to 19:00
Procedure: VHS viewing tape. Access to masters dependent on workload.
Description: Collection includes classic nostalgia movies complimented with interviews and rehearsals, behind-the-scenes, lost films, etc. Interviews with movie stars, candid films, footage of world leaders, space (NASA), music clips, nature and circus, cartoons, war and documentaries. Partly computerized. Rate card and catalogue available.

ICAIC

Calle 23, 1155 Vedado, Habana, Cuba
© +53 7 333862 / 34400 / 304666
Ⓕ +53 7 333032
〰 511419 ICAIC CU

Contacts: Leon Francisco, Rodriguez Antonio, Alfredo Calvino
Subjects: Historical archive, feature films, animation.
▦ 16mm, 35mm; Beta, Umatic. NTSC.
Research: By both staff and outside researchers.
☺ Mon–Fri 08:00 to 16:00
Procedure: VHS/Umatic/Betamax for viewing. Masters vary
– usually 1 week.
Description: Social, political and cultural footage from 1902
up to the present day with special emphasis on events from
1954 onwards. Features and short films covering all genres
and themes. Animation mainly for children. Partly
computerized. Rate card and catalogue available. English,
French and Russian spoken.

IMAGEWAYS

Second Floor, 412 West 48th Street, New York NY 10036,
USA
© +1 212 265 1287
Ⓕ +1 212 586 0339

Contacts: Adam Sargis, Kenneth Powell, Ray Sidwell
Subjects: Stock shots, newsreels, comedy, animation, classic
films, documentaries, industry, educational films, television.
▦ Film; 1″ videotape with timecoded 3/4″ cassettes.
Research: By staff. Appointment to visit.
Procedure: Timecoded cassette compiled. Masters copied
after selection.
Description: Stock footage library with material dating from
1905 to present day. Footage comes from newsreels, silent
films, cartoons, historical films, Hollywood features,
documentaries, industrial films, educational films, television
programmes and original shot material. Collection is
approximately 70% colour and 30% black and white.
Computerized. Rate card available. Minimum license fee
charged on delivery of master material.

INTERNATIONAL MEDIA RESOURCE EXCHANGE

124 Washington Place, New York, NY 10014, USA
© +1 212 463 0108
Ⓕ +1 212 243 3805

Contacts: Karen Ranucci
Subjects: Latin America, documentaries, animation, music.
▦ Most video formats. NTSC.
Research: By both staff and outside researchers.
Appointment to visit.
🕑 Mon-Fri 10:00 to 17:00
Procedure: Viewing on Umatic, VHS, Betamax. 2 weeks for access to masters, can rush.
Description: More than 500 films and videos of all genres made by Latin Americans including short fiction, features, documentaries, video art animations and music videos. Computerized. English and Spanish spoken.

JUDSON ROSEBUSH COMPANY

154 West 57th Street, New York, NY 10019-3321, USA
© +1 212 581 3000
Ⓕ +1 212 757 8283

Contacts: Judson Rosebush, Kristine Watt
Subjects: Animation.
▦ Video and computer programmes.
Research: By both staff and outside researchers.
🕑 Mon-Sat 08:00 to 20:00
Procedure: Viewing on CD-ROMs, MACs and video. 5 days for access to masters.
Description: The library specializes in computer animation dating from 1970 to 1990. Computerized. Catalogue and rate card available. English, Spanish and French spoken.

M.C. STUART & ASSOCIATES (MSCAA)

88 Highett Street, Richmond, Victoria 3121, Australia
ⓒ +61 3 429 8666
ⓕ +61 3 429 1839

Contacts: Max Stuart, Paul Stuart
Subjects: Natural history, leisure, sport, music, culture, documentaries, animation, childrens, feature films, entertainment.
☉ Mon-Fri 07:00 to 19:00
Description: MSCAA represent some 40 Australian producers syndicating their programmes to many markets. The types of programmes handled include documentaries, children's programmes, cartoons, feature films, light entertainment, music (modern and classical), the Arts, Australian rules football and leisure sports. Computerized. Rate card and catalogue available. Italian and French spoken.
Foreign Offices: UK, France, Spain, Austria, Norway, Italy, Germany, Greece, Malaysia, Hong Kong, Japan, Canada, USA, Singapore, Sri Lanka, Turkey, Jordan, Thailand.

NATIONAL LIBRARY OF AUSTRALIA

Film & Video Lending Service, Parkes Place, Canberra 2600, Australia
ⓒ +61 6 262 1361
ⓕ +61 6 262 1634

Contacts: Reference Officer
Subjects: National Archives, educational films, documentaries, feature films, animation.
▦ 16mm; Umatic, VHS. PAL, some NTSC.
Research: Researchers can visit, appointments recommended not essential.
☉ Mon-Fri 09:00 to 16:30
Procedure: Free loan to institutes, businesses and groups. No masters held.
Description: Over 23 500 instructional and educational documentary titles held covering most subject areas. Also a film and TV study collection with feature films, short fiction, animation and experimental film and video. Computerized. Full catalogue available on microfiche and screen studies catalogue in print form.

NEW ZEALAND FILM ARCHIVE

P.O. Box 11-449, First Floor, The Film Centre, Cnr. Cable
Street & Jervois Quay, Wellington, New Zealand
© +64 4 3847647
⑤ +64 4 3829595

Contacts: Bronwyn Taylor (public programmes), Diane Pivac
(documentation)
Subjects: National Archives, newsreels, documentaries,
feature films, animation.
▦ Film; video.
Research: By appointment only.
◷ Mon-Fri 09:00 to 17:00
Procedure: Access to view is available. Master material not
available.
Description: Held in the archive's collection are New Zealand
and overseas films from 1897 to the present day, comprising
fiction and feature films, shorts animated films,
documentaries, newsreels, video and television programmes.
A wide variety of promotional, critical and historical
documentation and information is also held for New Zealand
and overseas films. Copyright is not held by NZFA.
Computerized. Rate card available.

ORIGINAL FILMVIDEO LIBRARY

P.O. Box 3457, Anaheim, CA 92803, USA
© +1 714 526 4392
⑤ +1 714 526 4392

Contacts: Ronnie L. James
Subjects: Classic films, advertising, trailers, television,
animation.
▦ 16mm, 35mm.
Research: By staff only.
◷ Mon-Fri 10:00 to 16:00
Procedure: Viewing tapes available for small fee. All prints
on site.
Description: Over 10 000 original rare 16mm and 35mm
prints of vintage TV shows dating mainly from 1948 to 1970
and mostly produced by US companies. Many legendary
talents rediscovered in forgotten or undocumented
appearances on television, from Gloria Swanson to Richard
Burton. Also thousands of TV commercials, movie preview
trailers and other shorts. Transfers from prints can be made
on site to VHS and Umatic via the Elmo TRV-16G system.
Additionally there is an exhaustive reference library on TV
and movies. Selective catalogue available, collection
constantly being added to. Rates quoted based on title and
use.

SELECT EFFECTS – AUSTRALIA

11 Station Street, Naremburn, NSW 2065, Australia
ⓒ +61 2 437 5620
Ⓕ +61 2 901 4505

Contacts: Jill Freestone
Subjects: Special effects, computer imagery, time-lapse, animation.
🎞 16mm, 35mm; Beta SP. PAL.
Research: By outside researchers. Appointment to visit.
🕑 Mon–Fri 09:00 to 17:30
Procedure: VHS viewing tapes loaned. 1–2 hours for access to masters.
Description: Mainly computer generated effects but also time-lapse, animation and live action. Subjects covered include globes, fireworks, maps, grids, sport, health, entertainment, environment, music, space and hi-tech. This company represents US company Cascom International. Partly computerized. Catalogue showing a freeze frame of each effect in the library is available.
Foreign Offices: USA (Cascom International).

SHAMRA for Production and Distribution

P.O. Box 149, Damascus, Syria
ⓒ +963 11 665601
Ⓕ +963 11 662812
✉ 411404 SY

Contacts: Khaldoun Al Maleh
Subjects: Comedy, animation, drama.
🎞 Beta/Beta SP, 1", BVU, Umatic. PAL.
Research: Appointment to visit.
🕑 Sat–Thurs 09:00 to 21:00
Description: Arab speaking comedies, television series and plays. Also a collection of TV programmes and cartoon films dubbed into Arabic - rights held for distributoion to Arabic speaking TV stations. Computerized. English spoken.
Foreign Offices: Greece.

TWENTIETH CENTURY FOX

2121 Avenue of the Stars, Los Angeles, CA 90067, USA
ⓒ +1 310 203 4613
Ⓕ +1 310 203 4611

Contacts: Vary depending on requested material
Subjects: Feature films, television, animation.
Procedure: All requests must be in writing addressed to Los Angeles office.
Description: All clearances for Twentieth Century Fox product is handled in the Los Angeles office. Information required before contacting relevant person (by fax) is: name, address, telephone/fax of licensee; name and nature of programme; intended use of clip; title, description of scene and length of clip; media, territory, term and air dates required. For feature films, use of still photographs and audio bites contact: Rebecca Herrera, Fax: (310) 203 4118. For TV series (other than The Simpsons and Steven Bochco products) contact: Lisa Alcov or Laura Jenkins, Fax: (310) 203 1067. For The Simpsons and Bochco Shows contact: Suzanne Krajewki, Fax: (310) 277 9041.

WGBH FILM & VIDEO RESOURCE CENTER

125 Wester Avenue, Boston, MA 02134, USA
ⓒ +1 617 492 3079
Ⓕ +1 617 783 4243
✎ 710 330 6887

Contacts: Vladimir Stefanovic, Patricia Barraza
Subjects: Documentaries, natural history, science, medicine, animation, aviation.
▦ 16mm, 35mm; Beta/Beta SP, D2, 1″, Umatic. NTSC.
Research: By staff only.
🕓 Mon-Fri 09:00 to 17:00
Procedure: Viewing on VHS or Umatic as requested. 3 days for access to masters.
Description: WGBH is one of the largest documentary producing stations in the US Public Broadcasting System, producing over 30% of prime time PBS programmes. Having been in existence since 1955 the extensive library holds material covering subjects such as nature, science, scenics, animation, wildlife, high tech, health/surgery and flight. The majority of copyright is held by WGBH. Partly computerized. Catalogue and rate card available. English, Spanish and Macedonian spoken.

Apartheid

SOUTH AFRICAN NATIONAL FILM VIDEO & SOUND ARCHIVES

Private Bag X236, Pretoria 0001, South Africa
ⓒ +27 12 343 9767/8/9
ⓕ +27 12 344 5143

Contacts: Johan de Lange
Subjects: South Africa, apartheid, arts.
Most film formats; Beta/Beta SP, 1", Umatic, VHS. PAL.
Research: Research by appointment only - not open on Fridays to public.
Mon-Fri 08:00 to 16:00
Procedure: Viewing on premises on all formats. 3 days for access to masters.
Description: The collection contains films, videos, gramophone records, CDs, audio cassettes and documentation all relating to South Africa. There is also an information centre on the arts. Copyrights all reside with the original owners of the material except for a few exceptional cases. Partly computerized. Catalogue available. English and Afrikaans spoken.

VILLON FILMS

77 W 28 Avenue, Vancouver, BC V5Y 2K7, Canada
ⓒ +1 604 879 6042
ⓕ +1 604 879 6042

Contacts: Peter Davis
Subjects: Historical archive, documentaries, advertising, Africa, AIDS, apartheid, Cuba, culture, espionage, war.
Majority of material is 16mm. Some original video.
Research: Visits by appointment.
7 days, 24 hours
Procedure: Viewing of VHS and 16mm on premises, some video elsewhere.
Description: The collection comprises films made and collected by Peter including out-takes, commercials from the 1950s and 60s and valuable historical material. Subjects covered include Africa, AIDS, Rhodesia and Zimbabwe and especially South Africa 1900 to 1990; Catskills (Borscht Belt) 1900 to 1990; US covert activities, spies, the Cold War; D.H. Lawrence; Middle East late 1960s, 70s, 80s; US anti-war movement and counter culture 1960s and 70s; Britain early 1960s; World War II China; Native Americans (Crow and Navajo) 70s and 80s; Cuba 1960s. Partly computerized. Rates negotiable. English, French, Swedish and some Italian spoken.

Architecture

DOOMSDAY STUDIOS

212 James Street, Ottawa, Ontario K1R 5M7, Canada
ⓒ +1 613 230 9769
Ⓕ +1 613 230 6004

Contacts: Ramona Macdonald, Tony Kelleher
Subjects: Architecture, folklore, animation, feature films.
🎞 16mm, 35mm; 1", Umatic. PAL and NTSC.
Research: By staff.
🕑 Mon-Fri 09:00 to 17:00
Procedure: Viewing material on 16mm or cassette.
Description: The library has a collection of Nova Scotia folk art including black and white footage of a folk festival in the 1970s. They also have Lithuanian folk art, experimental animation and various features. English, French, Spanish, German, Russian and Lithuanian spoken.

Aviation

AIRLINE FILM & TV PROMOTIONS

13246 Weidner Street, Pacoima, CA 91331-2343, USA
© +1 818 899 1151
Ⓕ +1 818 896 5929

Contacts: Alf or Mikael Jacobsen
Subjects: Aviation, locations, leisure.
35mm.
Research: By staff. Visit by appointment.
Mon-Fri 08:00 to 17:00
Description: Footage of commercial airlines - take-offs, landings, in flight - worldwide. Establishing shots of many capital cities. Sports and recreational activities. Rate card available.

CAE-LINK CORPORATION

P.O. Box 1237, Binghamton, NY 13902-1237, USA
© +1 607 721 5850
Ⓕ +1 607 721 5574

Contacts: Paul Redfern
Subjects: Aviation.
Beta/Beta SP, D2. NTSC.
Research: Researchers can visit by appointment.
Mon-Fri 09:00 to 17:00
Procedure: Time coded VHS for viewing. 48 hours or less for access to masters.
Description: Extensive footage of flight, air traffic control and medical simulators, also some aircraft footage.

CAMEO FILM LIBRARY

10620 Burbank Blvd, N. Hollywood, CA 91607, USA
© +1 818 980 8700
Ⓕ +1 818 980 7113

Contacts: Marilyn Chielens, Steven Vrabel
Subjects: Stock shots, locations, aerial photography, aviation, military.
35mm.
Research: By staff only.
Mon-Fri 08:30 to 17:30
Description: A wide variety of stock shots including worldwide establishing shots, military aircraft, period and contemporary military, aerial footage, sunrises and sunsets, etc. Rate card available.

FRONT LINE

Suite 3 Senyo Building, 5th Floor, 3-1-9 Nakameguro,
Meguro-ku, Toyko 153, Japan
© +81 3 3760 6271
Ⓕ +81 3 3760 6012

Contacts: Seiichi Sugiura
Subjects: Stock shots, aviation, locations, natural history,
industry, space, time-lapse, transport, environmental.
🕐 Mon-Fri 10:00 to 18:00
Procedure: Viewing tapes loaned. Masters copied after
selection.
Description: Agents for UK company Index Stock Shots, USA
company Opus Global and Canadian company Fabulous
Footage in Japan.

HOT SHOTS COOL CUTS

1926 Broadway, New York, NY 10023, USA
© +1 212 799 9100
Ⓕ +1 212 799 9258

Contacts: Andrew Conti
Subjects: Stock shots, historical archive, aviation.
🎞 35mm.
Research: By staff. Researchers can visit by appointment
only.
🕐 Mon-Fri 09:30 to 18:00
Procedure: VHS and Umatic viewing tapes (PAL and NTSC).
24 hours for access to masters.
Description: Hot Shots exclusively represent an international
network of cinematographers with extensive contemporary
and archival holdings covering all topics imaginable including
the stock footage rights to the Pan Am film library and the
Hearst Entertainments historical collection. Catalogue and
rate card available. Computerized. English and Spanish
spoken.

IMAGES OF THE EAST

·19B Jalan 20/14, Petaling Jaya Selangor 46300, Malaysia
ⓒ +60 03 776 7199
ⓕ +60 03 776 4560

Contacts: Theresa Khoo
Subjects: Stock shots, aviation, locations, natural history, industry, space, time-lapse, transport, environmental.
▦ Beta SP, 1″, Umatic. PAL.
Research: By staff. Visits by appointment.
☉ Mon–Fri 08:30 to 17:45
Procedure: Viewing tapes loaned. Masters copied after selection, 3–4 days for access.
Description: Agents for UK company Index Stock Shots and German company Modern Video Library in Malaysia and Singapore. The library holds an A–Z of subject categories including landscape, destination and sports footage from Malaysia. Partly computerized. Rate card available. English spoken.

KESSER STOCK LIBRARY

21 SW 15 Road, Miami, Florida 33129, USA
ⓒ +1 305 358 7900
ⓕ +1 305 358 2209

Contacts: Emily Wilson, Charles Carrubba
Subjects: Stock shots, locations, space, agriculture, leisure, fishing, time-lapse, underwater photography, aviation.
Research: By staff.
☉ Mon–Fri 09:00 to 17:00
Description: Range of archival and contemporary stock shot material. Subjects include world destinations, wildlife, sunsets, fireworks, horseracing, time-lapse and underwater photography, agriculture, space, fishing, etc. Partly computerized. Rate card and brochure available.

LARRY DORN ASSOCIATES / WORLD BACKGROUNDS

Suite 306, 5820 Wilshire Boulevard, Los Angeles CA 90036,
USA
© +1 213 935 6266
Ⓕ +1 213 935 9523

Contacts: Linda Dorn
Subjects: Stock shots, locations, Americana, aerial
photography, underwater photography, aviation, transport,
space.
▥ 35mm originals; 1″ with matching 3/4″ and VHS videotapes.
Research: By staff. Appointment to visit.
☺ Mon-Fri 09:00 to 17:00
Procedure: Viewing tapes compiled. Masters copied on
selection.
Description: Period and contemporary stock footage.
European establishing shots, worldwide locations, Americana,
scenics, aerials, various airlines and international airports,
period wars, space, etc. Computerized. Rate card available.
Foreign Offices: France, Italy, UK.

PARAMOUNT PICTURES FILM LIBRARY

Hal Wallis Building, Room 108, 5555 Melrose Avenue,
Hollywood CA 90038, USA
© +1 213 956 5510
Ⓕ +1 213 956 1833

Contacts: Pat Harris
Subjects: Stock shots, aerial photography, transport,
aviation, locations, building, skylines, out-takes.
▥ 35mm.
Research: By staff only (no charge made). Appointment to
visit.
☺ Mon-Fri 09:00 to 18:00
Procedure: Film transferred to video at clients cost. 4-5
days for access to masters
Description: Out-takes and unused footage from
Paramount's features and television series spanning over 50
years. Over 9000 contemporary scenes catalogued in the
past year. Subjects vary from aerials of cities and
countrysides, stationary and moving process for cars, planes
and trains, buildings of every type, scenery to aviation,
amusements and skylines. Material is exclusively 35mm
including 3 strip technicolor. Rate card available.

PETRIFIED FILMS / THE IMAGE BANK

Room 204, 430 West 14th Street, New York NY 10014, USA
© +1 212 242 5461
© +1 212 691 8347

Contacts: Lori Cheatle, Rob Cates
Subjects: Historical archive, Hollywood, transport, consumerism, Americana, industry, war, aviation, feature film, out-takes.
35mm, 16mm; some on 1", D2, 3/4" with matching VHS.
Research: By staff. Visits by appointment.
☉ Mon–Fri 09:30 to 18:00
Procedure: Viewing tapes assembled. Masters copied after selection.
Description: Historical collection including pre-1951 Warner Brothers stock and pre-1965 Columbia Pictures stock. A-Z of subjects including action sequences, period recreations, establishing shots, projection backgrounds, cityscapes and worldwide locations. Industrial, military and aviation collections. Car culture and 1950s daily life in the US. Majority dates from 1920s to 1960s. Partly computerized. Rate card and catalogue available.
Foreign Offices: Contact local Image Bank office.

TELECINE INTERNATIONAL PRODUCTIONS

P.O. Box 8426, Universal City, CA 91608, USA
© +1 818 889 8246
© +1 818 889 5605

Contacts: Nick Archer
Subjects: Stock shots, locations, transport, aviation, time-lapse, landscapes.
35mm.
Research: By both staff and outside researchers.
☉ Mon–Fri 09:00 to 18:00
Procedure: Film/cassette viewing reels. Minimum royalty due for masters.
Description: Worldwide establishing shots, cityscapes and traffic from 1957 to present day, transportation, jets, buildings, scenics, moons, sunrises, suns, time-lapse clouds. Rate card and brochure available.

WGBH FILM & VIDEO RESOURCE CENTER

125 Wester Avenue, Boston, MA 02134, USA
© +1 617 492 3079
Ⓕ +1 617 783 4243
✍ 710 330 6887

Contacts: Vladimir Stefanovic, Patricia Barraza
Subjects: Documentaries, natural history, science, medicine,
animation, aviation.
▦ 16mm, 35mm; Beta/Beta SP, D2, 1″, Umatic. NTSC.
Research: By staff only.
☉ Mon–Fri 09:00 to 17:00
Procedure: Viewing on VHS or Umatic as requested. 3 days
for access to masters.
Description: WGBH is one of the largest documentary
producing stations in the US Public Broadcasting System,
producing over 30% of prime time PBS programmes. Having
been in existence since 1955 the extensive library holds
material covering subjects such as nature, science, scenics,
animation, wildlife, high tech, health/surgery and flight. The
majority of copyright is held by WGBH. Partly computerized.
Catalogue and rate card available. English, Spanish and
Macedonian spoken.

Biology

NEW YORK ZOOLOGICAL SOCIETY

The Wildlife Conservation Society Office of Media Studies,
185th Street and Southern Blvd, Bronx, NY 10460, USA
Ⓒ +1 718 220 5134
Ⓕ +1 718 220 7114

Contacts: Thomas Veltre
Subjects: Natural history, environmental, biology.
🎞 16mm, 35mm; most video formats. NTSC.
Research: Limited research by staff - $150 minimum for
VHS. Appointments.
🕑 Mon-Fri 10:00 to 17:00
Procedure: VHS tapes compiled dependent on workload. 2-3
days for access to masters.
Description: The collection is comprised of film shot at the
Bronx Zoo, NY aquarium and other NYZS facilities as well as
film from research expeditions sponsored by the society over
the last 80 years. Good close-ups of many rare species in
naturalistic settings, historical material on field research and
much good wildlife from East Africa in 1960s and 1970s.

Business

BROAD STREET PRODUCTIONS

10 West 19th Street, New York, NY 10011, USA
✆ +1 212 924 4700
Ⓕ +1 212 924 5085

Contacts: Jody Bergedick, David Fink
Subjects: Industry, skylines, business.
16mm. Most video formats. NTSC.
Research: By both staff and outside researchers. Appointment to visit.
Mon-Fri 09:00 to 18:00 (other days and hours on request)
Procedure: Timecoded VHS or Umatic viewing copies. Access to masters within 24 hours.
Description: The collection contains material relating to business and finance with footage of financial markets, industrial processes, city skylines, hi-tech communications imagery and business people in various situations. Partly computerized. Catalogue and rate card available.

Childrens

ARGO FILMS

43 Ben Yehuda St, Tel Aviv 69010, Israel
© +972 3 5228251
Ⓕ +972 3 5246910

Subjects: Feature films, documentaries, childrens.
☼ Sun-Thur 09:00 to 16:00
Description: Approximately 40 hours of programmes including feature films (contemporary Israel), documentaries (Ethiopian women) and children's shows (live and puppets).

KIDS TV

P.O. Box 8148, Symonds Street, Auckland 3, New Zealand
© +64 09 357 0724
Ⓕ +64 09 358 4809

Contacts: David Stewart
Subjects: Childrens, educational films.
▥ Beta/Beta SP, D2, 1″. PAL.
Research: By staff.
☼ Mon-Fri 08:00 to 18:00
Procedure: Timecoded VHS cassettes for viewing. Immediate access to masters.
Description: Programmes that target an age range from 1-19 years. Subjects covered are music, sports, current affairs and education for children and parents. Copyright owned by Kids TV. Computerized.

MAURITIUS BROADCASTING CORPORATION

1 Louis Pasteur Street, Forest Side, Mauritius
© +230 675001/2/3 6743743
Ⓕ +230 6757332
✎ 4230 MAUBROD IW

Contacts: Anne Marie Ginette Fabre
Subjects: National Archives, current affairs, religion, documentaries, childrens, music, personalities, sport.
▥ 16mm, 35mm; Beta/Beta SP, BVU, Umatic. PAL and SECAM.
Research: By staff. Outside researchers by appointment.
☼ 7 days 08:30 to 17:00
Procedure: Viewing on 16mm and video. 2 hours for access to masters.
Description: A wide range of programme material covering political, international and local events, religion, documentaries, television for children and teenagers, musicals, interviews and sports. English and French spoken.

M.C. STUART & ASSOCIATES (MSCAA)

88 Highett Street, Richmond, Victoria 3121, Australia
℃ +61 3 429 8666
Ⓕ +61 3 429 1839

Contacts: Max Stuart, Paul Stuart
Subjects: Natural history, leisure, sport, music, culture, documentaries, animation, childrens, feature films, entertainment.
🕓 Mon-Fri 07:00 to 19:00
Description: MSCAA represent some 40 Australian producers syndicating their programmes to many markets. The types of programmes handled include documentaries, children's programmes, cartoons, feature films, light entertainment, music (modern and classical), the Arts, Australian rules football and leisure sports. Computerized. Rate card and catalogue available. Italian and French spoken.
Foreign Offices: UK, France, Spain, Austria, Norway, Italy, Germany, Greece, Malaysia, Hong Kong, Japan, Canada, USA, Singapore, Sri Lanka, Turkey, Jordan, Thailand.

RADIO TELEVISION BRUNEI

Bandar Seri, Bandar Seri Begawan 2042, Brunei
℃ +673 2 243111 Ext. 224
Ⓕ +673 2 227204
〰 BU2720 RTBPROG

Contacts: Mr. H.J.M.D. Salleh
Subjects: Drama, comedy, documentaries, childrens.
▦ 16mm, 35mm; Video.
🕓 Mon-Thur and Sat 07:45 to 12:15, 13:30 to 16:30
Procedure: Umatic and VHS viewing material in PAL and NTSC.
Description: Television output including full range of programmes and series. English and Malay spoken.

Circus

HOLLYWOOD HOUSE VIDEO ARCHIVES / HOME ENTERTAINMENT HOLDINGS

Box 555, Bondi Beach, NSW 2026, Australia
Ⓒ +61 2 365 1055
Ⓕ +61 2 365 1577

Contacts: Joe Shellim
Subjects: Classic films, documentaries, music, space, film industry, animation, war, personalities, circus, natural history.
▦ Film; Beta, 1″, BVU, Umatic.
Research: By staff.
☉ Sun–Fri 10:00 to 19:00
Procedure: VHS viewing tape. Access to masters dependent on workload.
Description: Collection includes classic nostalgia movies complimented with interviews and rehearsals, behind-the-scenes, lost films, etc. Interviews with movie stars, candid films, footage of world leaders, space (NASA), music clips, nature and circus, cartoons, war and documentaries. Partly computerized. Rate card and catalogue available.

Classic films

AMAZING IMAGES

Suite 1581, 6671 Sunset Boulevard, Hollywood CA 90028, USA
℃ +1 213 962 1899
Ⓕ +1 213 962 1898

Contacts: Michael Peter Yakaitis
Subjects: Historical archive, newsreels, classic films, trailers, out-takes, personalities.
16mm, 35mm; video.
Research: By staff only.
Mon–Fri 09:30 to 18:00
Procedure: VHS or Umatic viewing copies. 24 hours for access to masters.
Description: The collection begins pre-1900 and includes old Hollywood stars of silent and sound motion pictures, locations around the globe, newsreels, historical events, world war, comedy, censorship, serial and weekly magazines, bloopers, Kodascopes, out-takes and film trailers. There is also a wide assortment of animal footage, celebrities and industrial material. Partly computerized. Rate card available.

ARCHIVE FILMS

530 West 25th Street, New York, NY 1001, USA
℃ +1 212 620 3955
Ⓕ +1 212 645 2137

Contacts: Patrick Montgomery
Subjects: Historical archive, newsreels, Hollywood, classic films, film industry, educational films.
35mm, 16mm; various video formats with matching cassettes.
Research: By staff. Appointment to visit.
Mon–Fri 09:00 to 18:00
Procedure: Viewing tapes assembled. 24–48 hours for access to masters.
Description: Over 5000 hours of newsreels, silent films, classic comedies, Hollywood features, historical dramas, documentaries and educational films. Represent The March of Time, The RKO Shorts Library, International Film Foundation, TV House and Videowest. Computerized. Rate card and catalogue available.
Foreign Offices: France, Germany, Italy, Japan, Netherlands, Sweden, UK, USA.

A.R.I.Q. FOOTAGE

One Main Street, East Hampton, New York 11964, USA
© +1 516 329 9200
Ⓕ +1 516 329 9260

Contacts: Joe Lauro,·Mart Heideman
Subjects: Historical archive, classic films, comedy, music, newsreels, industry, space.
Various film and video formats. All line standards available.
Research: By staff. Visits by appointment.
Mon–Fri 09:00 to 17:30
Procedure: Viewing material on VHS and Umatic. 24 hours for access to masters.
Description: Footage covers 1895 to 1990 with a very strong historical archive. Universal newsreel (1929 to 1967), musical performance footage including Jazz, Blues, Country, Rock and Roll, Pop from 1910 to 1990, silent films, industrial footage, space program, life styles and a range of general subject. Computerized. Rate card available.

CABLE FILMS & VIDEO

Country Club Station, Kansas City, MO 64113, USA
© +1 913 362 2804
Ⓕ +1 913 341 7365

Contacts: Herbert Miller
Subjects: Classic films, comedy.
Film; 1″, 3/4″, VHS.
Research: By staff.
Mon–Sat
Description: American and some foreign classic feature films dating from 1915. The majority of the material comes from the silent film era through to the 1930s and 40s. Excerpts they are able to offer include Charlie Chaplin, Buster Keaton, Douglas Fairbanks Snr. as well as It's A Wonderful Life and Night Of The Living Dead. Catalogue available.

EM GEE FILM LIBRARY

Suite 103, 6924 Canby Avenue, Reseda CA 91335, USA
© +1 818 881 8110
℉ +1 818 981 5506

Contacts: Murray Glass
Subjects: Public domain, classic films, feature films, comedy, documentaries, westerns, animation.
All film formats; VHS, Umatic. NTSC.
Research: By both staff and outside researchers.
Mon-Fri 08:30 to 17:00
Procedure: Viewing material on 16mm or VHS. 1 week for access to masters.
Description: Approximately 3000 titles in all genres - silent and sound, black and white and colour. Their speciality is in public domain material covering all subject areas including comedies, documentaries, westerns, animation and feature films. Partly computerized. Catalogue and rate card available.

HOLLYWOOD FILM REGISTRY

6926 Melrose Avenue, Hollywood, CA 90038, USA
© +1 213 937 7067
℉ +1 213 655 8889

Contacts: Dan Price
Subjects: Historical archive, stock shots, locations, personalities, Americana, documentaries, classic films, motor racing.
16mm, 35mm; most video formats.
Research: By both staff and outside researchers.
Appointment to visit.
Mon-Fri 10:30 to 17:30
Procedure: Viewing on VHS, Umatic, 35mm. 24 hours for access to masters.
Description: Encompasses 10 major collections. American Film Registry (from silent era on - institutional, travel, Imperial China...), Dennis Film Libraries (news, establishing shots, personalities, space...), Documentary Productions (Americana, motor sport), Keystone Collection (comedy), Paper Prints (1890s to 1910), Sand Castles (current establishing shots), Sandler Film Library (historical library used for stock by Hollywood producers since the 1930s), Slapstick & Gags (silent movies), Video & Film Stringers (current stock shots), Visual Dynamics (virtual encyclopaedic library up to the early 1970s). Partly computerized. Rate card available.

HOLLYWOOD HOUSE VIDEO ARCHIVES / HOME ENTERTAINMENT HOLDINGS

Box 555, Bondi Beach, NSW 2026, Australia
ⓒ +61 2 365 1055
ⓕ +61 2 365 1577

Contacts: Joe Shellim
Subjects: Classic films, documentaries, music, space, film industry, animation, war, personalities, circus, natural history.
Film; Beta, 1″, BVU, Umatic.
Research: By staff.
☺ Sun-Fri 10:00 to 19:00
Procedure: VHS viewing tape. Access to masters dependent on workload.
Description: Collection includes classic nostalgia movies complimented with interviews and rehearsals, behind-the-scenes, lost films, etc. Interviews with movie stars, candid films, footage of world leaders, space (NASA), music clips, nature and circus, cartoons, war and documentaries. Partly computerized. Rate card and catalogue available.

IMAGEWAYS

Second Floor, 412 West 48th Street, New York NY 10036, USA
ⓒ +1 212 265 1287
ⓕ +1 212 586 0339

Contacts: Adam Sargis, Kenneth Powell, Ray Sidwell
Subjects: Stock shots, newsreels, comedy, animation, classic films, documentaries, industry, educational films, television.
Film; 1″ videotape with timecoded 3/4″ cassettes.
Research: By staff. Appointment to visit.
Procedure: Timecoded cassette compiled. Masters copied after selection.
Description: Stock footage library with material dating from 1905 to present day. Footage comes from newsreels, silent films, cartoons, historical films, Hollywood features, documentaries, industrial films, educational films, television programmes and original shot material. Collection is approximately 70% colour and 30% black and white. Computerized. Rate card available. Minimum license fee charged on delivery of master material.

JOHN E. ALLEN

116 North Avenue, Park Ridge, NJ 07656, USA
ⓒ +1 201 391 3299
ⓕ +1 201 391 6335

Contacts: John E. Allen, Beverley Allen
Subjects: Historical archive, newsreels, war, Russia, industry, transport, classic films, educational films, travelogues.
▦ Mainly film; some video.
Research: By both staff and outside researchers.
🕐 Mon-Fri 09:00 to 18:00
Description: Kinograms from 1915 to 1931. Telenews 1947 to 1953. World War I and II, Spanish American War, Mexican Revolution, Russian Revolution, Hungarian Revolution, Spanish Civil War, Korean War, etc. Industry 1910 to 1950s, transportation, educational, ethnographic, travel, nature, features 1905 to 1950s, stills, posters and lobby cards. Partly computerized. Rate card available.

ORIGINAL FILMVIDEO LIBRARY

P.O. Box 3457, Anaheim, CA 92803, USA
ⓒ +1 714 526 4392
ⓕ +1 714 526 4392

Contacts: Ronnie L. James
Subjects: Classic films, advertising, trailers, television, animation.
▦ 16mm, 35mm.
Research: By staff only.
🕐 Mon-Fri 10:00 to 16:00
Procedure: Viewing tapes available for small fee. All prints on site.
Description: Over 10 000 original rare 16mm and 35mm prints of vintage TV shows dating mainly from 1948 to 1970 and mostly produced by US companies. Many legendary talents rediscovered in forgotten or undocumented appearances on television, from Gloria Swanson to Richard Burton. Also thousands of TV commercials, movie preview trailers and other shorts. Transfers from prints can be made on site to VHS and Umatic via the Elmo TRV-16G system. Additionally there is an exhaustive reference library on TV and movies. Selective catalogue available, collection constantly being added to. Rates quoted based on title and use.

STREAMLINE ARCHIVES

Suite 1314, 432 Park Avenue South, New York NY 10016, USA
ⓒ +1 212 696 2616
Ⓕ +1 212 696 0021

Contacts: Mark Trost
Subjects: Stock shots, newsreels, current affairs, classic films, feature films, educational, industry, sport, television, advertising, travelogues.

16mm, 35mm; most video formats. PAL, NTSC and SECAM.
Research: By staff only. Appointments for viewings.
Mon-Fri 09:30 to 19:30
Procedure: Viewing tapes assembled on VHS or Umatic. 24 hours for access to masters.
Description: Streamline's archives are being continually expanded including educational, government and industrial films, newsreels (from the turn of the century through to the early 1970s), silent comedies, television programmes and commercials, sports films, theatrical shorts, classic features and trailers as well as travel video and daily news footage (1986 to present) from Cablevision's award winning News 12 Long Island channel. Computerized. Rate card and catalogue available. English, Spanish and Japanese spoken.

VIDEO TAPE LIBRARY

Suite 2, 1509 N. Crescent Heights Blvd, Los Angeles CA 90046, USA
ⓒ +1 213 656 4330
Ⓕ +1 213 656 8746

Contacts: Melody St. John, Peggy Shannon
Subjects: Stock shots, current affairs, newsreels, locations, beauty, comedy, classic films, sport, leisure, environmental, medicine, out-takes.

20% film; 80% video.
Research: By both staff and outside researchers.
Mon-Fri 09:00 to 17:00
Procedure: 24 hour turnaround for research, preview and master footage.
Description: Enormous range of stock shot material ranging from archival footage (1898) to current news topics. Over 2 million shots on virtually every subject including locations, disasters, sports, medical, comedy, lifestyles, politics, time-lapse, film and television classics, newsreels from 1929 to 1967. Computerized. Rate card and brochure available.

VIDEO YESTERYEAR

Box C, Sandy Hook, CT 06482, USA
© +1 203 744 2476
Ⓕ +1 203 797 0819

Contacts: Jon Sonneborn
Subjects: Historical archive, classic films, television.
⊙ Mon-Fri 08:00 to 17:00
Description: Large collection of vintage film and television clips. Catalogue available.

WORLDVIEW ENTERTAINMENT

6 East 39th Street, New York, NY 10016, USA
© +1 212 679 8230
Ⓕ +1 212 686 0801

Contacts: Sandra Birnhak, Marcy Stuzin
Subjects: Historical archive, classic films, newsreels.
▦ 16mm, 35mm; all video formats. NTSC.
Research: By staff only. Appointment to visit.
⊙ Mon-Fri 09:30 to 18:00
Procedure: Umatic/VHS viewing tapes assembled.
Description: Large and comprehensive library of silent films. Archival and newsreel footage dating from the late 1890s to the 1950s. Mostly on card catalogue but in the process of computerization. Catalogue and rate card available.

Comedy

A.R.I.Q. FOOTAGE

One Main Street, East Hampton, New York 11964, USA
ⓒ +1 516 329 9200
ⓕ +1 516 329 9260

Contacts: Joe Lauro, Mart Heideman
Subjects: Historical archive, classic films, comedy, music, newsreels, industry, space.
▦ Various film and video formats. All line standards available.
Research: By staff. Visits by appointment.
☉ Mon-Fri 09:00 to 17:30
Procedure: Viewing material on VHS and Umatic. 24 hours for access to masters.
Description: Footage covers 1895 to 1990 with a very strong historical archive. Universal newsreel (1929 to 1967), musical performance footage including Jazz, Blues, Country, Rock and Roll, Pop from 1910 to 1990, silent films, industrial footage, space program, life styles and a range of general subject. Computerized. Rate card available.

CABLE FILMS & VIDEO

Country Club Station, Kansas City, MO 64113, USA
ⓒ +1 913 362 2804
ⓕ +1 913 341 7365

Contacts: Herbert Miller
Subjects: Classic films, comedy.
▦ Film; 1", 3/4", VHS.
Research: By staff.
☉ Mon-Sat
Description: American and some foreign classic feature films dating from 1915. The majority of the material comes from the silent film era through to the 1930s and 40s. Excerpts they are able to offer include Charlie Chaplin, Buster Keaton, Douglas Fairbanks Snr. as well as It's A Wonderful Life and Night Of The Living Dead. Catalogue available.

EM GEE FILM LIBRARY

Suite 103, 6924 Canby Avenue, Reseda CA 91335, USA
© +1 818 881 8110
Ⓕ +1 818 981 5506

Contacts: Murray Glass
Subjects: Public domain, classic films, feature films, comedy, documentaries, westerns, animation.
All film formats; VHS, Umatic. NTSC.
Research: By both staff and outside researchers.
🕑 Mon–Fri 08:30 to 17:00
Procedure: Viewing material on 16mm or VHS. 1 week for access to masters.
Description: Approximately 3000 titles in all genres - silent and sound, black and white and colour. Their speciality is in public domain material covering all subject areas including comedies, documentaries, westerns, animation and feature films. Partly computerized. Catalogue and rate card available.

FISH FILMS FOOTAGE WORLD

4548 Van Noord Avenue, Studio City, CA 91604-1013, USA
© +1 818 905 1071
Ⓕ +1 818 905 0301

Contacts: David Fishbein
Subjects: Historical archive, stock shots, time-lapse, underwater photography, Americana, locations, leisure, comedy, transport, industrial.
Research: By staff. Appointment to visit.
🕑 Mon–Fri 09:00 to 17:00
Description: Vintage and contemporary footage covering all subject areas. Time-lapse, underwater, scenics, aerials, sports, specializing in lifestyles, comedy, historic events, transportation, Americana, educational, travel, industrial, public domain. Partly computerized. Rate card and brochure available.

IMAGEWAYS

Second Floor, 412 West 48th Street, New York NY 10036,
USA
ⓒ +1 212 265 1287
Ⓕ +1 212 586 0339

Contacts: Adam Sargis, Kenneth Powell, Ray Sidwell
Subjects: Stock shots, newsreels, comedy, animation, classic
films, documentaries, industry, educational films, television.
Film; 1" videotape with timecoded 3/4" cassettes.
Research: By staff. Appointment to visit.
Procedure: Timecoded cassette compiled. Masters copied
after selection.
Description: Stock footage library with material dating from
1905 to present day. Footage comes from newsreels, silent
films, cartoons, historical films, Hollywood features,
documentaries, industrial films, educational films, television
programmes and original shot material. Collection is
approximately 70% colour and 30% black and white.
Computerized. Rate card available. Minimum license fee
charged on delivery of master material.

OASIS PICTURES

56 Shaftesbury Avenue, Toronto, Ontario M4T 1A3, Canada
ⓒ +1 416 925 4353
Ⓕ +1 416 967 1292

Contacts: Valerie Cabrera, Peter Emerson
Subjects: Drama, comedy, science, exploration, Africa,
environmental, adventure sports, folklore, stunts.
16mm, 35mm; Beta/Beta SP, D2, 1", Umatic. PAL and
NTSC.
Research: Usually done by staff. Appointment recommended
to visit.
🕐 Mon-Fri 09:00 to 18:00
Procedure: Viewing on VHS NTSC (some PAL available).
1-3 days for access to masters.
Description: The Oasis catalogue features a wide range of
comedy, family and action dramas plus documentaries with
subjects including exploration and adventure, gardening,
cottage living and its folklore, genetic engineering, fire
fighting, Africa, environmental change, stunt people, an
ancient aboriginal festival in South America, war reporters,
etc. Partly computerized. Catalogue available. English,
Spanish, Italian and French spoken.

RADIO TELEVISION BRUNEI

Bandar Seri, Bandar Seri Begawan 2042, Brunei
© +673 2 243111 Ext. 224
© +673 2 227204
/✓ BU2720 RTBPROG

Contacts: Mr. H.J.M.D. Salleh
Subjects: Drama, comedy, documentaries, childrens.
16mm, 35mm; Video.
Mon-Thur and Sat 07:45 to 12:15, 13:30 to 16:30
Procedure: Umatic and VHS viewing material in PAL and NTSC.
Description: Television output including full range of programmes and series. English and Malay spoken.

SHAMRA for Production and Distribution

P.O. Box 149, Damascus, Syria
© +963 11 665601
© +963 11 662812
/✓ 411404 SY

Contacts: Khaldoun Al Maleh
Subjects: Comedy, animation, drama.
Beta/Beta SP, 1", BVU, Umatic. PAL.
Research: Appointment to visit.
Sat-Thurs 09:00 to 21:00
Description: Arab speaking comedies, television series and plays. Also a collection of TV programmes and cartoon films dubbed into Arabic - rights held for distributoion to Arabic speaking TV stations. Computerized. English spoken.
Foreign Offices: Greece.

VIDEO TAPE LIBRARY

Suite 2, 1509 N. Crescent Heights Blvd, Los Angeles CA
90046, USA
© +1 213 656 4330
Ⓕ +1 213 656 8746

Contacts: Melody St. John, Peggy Shannon
Subjects: Stock shots, current affairs, newsreels, locations,
beauty, comedy, classic films, sport, leisure, environmental,
medicine, out-takes.
20% film; 80% video.
Research: By both staff and outside researchers.
Mon-Fri 09:00 to 17:00
Procedure: 24 hour turnaround for research, preview and
master footage.
Description: Enormous range of stock shot material ranging
from archival footage (1898) to current news topics. Over 2
million shots on virtually every subject including locations,
disasters, sports, medical, comedy, lifestyles, politics,
time-lapse, film and television classics, newsreels from 1929
to 1967. Computerized. Rate card and brochure available.

Computer imagery

CASCOM INTERNATIONAL

806 4th Avenue South, Nashville, TN 37210, USA
© +1 615 242 8900
Ⓕ +1 615 256 7890

Contacts: Victor Rumore
Subjects: Special effects, computer imagery, time-lapse, animation.
🎞 16mm, 35mm; Beta SP. PAL.
Research: By outside researchers. Appointment to visit.
🕑 Mon-Fri 09:00 to 17:30
Procedure: VHS viewing tapes loaned. 1-2 hours for access to masters.
Description: Mainly computer generated effects but also time-lapse, animation and live action. Subjects covered include globes, fireworks, maps, grids, sport, health, entertainment, environment, music, space and hi-tech. Catalogue showing a freeze frame of each effect in the library is available.
Foreign Offices: Australia (Select Effects).

DARINO FILMS

222 Park Avenue South, New York, NY 10003, USA
© +1 212 228 4024
Ⓕ +1 212 473 7448

Contacts: Ed Darino
Subjects: Special effects, computer imagery, trailers, stock shots, environmental.
Research: By staff. Appointment to visit.
🕑 Mon-Fri 09:00 to 17:00
Description: Darino Films hold a library of special effects comprised of computer graphics and animated backgrounds. They also have The Producers Library of approximately 10 hours of stock footage, environmental, historic, nature, cities, etc. In addition they have the Hollywood Vaults collection of 2500 trailers. Computerized. Rate card and brochure available.

SELECT EFFECTS – AUSTRALIA

11 Station Street, Naremburn, NSW 2065, Australia
ⓒ +61 2 437 5620
ⓕ +61 2 901 4505

Contacts: Jill Freestone
Subjects: Special effects, computer imagery, time-lapse, animation.
16mm, 35mm; Beta SP. PAL.
Research: By outside researchers. Appointment to visit.
Mon–Fri 09:00 to 17:30
Procedure: VHS viewing tapes loaned. 1–2 hours for access to masters.
Description: Mainly computer generated effects but also time-lapse, animation and live action. Subjects covered include globes, fireworks, maps, grids, sport, health, entertainment, environment, music, space and hi-tech. This company represents US company Cascom International. Partly computerized. Catalogue showing a freeze frame of each effect in the library is available.
Foreign Offices: USA (Cascom International).

STIMULUS / IMAGE RESEARCH

P.O. Box 170519, San Francisco, CA 94117, USA
ⓒ +1 415 558 8339
ⓕ +1 415 864 3897

Contacts: Grant Johnson
Subjects: Computer imagery, special effects, space, landscapes, science, educational films.
Beta/Beta SP, Umatic. NTSC (also various formats of stills).
Research: By staff only.
Mon–Fri 09:00 to 17:00
Procedure: VHS viewing cassettes, NTSC. 3 days for access to masters.
Description: Stimulus are producers of scientific and educational video programming. Their stock collection includes Western US scenics, landscapes, geological and computer generated terrain imagery. Also held is aerial, satellite and computer terrain imagery of full US, some world and planetary locations. Partly computerized.

Cookery

TIMES TELEVISION LIBRARY

The Time of India Building, 7 Bahadur Shah Zafar Marg, New Dehli 110 002, India
℡ +91 11 3722094/3351606/3352087
℻ +91 11 3715532/3715836
✎ 031-61337/38 INDIA IN

Contacts: Mr. Sanjay Sethi
Subjects: Drama, documentaries, industry, personalities, cookery, music, fashion, sport, science, environmental, culture.
▦ Most video formats. PAL.
Research: By both staff and outside researchers.
🕓 6 days, 10:00 to 17:00
Procedure: Viewing on VHS. 1-2 hours for access to BVU and Beta masters.
Description: Times Television was formed in 1986 and has produced and marketed a large range of programmes covering subjects relating to India including social issues, economy, business and industry, film industry awards, fashion, personalities, cuisine of Eastern and Western India, beauty contests, sport, science and the environment. They also hold various drama serials plus a few pop concerts including Bryan Adams and Jethro Tull. Partly computerized. English and Hindi spoken.
Foreign Offices: UK.

Crime

DOWNTOWN COMMUNITY TELEVISION

87 Lafayette Street, New York, NY 10013, USA
ⓒ +1 212 966 4510
ⓕ +1 212 219 0248

Contacts: Anita Tovich
Subjects: Current affairs, crime, civil rights, farming, immigration.
All material on video, various formats. NTSC.
Research: By staff. Appointment to visit.
☉ Mon-Fri 10:00 to 18:00
Procedure: Viewing material supplied from in-house editing facilities.
Description: Footage covers international political issues in Asia, Central America and the former Soviet Union. Subjects include crime, labour issues, urban issues, farm problems, human interest and Asian-American immigrants.
Computerized. Catalogue and rate card available. English, Spanish, Portuguese and French spoken.

Dance

FILMS OF INDIA

P.O. Box 48303, Los Angeles, CA 90048, USA
✆ +1 213 383 9217

Contacts: Mr R.A. Bagai
Subjects: Asian cinema, dance, drama, documentaries, culture, religion.
▦ Film.
Research: By staff. Appointment to visit.
🕐 Mon-Fri 09:30 to 17:30
Description: Feature films, shorts, drama, documentaries, religious films, etc. Ram Bagai also has extensive footage of Ghandi having acquired a large film library after his assassination. Brochure available.

Educational films

ARCHIVE FILMS

530 West 25th Street, New York, NY 1001, USA
© +1 212 620 3955
Ⓕ +1 212 645 2137

Contacts: Patrick Montgomery
Subjects: Historical archive, newsreels, Hollywood, classic films, film industry, educational films.
▦ 35mm, 16mm; various video formats with matching cassettes.
Research: By staff. Appointment to visit.
☺ Mon–Fri 09:00 to 18:00
Procedure: Viewing tapes assembled. 24–48 hours for access to masters.
Description: Over 5000 hours of newsreels, silent films, classic comedies, Hollywood features, historical dramas, documentaries and educational films. Represent The March of Time, The RKO Shorts Library, International Film Foundation, TV House and Videowest. Computerized. Rate card and catalogue available.
Foreign Offices: France, Germany, Italy, Japan, Netherlands, Sweden, UK, USA.

AUDIO VISUAL INSTITUTE, NATIONAL LIBRARY & ARCHIVE

P.O. Box 31519, Dar Es Salaam, Tanzania
© +255 51 72601/2/3/4

Contacts: M.I. Kange, Eva Sessoa
Subjects: National Archives, educational films, engineering, health, agriculture, tourism, current affairs.
▦ 16mm, 35mm.
Research: Permission and appointment needed prior to research.
☺ Mon–Fri 07:30 to 15:30
Procedure: On request.
Description: Copyright to materials in the collection is owned by respective producers of films. The library is not computerized. A book catalogue is issued.

DOKO VIDEO

33 Hayetzira Street, Ramat Gan 52521, Israel
© +972 3 5753555
Ⓕ +972 3 5753189

Contacts: Mrs Taly Kaufman
Subjects: Documentaries, war, Jewish history, travelogues, technology, educational films, social history, childrens'.
8mm; D2, BVU. All line standards available.
Research: By staff.
Sun-Thur 09:00 to 17:00
Procedure: VHS viewing copies supplied. 3-7 days for access to masters.
Description: Doko Video have a wide range of programmes available covering every aspect of Israel (history, religion, ethnic and social life, etc.). Titles available are listed in their catalogue under the following headings - battles for peace, holocaust and revival, follow the sun, biblical landscapes, innovative technology, Jerusalem, discovering the past, the social scene and children's program. Hebrew, English and French spoken.

FILM/AUDIO SERVICES

Suite 311, 430 West 14th Street, New York NY 10014, USA
© +1 212 645 2112
Ⓕ +1 212 255 4220

Contacts: Bob Summers, Mike Cocchi, Dean Cady
Subjects: Historical archive, travelogues, culture, educational films, industry, public domain.
Most film and video formats. NTSC.
Research: By staff preferably. Appointment to visit.
Mon-Fri 09:00 to 18:00 (or by appointment)
Procedure: Viewing material on VHS or 3/4" NTSC. 24 hours for access to masters.
Description: Worldwide travel footage dating from 1926 to 1980s; education and industrial films from the 1930s to 60s; historical actuality public domain material sourced from the National Archives and Library of Congress sold at less cost. Inexpensive and fast turnaround film to NTSC Beta SP and 1" tape in house. Partly computerized. Catalogue and rate card available. English and some Spanish spoken.

IMAGEWAYS

Second Floor, 412 West 48th Street, New York NY 10036,
USA
Ⓒ +1 212 265 1287
Ⓕ +1 212 586 0339

Contacts: Adam Sargis, Kenneth Powell, Ray Sidwell
Subjects: Stock shots, newsreels, comedy, animation, classic
films, documentaries, industry, educational films, television.
Film; 1" videotape with timecoded 3/4" cassettes.
Research: By staff. Appointment to visit.
Procedure: Timecoded cassette compiled. Masters copied
after selection.
Description: Stock footage library with material dating from
1905 to present day. Footage comes from newsreels, silent
films, cartoons, historical films, Hollywood features,
documentaries, industrial films, educational films, television
programmes and original shot material. Collection is
approximately 70% colour and 30% black and white.
Computerized. Rate card available. Minimum license fee
charged on delivery of master material.

JOHN E. ALLEN

116 North Avenue, Park Ridge, NJ 07656, USA
Ⓒ +1 201 391 3299
Ⓕ +1 201 391 6335

Contacts: John E. Allen, Beverley Allen
Subjects: Historical archive, newsreels, war, Russia, industry,
transport, classic films, educational films, travelogues.
Mainly film; some video.
Research: By both staff and outside researchers.
⊙ Mon-Fri 09:00 to 18:00
Description: Kinograms from 1915 to 1931. Telenews 1947
to 1953. World War I and II, Spanish American War, Mexican
Revolution, Russian Revolution, Hungarian Revolution,
Spanish Civil War, Korean War, etc. Industry 1910 to 1950s,
transportation, educational, ethnographic, travel, nature,
features 1905 to 1950s, stills, posters and lobby cards.
Partly computerized. Rate card available.

KIDS TV

P.O. Box 8148, Symonds Street, Auckland 3, New Zealand
℃ +64 09 357 0724
Ⓕ +64 09 358 4809

Contacts: David Stewart
Subjects: Childrens, educational films.
▦ Beta/Beta SP, D2, 1". PAL.
Research: By staff.
🕓 Mon-Fri 08:00 to 18:00
Procedure: Timecoded VHS cassettes for viewing. Immediate access to masters.
Description: Programmes that target an age range from 1-19 years. Subjects covered are music, sports, current affairs and education for children and parents. Copyright owned by Kids TV. Computerized.

METRO TELEVISION VIDEO ARCHIVE

Paddington Town Hall, P.O. Box 299, Paddington, NSW 2021, Australia
℃ +61 2 361 5318
Ⓕ +61 2 361 5320

Contacts: Helen Chapman, Peter Giles, Kate Ingham
Subjects: Documentaries, homosexuality, health, educational films.
▦ Videotape.
Research: By both staff and outside researchers. Appointment to visit.
🕓 Mon-Fri 09:00 to 17:00
Procedure: Umatic, SVHS, VHS, Jsystem viewing tapes supplied.
Description: A wide and varied selection of independent and community produced material. Documentaries, short dramas, experimental pieces, conferences, seminars, community events and demonstrations. Copyrights held for some of the archive, currently in the process of negotiating with various organizations for copyrights going back over the last 20 years. Partly computerized. Catalogue available.

NATIONAL LIBRARY OF AUSTRALIA

Film & Video Lending Service, Parkes Place, Canberra 2600, Australia
🖂 +61 6 262 1361
🖷 +61 6 262 1634

Contacts: Reference Officer
Subjects: National Archives, educational films, documentaries, feature films, animation.
🎞 16mm; Umatic, VHS. PAL, some NTSC.
Research: Researchers can visit, appointments recommended not essential.
🕑 Mon-Fri 09:00 to 16:30
Procedure: Free loan to institutes, businesses and groups. No masters held.
Description: Over 23 500 instructional and educational documentary titles held covering most subject areas. Also a film and TV study collection with feature films, short fiction, animation and experimental film and video. Computerized. Full catalogue available on microfiche and screen studies catalogue in print form.

PLANET PICTURES

P.O. Box 65862, Los Angeles, CA 90065, USA
🖂 +1 818 246 7700
🖷 +1 818 240 8391

Contacts: Jenny Hayden
Subjects: Documentaries, medicine, health, educational films, natural history, time-lapse.
🎞 Time-lapse on film; mainly video.
Research: By both staff and outside researchers. Appointment to visit.
🕑 Mon-Fri 09:00 to 18:00
Description: Over 400 hours of footage and completed documentaries on a variety of subjects - medicine and health, high technology, workplace, nature, timelapse, wildlife, adventure, arts and entertainment and people. Computerized. Brochure available.

RONIN FILMS

P.O. Box 1005, Civic Square, ACT 2608, Australia
© +616 248 0851
® +616 249 1640

Contacts: Michele Day, Maria Jacoveli, Carolyn Odgers
Subjects: Documentaries, educational films, Asian cinema, feature films.
▦ 16mm, 35mm; Beta/Beta SP, D2, 1″, Umatic. PAL and NTSC.
Research: By staff only.
☉ Mon-Fri 09:00 to 17:00
Procedure: Preview material on video, mainly PAL, some on NTSC.
Description: Imported and Australian features and documentaries as well as video and non-theatrical titles. Partly computerized. Catalogue and rate card available.

STIMULUS / IMAGE RESEARCH

P.O. Box 170519, San Francisco, CA 94117, USA
© +1 415 558 8339
® +1 415 864 3897

Contacts: Grant Johnson
Subjects: Computer imagery, special effects, space, landscapes, science, educational films.
▦ Beta/Beta SP, Umatic. NTSC (also various formats of stills).
Research: By staff only.
☉ Mon-Fri 09:00 to 17:00
Procedure: VHS viewing cassettes, NTSC. 3 days for access to masters.
Description: Stimulus are producers of scientific and educational video programming. Their stock collection includes Western US scenics, landscapes, geological and computer generated terrain imagery. Also held is aerial, satellite and computer terrain imagery of full US, some world and planetary locations. Partly computerized.

UNITED STUDIOS OF ISRAEL

Kesem St. 8, Herzlia 46100, Israel
© +972 52 550 151-7
Ⓕ +972 52 550 334

Contacts: Mirjana Gross
Subjects: Newsreels, documentaries, educational films, war, current affairs, culture.
35mm; BVU.
Sun-Thur 08:00 to 17:00
Description: Newsreels made in Israel from 1951 to 1971 covering events, wars, emigrations, new settlements and political life in the state. Documentary films on education, the army, water problems, Arab and Jewish life, etc. Brochure available. NB: Collections are also at the Spielberg Archive (Jerusalem) and the Harvard Judaica Department (Boston USA).

WILLIAM G. BEAL

512 Franklin Avenue, Pittsburgh, PA 15221, USA
© +1 412 243 7020
Ⓕ +1 412 243 4520

Contacts: William G. Beal
Subjects: Documentaries, educational films, industry, medicine, sailing.
80% film; 20% videotape.
Research: By staff. Appointment to visit.
Mon-Fri 09:00 to 17:00
Description: Footage from productions spanning the last 40 years. Productions made for clients in various industries including steel, glass, aluminum, ceramics, electronics, foundries, oil and gas and plastics. Documentaries made for hospitals, museums, colleges, universities and community organizations of all types. Special collection of tropical sailing subjects filmed in the Bahamas and Caribbean.

Engineering

AUDIO VISUAL INSTITUTE, NATIONAL LIBRARY & ARCHIVE

P.O. Box 31519, Dar Es Salaam, Tanzania
© +255 51 72601/2/3/4

Contacts: M.I. Kange, Eva Sessoa
Subjects: National Archives, educational films, engineering, health, agriculture, tourism, current affairs.
16mm, 35mm.
Research: Permission and appointment needed prior to research.
Mon-Fri 07:30 to 15:30
Procedure: On request.
Description: Copyright to materials in the collection is owned by respective producers of films. The library is not computerized. A book catalogue is issued.

Environmental

AL GIDDINGS – IMAGES UNLIMITED

8001 Capwell Drive, Oakland, CA 94621, USA
🕆 +1 510 562 8000
🕞 +1 510 562 8001

Contacts: Terry Thompson
Subjects: Natural history, underwater photography, environmental.
▦ 16mm, 35mm; most video formats. NTSC.
Research: By staff. Appointment to visit.
🕘 Mon–Fri 09:00 to 17:00
Procedure: Umatic/VHS tapes compiled or view at studio.
1–3 days for access to masters.
Description: Library of material made up from Al Giddings undersea and nature adventure television specials. Images range in diversity from whales and sharks to minute creatures, and from polar regions to tropical islands. Scenics, wildlife, nature and marine life from ocean floor to mountain top, tropics, desert, north and south poles, kelp forests, redwood forests, rainforest, storms, moons, divers, shipwrecks, etc. New footage from an expedition to the shipwrecked Titanic. Computerized. Brochure available.

BEYOND INFORMATION SERVICES

Beyond 2000, 34 Hotham Parade, Artarmon, NSW 2064, Australia
🕆 +61 2 438 5155
🕞 +61 2 439 6549

Contacts: Lisa Savage, Annette Overton
Subjects: Medicine, science, environmental, landscapes.
▦ Beta/Beta SP, 1″, Umatic. PAL.
Research: By staff only.
🕘 Mon–Fri 09:00 to 17:30
Procedure: Viewing tapes assembled.
Description: An extensive collection of footage from internationally acclaimed science and technology series, Beyond 2000. Footage covers subjects shot worldwide and includes medical breakthroughs, laboratory work, people, robotics, Australiana, hi-tech gadgets, environment, international rural and city landscapes, wildlife, etc. Computerized. Rate card available. English and French spoken.

CANADIAN BROADCASTING CORPORATION (CBC)

Box 500, Station A, Toronto, Ontario M5W 1E1, Canada
℄ +1 416 205 7608
Ⓕ +1 416 205 6736

Contacts: Roy Harris
Subjects: Stock shots, natural history, locations, medicine, environmental
▦ 16mm; Beta/Beta SP, 1″, Umatic. NTSC.
Research: By staff only.
☉ Mon–Fri 08:30 to 17:30
Procedure: Timecoded cassettes made to order. 2–3 days for access to masters.
Description: CBC's archive contains a wide range of programme material including natural history and environmental footage, medical research, cities of the world, history, etc. from Arctic life to ancient Yemini ruins. Computerized. Rate card available.

DARINO FILMS

222 Park Avenue South, New York, NY 10003, USA
℄ +1 212 228 4024
Ⓕ +1 212 473 7448

Contacts: Ed Darino
Subjects: Special effects, computer imagery, trailers, stock shots, environmental.
Research: By staff. Appointment to visit.
☉ Mon–Fri 09:00 to 17:00
Description: Darino Films hold a library of special effects comprised of computer graphics and animated backgrounds. They also have The Producers Library of approximately 10 hours of stock footage, environmental, historic, nature, cities, etc. In addition they have the Hollywood Vaults collection of 2500 trailers. Computerized. Rate card and brochure available.

FABULOUS FOOTAGE

4th Floor, 19 Mercer Street, Toronto, Ontario M5V 1H2, Canada
℗ +1 416 591 6955
Ⓕ +1 416 591 1666

Contacts: Steve Race, Patricia Harvey, Rhonda Olson, Julie Kovacs
Subjects: Stock shots, locations, culture, industry, medicine, military, music, environmental, leisure, transport, natural history, space, trailers.
Film; video (all film mastered onto tape).
Research: By both staff and outside researchers.
Mon-Fri 09:00 to 21:00
Description: Complete contemporary film and videotape library with a vast range of quality images. Subject headings include agriculture, buildings, cities, countries, cultural activities, industry and business, landmarks, landscapes, medical, military, music, natural phenomena, news, period recreations, professions, rain forests, recreation, space, special effects, spectacles, sports, transportation, underwater, water and wildlife. They also hold special collections of Nazi propaganda footage, Russian history, Russian space program, B-movies and trailers. Computerized. Rate card and catalogue available. NB: This is the head office, there is also an office in Vancouver, Canada Tel: (604) 684 8484, Fax: (604) 681 3299.
Foreign Offices: Argentina, Australia, Brazil, Canada, Chile, Germany, Indonesia, Japan, Malaysia, Philippines, Singapore, Mexico, Spain, USA.

FILM BANK STOCK FOOTAGE FILM & VIDEO LIBRARY

425 South Victory Boulevard, Burbank, CA 91502, USA
ⓒ +1 818 841 9176
ⓕ +1 818 567 4235

Contacts: Paula Lumbard, Elizabeth Canelake
Subjects: News, space, special effects, science, sport, medicine, time-lapse, aerial photography, natural history, animation, locations, environmental.
16mm, 35mm; most video formats. NTSC masters.
Research: By staff only. Researchers occasionally visit for big projects.
Mon-Fri 09:00 to 17:00
Procedure: Umatics loaned or VHS assembled. 24 hours for access to masters.
Description: Diverse collection of broadcast quality film and video images aimed at supplying the full range of client productions. Most subjects are covered in the library, the latest new collections being world locations, children of the world, environmental images (destruction, scientific and beauty shots), History of Flight, more space and solar flares, aerials across the US, agriculture and animals. Partly computerized. Catalogue and rate card available.

FRONT LINE

Suite 3 Senyo Building, 5th Floor, 3-1-9 Nakameguro, Meguro-ku, Toyko 153, Japan
ⓒ +81 3 3760 6271
ⓕ +81 3 3760 6012

Contacts: Seiichi Sugiura
Subjects: Stock shots, aviation, locations, natural history, industry, space, time-lapse, transport, environmental.
Mon-Fri 10:00 to 18:00
Procedure: Viewing tapes loaned. Masters copied after selection.
Description: Agents for UK company Index Stock Shots, USA company Opus Global and Canadian company Fabulous Footage in Japan.

IMAGES OF THE EAST

19B Jalan 20/14, Petaling Jaya Selangor 46300, Malaysia
© +60 03 776 7199
Ⓕ +60 03 776 4560

Contacts: Theresa Khoo
Subjects: Stock shots, aviation, locations, natural history, industry, space, time-lapse, transport, environmental.
Beta SP, 1″, Umatic. PAL.
Research: By staff. Visits by appointment.
Mon-Fri 08:30 to 17:45
Procedure: Viewing tapes loaned. Masters copied after selection, 3-4 days for access.
Description: Agents for UK company Index Stock Shots and German company Modern Video Library in Malaysia and Singapore. The library holds an A-Z of subject categories including landscape, destination and sports footage from Malaysia. Partly computerized. Rate card available. English spoken.

IMAGES PIXART

1973 Falardeau, Montreal, Quebec H2K 2L9, Canada
© +1 514 521 8776
Ⓕ +1 514 521 0541

Contacts: Emmanuelle de la Cressonniere
Subjects: Stock shots, environmental, culture, locations.
Betacam.
Research: By staff. Appointment to visit.
Mon-Fri 09:00 to 18:00
Description: Extensive collection of beauty shots of Canada from coast to coast. Also stock footage covering ecological and cultural issues in the province of Quebec for the last five years. Computerized. Rate card available.

MARINE GRAFICS

Box 2242, Chapel Hill, NC 27515, USA
℃ +1 919 362 8867
Ⓕ +1 919 362 8861

Contacts: Bill Lovin
Subjects: Underwater photography, environmental.
▦ 16mm neg with matching 1", original Beta SP and M2 (video NTSC).
Research: By staff.
Description: Underwater stock footage. Unusual marine life, behaviour, marine mammals, divers, shipwrecks, sharks, manta rays, dangerous marine life, scenics of the Caribbean and Pacific, beaches, ships, environmental damage, rainforest, Mayan ruins, Red Sea/Caribbean/South Pacific/Atlantic/Great Lakes/rivers. Rate card and brochure available. NB: Also represented by Energy Productions.
Foreign Offices: See Energy Productions listings.

MOONLIGHT PRODUCTIONS

3361 Saint Michael Court, Palo Alto, CA 94306, USA
℃ +1 415 961 7440
Ⓕ +1 415 961 7440

Contacts: Dr Lee Tepley
Subjects: Underwater photography, environmental.
▦ 16mm transferred to 1" + timecoded cassettes; some original video.
Research: By staff. Appointment to visit.
🕑 Mon- Fri 09:00 to 17:30
Description: Collected over the last 30 years, an extensive library of all types of undersea life, especially whales, dolphins and other large marine mammals. Also material of undersea lava flows and pollution. Partly computerized. Rates negotiable. Stock footage list available.

NATURAL SYMPHONIES

4 George Street, Redfern, NSW 2016, Australia
© +61 2 318 1577 / 46 55 1800
Ⓕ +61 2 318 1424 / 46 55 9434

Contacts: Neil O'Hare
Subjects: Underwater photography, natural history, culture, environmental.
Beta SP, D2, 1″. PAL.
Research: By staff mainly. Visits by appointment.
☉ Mon–Fri 09:00 to 17:00 (often contactable outside these times)
Procedure: Timecoded VHS or other formats available. 24 hours for access to masters.
Description: Shot in Australia and The South Pacific, the library ranges from aerial sequences to microscopic subjects including flora, fauna, marine life, tourist and research activities. All material is recorded on Betacam SP using BTS LDK 90 and 91 CCD cameras. Many of the sequences available are of animals, birds and locations that are extremely difficult to access and film owing to seasonal variations and remoteness. Material includes coral reefs, coral spawning, whales, dolphins and sea lions, Australian birds, animals, insects and reptiles, Australian environments and Aboriginal and islander culture. Computerized with database list on disk accessible by most word processors. Summary print outs and rate card available.

NBC NEWS ARCHIVES

30 Rockefeller Plaza, Room 902, New York, NY 10112, USA
© +1 212 664 3797
Ⓕ +1 212 957 8917

Contacts: Nancy Cole, Yuien Chin
Subjects: Current affairs, culture, religion, environmental, natural history, personalities, social history.
16mm, 35mm; most video formats. NTSC.
Research: By both staff and outside researchers. Appointment to visit.
☉ Mon–Fri 09:00 to 18:00
Procedure: Time-coded viewing material. Fast turnaround service.
Description: Over four decades of news events worldwide. The library covers social commentary, interviews, cultural, historical and religious programming, the environment, wildlife and stock shots for almost any subject imaginable. Computerized. Rate card available. Chinese and Spanish spoken.

NEW YORK ZOOLOGICAL SOCIETY

The Wildlife Conservation Society Office of Media Studies,
185th Street and Southern Blvd, Bronx, NY 10460, USA
℡ +1 718 220 5134
℻ +1 718 220 7114

Contacts: Thomas Veltre
Subjects: Natural history, environmental, biology.
🎞 16mm, 35mm; most video formats. NTSC.
Research: Limited research by staff - $150 minimum for
VHS. Appointments.
🕑 Mon-Fri 10:00 to 17:00
Procedure: VHS tapes compiled dependent on workload. 2-3
days for access to masters.
Description: The collection is comprised of film shot at the
Bronx Zoo, NY aquarium and other NYZS facilities as well as
film from research expeditions sponsored by the society over
the last 80 years. Good close-ups of many rare species in
naturalistic settings, historical material on field research and
much good wildlife from East Africa in 1960s and 1970s.

NOMAD FILMS INTERNATIONAL

Perth Business Centre, Stirling Street (P.O. Box 8240), Perth
6849, Australia
℡ +61 9 3881177
℻ +61 9 3811122

Contacts: Doug Stanley and Kate Faulkner
Subjects: Natural history, medicine, science, lifestyles,
locations, environmental, China, Jewish history, underwater
photography.
🎞 16mm; Beta/Beta SP, D2, 1", Umatic. PAL and NTSC.
Research: By staff only.
🕑 Mon-Fri 08:30 to 18:30
Procedure: VHS or Umatic PAL/NTSC viewing copies. 3 days
for access to masters.
Description: Enormous range of productions covering
wildlife, medical and scientific topics with worldwide
documentary series on people and places. Titles include The
Intruders, A Walk in the Sea and Crocodiles - the deadly
survivors (natural history), Land of the Dragon (Bhutan),
Dream Merchants of Asia (Taiwan, India, Japan, Hong Kong),
Journey to Hainan (China's most southerly province),
Breakthroughs (science, medicine and technology), Eye in
the Sky (satellite technology), Triumph of the Nomads
(Aborigines) to name a few. Glossy brochures available for
productions. Partly computerized.

OASIS PICTURES

56 Shaftesbury Avenue, Toronto, Ontario M4T 1A3, Canada
© +1 416 925 4353
⊕ +1 416 967 1292

Contacts: Valerie Cabrera, Peter Emerson
Subjects: Drama, comedy, science, exploration, Africa, environmental, adventure sports, folklore, stunts.
16mm, 35mm; Beta/Beta SP, D2, 1″, Umatic. PAL and NTSC.
Research: Usually done by staff. Appointment recommended to visit.
🕐 Mon-Fri 09:00 to 18:00
Procedure: Viewing on VHS NTSC (some PAL available). 1-3 days for access to masters.
Description: The Oasis catalogue features a wide range of comedy, family and action dramas plus documentaries with subjects including exploration and adventure, gardening, cottage living and its folklore, genetic engineering, fire fighting, Africa, environmental change, stunt people, an ancient aboriginal festival in South America, war reporters, etc. Partly computerized. Catalogue available. English, Spanish, Italian and French spoken.

RICHTER PRODUCTIONS

33 West 42nd Street, New York, NY 10036, USA
© +1 212 947 1395
⊕ +1 212 643 1208

Contacts: Robert Richter, Madeline Solano
Subjects: Environmental, Africa, Asia, Latin America.
16mm; most video formats. PAL and NTSC.
Research: Both both staff and outside researchers.
🕐 Mon-Fri 10:00 to 18:00
Procedure: Viewing material on VHS NTSC. 3 days for access to masters.
Description: The collection includes documentaries on environmental and social conditions mainly filmed in the developing world. Footage shows tropical rain forests and people of the forests in Asia, Africa and Latin America; also urban and rural scenes of people and living conditions in many developing world countries. Some restrictions on rights. Partly computerized. English, Spanish and some French spoken.

SOCIETE RADIO-CANADA

1400 Boulevard Rene-Levesque Est, Montreal, Quebec
H2L 2M2, Canada
℡ +1 514 597 7826
Ⓕ +1 514 597 7862

Contacts: Lucie Quenneville
Subjects: Current affairs, drama, environmental, stock shots.
Research: By staff. Appointment to visit.
☺ Mon-Fri 09:00 to 17:00
Description: SRC television is the only national French
network in Canada. The library has a full range of material
dating from 1952 including current affairs, news, drama,
environmental programmes and stock shot footage. Partly
computerized. Rate card and brochure available.

TIMES TELEVISION LIBRARY

The Time of India Building, 7 Bahadur Shah Zafar Marg, New
Dehli 110 002, India
℡ +91 11 3722094/3351606/3352087
Ⓕ +91 11 3715532/3715836
〽 031-61337/38 INDIA IN

Contacts: Mr. Sanjay Sethi
Subjects: Drama, documentaries, industry, personalities,
cookery, music, fashion, sport, science, environmental,
culture.
▦ Most video formats. PAL.
Research: By both staff and outside researchers.
☺ 6 days, 10:00 to 17:00
Procedure: Viewing on VHS. 1-2 hours for access to BVU
and Beta masters.
Description: Times Television was formed in 1986 and has
produced and marketed a large range of programmes
covering subjects relating to India including social issues,
economy, business and industry, film industry awards,
fashion, personalities, cuisine of Eastern and Western India,
beauty contests, sport, science and the environment. They
also hold various drama serials plus a few pop concerts
including Bryan Adams and Jethro Tull. Partly computerized.
English and Hindi spoken.
Foreign Offices: UK.

VIDEO TAPE LIBRARY

Suite 2, 1509 N. Crescent Heights Blvd, Los Angeles CA 90046, USA
ⓒ +1 213 656 4330
ⓕ +1 213 656 8746

Contacts: Melody St. John, Peggy Shannon
Subjects: Stock shots, current affairs, newsreels, locations, beauty, comedy, classic films, sport, leisure, environmental, medicine, out-takes.
▦ 20% film; 80% video.
Research: By both staff and outside researchers.
☉ Mon-Fri 09:00 to 17:00
Procedure: 24 hour turnaround for research, preview and master footage.
Description: Enormous range of stock shot material ranging from archival footage (1898) to current news topics. Over 2 million shots on virtually every subject including locations, disasters, sports, medical, comedy, lifestyles, politics, time-lapse, film and television classics, newsreels from 1929 to 1967. Computerized. Rate card and brochure available.

WORLDWIDE TELEVISION NEWS (WTN)

1995 Broadway, New York, NY 10023, USA
ⓒ +1 212 362 4440
ⓕ +1 212 496 1269
✐ 237853

Contacts: Vincent O'Reilly, David Seevers
Subjects: Current affairs, newsreels, environmental, sport.
▦ 16mm; Beta/Beta SP, D2, BVU, Umatic. NTSC. PAL - London office.
Research: By staff or outside researchers. Appointment to visit.
☉ Mon-Fri 09:00 to 19:00
Procedure: VHS dubb, other formats on request. 24 hours for access to masters.
Description: Dating from 1963 and formerly known as UPITN, WTN is the successor to the UPI-Movietonews collection. The library consists of mainly domestic and foreign news but also produces weekly features, an entertainment and sports service, the Earthfile Environment programme and Roving Report - a weekly service of five in-depth reports. Copyright is held for most material, others obtained on a case by case basis, restrictions may occur with sports and entertainment footage. Computerized. Catalogue of Roving Reports available plus rate card. English, Spanish and French spoken.

Espionage

VILLON FILMS

77 W 28 Avenue, Vancouver, BC V5Y 2K7, Canada
© +1 604 879 6042
Ⓕ +1 604 879 6042

Contacts: Peter Davis
Subjects: Historical archive, documentaries, advertising, Africa, AIDS, apartheid, Cuba, culture, espionage, war.
Majority of material is 16mm. Some original video.
Research: Visits by appointment.
7 days, 24 hours
Procedure: Viewing of VHS and 16mm on premises, some video elsewhere.
Description: The collection comprises films made and collected by Peter including out-takes, commercials from the 1950s and 60s and valuable historical material. Subjects covered include Africa, AIDS, Rhodesia and Zimbabwe and especially South Africa 1900 to 1990; Catskills (Borscht Belt) 1900 to 1990; US covert activities, spies, the Cold War; D.H. Lawrence; Middle East late 1960s, 70s, 80s; US anti-war movement and counter culture 1960s and 70s; Britain early 1960s; World War II China; Native Americans (Crow and Navajo) 70s and 80s; Cuba 1960s. Partly computerized. Rates negotiable. English, French, Swedish and some Italian spoken.

Film industry

ARCHIVE FILMS

530 West 25th Street, New York, NY 1001, USA
© +1 212 620 3955
Ⓕ +1 212 645 2137

Contacts: Patrick Montgomery
Subjects: Historical archive, newsreels, Hollywood, classic films, film industry, educational films.
35mm, 16mm; various video formats with matching cassettes.
Research: By staff. Appointment to visit.
Mon-Fri 09:00 to 18:00
Procedure: Viewing tapes assembled. 24-48 hours for access to masters.
Description: Over 5000 hours of newsreels, silent films, classic comedies, Hollywood features, historical dramas, documentaries and educational films. Represent The March of Time, The RKO Shorts Library, International Film Foundation, TV House and Videowest. Computerized. Rate card and catalogue available.
Foreign Offices: France, Germany, Italy, Japan, Netherlands, Sweden, UK, USA.

FILM & TELEVISION INSTITUTE (WA)

92 Adelaide Street, Fremantle, Western Australia 6160, Australia
© +61 9 335 1055
Ⓕ +61 9 335 1283

Contacts: Rita Shanahan
Subjects: Film industry, television.
Viewing material held on video only.
Research: By staff or outside researchers.
Tues-Fri 12:00 to 17:30
Description: The Institute does not sell footage but has a small specialist collection of books, journals and videos on the subject areas of film and television available for research purposes. There is particular emphasis on technical and business matters. All copyrights reside with the individual filmmakers. Partly computerized.

HOLLYWOOD HOUSE VIDEO ARCHIVES / HOME ENTERTAINMENT HOLDINGS

Box 555, Bondi Beach, NSW 2026, Australia
ⓒ +61 2 365 1055
Ⓕ +61 2 365 1577

Contacts: Joe Shellim
Subjects: Classic films, documentaries, music, space, film industry, animation, war, personalities, circus, natural history.
▦ Film; Beta, 1″, BVU, Umatic.
Research: By staff.
◷ Sun-Fri 10:00 to 19:00
Procedure: VHS viewing tape. Access to masters dependent on workload.
Description: Collection includes classic nostalgia movies complimented with interviews and rehearsals, behind-the-scenes, lost films, etc. Interviews with movie stars, candid films, footage of world leaders, space (NASA), music clips, nature and circus, cartoons, war and documentaries. Partly computerized. Rate card and catalogue available.

PRODUCERS LIBRARY SERVICE

1051 N. Cole Avenue, Hollywood, CA 90038, USA
ⓒ +1 213 465 0572
Ⓕ +1 213 465 1671

Contacts: Jeffrey Goodman, Richard Scott
Subjects: Stock shots, documentaries, film industry.
▦ Film; 200 videotape masters.
Research: By staff. Appointment to visit.
◷ Mon-Fri 09:00 to 17:30
Description: Hollywood history from 1910, specializing in the golden age of Hollywood. Represent Orion Pictures and TV stock footage, ABC Circle Films and many footage collections of filmmakers. Mainly computerized. Rate card and brochure available.

Folklore

DOOMSDAY STUDIOS

212 James Street, Ottawa, Ontario K1R 5M7, Canada
© +1 613 230 9769
Ⓕ +1 613 230 6004

Contacts: Ramona Macdonald, Tony Kelleher
Subjects: Architecture, folklore, animation, feature films.
16mm, 35mm; 1", Umatic. PAL and NTSC.
Research: By staff.
Mon–Fri 09:00 to 17:00
Procedure: Viewing material on 16mm or cassette.
Description: The library has a collection of Nova Scotia folk art including black and white footage of a folk festival in the 1970s. They also have Lithuanian folk art, experimental animation and various features. English, French, Spanish, German, Russian and Lithuanian spoken.

OASIS PICTURES

56 Shaftesbury Avenue, Toronto, Ontario M4T 1A3, Canada
© +1 416 925 4353
Ⓕ +1 416 967 1292

Contacts: Valerie Cabrera, Peter Emerson
Subjects: Drama, comedy, science, exploration, Africa, environmental, adventure sports, folklore, stunts.
16mm, 35mm; Beta/Beta SP, D2, 1", Umatic. PAL and NTSC.
Research: Usually done by staff. Appointment recommended to visit.
Mon–Fri 09:00 to 18:00
Procedure: Viewing on VHS NTSC (some PAL available). 1–3 days for access to masters.
Description: The Oasis catalogue features a wide range of comedy, family and action dramas plus documentaries with subjects including exploration and adventure, gardening, cottage living and its folklore, genetic engineering, fire fighting, Africa, environmental change, stunt people, an ancient aboriginal festival in South America, war reporters, etc. Partly computerized. Catalogue available. English, Spanish, Italian and French spoken.

Health

AUDIO VISUAL INSTITUTE, NATIONAL LIBRARY & ARCHIVE

P.O. Box 31519, Dar Es Salaam, Tanzania
© +255 51 72601/2/3/4

Contacts: M.I. Kange, Eva Sessoa
Subjects: National Archives, educational films, engineering, health, agriculture, tourism, current affairs.
🎞 16mm, 35mm.
Research: Permission and appointment needed prior to research.
🕐 Mon-Fri 07:30 to 15:30
Procedure: On request.
Description: Copyright to materials in the collection is owned by respective producers of films. The library is not computerized. A book catalogue is issued.

METRO TELEVISION VIDEO ARCHIVE

Paddington Town Hall, P.O. Box 299, Paddington, NSW 2021, Australia
© +61 2 361 5318
🅕 +61 2 361 5320

Contacts: Helen Chapman, Peter Giles, Kate Ingham
Subjects: Documentaries, homosexuality, health, educational films.
🎞 Videotape.
Research: By both staff and outside researchers. Appointment to visit.
🕐 Mon-Fri 09:00 to 17:00
Procedure: Umatic, SVHS, VHS, Jsystem viewing tapes supplied.
Description: A wide and varied selection of independent and community produced material. Documentaries, short dramas, experimental pieces, conferences, seminars, community events and demonstrations. Copyrights held for some of the archive, currently in the process of negotiating with various organizations for copyrights going back over the last 20 years. Partly computerized. Catalogue available.

PLANET PICTURES

P.O. Box 65862, Los Angeles, CA 90065, USA
ⓒ +1 818 246 7700
Ⓕ +1 818 240 8391

Contacts: Jenny Hayden
Subjects: Documentaries, medicine, health, educational films, natural history, time-lapse.
▦ Time-lapse on film; mainly video.
Research: By both staff and outside researchers. Appointment to visit.
🕑 Mon-Fri 09:00 to 18:00
Description: Over 400 hours of footage and completed documentaries on a variety of subjects - medicine and health, high technology, workplace, nature, timelapse, wildlife, adventure, arts and entertainment and people. Computerized. Brochure available.

PYRAMID FILM & VIDEO

2801 Colorado Avenue, Santa Monica, CA 90404, USA
ⓒ +1 310 828 7577
Ⓕ +1 310 453 9083

Contacts: Arthur C. Passante
Subjects: Documentaries, natural history, medicine, health, sport, arts, entertainment.
Research: By both staff and outside researchers. Appointment to visit.
🕑 Mon-Fri 08:00 to 17:00
Procedure: VHS or 16mm for viewing. 1 week average for access to masters.
Description: Over 500 titles of speciality short films covering nature, medicine, health, sports/action, documentary, history, art, media studies and entertainment. Catalogue and rate card available.
Foreign Offices: 80 worldwide distributors but all stock footage licensing is handled by this office.

STOCK SHOTS

1085 Louise Avenue, San Jose, CA 95125, USA
© +1 408 971 1325
Ⓕ +1 408 723 3846

Contacts: Tom Mertens
Subjects: Transport, agriculture, locations, medicine, health.
▦ 20 000 feet of film; 500 hours of videotape.
Research: By staff.
🕑 Mon-Fri 10:00 to 16:00
Description: Silicon Valley, San Francisco aerials, rail transit, agriculture, Europe, Asian, Africa collection filmed 1945 to 1975. Also incorporates The Justin Byers Film Collection. Partly computerized. Rate card available.

Homosexuality

METRO TELEVISION VIDEO ARCHIVE

Paddington Town Hall, P.O. Box 299, Paddington, NSW 2021, Australia
Ⓒ +61 2 361 5318
Ⓕ +61 2 361 5320

Contacts: Helen Chapman, Peter Giles, Kate Ingham
Subjects: Documentaries, homosexuality, health, educational films.
Videotape.
Research: By both staff and outside researchers. Appointment to visit.
Mon-Fri 09:00 to 17:00
Procedure: Umatic, SVHS, VHS, Jsystem viewing tapes supplied.
Description: A wide and varied selection of independent and community produced material. Documentaries, short dramas, experimental pieces, conferences, seminars, community events and demonstrations. Copyrights held for some of the archive, currently in the process of negotiating with various organizations for copyrights going back over the last 20 years. Partly computerized. Catalogue available.

Horse racing

HISTORIC THOROUGHBRED COLLECTIONS

35 Monterey Lane, Sierra Madre, CA 91024, USA
℆ +1 818 355 4361

Contacts: Joe Burnham, Thom Murray
Subjects: Horse racing.
16mm, 35mm; Beta/Beta SP, 1″, Umatic. NTSC.
Research: Visits by appointment.
No formal hours. Answerphone service at all times.
Procedure: Timecoded cassettes available to serious customers.
Description: Collection specializes in US thoroughbred racing from 1930 to 1987 featuring famous horses such as Triple Crown winners. Establishing shots of most famous US tracks, for example Churchill Downs, Belmont, Saratoga, Santa Anita, Hollywood Park and Del Mar. Original material all film, colour since 1950s; much transferred to video. Partly computerized.

Immigration

DOWNTOWN COMMUNITY TELEVISION

87 Lafayette Street, New York, NY 10013, USA
© +1 212 966 4510
Ⓕ +1 212 219 0248

Contacts: Anita Tovich
Subjects: Current affairs, crime, civil rights, farming, immigration.
All material on video, various formats. NTSC.
Research: By staff. Appointment to visit.
⊘ Mon-Fri 10:00 to 18:00
Procedure: Viewing material supplied from in-house editing facilities.
Description: Footage covers international political issues in Asia, Central America and the former Soviet Union. Subjects include crime, labour issues, urban issues, farm problems, human interest and Asian-American immigrants.
Computerized. Catalogue and rate card available. English, Spanish, Portuguese and French spoken.

Industry

A.R.I.Q. FOOTAGE

One Main Street, East Hampton, New York 11964, USA
℡ +1 516 329 9200
℻ +1 516 329 9260

Contacts: Joe Lauro, Mart Heideman
Subjects: Historical archive, classic films, comedy, music, newsreels, industry, space.
▦ Various film and video formats. All line standards available.
Research: By staff. Visits by appointment.
🕐 Mon-Fri 09:00 to 17:30
Procedure: Viewing material on VHS and Umatic. 24 hours for access to masters.
Description: Footage covers 1895 to 1990 with a very strong historical archive. Universal newsreel (1929 to 1967), musical performance footage including Jazz, Blues, Country, Rock and Roll, Pop from 1910 to 1990, silent films, industrial footage, space program, life styles and a range of general subject. Computerized. Rate card available.

BROAD STREET PRODUCTIONS

10 West 19th Street, New York, NY 10011, USA
℡ +1 212 924 4700
℻ +1 212 924 5085

Contacts: Jody Bergedick, David Fink
Subjects: Industry, skylines, business.
▦ 16mm. Most video formats. NTSC.
Research: By both staff and outside researchers. Appointment to visit.
🕐 Mon-Fri 09:00 to 18:00 (other days and hours on request)
Procedure: Timecoded VHS or Umatic viewing copies. Access to masters within 24 hours.
Description: The collection contains material relating to business and finance with footage of financial markets, industrial processes, city skylines, hi-tech communications imagery and business people in various situations. Partly computerized. Catalogue and rate card available.

CENTRAL COAST MEDIA HOLDINGS (CCM GROUP)

1st Floor, 56 The Entrance Road, The Entrance, NSW 2261,
Australia
Ⓒ +61 43 331122
Ⓕ +61 43 341017

Contacts: Mark and Michelle Falzon
Subjects: Industry, natural history, aerial photography,
lifestyles, landscapes.
▦ 16mm; Beta. PAL.
Research: By staff. Appointment to visit.
☺ Mon-Fri 08:00 to 18:00
Procedure: Timecoded VHS available. Masters as reasonably
required.
Description: Comprehensive range of Australian floral and
landscape material on 16mm and Betacam plus a range of
corporate industrial imagery. The collection specializes in
central coast and New South Wales footage with aerial and
lifestyle, etc. shots. Rate card and catalogue available.

FABULOUS FOOTAGE

4th Floor, 19 Mercer Street, Toronto, Ontario M5V 1H2,
Canada
Ⓒ +1 416 591 6955
Ⓕ +1 416 591 1666

Contacts: Steve Race, Patricia Harvey, Rhonda Olson, Julie
Kovacs
Subjects: Stock shots, locations, culture, industry, medicine,
military, music, environmental, leisure, transport, natural
history, space, trailers.
▦ Film; video (all film mastered onto tape).
Research: By both staff and outside researchers.
☺ Mon-Fri 09:00 to 21:00
Description: Complete contemporary film and videotape
library with a vast range of quality images. Subject headings
include agriculture, buildings, cities, countries, cultural
activities, industry and business, landmarks, landscapes,
medical, military, music, natural phenomena, news, period
recreations, professions, rain forests, recreation, space,
special effects, spectacles, sports, transportation,
underwater, water and wildlife. They also hold special
collections of Nazi propaganda footage, Russian history,
Russian space program, B-movies and trailers. Computerized.
Rate card and catalogue available. NB: This is the head
office, there is also an office in Vancouver, Canada Tel:
(604) 684 8484, Fax: (604) 681 3299.
Foreign Offices: Argentina, Australia, Brazil, Canada, Chile,
Germany, Indonesia, Japan, Malaysia, Philippines, Singapore,
Mexico, Spain, USA.

FILM/AUDIO SERVICES

Suite 311, 430 West 14th Street, New York NY 10014, USA
ⓒ +1 212 645 2112
ⓕ +1 212 255 4220

Contacts: Bob Summers, Mike Cocchi, Dean Cady
Subjects: Historical archive, travelogues, culture, educational
films, industry, public domain.
▦ Most film and video formats. NTSC.
Research: By staff preferably. Appointment to visit.
🕑 Mon-Fri 09:00 to 18:00 (or by appointment)
Procedure: Viewing material on VHS or 3/4" NTSC. 24
hours for access to masters.
Description: Worldwide travel footage dating from 1926 to
1980s; education and industrial films from the 1930s to 60s;
historical actuality public domain material sourced from the
National Archives and Library of Congress sold at less cost.
Inexpensive and fast turnaround film to NTSC Beta SP and
1" tape in house. Partly computerized. Catalogue and rate
card available. English and some Spanish spoken.

FRONT LINE

Suite 3 Senyo Building, 5th Floor, 3-1-9 Nakameguro,
Meguro-ku, Toyko 153, Japan
ⓒ +81 3 3760 6271
ⓕ +81 3 3760 6012

Contacts: Seiichi Sugiura
Subjects: Stock shots, aviation, locations, natural history,
industry, space, time-lapse, transport, environmental.
🕑 Mon-Fri 10:00 to 18:00
Procedure: Viewing tapes loaned. Masters copied after
selection.
Description: Agents for UK company Index Stock Shots, USA
company Opus Global and Canadian company Fabulous
Footage in Japan.

HIPS FILM & VIDEO PRODUCTIONS

257 Coventry Street, South Melbourne, Victoria 3205, Australia
© +61 3 699 9427
Ⓕ +61 3 699 9392

Contacts: John Hipwell
Subjects: Energy conservation, industry.
16mm; Beta/Beta SP, Hi 8. PAL.
Research: By staff. Visits by appointment.
Mon-Fri 09:00 to 17:30
Procedure: Access to masters normally 48 hours.
Description: Productions deal with the subject of energy management and conservation showing several of the latest developments. Computerized. Rates on application.

IMAGES OF THE EAST

19B Jalan 20/14, Petaling Jaya Selangor 46300, Malaysia
© +60 03 776 7199
Ⓕ +60 03 776 4560

Contacts: Theresa Khoo
Subjects: Stock shots, aviation, locations, natural history, industry, space, time-lapse, transport, environmental.
Beta SP, 1", Umatic. PAL.
Research: By staff. Visits by appointment.
Mon-Fri 08:30 to 17:45
Procedure: Viewing tapes loaned. Masters copied after selection, 3-4 days for access.
Description: Agents for UK company Index Stock Shots and German company Modern Video Library in Malaysia and Singapore. The library holds an A-Z of subject categories including landscape, destination and sports footage from Malaysia. Partly computerized. Rate card available. English spoken.

IMAGEWAYS

Second Floor, 412 West 48th Street, New York NY 10036, USA
© +1 212 265 1287
Ⓕ +1 212 586 0339

Contacts: Adam Sargis, Kenneth Powell, Ray Sidwell
Subjects: Stock shots, newsreels, comedy, animation, classic films, documentaries, industry, educational films, television.
🎞 Film; 1" videotape with timecoded 3/4" cassettes.
Research: By staff. Appointment to visit.
Procedure: Timecoded cassette compiled. Masters copied after selection.
Description: Stock footage library with material dating from 1905 to present day. Footage comes from newsreels, silent films, cartoons, historical films, Hollywood features, documentaries, industrial films, educational films, television programmes and original shot material. Collection is approximately 70% colour and 30% black and white. Computerized. Rate card available. Minimum license fee charged on delivery of master material.

JACK CHISHOLM FILM PRODUCTIONS

Suite 50, 99 Atlantic Avenue, Toronto, Ontario M6K 3J8, Canada
© +1 416 588 5200
Ⓕ +1 416 588 5324

Contacts: Peter Robinson
Subjects: Stock shots, historical archive, locations, time-lapse, current affairs, newsreels, natural history, industry, science.
🎞 16mm, 35mm; Beta/Beta SP, 1", Umatic, SVHS, some digital. NTSC.
Research: By staff only.
🕓 Mon-Fri 09:00 to 17:30
Procedure: Umatic or VHS viewing copies. 24 hours for access to masters.
Description: The stock footage library contains archive material dating from 1896 up to present day. Subjects cover major events around the world, wildlife, foreign locations, industry and science as well as quality shots of clouds, sunsets, time-lapse flowers, etc. The collection comprises of 10 000 hours of video footage and 4 million feet of film. They hold 35mm neg of across Canada scenics plus the Millenium television series. Computerized. Rate card available. English and Italian spoken.

JOHN E. ALLEN

116 North Avenue, Park Ridge, NJ 07656, USA
© +1 201 391 3299
Ⓕ +1 201 391 6335

Contacts: John E. Allen, Beverley Allen
Subjects: Historical archive, newsreels, war, Russia, industry, transport, classic films, educational films, travelogues.
Mainly film; some video.
Research: By both staff and outside researchers.
Mon–Fri 09:00 to 18:00
Description: Kinograms from 1915 to 1931. Telenews 1947 to 1953. World War I and II, Spanish American War, Mexican Revolution, Russian Revolution, Hungarian Revolution, Spanish Civil War, Korean War, etc. Industry 1910 to 1950s, transportation, educational, ethnographic, travel, nature, features 1905 to 1950s, stills, posters and lobby cards. Partly computerized. Rate card available.

NORTHSTAR PRODUCTIONS

3003 "O" Street NW, Washington DC 20007, USA
© +1 202 338 7337
Ⓕ +1 202 337 4387

Contacts: Don North
Subjects: War, locations, industry, leisure.
Videotape.
Research: By both staff and outside researchers.
Appointment to visit.
7 days
Description: Footage of various international war zones including Afghanistan (1987 combat), El Salvador (Guerilla war 1983 to 1990), Nicaragua, Middle East (Beirut siege 1982), Gulf War and rebuilding of Kuwait, Vietnam (1967 to 1990), Sarajevo. Also footage from Hong Kong, Austria, Prague, Washington DC, Estonia (Balkans independence movement), Finland (modern and World War II) etc. Partly computerized. Brochure available.

PETRIFIED FILMS / THE IMAGE BANK

Room 204, 430 West 14th Street, New York NY 10014, USA
© +1 212 242 5461
Ⓕ +1 212 691 8347

Contacts: Lori Cheatle, Rob Cates
Subjects: Historical archive, Hollywood, transport, consumerism, Americana, industry, war, aviation, feature film, out-takes.
🎞 35mm, 16mm; some on 1", D2, 3/4" with matching VHS.
Research: By staff. Visits by appointment.
🕐 Mon-Fri 09:30 to 18:00
Procedure: Viewing tapes assembled. Masters copied after selection.
Description: Historical collection including pre-1951 Warner Brothers stock and pre-1965 Columbia Pictures stock. A-Z of subjects including action sequences, period recreations, establishing shots, projection backgrounds, cityscapes and worldwide locations. Industrial, military and aviation collections. Car culture and 1950s daily life in the US. Majority dates from 1920s to 1960s. Partly computerized. Rate card and catalogue available.
Foreign Offices: Contact local Image Bank office.

SECOND LINE SEARCH

1926 Broadway, New York, NY 10023, USA
© +1 212 787 7500
Ⓕ +1 212 787 7636

Contacts: Susan Luchars, George Bartko
Subjects: Locations, historical archive, sport, natural history, aerial photography, time-lapse, Americana, out-takes, industry, lifestyles.
🎞 Variety of film and video formats.
Research: By staff.
🕐 Mon-Fri 09:30 to 18:00
Procedure: Umatic viewing cassettes (NTSC or PAL). 2-3 days for access to masters.
Description: A variety of material including scenics, archival footage, sports, wildlife, news, aerials, international locations, Americana, oddities/bloopers, industry, technology, lifestyle and time-lapse. Computerized. French, Spanish, Portuguese, Italian and German spoken.

SOURCE STOCK FOOTAGE LIBRARY, THE

738 N. Constitution Drive, Tuscon, Arizona 85748, USA
© +1 602 298 4810
⑤ +1 602 290 8831

Contacts: John Willwater, Bill and Lynne Briggs
Subjects: Stock shots, natural history, industry, time-lapse, locations, mining.
Research: By staff.
☉ Mon–Fri 08:00 to 17:00
Description: Scenics, time-lapse, clouds and suns, animals, petrochemical and mining industrial, US and international destinations, desert plants and animals, cowboys, Phoenix, Tuscson, Alaskan wilderness and animals. Computerized. Rate card and brochure available.

STREAMLINE ARCHIVES

Suite 1314, 432 Park Avenue South, New York NY 10016, USA
© +1 212 696 2616
⑤ +1 212 696 0021

Contacts: Mark Trost
Subjects: Stock shots, newsreels, current affairs, classic films, feature films, educational, industry, sport, television, advertising, travelogues.
🎞 16mm, 35mm; most video formats. PAL, NTSC and SECAM.
Research: By staff only. Appointments for viewings.
☉ Mon–Fri 09:30 to 19:30
Procedure: Viewing tapes assembled on VHS or Umatic. 24 hours for access to masters.
Description: Streamline's archives are being continually expanded including educational, government and industrial films, newsreels (from the turn of the century through to the early 1970s), silent comedies, television programmes and commercials, sports films, theatrical shorts, classic features and trailers as well as travel video and daily news footage (1986 to present) from Cablevision's award winning News 12 Long Island channel. Computerized. Rate card and catalogue available. English, Spanish and Japanese spoken.

TIMES TELEVISION LIBRARY

The Time of India Building, 7 Bahadur Shah Zafar Marg, New Dehli 110 002, India
℄ +91 11 3722094/3351606/3352087
Ⓕ +91 11 3715532/3715836
⟋ 031-61337/38 INDIA IN

Contacts: Mr. Sanjay Sethi
Subjects: Drama, documentaries, industry, personalities, cookery, music, fashion, sport, science, environmental, culture.
▦ Most video formats. PAL.
Research: By both staff and outside researchers.
◷ 6 days, 10:00 to 17:00
Procedure: Viewing on VHS. 1-2 hours for access to BVU and Beta masters.
Description: Times Television was formed in 1986 and has produced and marketed a large range of programmes covering subjects relating to India including social issues, economy, business and industry, film industry awards, fashion, personalities, cuisine of Eastern and Western India, beauty contests, sport, science and the environment. They also hold various drama serials plus a few pop concerts including Bryan Adams and Jethro Tull. Partly computerized. English and Hindi spoken.
Foreign Offices: UK.

WILLIAM G. BEAL

512 Franklin Avenue, Pittsburgh, PA 15221, USA
℄ +1 412 243 7020
Ⓕ +1 412 243 4520

Contacts: William G. Beal
Subjects: Documentaries, educational films, industry, medicine, sailing.
▦ 80% film; 20% videotape.
Research: By staff. Appointment to visit.
◷ Mon-Fri 09:00 to 17:00
Description: Footage from productions spanning the last 40 years. Productions made for clients in various industries including steel, glass, aluminum, ceramics, electronics, foundries, oil and gas and plastics. Documentaries made for hospitals, museums, colleges, universities and community organizations of all types. Special collection of tropical sailing subjects filmed in the Bahamas and Caribbean.

WPA FILM LIBRARY

5525 W. 159th Street, Oak Forest, IL 60452, USA
ⓒ +1 708 535 1540
Ⓕ +1 708 535 1541

Contacts: Michael Mertz
Subjects: Historical archive, newsreels, industry, Americana, music, transport, fashion, locations, natural history.
10 000 hours film; 2000 hours videotape.
Research: By both staff and outside researchers.
Mon-Fri 8:30 to 17:00
Description: Complete historical materials from 1896 to the present day. Specialities include newsreels, Americana from the 1940s and 50s, early rock and roll performances (Hullabaloo in 1964/5, The Music Scene in 1969/70), UFOs, automobiles, fashions, American Civil Rights, contemporary geographic materials, nature and wildlife, American industry collection from the 1940s to the present day. Also represent British Pathe News for North America only. Partly computerized. Rate card and brochure available.

Landscapes

BEYOND INFORMATION SERVICES

Beyond 2000, 34 Hotham Parade, Artarmon, NSW 2064,
Australia
© +61 2 438 5155
Ⓕ +61 2 439 6549

Contacts: Lisa Savage, Annette Overton
Subjects: Medicine, science, environmental, landscapes.
Beta/Beta SP, 1", Umatic. PAL.
Research: By staff only.
Mon–Fri 09:00 to 17:30
Procedure: Viewing tapes assembled.
Description: An extensive collection of footage from
internationally acclaimed science and technology series,
Beyond 2000. Footage covers subjects shot worldwide and
includes medical breakthroughs, laboratory work, people,
robotics, Australiana, hi-tech gadgets, environment,
international rural and city landscapes, wildlife, etc.
Computerized. Rate card available. English and French
spoken.

CENTRAL COAST MEDIA HOLDINGS (CCM GROUP)

1st Floor, 56 The Entrance Road, The Entrance, NSW 2261,
Australia
© +61 43 331122
Ⓕ +61 43 341017

Contacts: Mark and Michelle Falzon
Subjects: Industry, natural history, aerial photography,
lifestyles, landscapes.
16mm; Beta. PAL.
Research: By staff. Appointment to visit.
Mon–Fri 08:00 to 18:00
Procedure: Timecoded VHS available. Masters as reasonably
required.
Description: Comprehensive range of Australian floral and
landscape material on 16mm and Betacam plus a range of
corporate industrial imagery. The collection specializes in
central coast and New South Wales footage with aerial and
lifestyle, etc. shots. Rate card and catalogue available.

CVA FILM & TELEVISION

P.O. Box 25, West Perth, Western Australia 6872, Australia
ⓒ +61 9 481 6107
Ⓕ +61 9 481 6107

Contacts: Sue Taylor, Derek Longhurst
Subjects: Mining, landscapes.
🎞 16mm; D2, 1", BVU, Umatic. PAL.
Research: By staff only.
🕑 Mon-Fri 08:30 to 18:00
Procedure: PAL or NTSC VHS viewing cassettes. 1 week for access to masters.
Description: Extensive footage of different types of mining in Western Australia - particularly gold, iron ore and coal (underground and open cut). Various landscape shots of Perth and Western Australia. Computerized. German, French and Italian spoken.

DELTA PRODUCTIONS

P.O. Box 4836, Darwin, NT 0801, Australia
ⓒ +61 89 817435 / 817568
Ⓕ +61 89 813213

Contacts: Bob West
Subjects: Historical archive, landscapes, tourism.
🎞 BVU, Beta/Beta SP, SVHS. PAL.
Research: By staff. Appointment to visit.
🕑 Mon-Fri 08:30 to 17:00
Procedure: Access to masters in 2-3 days.
Description: Main area covered is the Northern Territory of Australia with footage covering special events since 1982 and all major tourist locations and attractions. Delta also have some historical material dating from the 1920s to 1940s. Partly computerized.

ENERGY PRODUCTIONS' TIMESCAPE IMAGE LIBRARY

4th Floor, 12700 Ventura Boulevard, Studio City, CA 91604
USA
© +1 818 508 1444
Ⓕ +1 818 508 1293

Contacts: Joan Sargent, Randy Gitsch
Subjects: Americana, sport, time-lapse, macro photography,
natural history, locations, fashion, culture, landscapes,
lifestyles, special effects.
16mm, 35mm, 70mm; most video formats.
Research: By staff. Visits by appointment.
Mon-Fri 09.00 to 18.00
Procedure: Viewing tapes assembled. Masters copied after
selection.
Description: Energy Productions hold the Timescape Image
Library, a huge library of stock material encompassing sports,
wildlife, landmarks, cities, seascapes, macro/micro
photography, fashion, underwater, botany, computer imagery
and daily life from around the world. Also available via this
office is The Playboy Fashion Collection, Namco Computer
Imagery, Warren Miller Films and Sports Library, Windham
Hills Video and Film Library and Bob Landis Wildlife.
Computerized. Rate card and brochure available. NB: Energy
also have a New York office, Tel: (212) 686 4900, Fax:
(212) 686 4998.Mon-Fri 09:00 to 18:00
Foreign Offices: France, Germany, Italy, Japan, Spain,
Sweden, Turkey, Israel, UK, USA.

FILM & VIDEO STOCK SHOTS

Suite E, 10700 Ventura Boulevard, Studio City CA 91604,
USA
© +1 818 760 2098
Ⓕ +1 818 760 3294

Contacts: Stephanie Siebert, William Bolls
Subjects: Stock shots, current affairs, leisure, natural history,
time-lapse, locations, macro photography, animation, culture,
landscapes.
Film; videotape.
Research: By staff. Appointment to visit.
Mon-Fri 09:00 to 17:00
Description: Huge selection of both current and archival film
and videotape original images. Subjects include news events,
action sports, nature and wildlife, time-lapse cinematography,
landscapes and cityscapes, microscopy, cartoons, lifestyles
and travel footage. Next business day turnaround on master
footage orders and competitive rates. Computerized.
Brochure and rate card available.

STIMULUS / IMAGE RESEARCH

P.O. Box 170519, San Francisco, CA 94117, USA
© +1 415 558 8339
Ⓕ +1 415 864 3897

Contacts: Grant Johnson
Subjects: Computer imagery, special effects, space, landscapes, science, educational films.
▦ Beta/Beta SP, Umatic. NTSC (also various formats of stills).
Research: By staff only.
🕐 Mon-Fri 09:00 to 17:00
Procedure: VHS viewing cassettes, NTSC. 3 days for access to masters.
Description: Stimulus are producers of scientific and educational video programming. Their stock collection includes Western US scenics, landscapes, geological and computer generated terrain imagery. Also held is aerial, satellite and computer terrain imagery of full US, some world and planetary locations. Partly computerized.

TELECINE INTERNATIONAL PRODUCTIONS

P.O. Box 8426, Universal City, CA 91608, USA
© +1 818 889 8246
Ⓕ +1 818 889 5605

Contacts: Nick Archer
Subjects: Stock shots, locations, transport, aviation, time-lapse, landscapes.
▦ 35mm.
Research: By both staff and outside researchers.
🕐 Mon-Fri 09:00 to 18:00
Procedure: Film/cassette viewing reels. Minimum royalty due for masters.
Description: Worldwide establishing shots, cityscapes and traffic from 1957 to present day, transportation, jets, buildings, scenics, moons, sunrises, suns, time-lapse clouds. Rate card and brochure available.

Locations

ACTION SPORTS / SCOTT DITTRICH FILMS

P.O. Box 301, Malibu, CA 90265, USA
© +1 310 459 2526
Ⓕ +1 310 456 1743

Contacts: Patrick
Subjects: Adventure sports, leisure, locations.
Film.
Research: By both staff and outside researchers.
Appointment to visit.
Mon-Fri 09:00 to 17:00
Description: Actions sports footage - surf, snow, waterskiing, mountain biking, kayak, skating, rollerblading, windsurfing, waves, snowboarding, etc. Also location shots such as sunsets, Los Angeles and tropical. Partly computerized. Rate card and catalogue available.

AIRLINE FILM & TV PROMOTIONS

13246 Weidner Street, Pacoima, CA 91331-2343, USA
© +1 818 899 1151
Ⓕ +1 818 896 5929

Contacts: Alf or Mikael Jacobsen
Subjects: Aviation, locations, leisure.
35mm.
Research: By staff. Visit by appointment.
Mon-Fri 08:00 to 17:00
Description: Footage of commercial airlines - take-offs, landings, in flight - worldwide. Establishing shots of many capital cities. Sports and recreational activities. Rate card available.

A.M. STOCK EXCHANGE, THE

Suite 207, 4741 Laurel Cyn. Bl., N. Hollywood CA 91607, USA
ℂ +1 818 762 7865
Ⓕ +1 818 762 7886

Contacts: Chris Angelich
Subjects: Stock shots, locations.
▦ 35mm, 16mm; 3/4" master videotape.
Research: By staff.
🕐 Mon-Fri 09:00 to 18:00
Description: Stock footage library with a wide variety of modern shots. They will also do custom stock shots for clients. Shots include skylines, buildings, schools, colleges, restaurants, houses, cities - Los Angeles, San Francisco, Palm Springs, New York, Washington DC, Philadelphia, Chicago, Detroit, Atlanta, etc. Computerized. Rate card available.

AUSTRALIAN BROADCASTING CORPORATION (ABC)

ABC TV Library Sales, GPO Box 9994, Sydney, NSW 2000, Australia
ℂ +61 2 950 3269 / 3284
Ⓕ +61 2 950 3277

Contacts: Cyrus Irani, Richard Carter
Subjects: Current affairs, stock shots, natural history, sport, lifestyles, locations.
▦ 16mm; Beta/Beta SP, 1", BVU, Umatic.
Research: By staff only. Clients may view in the office.
🕐 Mon-Fri 09:00 to 17:30
Procedure: VHS or Umatic viewing tapes supplied. 24 hours for access to masters.
Description: The ABC is the major government broadcaster holding Australian and international news and current affairs footage dating from 1960. They also hold a large stock footage library covering over 4000 subjects including a natural history collection, sport, lifestyle and location material. ABC are also agents for the Reuters/Visnews and Qantas libraries. Computerized. Rate card available. NB: ABC also have offices in Adelaide, Brisbane, Darwin, Melbourne, Perth and Hobart (Tasmania).

CAMEO FILM LIBRARY

10620 Burbank Blvd, N. Hollywood, CA 91607, USA
© +1 818 980 8700
Ⓕ +1 818 980 7113

Contacts: Marilyn Chielens, Steven Vrabel
Subjects: Stock shots, locations, aerial photography, aviation, military.
⊞ 35mm.
Research: By staff only.
⊘ Mon-Fri 08:30 to 17:30
Description: A wide variety of stock shots including worldwide establishing shots, military aircraft, period and contemporary military, aerial footage, sunrises and sunsets, etc. Rate card available.

CANADIAN BROADCASTING CORPORATION (CBC)

Box 500, Station A, Toronto, Ontario M5W 1E1, Canada
© +1 416 205 7608
Ⓕ +1 416 205 6736

Contacts: Roy Harris
Subjects: Stock shots, natural history, locations, medicine, environmental.
⊞ 16mm; Beta/Beta SP, 1", Umatic. NTSC.
Research: By staff only.
⊘ Mon-Fri 08:30 to 17:30
Procedure: Timecoded cassettes made to order. 2-3 days for access to masters.
Description: CBC's archive contains a wide range of programme material including natural history and environmental footage, medical research, cities of the world, history, etc. from Arctic life to ancient Yemini ruins. Computerized. Rate card available.

CARLETON PRODUCTIONS

1500 Merivale Road, Ottawa, Ontario K2E 6Z5, Canada
© +1 613 224 1313 Ext. 330, 309
Ⓕ +1 613 224 9074

Contacts: Pat Billings, Randi Hansen, Dianne Van Velthoven, Mark Ross
Subjects: Locations, current affairs, sports.
⊞ 3/4" master videotape.
Research: By staff.
⊘ Mon-Fri 08:00 to 17:00
Description: Footage from across Canada (mostly from the capital area Ottawa), scenery, politics, special events and sports. Partly computerized (covering the last three years).

CINEMA NETWORK (CINENET)

Suite 111, 2235 First Street, Simi Valley CA 93065, USA
© +1 805 527 0093
Ⓕ +1 805 527 0305

Contacts: Richard Spruiell, Jim Jarrard
Subjects: Stock shots, natural history, locations, sport, time-lapse, underwater photography.
35mm, 16mm; NTSC videotape.
Research: By staff. Appointment to visit.
Procedure: Viewing tapes compiled. Masters copied after payment received.
Description: Stock footage library with very comprehensive A–Z listing of subjects - almost every topic you can think of is covered in their brochure, they also undertake custom filming. Computerized on Cinemind software. Rate card and brochure available.

COE FILM ASSOCIATES

65 East 96th Street, New York, NY 10128, USA
© +1 212 831 5355
Ⓕ +1 212 996 6728

Contacts: Arlene Gross
Subjects: Natural history, locations, Americana, documentaries, drama.
16mm; Beta/Beta SP, 1″, BVU, Umatic. PAL and NTSC.
Research: By staff only.
☉ Mon–Fri 09:30 to 17:30
Procedure: Umatic/VHS NTSC or PAL loaned. 24 hours for access to masters.
Description: Footage derives from documentaries and dramas produced by Coe Film Associates and covers nature, wildlife, destinations, Americana and New York City. Computerized. English, Spanish and French spoken.

ENERGY PRODUCTIONS' TIMESCAPE IMAGE LIBRARY

4th Floor, 12700 Ventura Boulevard, Studio City, CA 91604
USA
℡ +1 818 508 1444
Ⓕ +1 818 508 1293

Contacts: Joan Sargent, Randy Gitsch
Subjects: Americana, sport, time-lapse, macro photography,
natural history, locations, fashion, culture, landscapes,
lifestyles, special effects.
🎞 16mm, 35mm, 70mm; most video formats.
Research: By staff. Visits by appointment.
🕓 Mon–Fri 09.00 to 18.00
Procedure: Viewing tapes assembled. Masters copied after
selection.
Description: Energy Productions hold the Timescape Image
Library, a huge library of stock material encompassing sports,
wildlife, landmarks, cities, seascapes, macro/micro
photography, fashion, underwater, botany, computer imagery
and daily life from around the world. Also available via this
office is The Playboy Fashion Collection, Namco Computer
Imagery, Warren Miller Films and Sports Library, Windham
Hills Video and Film Library and Bob Landis Wildlife.
Computerized. Rate card and brochure available. NB: Energy
also have a New York office, Tel: (212) 686 4900, Fax:
(212) 686 4998.Mon–Fri 09:00 to 18:00
Foreign Offices: France, Germany, Italy, Japan, Spain,
Sweden, Turkey, Israel, UK, USA.

FABULOUS FOOTAGE

4th Floor, 19 Mercer Street, Toronto, Ontario M5V 1H2, Canada
© +1 416 591 6955
Ⓕ +1 416 591 1666

Contacts: Steve Race, Patricia Harvey, Rhonda Olson, Julie Kovacs
Subjects: Stock shots, locations, culture, industry, medicine, military, music, environmental, leisure, transport, natural history, space, trailers.
▦ Film; video (all film mastered onto tape).
Research: By both staff and outside researchers.
☉ Mon-Fri 09:00 to 21:00
Description: Complete contemporary film and videotape library with a vast range of quality images. Subject headings include agriculture, buildings, cities, countries, cultural activities, industry and business, landmarks, landscapes, medical, military, music, natural phenomena, news, period recreations, professions, rain forests, recreation, space, special effects, spectacles, sports, transportation, underwater, water and wildlife. They also hold special collections of Nazi propaganda footage, Russian history, Russian space program, B-movies and trailers. Computerized. Rate card and catalogue available. NB: This is the head office, there is also an office in Vancouver, Canada Tel: (604) 684 8484, Fax: (604) 681 3299.
Foreign Offices: Argentina, Australia, Brazil, Canada, Chile, Germany, Indonesia, Japan, Malaysia, Philippines, Singapore, Mexico, Spain, USA.

FILM & VIDEO STOCK SHOTS

Suite E, 10700 Ventura Boulevard, Studio City CA 91604, USA
℡ +1 818 760 2098
🆎 +1 818 760 3294

Contacts: Stephanie Siebert, William Bolls
Subjects: Stock shots, current affairs, leisure, natural history, time-lapse, locations, macro photography, animation, culture, landscapes.
▦ Film; videotape.
Research: By staff. Appointment to visit.
🕓 Mon–Fri 09:00 to 17:00
Description: Huge selection of both current and archival film and videotape original images. Subjects include news events, action sports, nature and wildlife, time-lapse cinematography, landscapes and cityscapes, microscopy, cartoons, lifestyles and travel footage. Next business day turnaround on master footage orders and competitive rates. Computerized. Brochure and rate card available.

FILM BANK STOCK FOOTAGE FILM & VIDEO LIBRARY

425 South Victory Boulevard, Burbank, CA 91502, USA
℡ +1 818 841 9176
🆎 +1 818 567 4235

Contacts: Paula Lumbard, Elizabeth Canelake
Subjects: News, space, special effects, science, sport, medicine, time-lapse, aerial photography, natural history, animation, locations, environmental.
▦ 16mm, 35mm; most video formats. NTSC masters.
Research: By staff only. Researchers occasionally visit for big projects.
🕓 Mon–Fri 09:00 to 17:00
Procedure: Umatics loaned or VHS assembled. 24 hours for access to masters.
Description: Diverse collection of broadcast quality film and video images aimed at supplying the full range of client productions. Most subjects are covered in the library, the latest new collections being world locations, children of the world, environmental images (destruction, scientific and beauty shots), History of Flight, more space and solar flares, aerials across the US, agriculture and animals. Partly computerized. Catalogue and rate card available.

FILM WORLD

2 Whiting Street, P.O. Box 313, Artarmon, NSW 2064,
Australia
ⓒ +61 2 438 1888
ⓕ +61 2 439 8541

Contacts: Naomi Saville
Subjects: Newsreels, locations, natural history, lifestyles,
tourism, travelogues.
🎞 Film; Beta/Beta SP, 1″, D1. PAL and NTSC.
Research: By both staff and outside researchers.
Appointment to visit.
🕓 Mon-Fri 08:30 to 17:30
Procedure: VHS or Umatic viewing cassettes. 24 hours for
access to masters.
Description: Over 3000 hours of footage covering archival
news material, contemporary landscapes, wildlife and
lifestyles. Film World are exclusive agents for the Cinesound
and Movietone newsreel collection, Australian Tourist
Commission, Queensland Tourist & Travel Corporation,
Canadian company Fabulous Footage and many more.
Computerized. Subject headings list and rate card available.

FISH FILMS FOOTAGE WORLD

4548 Van Noord Avenue, Studio City, CA 91604-1013, USA
ⓒ +1 818 905 1071
ⓕ +1 818 905 0301

Contacts: David Fishbein
Subjects: Historical archive, stock shots, time-lapse,
underwater photography, Americana, locations, leisure,
comedy, transport, industrial.
Research: By staff. Appointment to visit.
🕓 Mon-Fri 09:00 to 17:00
Description: Vintage and contemporary footage covering all
subject areas. Time-lapse, underwater, scenics, aerials,
sports, specializing in lifestyles, comedy, historic events,
transportation, Americana, educational, travel, industrial,
public domain. Partly computerized. Rate card and brochure
available.

FRONT LINE

Suite 3 Senyo Building, 5th Floor, 3-1-9 Nakameguro,
Meguro-ku, Toyko 153, Japan
ⓒ +81 3 3760 6271
Ⓕ +81 3 3760 6012

Contacts: Seiichi Sugiura
Subjects: Stock shots, aviation, locations, natural history,
industry, space, time-lapse, transport, environmental.
🕐 Mon-Fri 10:00 to 18:00
Procedure: Viewing tapes loaned. Masters copied after
selection.
Description: Agents for UK company Index Stock Shots, USA
company Opus Global and Canadian company Fabulous
Footage in Japan.

GLOBAL VILLAGE STOCK FOOTAGE LIBRARY

1717 Darby Road, Sebastopol, CA 95472, USA
ⓒ +1 707 829 9542
Ⓕ +1 707 829 9542

Contacts: Michael Heumann, Marcia Ludwig
Subjects: Travelogues, locations, culture, stock shots.
▦ Beta/Beta SP, Umatic. NTSC.
Research: By staff on database - response by fax.
🕐 7 days 24 hours a day.
Procedure: Viewing on Umatic or VHS NTSC. 48 hours for
access to masters.
Description: Global Village is a collection of video stock
images gathered from around the world for the travel
programmes distributed by International Video Network,
Rand McNally Videos, Reader's Digest Videos and the
Discovery Channel "World Away" series. They are also a
clearing house and referral service for collections belonging
to other producers and various public domain image libraries.
Computerized database covering over 10 000 subjects
available free plus rate card. English and German spoken.

HOLLYWOOD FILM REGISTRY

6926 Melrose Avenue, Hollywood, CA 90038, USA
ⓒ +1 213 937 7067
ⓕ +1 213 655 8889

Contacts: Dan Price
Subjects: Historical archive, stock shots, locations, personalities, Americana, documentaries, classic films, motor racing.
🎞 16mm, 35mm; most video formats.
Research: By both staff and outside researchers. Appointment to visit.
🕐 Mon-Fri 10:30 to 17:30
Procedure: Viewing on VHS, Umatic, 35mm. 24 hours for access to masters.
Description: Encompasses 10 major collections. American Film Registry (from silent era on - institutional, travel, Imperial China...), Dennis Film Libraries (news, establishing shots, personalities, space...), Documentary Productions (Americana, motor sport), Keystone Collection (comedy), Paper Prints (1890s to 1910), Sand Castles (current establishing shots), Sandler Film Library (historical library used for stock by Hollywood producers since the 1930s), Slapstick & Gags (silent movies), Video & Film Stringers (current stock shots), Visual Dynamics (virtual encyclopaedic library up to the early 1970s). Partly computerized. Rate card available.

IMAGE BANK / FILM DIVISION

4th Floor, 111 Fifth Avenue, New York NY 10003, USA
© +1 212 529 6700
℉ +1 212 529 8889

Contacts: Brian Mitchell
Subjects: Stock shots, aerial photography, time-lapse, lifestyles, natural history, locations, sport.
All film and video formats and line standards held.
Research: By both staff and outside researchers. Appointment to visit.
Mon-Fri 09:00 to 17:00
Procedure: 3/4"/VHS (any line standard) for viewing. 24 hours for access to masters.
Description: Vast collection of stock material, contemporary and archival, acquired from Turner Broadcasting, Ocean Images, I.R.E., Pigeon Productions, MacGillivray Freeman Films, Dentsu Prox., McDonnell Douglas, Nature Conservancy, etc. Offices worldwide and major cities of North America - Chicago, Detroit, Mexico, Minneapolis, Atlanta, Dallas and Los Angeles. Computerized. English, French, Spanish, Italian, German and Greek spoken in the NEW YORK HEADQUARTERS.
Foreign Offices: Argentina, Brazil, Chile, Colombia, Australia, Canada, Hong Kong, Indonesia, Korea, Japan, Malaysia, Philippines, Singapore, Taiwan, Thailand, South Africa, UK, USA.

IMAGES OF THE EAST

19B Jalan 20/14, Petaling Jaya Selangor 46300, Malaysia
© +60 03 776 7199
℉ +60 03 776 4560

Contacts: Theresa Khoo
Subjects: Stock shots, aviation, locations, natural history, industry, space, time-lapse, transport, environmental.
Beta SP, 1", Umatic. PAL.
Research: By staff. Visits by appointment.
Mon-Fri 08:30 to 17:45
Procedure: Viewing tapes loaned. Masters copied after selection, 3-4 days for access.
Description: Agents for UK company Index Stock Shots and German company Modern Video Library in Malaysia and Singapore. The library holds an A-Z of subject categories including landscape, destination and sports footage from Malaysia. Partly computerized. Rate card available. English spoken.

IMAGES PIXART

1973 Falardeau, Montreal, Quebec H2K 2L9, Canada
Ⓒ +1 514 521 8776
Ⓕ +1 514 521 0541

Contacts: Emmanuelle de la Cressonniere
Subjects: Stock shots, environmental, culture, locations.
Betacam.
Research: By staff. Appointment to visit.
Mon-Fri 09:00 to 18:00
Description: Extensive collection of beauty shots of Canada from coast to coast. Also stock footage covering ecological and cultural issues in the province of Quebec for the last five years. Computerized. Rate card available.

INTERNATIONAL VIDEO NETWORK (IVN)

Worldwide Stock Footage Library,
2242 Camino Ramon, San Ramon, CA 94583, USA
Ⓒ +1 510 866 1344 Ext. 217
Ⓕ +1 510 866 0614

Subjects: Locations, travelogues, leisure.
16mm; 1", Beta SP with matching VHS.
Research: By staff only.
Mon-Fri 09:00 to 18:00
Procedure: Viewing tapes loaned. Masters copied after selection.
Description: Over 100 hours of destination footage, countries and cities all over the world. Also includes adventure and sporting activities. Partly computerized. Rate card and catalogue available.
Foreign Offices: UK.

JACK CHISHOLM FILM PRODUCTIONS

Suite 50, 99 Atlantic Avenue, Toronto, Ontario M6K 3J8, Canada
© +1 416 588 5200
Ⓕ +1 416 588 5324

Contacts: Peter Robinson
Subjects: Stock shots, historical archive, locations, time-lapse, current affairs, newsreels, natural history, industry, science.
🎞 16mm, 35mm; Beta/Beta SP, 1", Umatic, SVHS, some digital. NTSC.
Research: By staff only.
🕐 Mon–Fri 09:00 to 17:30
Procedure: Umatic or VHS viewing copies. 24 hours for access to masters.
Description: The stock footage library contains archive material dating from 1896 up to present day. Subjects cover major events around the world, wildlife, foreign locations, industry and science as well as quality shots of clouds, sunsets, time-lapse flowers, etc. The collection comprises of 10 000 hours of video footage and 4 million feet of film. They hold 35mm neg of across Canada scenics plus the Millenium television series. Computerized. Rate card available. English and Italian spoken.

KESSER STOCK LIBRARY

21 SW 15 Road, Miami, Florida 33129, USA
© +1 305 358 7900
Ⓕ +1 305 358 2209

Contacts: Emily Wilson, Charles Carrubba
Subjects: Stock shots, locations, space, agriculture, leisure, fishing, time-lapse, underwater photography, aviation.
Research: By staff.
🕐 Mon–Fri 09:00 to 17:00
Description: Range of archival and contemporary stock shot material. Subjects include world destinations, wildlife, sunsets, fireworks, horseracing, time-lapse and underwater photography, agriculture, space, fishing, etc. Partly computerized. Rate card and brochure available.

LARRY DORN ASSOCIATES / WORLD BACKGROUNDS

Suite 306, 5820 Wilshire Boulevard, Los Angeles CA 90036, USA
Ⓒ +1 213 935 6266
Ⓕ +1 213 935 9523

Contacts: Linda Dorn
Subjects: Stock shots, locations, Americana, aerial photography, underwater photography, aviation, transport, space.

▦ 35mm originals; 1″ with matching 3/4″ and VHS videotapes.
Research: By staff. Appointment to visit.
☉ Mon–Fri 09:00 to 17:00
Procedure: Viewing tapes compiled. Masters copied on selection.
Description: Period and contemporary stock footage. European establishing shots, worldwide locations, Americana, scenics, aerials, various airlines and international airports, period wars, space, etc. Computerized. Rate card available.
Foreign Offices: France, Italy, UK.

NOMAD FILMS INTERNATIONAL

Perth Business Centre, Stirling Street (P.O. Box 8240), Perth 6849, Australia
Ⓒ +61 9 3881177
Ⓕ +61 9 3811122

Contacts: Doug Stanley and Kate Faulkner
Subjects: Natural history, medicine, science, lifestyles, locations, environmental, China, Jewish history, underwater photography.

▦ 16mm; Beta/Beta SP, D2, 1″, Umatic. PAL and NTSC.
Research: By staff only.
☉ Mon–Fri 08:30 to 18:30
Procedure: VHS or Umatic PAL/NTSC viewing copies. 3 days for access to masters.
Description: Enormous range of productions covering wildlife, medical and scientific topics with worldwide documentary series on people and places. Titles include The Intruders, A Walk in the Sea and Crocodiles – the deadly survivors (natural history), Land of the Dragon (Bhutan), Dream Merchants of Asia (Taiwan, India, Japan, Hong Kong), Journey to Hainan (China's most southerly province), Breakthroughs (science, medicine and technology), Eye in the Sky (satellite technology), Triumph of the Nomads (Aborigines) to name a few. Glossy brochures available for productions. Partly computerized.

NORTHSTAR PRODUCTIONS

3003 "O" Street NW, Washington DC 20007, USA
Ⓒ +1 202 338 7337
Ⓕ +1 202 337 4387

Contacts: Don North
Subjects: War, locations, industry, leisure.
▦ Videotape.
Research: By both staff and outside researchers.
Appointment to visit.
🕔 7 days
Description: Footage of various international war zones
including Afghanistan (1987 combat), El Salvador (Guerilla
war 1983 to 1990), Nicaragua, Middle East (Beirut siege
1982), Gulf War and rebuilding of Kuwait, Vietnam (1967 to
1990), Sarajevo. Also footage from Hong Kong, Austria,
Prague, Washington DC, Estonia (Balkans independence
movement), Finland (modern and World War II) etc. Partly
computerized. Brochure available.

PARAMOUNT PICTURES FILM LIBRARY

Hal Wallis Building, Room 108, 5555 Melrose Avenue,
Hollywood CA 90038, USA
Ⓒ +1 213 956 5510
Ⓕ +1 213 956 1833

Contacts: Pat Harris
Subjects: Stock shots, aerial photography, transport,
aviation, locations, building, skylines, out-takes.
▦ 35mm.
Research: By staff only (no charge made). Appointment to
visit.
🕔 Mon-Fri 09:00 to 18:00
Procedure: Film transferred to video at clients cost. 4-5
days for access to masters
Description: Out-takes and unused footage from
Paramount's features and television series spanning over 50
years. Over 9000 contemporary scenes catalogued in the
past year. Subjects vary from aerials of cities and
countrysides, stationary and moving process for cars, planes
and trains, buildings of every type, scenery to aviation,
amusements and skylines. Material is exclusively 35mm
including 3 strip technicolor. Rate card available.

PAUL ZWICK PRODUCTIONS

P.O. Box 91134, Auckland Park 2006, South Africa
ⓒ +27 11 789 6390/1
ⓕ +27 11 789 6044

Contacts: Paul Zwick
Subjects: Natural history, locations.
▦ Beta/Beta SP. PAL.
Research: By staff. Visits by appointment.
☼ Mon-Fri 08:30 to 18:00
Procedure: Timecoded VHS tapes compiled. 3 hours for access to masters.
Description: Various wildlife scenes of southern African game reserves, extensive footage of Indian Ocean islands - Mauritius and Comores, also footage of major US cities - New York, Las Vegas, San Francisco, etc. Computerized. English, Afrikaans and Hungarian spoken.

ROBERT BOCKING PRODUCTIONS

75 Hucknall Road, Downsview, Ontario M3J IWI, Canada
ⓒ +1 416 631 9845

Contacts: Robert Bocking
Subjects: Natural history, locations.
▦ Videotape.
☼ Mon-Fri 09:00 to 17:00
Description: Nature footage and scenics from North America, Costa Rica to the Arctic, Atlantic to the Pacific. Partly computerized. Rate card and catalogue available.

SECOND LINE SEARCH

1926 Broadway, New York, NY 10023, USA
ⓒ +1 212 787 7500
ⓕ +1 212 787 7636

Contacts: Susan Luchars, George Bartko
Subjects: Locations, historical archive, sport, natural history, aerial photography, time-lapse, Americana, out-takes, industry, lifestyles.
▦ Variety of film and video formats.
Research: By staff.
☼ Mon-Fri 09:30 to 18:00
Procedure: Umatic viewing cassettes (NTSC or PAL). 2-3 days for access to masters.
Description: A variety of material including scenics, archival footage, sports, wildlife, news, aerials, international locations, Americana, oddities/bloopers, industry, technology, lifestyle and time-lapse. Computerized. French, Spanish, Portuguese, Italian and German spoken.

SOURCE STOCK FOOTAGE LIBRARY, THE

738 N. Constitution Drive, Tuscon, Arizona 85748, USA
ⓒ +1 602 298 4810
Ⓕ +1 602 290 8831

Contacts: John Willwater, Bill and Lynne Briggs
Subjects: Stock shots, natural history, industry, time-lapse, locations, mining.
Research: By staff.
🕓 Mon-Fri 08:00 to 17:00
Description: Scenics, time-lapse, clouds and suns, animals, petrochemical and mining industrial, US and international destinations, desert plants and animals, cowboys, Phoenix, Tuscson, Alaskan wilderness and animals. Computerized. Rate card and brochure available.

STOCK OPTIONS

P.O. Box 87622, Houghton 2041, South Africa
ⓒ +27 11 788 7248 / 880 1287
Ⓕ +27 11 788 9996

Contacts: Margi Sheard, Sandee Daniell
Subjects: Natural history, travelogues, locations, anthropology, aerial photography.
🎞 16mm, 35mm; Beta SP, 1", D1. PAL, some NTSC masters available.
Research: By both staff and outside researchers. Appointment to visit.
🕓 Mon-Fri 08:30 to 17:30 (contactable until 22:00 by telephone)
Procedure: Umatic/VHS for viewing. 2 hours for local access to masters.
Description: Stock Options have African wildlife material (16mm and Beta SP), African landscapes, seascapes including aerial footage (16mm and 35mm), ethnic tribes and customs and international travel footage (Beta SP). Computerized. Catalogue and rate card available.
Foreign Offices: Represented by Index Stock Shots in London, Energy Productions in Los Angeles and Film World Research in Sydney.

STOCK SHOTS

1085 Louise Avenue, San Jose, CA 95125, USA
ⓒ +1 408 971 1325
Ⓕ +1 408 723 3846

Contacts: Tom Mertens
Subjects: Transport, agriculture, locations, medicine, health.
20 000 feet of film; 500 hours of videotape.
Research: By staff.
Mon-Fri 10:00 to 16:00
Description: Silicon Valley, San Francisco aerials, rail transit, agriculture, Europe, Asian, Africa collection filmed 1945 to 1975. Also incorporates The Justin Byers Film Collection. Partly computerized. Rate card available.

STUART JEWELL PRODUCTIONS

2040 Garden Lane, Costa Mesa, CA 92627, USA
ⓒ +1 714 548 7234
Ⓕ +1 818 508 1293 (agents fax)

Contacts: Agent Energy Productions
Subjects: Documentaries, natural history, culture, locations, time-lapse, aerial photography, steam trains.
16mm, 35mm; Beta SP, D2 1", BVU. NTSC.
Description: Series of worldwide documentaries mostly natural history subjects - titles include Rolling to Guatemala, Following the Oregon Trail, Winter in Yellowstone, Teton and Mount. Rainer National Parks, The Great Aerial Odyssey, locations including Alaska, Hawaii, Borneo, Thailand, Africa, Egypt, India, Nepal plus steam trains in America, Canada, Australia and Guatemala. Partly computerized. NB: Represented by Energy Productions.
Foreign Offices: Contact local Energy Productions office.

TELECINE INTERNATIONAL PRODUCTIONS

P.O. Box 8426, Universal City, CA 91608, USA
℡ +1 818 889 8246
Ⓕ +1 818 889 5605

Contacts: Nick Archer
Subjects: Stock shots, locations, transport, aviation,
time-lapse, landscapes.
▦ 35mm.
Research: By both staff and outside researchers.
🕓 Mon-Fri 09:00 to 18:00
Procedure: Film/cassette viewing reels. Minimum royalty
due for masters.
Description: Worldwide establishing shots, cityscapes and
traffic from 1957 to present day, transportation, jets,
buildings, scenics, moons, sunrises, suns, time-lapse clouds.
Rate card and brochure available.

VIDEO TAPE LIBRARY

Suite 2, 1509 N. Crescent Heights Blvd, Los Angeles CA
90046, USA
℡ +1 213 656 4330
Ⓕ +1 213 656 8746

Contacts: Melody St. John, Peggy Shannon
Subjects: Stock shots, current affairs, newsreels, locations,
beauty, comedy, classic films, sport, leisure, environmental,
medicine, out-takes.
▦ 20% film; 80% video.
Research: By both staff and outside researchers.
🕓 Mon-Fri 09:00 to 17:00
Procedure: 24 hour turnaround for research, preview and
master footage.
Description: Enormous range of stock shot material ranging
from archival footage (1898) to current news topics. Over 2
million shots on virtually every subject including locations,
disasters, sports, medical, comedy, lifestyles, politics,
time-lapse, film and television classics, newsreels from 1929
to 1967. Computerized. Rate card and brochure available.

WPA FILM LIBRARY

5525 W. 159th Street, Oak Forest, IL 60452, USA
ⓒ +1 708 535 1540
Ⓕ +1 708 535 1541

Contacts: Michael Mertz
Subjects: Historical archive, newsreels, industry, Americana, music, transport, fashion, locations, natural history.
10 000 hours film; 2000 hours videotape.
Research: By both staff and outside researchers.
🕓 Mon- Fri 8:30 to 17:00
Description: Complete historical materials from 1896 to the present day. Specialities include newsreels, Americana from the 1940s and 50s, early rock and roll performances (Hullabaloo in 1964/5, The Music Scene in 1969/70), UFOs, automobiles, fashions, American Civil Rights, contemporary geographic materials, nature and wildlife, American industry collection from the 1940s to the present day. Also represent British Pathe News for North America only. Partly computerized. Rate card and brochure available.

Macro photography

ENERGY PRODUCTIONS' TIMESCAPE IMAGE LIBRARY

4th Floor, 12700 Ventura Boulevard, Studio City, CA 91604 USA
© +1 818 508 1444
Ⓕ + 1 818 508 1293

Contacts: Joan Sargent, Randy Gitsch
Subjects: Americana, sport, time-lapse, macro photography, natural history, locations, fashion, culture, landscapes, lifestyles, special effects.

▦ 16mm, 35mm, 70mm; most video formats.
Research: By staff. Visits by appointment.
☉ Mon-Fri 09.00 to 18.00
Procedure: Viewing tapes assembled. Masters copied after selection.
Description: Energy Productions hold the Timescape Image Library, a huge library of stock material encompassing sports, wildlife, landmarks, cities, seascapes, macro/micro photography, fashion, underwater, botany, computer imagery and daily life from around the world. Also available via this office is The Playboy Fashion Collection, Namco Computer Imagery, Warren Miller Films and Sports Library, Windham Hills Video and Film Library and Bob Landis Wildlife. Computerized. Rate card and brochure available. NB: Energy also have a New York office, Tel: (212) 686 4900, Fax: (212) 686 4998.Mon-Fri 09:00 to 18:00
Foreign Offices: France, Germany, Italy, Japan, Spain, Sweden, Turkey, Israel, UK, USA.

FILM & VIDEO STOCK SHOTS

Suite E, 10700 Ventura Boulevard, Studio City CA 91604, USA
Ⓒ +1 818 760 2098
Ⓕ +1 818 760 3294

Contacts: Stephanie Siebert, William Bolls
Subjects: Stock shots, current affairs, leisure, natural history, time-lapse, locations, macro photography, animation, culture, landscapes.

▦ Film; videotape.

Research: By staff. Appointment to visit.

☉ Mon- Fri 09:00 to 17:00

Description: Huge selection of both current and archival film and videotape original images. Subjects include news events, action sports, nature and wildlife, time-lapse cinematography, landscapes and cityscapes, microscopy, cartoons, lifestyles and travel footage. Next business day turnaround on master footage orders and competitive rates. Computerized. Brochure and rate card available.

Maritime

MYSTIC SEAPORT MUSEUM

Film & Video Archives, 75 Greenmanville Avenue, P.O. Box
6000, Mystic, CT 06355-0990, USA
© +1 203 572 5379
Ⓕ +1 203 572 5328

Contacts: Suki Williams
Subjects: Maritime, sailing.
▦ 16mm; videotape. NTSC.
Research: By staff preferably - space limited.
☉ Mon-Fri 09:00 to 17:00
Description: A collection of maritime images by both
professionals and amateurs. Material includes square riggers,
J boats, yachting, seafaring, ocean races, America's Cup
races, shipbuilding and restoration. Whaling footage from
1917, New England lighthouses, recreational boating and
other subjects of interest. The collection also includes many
international ports and islands. Partly computerized.
Catalogue of completed programmes available.

Medicine

BEYOND INFORMATION SERVICES

Beyond 2000, 34 Hotham Parade, Artarmon, NSW 2064, Australia
© +61 2 438 5155
Ⓕ +61 2 439 6549

Contacts: Lisa Savage, Annette Overton
Subjects: Medicine, science, environmental, landscapes. Beta/Beta SP, 1″, Umatic. PAL.
Research: By staff only.
🕓 Mon–Fri 09:00 to 17:30
Procedure: Viewing tapes assembled.
Description: An extensive collection of footage from internationally acclaimed science and technology series, Beyond 2000. Footage covers subjects shot worldwide and includes medical breakthroughs, laboratory work, people, robotics, Australiana, hi-tech gadgets, environment, international rural and city landscapes, wildlife, etc. Computerized. Rate card available. English and French spoken.

CANADIAN BROADCASTING CORPORATION (CBC)

Box 500, Station A, Toronto, Ontario M5W 1E1, Canada
© +1 416 205 7608
Ⓕ +1 416 205 6736

Contacts: Roy Harris
Subjects: Stock shots, natural history, locations, medicine, environmental
🕓 16mm; Beta/Beta SP, 1″, Umatic. NTSC.
Research: By staff only.
🕓 Mon–Fri 08:30 to 17:30
Procedure: Timecoded cassettes made to order. 2–3 days for access to masters.
Description: CBC's archive contains a wide range of programme material including natural history and environmental footage, medical research, cities of the world, history, etc. from Arctic life to ancient Yemini ruins. Computerized. Rate card available.

FABULOUS FOOTAGE

4th Floor, 19 Mercer Street, Toronto, Ontario M5V 1H2,
Canada
© +1 416 591 6955
Ⓕ +1 416 591 1666

Contacts: Steve Race, Patricia Harvey, Rhonda Olson, Julie
Kovacs
Subjects: Stock shots, locations, culture, industry, medicine,
military, music, environmental, leisure, transport, natural
history, space, trailers.
Film; video (all film mastered onto tape).
Research: By both staff and outside researchers.
Mon-Fri 09:00 to 21:00
Description: Complete contemporary film and videotape
library with a vast range of quality images. Subject headings
include agriculture, buildings, cities, countries, cultural
activities, industry and business, landmarks, landscapes,
medical, military, music, natural phenomena, news, period
recreations, professions, rain forests, recreation, space,
special effects, spectacles, sports, transportation,
underwater, water and wildlife. They also hold special
collections of Nazi propaganda footage, Russian history,
Russian space program, B-movies and trailers. Computerized.
Rate card and catalogue available. NB: This is the head
office, there is also an office in Vancouver, Canada Tel:
(604) 684 8484, Fax: (604) 681 3299.
Foreign Offices: Argentina, Australia, Brazil, Canada, Chile,
Germany, Indonesia, Japan, Malaysia, Philippines, Singapore,
Mexico, Spain, USA.

FILM BANK STOCK FOOTAGE FILM & VIDEO LIBRARY

425 South Victory Boulevard, Burbank, CA 91502, USA
ℂ +1 818 841 9176
Ⓕ +1 818 567 4235

Contacts: Paula Lumbard, Elizabeth Canelake
Subjects: News, space, special effects, science, sport, medicine, time-lapse, aerial photography, natural history, animation, locations, environmental.

16mm, 35mm; most video formats. NTSC masters.
Research: By staff only. Researchers occasionally visit for big projects.

Mon–Fri 09:00 to 17:00
Procedure: Umatics loaned or VHS assembled. 24 hours for access to masters.
Description: Diverse collection of broadcast quality film and video images aimed at supplying the full range of client productions. Most subjects are covered in the library, the latest new collections being world locations, children of the world, environmental images (destruction, scientific and beauty shots), History of Flight, more space and solar flares, aerials across the US, agriculture and animals. Partly computerized. Catalogue and rate card available.

NOMAD FILMS INTERNATIONAL

Perth Business Centre, Stirling Street (P.O. Box 8240), Perth 6849, Australia
ℂ +61 9 3881177
Ⓕ +61 9 3811122

Contacts: Doug Stanley and Kate Faulkner
Subjects: Natural history, medicine, science, lifestyles, locations, environmental, China, Jewish history, underwater photography.

16mm; Beta/Beta SP, D2, 1″, Umatic. PAL and NTSC.
Research: By staff only.

Mon–Fri 08:30 to 18:30
Procedure: VHS or Umatic PAL/NTSC viewing copies. 3 days for access to masters.
Description: Enormous range of productions covering wildlife, medical and scientific topics with worldwide documentary series on people and places. Titles include The Intruders, A Walk in the Sea and Crocodiles - the deadly survivors (natural history), Land of the Dragon (Bhutan), Dream Merchants of Asia (Taiwan, India, Japan, Hong Kong), Journey to Hainan (China's most southerly province), Breakthroughs (science, medicine and technology), Eye in the Sky (satellite technology), Triumph of the Nomads (Aborigines) to name a few. Glossy brochures available for productions. Partly computerized.

PLANET PICTURES

P.O. Box 65862, Los Angeles, CA 90065, USA
(C) +1 818 246 7700
(F) +1 818 240 8391

Contacts: Jenny Hayden
Subjects: Documentaries, medicine, health, educational films, natural history, time-lapse.
▦ Time-lapse on film; mainly video.
Research: By both staff and outside researchers.
Appointment to visit.
☉ Mon-Fri 09:00 to 18:00
Description: Over 400 hours of footage and completed documentaries on a variety of subjects - medicine and health, high technology, workplace, nature, timelapse, wildlife, adventure, arts and entertainment and people. Computerized. Brochure available.

PYRAMID FILM & VIDEO

2801 Colorado Avenue, Santa Monica, CA 90404, USA
(C) +1 310 828 7577
(F) +1 310 453 9083

Contacts: Arthur C. Passante
Subjects: Documentaries, natural history, medicine, health, sport, arts, entertainment.
Research: By both staff and outside researchers.
Appointment to visit.
☉ Mon-Fri 08:00 to 17:00
Procedure: VHS or 16mm for viewing. 1 week average for access to masters.
Description: Over 500 titles of speciality short films covering nature, medicine, health, sports/action, documentary, history, art, media studies and entertainment. Catalogue and rate card available.
Foreign Offices: 80 worldwide distributors but all stock footage licensing is handled by this office.

STOCK SHOTS

1085 Louise Avenue, San Jose, CA 95125, USA
© +1 408 971 1325
Ⓕ +1 408 723 3846

Contacts: Tom Mertens
Subjects: Transport, agriculture, locations, medicine, health.
20 000 feet of film; 500 hours of videotape.
Research: By staff.
⊙ Mon–Fri 10:00 to 16:00
Description: Silicon Valley, San Francisco aerials, rail transit, agriculture, Europe, Asian, Africa collection filmed 1945 to 1975. Also incorporates The Justin Byers Film Collection. Partly computerized. Rate card available.

VIDEO TAPE LIBRARY

Suite 2, 1509 N. Crescent Heights Blvd, Los Angeles CA 90046, USA
© +1 213 656 4330
Ⓕ +1 213 656 8746

Contacts: Melody St. John, Peggy Shannon
Subjects: Stock shots, current affairs, newsreels, locations, beauty, comedy, classic films, sport, leisure, environmental, medicine, out-takes.
20% film; 80% video.
Research: By both staff and outside researchers.
⊙ Mon–Fri 09:00 to 17:00
Procedure: 24 hour turnaround for research, preview and master footage.
Description: Enormous range of stock shot material ranging from archival footage (1898) to current news topics. Over 2 million shots on virtually every subject including locations, disasters, sports, medical, comedy, lifestyles, politics, time-lapse, film and television classics, newsreels from 1929 to 1967. Computerized. Rate card and brochure available.

WGBH FILM & VIDEO RESOURCE CENTER

125 Wester Avenue, Boston, MA 02134, USA
© +1 617 492 3079
Ⓕ +1 617 783 4243
710 330 6887

Contacts: Vladimir Stefanovic, Patricia Barraza
Subjects: Documentaries, natural history, science, medicine, animation, aviation.
16mm, 35mm; Beta/Beta SP, D2, 1″, Umatic. NTSC.
Research: By staff only.
Mon-Fri 09:00 to 17:00
Procedure: Viewing on VHS or Umatic as requested. 3 days for access to masters.
Description: WGBH is one of the largest documentary producing stations in the US Public Broadcasting System, producing over 30% of prime time PBS programmes. Having been in existence since 1955 the extensive library holds material covering subjects such as nature, science, scenics, animation, wildlife, high tech, health/surgery and flight. The majority of copyright is held by WGBH. Partly computerized. Catalogue and rate card available. English, Spanish and Macedonian spoken.

WILLIAM G. BEAL

512 Franklin Avenue, Pittsburgh, PA 15221, USA
© +1 412 243 7020
Ⓕ +1 412 243 4520

Contacts: William G. Beal
Subjects: Documentaries, educational films, industry, medicine, sailing.
80% film; 20% videotape.
Research: By staff. Appointment to visit.
Mon-Fri 09:00 to 17:00
Description: Footage from productions spanning the last 40 years. Productions made for clients in various industries including steel, glass, aluminum, ceramics, electronics, foundries, oil and gas and plastics. Documentaries made for hospitals, museums, colleges, universities and community organizations of all types. Special collection of tropical sailing subjects filmed in the Bahamas and Caribbean.

Military

CAMEO FILM LIBRARY

10620 Burbank Blvd, N. Hollywood, CA 91607, USA
Ⓒ +1 818 980 8700
Ⓕ +1 818 980 7113

Contacts: Marilyn Chielens, Steven Vrabel
Subjects: Stock shots, locations, aerial photography, aviation, military.
🎞 35mm.
Research: By staff only.
🕐 Mon-Fri 08:30 to 17:30
Description: A wide variety of stock shots including worldwide establishing shots, military aircraft, period and contemporary military, aerial footage, sunrises and sunsets, etc. Rate card available.

FABULOUS FOOTAGE

4th Floor, 19 Mercer Street, Toronto, Ontario M5V 1H2, Canada
Ⓒ +1 416 591 6955
Ⓕ +1 416 591 1666

Contacts: Steve Race, Patricia Harvey, Rhonda Olson, Julie Kovacs
Subjects: Stock shots, locations, culture, industry, medicine, military, music, environmental, leisure, transport, natural history, space, trailers.
🎞 Film; video (all film mastered onto tape).
Research: By both staff and outside researchers.
🕐 Mon-Fri 09:00 to 21:00
Description: Complete contemporary film and videotape library with a vast range of quality images. Subject headings include agriculture, buildings, cities, countries, cultural activities, industry and business, landmarks, landscapes, medical, military, music, natural phenomena, news, period recreations, professions, rain forests, recreation, space, special effects, spectacles, sports, transportation, underwater, water and wildlife. They also hold special collections of Nazi propaganda footage, Russian history, Russian space program, B-movies and trailers. Computerized. Rate card and catalogue available. NB: This is the head office, there is also an office in Vancouver, Canada Tel: (604) 684 8484, Fax: (604) 681 3299.
Foreign Offices: Argentina, Australia, Brazil, Canada, Chile, Germany, Indonesia, Japan, Malaysia, Philippines, Singapore, Mexico, Spain, USA.

Music

A.R.I.Q. FOOTAGE

One Main Street, East Hampton, New York 11964, USA
ℂ +1 516 329 9200
Ⓕ +1 516 329 9260

Contacts: Joe Lauro, Mart Heideman
Subjects: Historical archive, classic films, comedy, music, newsreels, industry, space.

▦ Various film and video formats. All line standards available.
Research: By staff. Visits by appointment.

🕑 Mon–Fri 09:00 to 17:30
Procedure: Viewing material on VHS and Umatic. 24 hours for access to masters.
Description: Footage covers 1895 to 1990 with a very strong historical archive. Universal newsreel (1929 to 1967), musical performance footage including Jazz, Blues, Country, Rock and Roll, Pop from 1910 to 1990, silent films, industrial footage, space program, life styles and a range of general subject. Computerized. Rate card available.

FABULOUS FOOTAGE

4th Floor, 19 Mercer Street, Toronto, Ontario M5V 1H2,
Canada
© +1 416 591 6955
Ⓕ +1 416 591 1666

Contacts: Steve Race, Patricia Harvey, Rhonda Olson, Julie
Kovacs
Subjects: Stock shots, locations, culture, industry, medicine,
military, music, environmental, leisure, transport, natural
history, space, trailers.
Film; video (all film mastered onto tape).
Research: By both staff and outside researchers.
☼ Mon-Fri 09:00 to 21:00
Description: Complete contemporary film and videotape
library with a vast range of quality images. Subject headings
include agriculture, buildings, cities, countries, cultural
activities, industry and business, landmarks, landscapes,
medical, military, music, natural phenomena, news, period
recreations, professions, rain forests, recreation, space,
special effects, spectacles, sports, transportation,
underwater, water and wildlife. They also hold special
collections of Nazi propaganda footage, Russian history,
Russian space program, B-movies and trailers. Computerized.
Rate card and catalogue available. NB: This is the head
office, there is also an office in Vancouver, Canada Tel:
(604) 684 8484, Fax: (604) 681 3299.
Foreign Offices: Argentina, Australia, Brazil, Canada, Chile,
Germany, Indonesia, Japan, Malaysia, Philippines, Singapore,
Mexico, Spain, USA.

HOLLYWOOD HOUSE VIDEO ARCHIVES / HOME ENTERTAINMENT HOLDINGS

Box 555, Bondi Beach, NSW 2026, Australia
ⓒ +61 2 365 1055
ⓕ +61 2 365 1577

Contacts: Joe Shellim
Subjects: Classic films, documentaries, music, space, film industry, animation, war, personalities, circus, natural history.
▦ Film; Beta, 1", BVU, Umatic.
Research: By staff.
◷ Sun-Fri 10:00 to 19:00
Procedure: VHS viewing tape. Access to masters dependent on workload.
Description: Collection includes classic nostalgia movies complimented with interviews and rehearsals, behind-the-scenes, lost films, etc. Interviews with movie stars, candid films, footage of world leaders, space (NASA), music clips, nature and circus, cartoons, war and documentaries. Partly computerized. Rate card and catalogue available.

INTERNATIONAL MEDIA RESOURCE EXCHANGE

124 Washington Place, New York, NY 10014, USA
ⓒ +1 212 463 0108
ⓕ +1 212 243 3805

Contacts: Karen Ranucci
Subjects: Latin America, documentaries, animation, music.
▦ Most video formats. NTSC.
Research: By both staff and outside researchers. Appointment to visit.
◷ Mon-Fri 10:00 to 17:00
Procedure: Viewing on Umatic, VHS, Betamax. 2 weeks for access to masters, can rush.
Description: More than 500 films and videos of all genres made by Latin Americans including short fiction, features, documentaries, video art animations and music videos. Computerized. English and Spanish spoken.

MAURITIUS BROADCASTING CORPORATION

1 Louis Pasteur Street, Forest Side, Mauritius
℃ +230 675001/2/3 6743743
Ⓕ +230 6757332
⚹ 4230 MAUBROD IW

Contacts: Anne Marie Ginette Fabre
Subjects: National Archives, current affairs, religion, documentaries, childrens, music, personalities, sport.
16mm, 35mm; Beta/Beta SP, BVU, Umatic. PAL and SECAM.
Research: By staff. Outside researchers by appointment.
🕐 7 days 08:30 to 17:00
Procedure: Viewing on 16mm and video. 2 hours for access to masters.
Description: A wide range of programme material covering political, international and local events, religion, documentaries, television for children and teenagers, musicals, interviews and sports. English and French spoken.

M.C. STUART & ASSOCIATES (MSCAA)

88 Highett Street, Richmond, Victoria 3121, Australia
℃ +61 3 429 8666
Ⓕ +61 3 429 1839

Contacts: Max Stuart, Paul Stuart
Subjects: Natural history, leisure, sport, music, culture, documentaries, animation, childrens, feature films, entertainment.
🕐 Mon-Fri 07:00 to 19:00
Description: MSCAA represent some 40 Australian producers syndicating their programmes to many markets. The types of programmes handled include documentaries, children's programmes, cartoons, feature films, light entertainment, music (modern and classical), the Arts, Australian rules football and leisure sports. Computerized. Rate card and catalogue available. Italian and French spoken.
Foreign Offices: UK, France, Spain, Austria, Norway, Italy, Germany, Greece, Malaysia, Hong Kong, Japan, Canada, USA, Singapore, Sri Lanka, Turkey, Jordan, Thailand.

TIMES TELEVISION LIBRARY

The Time of India Building, 7 Bahadur Shah Zafar Marg, New
Dehli 110 002, India
℡ +91 11 3722094/3351606/3352087
℻ +91 11 3715532/3715836
✒ 031-61337/38 INDIA IN

Contacts: Mr. Sanjay Sethi
Subjects: Drama, documentaries, industry, personalities,
cookery, music, fashion, sport, science, environmental,
culture.
▥ Most video formats. PAL.
Research: By both staff and outside researchers.
🕐 6 days, 10:00 to 17:00
Procedure: Viewing on VHS. 1-2 hours for access to BVU
and Beta masters.
Description: Times Television was formed in 1986 and has
produced and marketed a large range of programmes
covering subjects relating to India including social issues,
economy, business and industry, film industry awards,
fashion, personalities, cuisine of Eastern and Western India,
beauty contests, sport, science and the environment. They
also hold various drama serials plus a few pop concerts
including Bryan Adams and Jethro Tull. Partly computerized.
English and Hindi spoken.
Foreign Offices: UK.

WPA FILM LIBRARY

5525 W. 159th Street, Oak Forest, IL 60452, USA
℡ +1 708 535 1540
℻ +1 708 535 1541

Contacts: Michael Mertz
Subjects: Historical archive, newsreels, industry, Americana,
music, transport, fashion, locations, natural history.
▥ 10 000 hours film; 2000 hours videotape.
Research: By both staff and outside researchers.
🕐 Mon-Fri 8:30 to 17:00
Description: Complete historical materials from 1896 to the
present day. Specialities include newsreels, Americana from
the 1940s and 50s, early rock and roll performances
(Hullabaloo in 1964/5, The Music Scene in 1969/70), UFOs,
automobiles, fashions, American Civil Rights, contemporary
geographic materials, nature and wildlife, American industry
collection from the 1940s to the present day. Also represent
British Pathe News for North America only. Partly
computerized. Rate card and brochure available.

ZAMBIA NATIONAL BROADCASTING CORPORATION

Library Services, P.O. Box 50015, Lusaka, Zambia
© +260 1 252793
ZA 41221

Contacts: J.R. Chanda
Subjects: Current affairs, culture, music, drama, sport. Film; videotape.
Research: By both staff and outside researchers. Requests in writing.
Mon-Fri 08:00 to 17:30, Sat-Sun 08:00 to 13:00
Description: The political development of Zambia, economic and business issues affecting the Zambian economy plus traditional music, dance and locations. Drama from Zambia, sport, etc. Also represent URTNA in Africa. Computerized.

Natural history

ACTION SPORTS ADVENTURE (ASA)

1926 Broadway, New York, NY 10023, USA
ⓒ +1 212 721 2800
Ⓕ +1 212 721 0191

Contacts: Rob Pavlin, Jill Schiffman
Subjects: Sport, Olympics, historical archive, leisure, natural history.
▦ Various film and video formats/line standards available.
Research: By staff.
🕐 Mon-Fri 09:30 to 18:30
Procedure: Time-coded VHS and 3/4" cassettes. 24 hours for access to masters.
Description: The library holds important historical collections of footage from the world's best known sports cinematographers and exclusively represents various sports leagues, teams and governing bodies. ASA are the official filmmakers and exclusive stock footage representatives for the US Soccer Federation. All major sports such as basketball, football, soccer, hockey, as well as Olympic disciplines, recreational and aesthetic sports are covered together with wildlife and nature footage. Computerized. Demo reel and promotional material available. English and Spanish spoken.

AL GIDDINGS – IMAGES UNLIMITED

8001 Capwell Drive, Oakland, CA 94621, USA
ⓒ +1 510 562 8000
Ⓕ +1 510 562 8001

Contacts: Terry Thompson
Subjects: Natural history, underwater photography, environmental.
▦ 16mm, 35mm; most video formats. NTSC.
Research: By staff. Appointment to visit.
🕐 Mon-Fri 09:00 to 17:00
Procedure: Umatic/VHS tapes compiled or view at studio. 1-3 days for access to masters.
Description: Library of material made up from Al Giddings undersea and nature adventure television specials. Images range in diversity from whales and sharks to minute creatures, and from polar regions to tropical islands. Scenics, wildlife, nature and marine life from ocean floor to mountain top, tropics, desert, north and south poles, kelp forests, redwood forests, rainforest, storms, moons, divers, shipwrecks, etc. New footage from an expedition to the shipwrecked Titanic. Computerized. Brochure available.

AUSTRALIAN BROADCASTING CORPORATION (ABC)

ABC TV Library Sales, GPO Box 9994, Sydney, NSW 2000, Australia
ℂ +61 2 950 3269 / 3284
Ⓕ +61 2 950 3277

Contacts: Cyrus Irani, Richard Carter
Subjects: Current affairs, stock shots, natural history, sport, lifestyles, locations.
▦ 16mm; Beta/Beta SP, 1", BVU, Umatic.
Research: By staff only. Clients may view in the office.
☉ Mon–Fri 09:00 to 17:30
Procedure: VHS or Umatic viewing tapes supplied. 24 hours for access to masters.
Description: The ABC is the major government broadcaster holding Australian and international news and current affairs footage dating from 1960. They also hold a large stock footage library covering over 4000 subjects including a natural history collection, sport, lifestyle and location material. ABC are also agents for the Reuters/Visnews and Qantas libraries. Computerized. Rate card available. NB: ABC also have offices in Adelaide, Brisbane, Darwin, Melbourne, Perth and Hobart (Tasmania).

CAMERAPIX

P.O. Box 45048, Nairobi, Kenya
ℂ +254 2 223511 / 334398
Ⓕ +254 2 217244
✎ 22576

Contacts: Mohamed Amin, Salim Amin
Subjects: Current affairs, natural history, culture.
▦ Videotape.
Research: By staff.
☉ Mon–Fri 08:00 to 17:00
Description: News, current affairs, wildlife and culture of Africa contained on approximately 6000 master videotapes.

CANADIAN BROADCASTING CORPORATION (CBC)

Box 500, Station A, Toronto, Ontario M5W 1E1, Canada
© +1 416 205 7608
Ⓕ +1 416 205 6736

Contacts: Roy Harris
Subjects: Stock shots, natural history, locations, medicine, environmental
🎞 16mm; Beta/Beta SP, 1″, Umatic. NTSC.
Research: By staff only.
🕓 Mon-Fri 08:30 to 17:30
Procedure: Timecoded cassettes made to order. 2-3 days for access to masters.
Description: CBC's archive contains a wide range of programme material including natural history and environmental footage, medical research, cities of the world, history, etc. from Arctic life to ancient Yemini ruins. Computerized. Rate card available.

CENTRAL COAST MEDIA HOLDINGS (CCM GROUP)

1st Floor, 56 The Entrance Road, The Entrance, NSW 2261, Australia
© +61 43 331122
Ⓕ +61 43 341017

Contacts: Mark and Michelle Falzon
Subjects: Industry, natural history, aerial photography, lifestyles, landscapes.
🎞 16mm; Beta. PAL.
Research: By staff. Appointment to visit.
🕓 Mon-Fri 08:00 to 18:00
Procedure: Timecoded VHS available. Masters as reasonably required.
Description: Comprehensive range of Australian floral and landscape material on 16mm and Betacam plus a range of corporate industrial imagery. The collection specializes in central coast and New South Wales footage with aerial and lifestyle, etc. shots. Rate card and catalogue available.

CINEMA NETWORK (CINENET)

Suite 111, 2235 First Street, Simi Valley CA 93065, USA
© +1 805 527 0093
Ⓕ +1 805 527 0305

Contacts: Richard Spruiell, Jim Jarrard
Subjects: Stock shots, natural history, locations, sport, time-lapse, underwater photography.
▦ 35mm, 16mm; NTSC videotape.
Research: By staff. Appointment to visit.
Procedure: Viewing tapes compiled. Masters copied after payment received.
Description: Stock footage library with very comprehensive A-Z listing of subjects - almost every topic you can think of is covered in their brochure, they also undertake custom filming. Computerized on Cinemind software. Rate card and brochure available.

COE FILM ASSOCIATES

65 East 96th Street, New York, NY 10128, USA
© +1 212 831 5355
Ⓕ +1 212 996 6728

Contacts: Arlene Gross
Subjects: Natural history, locations, Americana, documentaries, drama.
▦ 16mm; Beta/Beta SP, 1″, BVU, Umatic. PAL and NTSC.
Research: By staff only.
☺ Mon-Fri 09:30 to 17:30
Procedure: Umatic/VHS NTSC or PAL loaned. 24 hours for access to masters.
Description: Footage derives from documentaries and dramas produced by Coe Film Associates and covers nature, wildlife, destinations, Americana and New York City. Computerized. English, Spanish and French spoken.

ENERGY PRODUCTIONS' TIMESCAPE IMAGE LIBRARY

4th Floor, 12700 Ventura Boulevard, Studio City, CA 91604 USA
ⓒ +1 818 508 1444
ⓕ +1 818 508 1293

Contacts: Joan Sargent, Randy Gitsch
Subjects: Americana, sport, time-lapse, macro photography, natural history, locations, fashion, culture, landscapes, lifestyles, special effects.
▥ 16mm, 35mm, 70mm; most video formats.
Research: By staff. Visits by appointment.
☺ Mon-Fri 09.00 to 18.00
Procedure: Viewing tapes assembled. Masters copied after selection.
Description: Energy Productions hold the Timescape Image Library, a huge library of stock material encompassing sports, wildlife, landmarks, cities, seascapes, macro/micro photography, fashion, underwater, botany, computer imagery and daily life from around the world. Also available via this office is The Playboy Fashion Collection, Namco Computer Imagery, Warren Miller Films and Sports Library, Windham Hills Video and Film Library and Bob Landis Wildlife. Computerized. Rate card and brochure available. NB: Energy also have a New York office, Tel: (212) 686 4900, Fax: (212) 686 4998.Mon-Fri 09:00 to 18:00
Foreign Offices: France, Germany, Italy, Japan, Spain, Sweden, Turkey, Israel, UK, USA.

FABULOUS FOOTAGE

4th Floor, 19 Mercer Street, Toronto, Ontario M5V 1H2,
Canada
© +1 416 591 6955
Ⓕ +1 416 591 1666

Contacts: Steve Race, Patricia Harvey, Rhonda Olson, Julie
Kovacs
Subjects: Stock shots, locations, culture, industry, medicine,
military, music, environmental, leisure, transport, natural
history, space, trailers.
▦ Film; video (all film mastered onto tape).
Research: By both staff and outside researchers.
☉ Mon- Fri 09:00 to 21:00
Description: Complete contemporary film and videotape
library with a vast range of quality images. Subject headings
include agriculture, buildings, cities, countries, cultural
activities, industry and business, landmarks, landscapes,
medical, military, music, natural phenomena, news, period
recreations, professions, rain forests, recreation, space,
special effects, spectacles, sports, transportation,
underwater, water and wildlife. They also hold special
collections of Nazi propaganda footage, Russian history,
Russian space program, B-movies and trailers. Computerized.
Rate card and catalogue available. NB: This is the head
office, there is also an office in Vancouver, Canada Tel:
(604) 684 8484, Fax: (604) 681 3299.
Foreign Offices: Argentina, Australia, Brazil, Canada, Chile,
Germany, Indonesia, Japan, Malaysia, Philippines, Singapore,
Mexico, Spain, USA.

FILM & VIDEO STOCK SHOTS

Suite E, 10700 Ventura Boulevard, Studio City CA 91604,
USA
© +1 818 760 2098
Ⓕ +1 818 760 3294

Contacts: Stephanie Siebert, William Bolls
Subjects: Stock shots, current affairs, leisure, natural history,
time-lapse, locations, macro photography, animation, culture,
landscapes.
▦ Film; videotape.
Research: By staff. Appointment to visit.
🕘 Mon-Fri 09:00 to 17:00
Description: Huge selection of both current and archival film
and videotape original images. Subjects include news events,
action sports, nature and wildlife, time-lapse cinematography,
landscapes and cityscapes, microscopy, cartoons, lifestyles
and travel footage. Next business day turnaround on master
footage orders and competitive rates. Computerized.
Brochure and rate card available.

FILM BANK STOCK FOOTAGE FILM & VIDEO LIBRARY

425 South Victory Boulevard, Burbank, CA 91502, USA
© +1 818 841 9176
Ⓕ +1 818 567 4235

Contacts: Paula Lumbard, Elizabeth Canelake
Subjects: News, space, special effects, science, sport,
medicine, time-lapse, aerial photography, natural history,
animation, locations, environmental.
▦ 16mm, 35mm; most video formats. NTSC masters.
Research: By staff only. Researchers occasionally visit for big
projects.
🕘 Mon-Fri 09:00 to 17:00
Procedure: Umatics loaned or VHS assembled. 24 hours for
access to masters.
Description: Diverse collection of broadcast quality film and
video images aimed at supplying the full range of client
productions. Most subjects are covered in the library, the
latest new collections being world locations, children of the
world, environmental images (destruction, scientific and
beauty shots), History of Flight, more space and solar flares,
aerials across the US, agriculture and animals. Partly
computerized. Catalogue and rate card available.

FILM WORLD

2 Whiting Street, P.O. Box 313, Artarmon, NSW 2064,
Australia
© +61 2 438 1888
Ⓕ +61 2 439 8541

Contacts: Naomi Saville
Subjects: Newsreels, locations, natural history, lifestyles,
tourism, travelogues.
Film; Beta/Beta SP, 1", D1. PAL and NTSC.
Research: By both staff and outside researchers.
Appointment to visit.
Mon- Fri 08:30 to 17:30
Procedure: VHS or Umatic viewing cassettes. 24 hours for
access to masters.
Description: Over 3000 hours of footage covering archival
news material, contemporary landscapes, wildlife and
lifestyles. Film World are exclusive agents for the Cinesound
and Movietone newsreel collection, Australian Tourist
Commission, Queensland Tourist & Travel Corporation,
Canadian company Fabulous Footage and many more.
Computerized. Subject headings list and rate card available.

FILMSEARCH AUSTRALASIA

P.O. Box 46, Lindfield, NSW 2070, Australia
© +61 2 4162633
Ⓕ +61 2 4162554

Contacts: Chris Rowell
Subjects: Natural history, underwater photography, Asia.
16mm, 35mm; Beta SP, D2, 1". PAL.
Research: By both staff and outside researchers.
Appointment to visit.
Mon- Fri 09:00 to 17:00
Procedure: Timecoded PAL cassettes for viewing. 3 days for
access to masters.
Description: Australian flora and fauna, underwater footage,
some contemporary material and Asian footage.
Computerized. Rate card available.

FRONT LINE

Suite 3 Senyo Building, 5th Floor, 3-1-9 Nakameguro,
Meguro-ku, Toyko 153, Japan
℡ +81 3 3760 6271
℻ +81 3 3760 6012

Contacts: Seiichi Sugiura
Subjects: Stock shots, aviation, locations, natural history,
industry, space, time-lapse, transport, environmental.
🕐 Mon-Fri 10:00 to 18:00
Procedure: Viewing tapes loaned. Masters copied after
selection.
Description: Agents for UK company Index Stock Shots, USA
company Opus Global and Canadian company Fabulous
Footage in Japan.

HOLLYWOOD HOUSE VIDEO ARCHIVES / HOME
ENTERTAINMENT HOLDINGS

Box 555, Bondi Beach, NSW 2026, Australia
℡ +61 2 365 1055
℻ +61 2 365 1577

Contacts: Joe Shellim
Subjects: Classic films, documentaries, music, space, film
industry, animation, war, personalities, circus, natural
history.
🎞 Film; Beta, 1″, BVU, Umatic.
Research: By staff.
🕐 Sun-Fri 10:00 to 19:00
Procedure: VHS viewing tape. Access to masters dependent
on workload.
Description: Collection includes classic nostalgia movies
complimented with interviews and rehearsals,
behind-the-scenes, lost films, etc. Interviews with movie
stars, candid films, footage of world leaders, space (NASA),
music clips, nature and circus, cartoons, war and
documentaries. Partly computerized. Rate card and catalogue
available.

IMAGE BANK / FILM DIVISION

4th Floor, 111 Fifth Avenue, New York NY 10003, USA
ⓒ +1 212 529 6700
Ⓕ +1 212 529 8889

Contacts: Brian Mitchell
Subjects: Stock shots, aerial photography, time-lapse, lifestyles, natural history, locations, sport.
All film and video formats and line standards held.
Research: By both staff and outside researchers. Appointment to visit.
🕐 Mon-Fri 09:00 to 17:00
Procedure: 3/4"/VHS (any line standard) for viewing. 24 hours for access to masters.
Description: Vast collection of stock material, contemporary and archival, acquired from Turner Broadcasting, Ocean Images, I.R.E., Pigeon Productions, MacGillivray Freeman Films, Dentsu Prox., McDonnell Douglas, Nature Conservancy, etc. Offices worldwide and major cities of North America - Chicago, Detroit, Mexico, Minneapolis, Atlanta, Dallas and Los Angeles. Computerized. English, French, Spanish, Italian, German and Greek spoken in the NEW YORK HEADQUARTERS.
Foreign Offices: Argentina, Brazil, Chile, Colombia, Australia, Canada, Hong Kong, Indonesia, Korea, Japan, Malaysia, Philippines, Singapore, Taiwan, Thailand, South Africa, UK, USA.

IMAGES OF THE EAST

19B Jalan 20/14, Petaling Jaya Selangor 46300, Malaysia
ⓒ +60 03 776 7199
Ⓕ +60 03 776 4560

Contacts: Theresa Khoo
Subjects: Stock shots, aviation, locations, natural history, industry, space, time-lapse, transport, environmental.
Beta SP, 1", Umatic. PAL.
Research: By staff. Visits by appointment.
🕐 Mon-Fri 08:30 to 17:45
Procedure: Viewing tapes loaned. Masters copied after selection, 3-4 days for access.
Description: Agents for UK company Index Stock Shots and German company Modern Video Library in Malaysia and Singapore. The library holds an A-Z of subject categories including landscape, destination and sports footage from Malaysia. Partly computerized. Rate card available. English spoken.

JACK CHISHOLM FILM PRODUCTIONS

Suite 50, 99 Atlantic Avenue, Toronto, Ontario M6K 3J8,
Canada
℄ +1 416 588 5200
℻ +1 416 588 5324

Contacts: Peter Robinson
Subjects: Stock shots, historical archive, locations,
time-lapse, current affairs, newsreels, natural history,
industry, science.
▦ 16mm, 35mm; Beta/Beta SP, 1", Umatic, SVHS, some
digital. NTSC.
Research: By staff only.
🕐 Mon-Fri 09:00 to 17:30
Procedure: Umatic or VHS viewing copies. 24 hours for
access to masters.
Description: The stock footage library contains archive
material dating from 1896 up to present day. Subjects cover
major events around the world, wildlife, foreign locations,
industry and science as well as quality shots of clouds,
sunsets, time-lapse flowers, etc. The collection comprises of
10 000 hours of video footage and 4 million feet of film.
They hold 35mm neg of across Canada scenics plus the
Millenium television series. Computerized. Rate card
available. English and Italian spoken.

M.C. STUART & ASSOCIATES (MSCAA)

88 Highett Street, Richmond, Victoria 3121, Australia
℄ +61 3 429 8666
℻ +61 3 429 1839

Contacts: Max Stuart, Paul Stuart
Subjects: Natural history, leisure, sport, music, culture,
documentaries, animation, childrens, feature films,
entertainment.
🕐 Mon-Fri 07:00 to 19:00
Description: MSCAA represent some 40 Australian producers
syndicating their programmes to many markets. The types of
programmes handled include documentaries, children's
programmes, cartoons, feature films, light entertainment,
music (modern and classical), the Arts, Australian rules
football and leisure sports. Computerized. Rate card and
catalogue available. Italian and French spoken.
Foreign Offices: UK, France, Spain, Austria, Norway, Italy,
Germany, Greece, Malaysia, Hong Kong, Japan, Canada,
USA, Singapore, Sri Lanka, Turkey, Jordan, Thailand.

NATURAL SYMPHONIES

4 George Street, Redfern, NSW 2016, Australia
ⓒ +61 2 318 1577 / 46 55 1800
ⓕ +61 2 318 1424 / 46 55 9434

Contacts: Neil O'Hare
Subjects: Underwater photography, natural history, culture, environmental.
🎞 Beta SP, D2, 1″. PAL.
Research: By staff mainly. Visits by appointment.
🕐 Mon-Fri 09:00 to 17:00 (often contactable outside these times)
Procedure: Timecoded VHS or other formats available. 24 hours for access to masters.
Description: Shot in Australia and The South Pacific, the library ranges from aerial sequences to microscopic subjects including flora, fauna, marine life, tourist and research activities. All material is recorded on Betacam SP using BTS LDK 90 and 91 CCD cameras.. Many of the sequences available are of animals, birds and locations that are extremely difficult to access and film owing to seasonal variations and remoteness. Material includes coral reefs, coral spawning, whales, dolphins and sea lions, Australian birds, animals, insects and reptiles, Australian environments and Aboriginal and islander culture. Computerized with database list on disk accessible by most word processors. Summary print outs and rate card available.

NBC NEWS ARCHIVES

30 Rockefeller Plaza, Room 902, New York, NY 10112, USA
ⓒ +1 212 664 3797
ⓕ +1 212 957 8917

Contacts: Nancy Cole, Yuien Chin
Subjects: Current affairs, culture, religion, environmental, natural history, personalities, social history.
🎞 16mm, 35mm; most video formats. NTSC.
Research: By both staff and outside researchers. Appointment to visit.
🕐 Mon-Fri 09:00 to 18:00
Procedure: Time-coded viewing material. Fast turnaround service.
Description: Over four decades of news events worldwide. The library covers social commentary, interviews, cultural, historical and religious programming, the environment, wildlife and stock shots for almost any subject imaginable. Computerized. Rate card available. Chinese and Spanish spoken.

NEW YORK ZOOLOGICAL SOCIETY

The Wildlife Conservation Society Office of Media Studies,
185th Street and Southern Blvd, Bronx, NY 10460, USA
ⓒ +1 718 220 5134
Ⓕ +1 718 220 7114

Contacts: Thomas Veltre
Subjects: Natural history, environmental, biology.
▦ 16mm, 35mm; most video formats. NTSC.
Research: Limited research by staff - $150 minimum for
VHS. Appointments.
🕓 Mon–Fri 10:00 to 17:00
Procedure: VHS tapes compiled dependent on workload. 2–3
days for access to masters.
Description: The collection is comprised of film shot at the
Bronx Zoo, NY aquarium and other NYZS facilities as well as
film from research expeditions sponsored by the society over
the last 80 years. Good close-ups of many rare species in
naturalistic settings, historical material on field research and
much good wildlife from East Africa in 1960s and 1970s.

NEW ZEALAND TELEVISION ARCHIVE

Television New Zealand, P.O. Box 3819, Auckland, New
Zealand
ⓒ +64 9 375 0942
Ⓕ +64 9 375 0872

Contacts: Jane Hiscotte, Alan Ferris
Subjects: Current affairs, newsreels, documentaries, natural
history, leisure, stock shots.
▦ Film; videotape.
Research: By staff.
🕓 Mon–Fri 08:00 to 18:00
Procedure: Print outs available for each request.
Description: News, current affairs, stock shots and general
programming from New Zealand Television dating from 1960.
Newsreels and documentaries purchased from the National
Film Unit (1940 to 1965). The archive also specialize in
natural history footage, spectacular scenery and recreational
sports action. 80% computerized.

NOMAD FILMS INTERNATIONAL

Perth Business Centre, Stirling Street (P.O. Box 8240), Perth 6849, Australia
ⓒ +61 9 3881177
ⓕ +61 9 3811122

Contacts: Doug Stanley and Kate Faulkner
Subjects: Natural history, medicine, science, lifestyles, locations, environmental, China, Jewish history, underwater photography.

🎞 16mm; Beta/Beta SP, D2, 1″, Umatic. PAL and NTSC.
Research: By staff only.
🕐 Mon-Fri 08:30 to 18:30
Procedure: VHS or Umatic PAL/NTSC viewing copies. 3 days for access to masters.
Description: Enormous range of productions covering wildlife, medical and scientific topics with worldwide documentary series on people and places. Titles include The Intruders, A Walk in the Sea and Crocodiles - the deadly survivors (natural history), Land of the Dragon (Bhutan), Dream Merchants of Asia (Taiwan, India, Japan, Hong Kong), Journey to Hainan (China's most southerly province), Breakthroughs (science, medicine and technology), Eye in the Sky (satellite technology), Triumph of the Nomads (Aborigines) to name a few. Glossy brochures available for productions. Partly computerized.

OLIVER FILMS

508 City Road, South Melbourne, Victoria 3205, Australia
ⓒ +61 3 690 3300
ⓕ +61 3 699 4640

Contacts: Frank Howson, Peter McBain
Subjects: Stock shots, natural history.

🎞 35mm.
Research: By staff only.
🕐 Mon-Fri 09:00 to 18:00
Procedure: VHS viewing material can be supplied. Access to masters varies.
Description: Small but expanding collection of out-takes from feature films produced by Oliver Films. Stock footage of Melbourne and surrounding areas, also some Fiji jungle footage. Partly computerized. Catalogue and rate card available.

PAUL ZWICK PRODUCTIONS

P.O. Box 91134, Auckland Park 2006, South Africa
℃ +27 11 789 6390/1
Ⓕ +27 11 789 6044

Contacts: Paul Zwick
Subjects: Natural history, locations.
▦ Beta/Beta SP. PAL.
Research: By staff. Visits by appointment.
🕑 Mon-Fri 08:30 to 18:00
Procedure: Timecoded VHS tapes compiled. 3 hours for access to masters.
Description: Various wildlife scenes of southern African game reserves, extensive footage of Indian Ocean islands - Mauritius and Comores, also footage of major US cities - New York, Las Vegas, San Francisco, etc. Computerized. English, Afrikaans and Hungarian spoken.

PLANET PICTURES

P.O. Box 65862, Los Angeles, CA 90065, USA
℃ +1 818 246 7700
Ⓕ +1 818 240 8391

Contacts: Jenny Hayden
Subjects: Documentaries, medicine, health, educational films, natural history, time-lapse.
▦ Time-lapse on film; mainly video.
Research: By both staff and outside researchers. Appointment to visit.
🕑 Mon-Fri 09:00 to 18:00
Description: Over 400 hours of footage and completed documentaries on a variety of subjects - medicine and health, high technology, workplace, nature, timelapse, wildlife, adventure, arts and entertainment and people. Computerized. Brochure available.

PYRAMID FILM & VIDEO

2801 Colorado Avenue, Santa Monica, CA 90404, USA
ⓒ +1 310 828 7577
ⓕ +1 310 453 9083

Contacts: Arthur C. Passante
Subjects: Documentaries, natural history, medicine, health, sport, arts, entertainment.
Research: By both staff and outside researchers.
Appointment to visit.
☉ Mon- Fri 08:00 to 17:00
Procedure: VHS or 16mm for viewing. 1 week average for access to masters.
Description: Over 500 titles of speciality short films covering nature, medicine, health, sports/action, documentary, history, art, media studies and entertainment. Catalogue and rate card available.
Foreign Offices: 80 worldwide distributors but all stock footage licensing is handled by this office.

QUALICUM FILM PRODUCTIONS

6340 Island Highway West, Qualicum Beach, BC V9K 2E5, Canada
ⓒ +1 604 757 8390
ⓕ +1 604 757 8844

Contacts: Dick Harvey
Subjects: Natural history, underwater photography, fishing.
16mm; Beta/Beta SP. NTSC.
Research: By both staff and outside researchers.
Appointment to visit.
☉ 7 days 08:00 to 18:00
Procedure: VHS or Umatic viewing cassettes. Same day for access to masters.
Description: Qualicum specialize in nature and wildlife photography, their particular interest over the last 30 years being rivers. Material includes extensive footage of salmon (migration, underwater, spawning, all species) also black bears, eagles on rivers, ocean, underwater herring etc.

REEFSCENES AUSTRALIA

P.O. Box 2427, Australia
ⓒ +61 77 214819
ⓕ +61 77 713341

Contacts: Steve Gardner
Subjects: Underwater photography, natural history.
▦ Beta SP, D2, Digital Beta, Hi 8. PAL.
Research: By staff only.
☉ Mon-Fri 09:00 to 17:00
Procedure: Time coded VHS available. 48 hours for access to masters.
Description: Underwater, coral reef and marine related footage shot on Beta SP and Digital Betacam widescreen 16:9 format. Also natural history, underwater models and human related topics. Computerized. English, Pidgin and Norwegian spoken.

ROBERT BOCKING PRODUCTIONS

75 Hucknall Road, Downsview, Ontario M3J IWI, Canada
ⓒ +1 416 631 9845

Contacts: Robert Bocking
Subjects: Natural history, locations.
▦ Videotape.
☉ Mon-Fri 09:00 to 17:00
Description: Nature footage and scenics from North America, Costa Rica to the Arctic, Atlantic to the Pacific. Partly computerized. Rate card and catalogue available.

SECOND LINE SEARCH

1926 Broadway, New York, NY 10023, USA
ⓒ +1 212 787 7500
ⓕ +1 212 787 7636

Contacts: Susan Luchars, George Bartko
Subjects: Locations, historical archive, sport, natural history, aerial photography, time-lapse, Americana, out-takes, industry, lifestyles.
▦ Variety of film and video formats.
Research: By staff.
☉ Mon-Fri 09:30 to 18:00
Procedure: Umatic viewing cassettes (NTSC or PAL). 2-3 days for access to masters.
Description: A variety of material including scenics, archival footage, sports, wildlife, news, aerials, international locations, Americana, oddities/bloopers, industry, technology, lifestyle and time-lapse. Computerized. French, Spanish, Portuguese, Italian and German spoken.

SOURCE STOCK FOOTAGE LIBRARY, THE

738 N. Constitution Drive, Tuscon, Arizona 85748, USA
ⓒ +1 602 298 4810
ⓕ +1 602 290 8831

Contacts: John Willwater, Bill and Lynne Briggs
Subjects: Stock shots, natural history, industry, time-lapse, locations, mining.
Research: By staff.
🕐 Mon-Fri 08:00 to 17:00
Description: Scenics, time-lapse, clouds and suns, animals, petrochemical and mining industrial, US and international destinations, desert plants and animals, cowboys, Phoenix, Tuscson, Alaskan wilderness and animals. Computerized. Rate card and brochure available.

STOCK OPTIONS

P.O. Box 87622, Houghton 2041, South Africa
ⓒ +27 11 788 7248 / 880 1287
ⓕ +27 11 788 9996

Contacts: Margi Sheard, Sandee Daniell
Subjects: Natural history, travelogues, locations, anthropology, aerial photography.
🎞 16mm, 35mm; Beta SP, 1", D1. PAL, some NTSC masters available.
Research: By both staff and outside researchers.
Appointment to visit.
🕐 Mon-Fri 08:30 to 17:30 (contactable until 22:00 by telephone)
Procedure: Umatic/VHS for viewing. 2 hours for local access to masters.
Description: Stock Options have African wildlife material (16mm and Beta SP), African landscapes, seascapes including aerial footage (16mm and 35mm), ethnic tribes and customs and international travel footage (Beta SP). Computerized. Catalogue and rate card available.
Foreign Offices: Represented by Index Stock Shots in London, Energy Productions in Los Angeles and Film World Research in Sydney.

STORYTELLER PRODUCTIONS

11 Morrison Way, Willetton, WA 6155, Australia
© +61 9 354 2903
Ⓕ +61 9 457 2583

Contacts: Mike Searle
Subjects: Natural history.
▦ Film; videotape.
Research: By both staff and outside researchers by
appointment.
🕓 Mon-Fri 09:00 to 17:00
Description: Large collection of natural history footage
featuring endangered species from around the world. Rare
animals such as Australia's rarest animal the western swamp
tortoise. Whales, whale strandings, dolphins, aye aye, tigers,
elephants, crickets, spiders, snails, bandicoots, etc. Also hold
footage collections of USS Missouri, Australian Aboriginal
Dancers and Spitfire Dig. Partly computerized.

STUART JEWELL PRODUCTIONS

2040 Garden Lane, Costa Mesa, CA 92627, USA
© +1 714 548 7234
Ⓕ +1 818 508 1293 (agents fax)

Contacts: Agent Energy Productions
Subjects: Documentaries, natural history, culture, locations,
time-lapse, aerial photography, steam trains.
▦ 16mm, 35mm; Beta SP, D2 1", BVU. NTSC.
Description: Series of worldwide documentaries mostly
natural history subjects - titles include Rolling to Guatemala,
Following the Oregon Trail, Winter in Yellowstone, Teton and
Mount. Rainer National Parks, The Great Aerial Odyssey,
locations including Alaska, Hawaii, Borneo, Thailand, Africa,
Egypt, India, Nepal plus steam trains in America, Canada,
Australia and Guatemala. Partly computerized. NB:
Represented by Energy Productions.
Foreign Offices: Contact local Energy Productions office.

THOMAS HORTON ASSOCIATES

222 Sierra Road, Ojai, CA 93023, USA
℃ +1 805 646 7866

Contacts: Jean Garner
Subjects: Documentaries, adventure sports, exploration, natural history, underwater photography, Africa.
16mm, 35mm; most video formats. PAL and NTSC.
Research: By both staff and outside researchers. Appointment to visit.
☉ Mon- Fri 08:00 to 18:00
Procedure: Viewing on NTSC Umatic or VHS. 3 days for access to masters.
Description: Series of documentaries titled Search For Adventure (over 39 one-hour programmes) including adventure sports, exploration, nature and underwater footage. The collection also includes 18 hours of 16mm footage shot in Spring 1993 of African animals and people in South and Central Africa. Catalogue and rate card available. Spanish, French and German spoken.

WGBH FILM & VIDEO RESOURCE CENTER

125 Wester Avenue, Boston, MA 02134, USA
℃ +1 617 492 3079
Ⓕ +1 617 783 4243
✉ 710 330 6887

Contacts: Vladimir Stefanovic, Patricia Barraza
Subjects: Documentaries, natural history, science, medicine, animation, aviation.
16mm, 35mm; Beta/Beta SP, D2, 1″, Umatic. NTSC.
Research: By staff only.
☉ Mon- Fri 09:00 to 17:00
Procedure: Viewing on VHS or Umatic as requested. 3 days for access to masters.
Description: WGBH is one of the largest documentary producing stations in the US Public Broadcasting System, producing over 30% of prime time PBS programmes. Having been in existence since 1955 the extensive library holds material covering subjects such as nature, science, scenics, animation, wildlife, high tech, health/surgery and flight. The majority of copyright is held by WGBH..Partly computerized. Catalogue and rate card available. English, Spanish and Macedonian spoken.

WPA FILM LIBRARY

5525 W. 159th Street, Oak Forest, IL 60452, USA
© +1 708 535 1540
⊕ +1 708 535 1541

Contacts: Michael Mertz
Subjects: Historical archive, newsreels, industry, Americana, music, transport, fashion, locations, natural history.
🎞 10 000 hours film; 2000 hours videotape.
Research: By both staff and outside researchers.
☺ Mon–Fri 8:30 to 17:00
Description: Complete historical materials from 1896 to the present day. Specialities include newsreels, Americana from the 1940s and 50s, early rock and roll performances (Hullabaloo in 1964/5, The Music Scene in 1969/70), UFOs, automobiles, fashions, American Civil Rights, contemporary geographic materials, nature and wildlife, American industry collection from the 1940s to the present day. Also represent British Pathe News for North America only. Partly computerized. Rate card and brochure available.

Newsreels

AMAZING IMAGES

Suite 1581, 6671 Sunset Boulevard, Hollywood CA 90028, USA
ℂ +1 213 962 1899
Ⓕ +1 213 962 1898

Contacts: Michael Peter Yakaitis
Subjects: Historical archive, newsreels, classic films, trailers, out-takes, personalities.
🎞 16mm, 35mm; video.
Research: By staff only.
🕐 Mon–Fri 09:30 to 18:00
Procedure: VHS or Umatic viewing copies. 24 hours for access to masters.
Description: The collection begins pre-1900 and includes old Hollywood stars of silent and sound motion pictures, locations around the globe, newsreels, historical events, world war, comedy, censorship, serial and weekly magazines, bloopers, Kodascopes, out-takes and film trailers. There is also a wide assortment of animal footage, celebrities and industrial material. Partly computerized. Rate card available.

ARCHIVE FILMS

530 West 25th Street, New York, NY 1001, USA
ℂ +1 212 620 3955
Ⓕ +1 212 645 2137

Contacts: Patrick Montgomery
Subjects: Historical archive, newsreels, Hollywood, classic films, film industry, educational films.
🎞 35mm, 16mm; various video formats with matching cassettes.
Research: By staff. Appointment to visit.
🕐 Mon–Fri 09:00 to 18:00
Procedure: Viewing tapes assembled. 24–48 hours for access to masters.
Description: Over 5000 hours of newsreels, silent films, classic comedies, Hollywood features, historical dramas, documentaries and educational films. Represent The March of Time, The RKO Shorts Library, International Film Foundation, TV House and Videowest. Computerized. Rate card and catalogue available.
Foreign Offices: France, Germany, Italy, Japan, Netherlands, Sweden, UK, USA.

A.R.I.Q. FOOTAGE

One Main Street, East Hampton, New York 11964, USA
© +1 516 329 9200
Ⓕ +1 516 329 9260

Contacts: Joe Lauro, Mart Heideman
Subjects: Historical archive, classic films, comedy, music, newsreels, industry, space.
▦ Various film and video formats. All line standards available.
Research: By staff. Visits by appointment.
☉ Mon-Fri 09:00 to 17:30
Procedure: Viewing material on VHS and Umatic. 24 hours for access to masters.
Description: Footage covers 1895 to 1990 with a very strong historical archive. Universal newsreel (1929 to 1967), musical performance footage including Jazz, Blues, Country, Rock and Roll, Pop from 1910 to 1990, silent films, industrial footage, space program, life styles and a range of general subject. Computerized. Rate card available.

BUDGET FILMS STOCK FOOTAGE

4590 Santa Monica Blvd, Los Angeles, CA 90029, USA
© +1 213 660 0187
Ⓕ +1 213 660 5571

Contacts: Layne Murphy
Subjects: Historical archive, newsreels, documentaries.
▦ Film; videotape.
Research: By staff. Visits by appointment.
☉ Mon-Fri 09:00 to 17:00
Description: Vintage footage dating from the 1890s through to 1970s. The library contains theatrical, news, documentary and experimental and television materials.

FILM WORLD

2 Whiting Street, P.O. Box 313, Artarmon, NSW 2064,
Australia
© +61 2 438 1888
Ⓕ +61 2 439 8541

Contacts: Naomi Saville
Subjects: Newsreels, locations, natural history, lifestyles,
tourism, travelogues.

▦ Film; Beta/Beta SP, 1", D1. PAL and NTSC.
Research: By both staff and outside researchers.
Appointment to visit.

☉ Mon-Fri 08:30 to 17:30
Procedure: VHS or Umatic viewing cassettes. 24 hours for
access to masters.
Description: Over 3000 hours of footage covering archival
news material, contemporary landscapes, wildlife and
lifestyles. Film World are exclusive agents for the Cinesound
and Movietone newsreel collection, Australian Tourist
Commission, Queensland Tourist & Travel Corporation,
Canadian company Fabulous Footage and many more.
Computerized. Subject headings list and rate card available.

FRANKLIN D. ROOSEVELT LIBRARY

511 Albany Post Road, Hyde Park, NY 12538, USA
© +1 914 229 8114
Ⓕ +1 914 229 0872

Contacts: Mark Renovitch
Subjects: Historical archive, newsreels, amateur films.

▦ 16mm, 35mm.
Research: Limited research by staff. Appointment to visit
advised.

☉ Mon-Fri 08:45 to 17:00
Procedure: Viewing material not supplied. 2 weeks for
access to masters.
Description: The collection contains newsreels and home
movie footage of Franklin and Eleanor D. Roosevelt. Some of
the material is public domain but most is copyrighted by
other institutions.

FUNDACION CINEMATECA ARGENTINA

2nd Floor, Corrientes 2092, Buenos Aires 1045, Argentina
ⓒ +54 1 953 3755 / 7163
ⓕ +54 1 951 8558

Contacts: Guillermo or Paulina Fernandez Jurade
Subjects: National Archives, feature films, documentaries, newsreels.
▦ 35mm, 16mm; video.
Research: Appointment necessary.
☺ Mon-Fri 10:00 to 17:00
Procedure: Problems at present with duplication of material.
Description: The library holds feature films, documentaries and newsreels. Not all copyrights are held.

IMAGEWAYS

Second Floor, 412 West 48th Street, New York NY 10036, USA
ⓒ +1 212 265 1287
ⓕ +1 212 586 0339

Contacts: Adam Sargis, Kenneth Powell, Ray Sidwell
Subjects: Stock shots, newsreels, comedy, animation, classic films, documentaries, industry, educational films, television.
▦ Film; 1" videotape with timecoded 3/4" cassettes.
Research: By staff. Appointment to visit.
Procedure: Timecoded cassette compiled. Masters copied after selection.
Description: Stock footage library with material dating from 1905 to present day. Footage comes from newsreels, silent films, cartoons, historical films, Hollywood features, documentaries, industrial films, educational films, television programmes and original shot material. Collection is approximately 70% colour and 30% black and white. Computerized. Rate card available. Minimum license fee charged on delivery of master material.

JACK CHISHOLM FILM PRODUCTIONS

Suite 50, 99 Atlantic Avenue, Toronto, Ontario M6K 3J8, Canada
Ⓒ +1 416 588 5200
Ⓕ +1 416 588 5324

Contacts: Peter Robinson
Subjects: Stock shots, historical archive, locations, time-lapse, current affairs, newsreels, natural history, industry, science.
🎞 16mm, 35mm; Beta/Beta SP, 1", Umatic, SVHS, some digital. NTSC.
Research: By staff only.
🕐 Mon–Fri 09:00 to 17:30
Procedure: Umatic or VHS viewing copies. 24 hours for access to masters.
Description: The stock footage library contains archive material dating from 1896 up to present day. Subjects cover major events around the world, wildlife, foreign locations, industry and science as well as quality shots of clouds, sunsets, time-lapse flowers, etc. The collection comprises of 10 000 hours of video footage and 4 million feet of film. They hold 35mm neg of across Canada scenics plus the Millenium television series. Computerized. Rate card available. English and Italian spoken.

JOHN E. ALLEN

116 North Avenue, Park Ridge, NJ 07656, USA
Ⓒ +1 201 391 3299
Ⓕ +1 201 391 6335

Contacts: John E. Allen, Beverley Allen
Subjects: Historical archive, newsreels, war, Russia, industry, transport, classic films, educational films, travelogues.
🎞 Mainly film; some video.
Research: By both staff and outside researchers.
🕐 Mon–Fri 09:00 to 18:00
Description: Kinograms from 1915 to 1931. Telenews 1947 to 1953. World War I and II, Spanish American War, Mexican Revolution, Russian Revolution, Hungarian Revolution, Spanish Civil War, Korean War, etc. Industry 1910 to 1950s, transportation, educational, ethnographic, travel, nature, features 1905 to 1950s, stills, posters and lobby cards. Partly computerized. Rate card available.

NEW ZEALAND FILM ARCHIVE

P.O. Box 11-449, First Floor, The Film Centre, Cnr. Cable Street & Jervois Quay, Wellington, New Zealand
ⓒ +64 4 3847647
ⓕ +64 4 3829595

Contacts: Bronwyn Taylor (public programmes), Diane Pivac (documentation)
Subjects: National Archives, newsreels, documentaries, feature films, animation.
▦ Film; video.
Research: By appointment only.
🕐 Mon-Fri 09:00 to 17:00
Procedure: Access to view is available. Master material not available.
Description: Held in the archive's collection are New Zealand and overseas films from 1897 to the present day, comprising fiction and feature films, shorts animated films, documentaries, newsreels, video and television programmes. A wide variety of promotional, critical and historical documentation and information is also held for New Zealand and overseas films. Copyright is not held by NZFA. Computerized. Rate card available.

NEW ZEALAND TELEVISION ARCHIVE

Television New Zealand, P.O. Box 3819, Auckland, New Zealand
ⓒ +64 9 375 0942
ⓕ +64 9 375 0872

Contacts: Jane Hiscotte, Alan Ferris
Subjects: Current affairs, newsreels, documentaries, natural history, leisure, stock shots.
▦ Film; videotape.
Research: By staff.
🕐 Mon-Fri 08:00 to 18:00
Procedure: Print outs available for each request.
Description: News, current affairs, stock shots and general programming from New Zealand Television dating from 1960. Newsreels and documentaries purchased from the National Film Unit (1940 to 1965). The archive also specialize in natural history footage, spectacular scenery and recreational sports action. 80% computerized.

NEWSREEL VIDEO SERVICE

7329 Donna Avenue, Reseda, CA 91335, USA
© +1 818 344 7107
Ⓕ +1 818 996 4856

Contacts: Lois Arnote
Subjects: Newsreels, current affairs, stunts, fires.
▥ Videotape.
Research: By staff. Appointment to visit.
☉ 7 days 09:00 to 21:00
Description: News footage of LA gangs, LA riot footage
(approx. 10 hours), gang shootings in progress, SWAT teams,
FBI raids, movie celebrities, movie stunts and river rescues.
Newsreel also specialize in footage of fires, commercial
structure fires, house fires, car fires, bush fires, oil well fires
and high rise building fires - plenty of spectacular flames.
Computerized. Promotional video available.

OPUS GLOBAL / THE ELECTRONIC LIBRARY

1133 N. Highland Avenue, Hollywood, CA 90038, USA
© +1 213 993 9888
Ⓕ +1 213 993 9899

Contacts: Todd Stubner, Masih Madani
Subjects: Stock shots, time-lapse, feature films, advertising,
newsreels.
▥ Most film and video formats. NTSC.
Research: By staff and outside researchers. Appointment to
visit.
☉ 7 days 24 hours
Procedure: Viewing on VHS, Umatic, CD-ROM. Less than 24
hours for access to masters.
Description: Contemporary and archival collection ranging
from material specially shot for stock footage (real time and
time altered) and out-takes from productions to vintage
newsreels, feature films and commercials. The electronic
library contains more than two million scenes catalogued by
a unique object and relational database. Queries can be
made on the content of image, the patterns, colours, texture
and shapes of image objects, related layout and position
information as well as keywords. Images are available in all
formats including MPEG and JPEG for use in all mediums
including CD-ROM. Stills, sound effects and music are also
supplied. Fully computerized. Rate card and catalogue
available electronically.
Foreign Offices: Represented by Front Line in Japan.

SHERMAN GRINBERG FILM LIBRARIES

630 9th Avenue, New York, NY 10036, USA
ⓒ +1 212 765 5170
Ⓕ +1 212 262 1532

Contacts: Nancy Casey, Bernard Chertok
Subjects: Current affairs, newsreels, advertising, stock shots.
▦ 16mm, 35mm; most video formats. NTSC.
Research: By both staff and outside researchers.
Appointment to visit.
🕐 Mon-Fri 09:30 to 17:30
Procedure: Viewing as specified by client. 1-2 days for access to masters.
Description: A comprehensive collection of news coverage of the 20th Century, the library encorporates ABC Network News, Pathe News and Paramount News. Also represented are major libraries such as 20th Century Fox and HBO. Thirty years of television commercials are also available. Sherman Grinberg also have an office in Los Angeles at 1040 N. McCadden Place Tel: (213) 464 7491, Fax: (213) 462 5352, contacts: Bill Brewington, Linda Grinberg. Partly computerized. Catalogue and rate card available.

STEVEN SPIELBERG JEWISH FILM ARCHIVE

Law Building, The Hebrew University of Jerusalem, Mount Scopus, Jerusalem 91905, Israel
ⓒ +972 2 882513
Ⓕ +972 2 322545

Contacts: Marilyn Koolik
Subjects: National Archives, Jewish history, newsreels.
▦ Film; videocassettes.
Research: By both staff and outside researchers. Visits by appointment.
🕐 Sun-Thur 09:00 to 17:00
Description: Founded in 1969 the Spielberg archive maintains and acquires film and video material relating to Jewish and Israeli subjects. Newsreels include the Agadati Collection (1932 to 1956), the Carmel newsreels shot by Natan Axelrod (1905 to 1987), the Carmel-Herzliya and Geva newsreels. Computerized. Rate card available.

STREAMLINE ARCHIVES

Suite 1314, 432 Park Avenue South, New York NY 10016, USA
ⓒ +1 212 696 2616
ⓕ +1 212 696 0021

Contacts: Mark Trost
Subjects: Stock shots, newsreels, current affairs, classic films, feature films, educational, industry, sport, television, advertising, travelogues.

🎞 16mm, 35mm; most video formats. PAL, NTSC and SECAM.
Research: By staff only. Appointments for viewings.
🕐 Mon-Fri 09:30 to 19:30
Procedure: Viewing tapes assembled on VHS or Umatic. 24 hours for access to masters.
Description: Streamline's archives are being continually expanded including educational, government and industrial films, newsreels (from the turn of the century through to the early 1970s), silent comedies, television programmes and commercials, sports films, theatrical shorts, classic features and trailers as well as travel video and daily news footage (1986 to present) from Cablevision's award winning News 12 Long Island channel. Computerized. Rate card and catalogue available. English, Spanish and Japanese spoken.

UCLA FILM & TELEVISION ARCHIVE RESEARCH & STUDY CENTER

46 Powell Library, 405 Hilgard Avenue, Los Angeles, CA 90024-1517, USA
ⓒ +1 310 206 5388
ⓕ +1 310 206 5392

Subjects: Newsreels, current affairs.
🎞 Variety of film and video formats.
Research: Researchers can visit premises. Appointment necessary to view.
🕐 Mon-Fri 08:30 to 17:00
Procedure: Viewing on VHS or 35mm.
Description: 200 000 film and television programmes and over 27 million feet of newsreel footage. The collection also includes news and public affairs programmes. Copyright is held for some items only. Computerized.

UNITED STUDIOS OF ISRAEL

Kesem St. 8, Herzlia 46100, Israel
ⓒ +972 52 550 151-7
ⓕ +972 52 550 334

Contacts: Mirjana Gross
Subjects: Newsreels, documentaries, educational films, war, current affairs, culture.
🎞 35mm; BVU.
🕐 Sun-Thur 08:00 to 17:00
Description: Newsreels made in Israel from 1951 to 1971 covering events, wars, emigrations, new settlements and political life in the state. Documentary films on education, the army, water problems, Arab and Jewish life, etc. Brochure available. NB: Collections are also at the Spielberg Archive (Jerusalem) and the Harvard Judaica Department (Boston USA).

UNIVERSITY OF SOUTH CAROLINA NEWSFILM LIBRARY

Instructional Services Center, Columbia, South Carolina 29208, USA
ⓒ +1 803 777 6841
ⓕ +1 803 777 6841

Contacts: Andrew Murdoch, Don McCallister
Subjects: Newsreels, out-takes.
🎞 16mm, 35mm; most video formats. NTSC.
Research: Copies of story descriptions sent free.
Appointment to visit.
🕐 Mon-Fri 08:00 to 17:00
Procedure: Umatic or VHS timecoded viewing cassettes. Masters vary.
Description: The University is in the process of receiving the Movietone Newsreel collection from 20th Century Fox. At present they have the out-takes from 1919 to 1934 plus the newsreels and their associated out-takes from September 1942 to August 1944. They are also acquiring other film collections, the most significant being the local TV news - NBC affiliate WIS-TV, this footage dates from 1959 through to the mid 1970s documenting many of the important events and personalities in South Carolina during that time. Computerized. Rate card available.

VIDEO TAPE LIBRARY

Suite 2, 1509 N. Crescent Heights Blvd, Los Angeles CA
90046, USA
© +1 213 656 4330
⑤ +1 213 656 8746

Contacts: Melody St. John, Peggy Shannon
Subjects: Stock shots, current affairs, newsreels, locations,
beauty, comedy, classic films, sport, leisure, environmental,
medicine, out-takes.

20% film; 80% video.

Research: By both staff and outside researchers.

Mon-Fri 09:00 to 17:00

Procedure: 24 hour turnaround for research, preview and
master footage.

Description: Enormous range of stock shot material ranging
from archival footage (1898) to current news topics. Over 2
million shots on virtually every subject including locations,
disasters, sports, medical, comedy, lifestyles, politics,
time-lapse, film and television classics, newsreels from 1929
to 1967. Computerized. Rate card and brochure available.

WORLDVIEW ENTERTAINMENT

6 East 39th Street, New York, NY 10016, USA
© +1 212 679 8230
⑤ +1 212 686 0801

Contacts: Sandra Birnhak, Marcy Stuzin
Subjects: Historical archive, classic films, newsreels.

16mm, 35mm; all video formats. NTSC.

Research: By staff only. Appointment to visit.

Mon-Fri 09:30 to 18:00

Procedure: Umatic/VHS viewing tapes assembled.

Description: Large and comprehensive library of silent films.
Archival and newsreel footage dating from the late 1890s to
the 1950s. Mostly on card catalogue but in the process of
computerization. Catalogue and rate card available.

WORLDWIDE TELEVISION NEWS (WTN)

1995 Broadway, New York, NY 10023, USA
C +1 212 362 4440
F +1 212 496 1269
N 237853

Contacts: Vincent O'Reilly, David Seevers
Subjects: Current affairs, newsreels, environmental, sport.
16mm; Beta/Beta SP, D2, BVU, Umatic. NTSC. PAL -
London office.
Research: By staff or outside researchers. Appointment to
visit.
Mon-Fri 09:00 to 19:00
Procedure: VHS dubb, other formats on request. 24 hours
for access to masters.
Description: Dating from 1963 and formerly known as
UPITN, WTN is the successor to the UPI-Movietonews
collection. The library consists of mainly domestic and
foreign news but also produces weekly features, an
entertainment and sports service, the Earthfile Environment
programme and Roving Report - a weekly service of five
in-depth reports. Copyright is held for most material, others
obtained on a case by case basis, restrictions may occur with
sports and entertainment footage. Computerized. Catalogue
of Roving Reports available plus rate card. English, Spanish
and French spoken.

WPA FILM LIBRARY

5525 W. 159th Street, Oak Forest, IL 60452, USA
C +1 708 535 1540
F +1 708 535 1541

Contacts: Michael Mertz
Subjects: Historical archive, newsreels, industry, Americana,
music, transport, fashion, locations, natural history.
10 000 hours film; 2000 hours videotape.
Research: By both staff and outside researchers.
Mon-Fri 8:30 to 17:00
Description: Complete historical materials from 1896 to the
present day. Specialities include newsreels, Americana from
the 1940s and 50s, early rock and roll performances
(Hullabaloo in 1964/5, The Music Scene in 1969/70), UFOs,
automobiles, fashions, American Civil Rights, contemporary
geographic materials, nature and wildlife, American industry
collection from the 1940s to the present day. Also represent
British Pathe News for North America only. Partly
computerized. Rate card and brochure available.

Out-takes

AMAZING IMAGES

Suite 1581, 6671 Sunset Boulevard, Hollywood CA 90028, USA
ⓒ +1 213 962 1899
ⓕ +1 213 962 1898

Contacts: Michael Peter Yakaitis
Subjects: Historical archive, newsreels, classic films, trailers, out-takes, personalities.
▦ 16mm, 35mm; video.
Research: By staff only.
☉ Mon–Fri 09:30 to 18:00
Procedure: VHS or Umatic viewing copies. 24 hours for access to masters.
Description: The collection begins pre-1900 and includes old Hollywood stars of silent and sound motion pictures, locations around the globe, newsreels, historical events, world war, comedy, censorship, serial and weekly magazines, bloopers, Kodascopes, out-takes and film trailers. There is also a wide assortment of animal footage, celebrities and industrial material. Partly computerized. Rate card available.

PARAMOUNT PICTURES FILM LIBRARY

Hal Wallis Building, Room 108, 5555 Melrose Avenue, Hollywood CA 90038, USA
ⓒ +1 213 956 5510
ⓕ +1 213 956 1833

Contacts: Pat Harris
Subjects: Stock shots, aerial photography, transport, aviation, locations, building, skylines, out-takes.
▦ 35mm.
Research: By staff only (no charge made). Appointment to visit.
☉ Mon–Fri 09:00 to 18:00
Procedure: Film transferred to video at clients cost. 4–5 days for access to masters
Description: Out-takes and unused footage from Paramount's features and television series spanning over 50 years. Over 9000 contemporary scenes catalogued in the past year. Subjects vary from aerials of cities and countrysides, stationary and moving process for cars, planes and trains, buildings of every type, scenery to aviation, amusements and skylines. Material is exclusively 35mm including 3 strip technicolor. Rate card available.

PETRIFIED FILMS / THE IMAGE BANK

Room 204, 430 West 14th Street, New York NY 10014, USA
© +1 212 242 5461
Ⓕ +1 212 691 8347

Contacts: Lori Cheatle, Rob Cates
Subjects: Historical archive, Hollywood, transport, consumerism, Americana, industry, war, aviation, feature film, out-takes.
▦ 35mm, 16mm; some on 1", D2, 3/4" with matching VHS.
Research: By staff. Visits by appointment.
☺ Mon- Fri 09:30 to 18:00
Procedure: Viewing tapes assembled. Masters copied after selection.
Description: Historical collection including pre-1951 Warner Brothers stock and pre-1965 Columbia Pictures stock. A-Z of subjects including action sequences, period recreations, establishing shots, projection backgrounds, cityscapes and worldwide locations. Industrial, military and aviation collections. Car culture and 1950s daily life in the US. Majority dates from 1920s to 1960s. Partly computerized. Rate card and catalogue available.
Foreign Offices: Contact local Image Bank office.

SECOND LINE SEARCH

1926 Broadway, New York, NY 10023, USA
© +1 212 787 7500
Ⓕ +1 212 787 7636

Contacts: Susan Luchars, George Bartko
Subjects: Locations, historical archive, sport, natural history, aerial photography, time-lapse, Americana, out-takes, industry, lifestyles.
▦ Variety of film and video formats.
Research: By staff.
☺ Mon- Fri 09:30 to 18:00
Procedure: Umatic viewing cassettes (NTSC or PAL). 2-3 days for access to masters.
Description: A variety of material including scenics, archival footage, sports, wildlife, news, aerials, international locations, Americana, oddities/bloopers, industry, technology, lifestyle and time-lapse. Computerized. French, Spanish, Portuguese, Italian and German spoken.

UNIVERSITY OF SOUTH CAROLINA NEWSFILM LIBRARY

Instructional Services Center, Columbia, South Carolina
29208, USA
ⓒ +1 803 777 6841
Ⓕ +1 803 777 6841

Contacts: Andrew Murdoch, Don McCallister
Subjects: Newsreels, out-takes.
16mm, 35mm; most video formats. NTSC.
Research: Copies of story descriptions sent free.
Appointment to visit.
🕓 Mon–Fri 08:00 to 17:00
Procedure: Umatic or VHS timecoded viewing cassettes.
Masters vary.
Description: The University is in the process of receiving the
Movietone Newsreel collection from 20th Century Fox. At
present they have the out-takes from 1919 to 1934 plus the
newsreels and their associated out-takes from September
1942 to August 1944. They are also acquiring other film
collections, the most significant being the local TV news -
NBC affiliate WIS-TV, this footage dates from 1959 through
to the mid 1970s documenting many of the important events
and personalities in South Carolina during that time.
Computerized. Rate card available.

VIDEO TAPE LIBRARY

Suite 2, 1509 N. Crescent Heights Blvd, Los Angeles CA
90046, USA
ⓒ +1 213 656 4330
Ⓕ +1 213 656 8746

Contacts: Melody St. John, Peggy Shannon
Subjects: Stock shots, current affairs, newsreels, locations,
beauty, comedy, classic films, sport, leisure, environmental,
medicine, out-takes.
20% film; 80% video.
Research: By both staff and outside researchers.
🕓 Mon–Fri 09:00 to 17:00
Procedure: 24 hour turnaround for research, preview and
master footage.
Description: Enormous range of stock shot material ranging
from archival footage (1898) to current news topics. Over 2
million shots on virtually every subject including locations,
disasters, sports, medical, comedy, lifestyles, politics,
time-lapse, film and television classics, newsreels from 1929
to 1967. Computerized. Rate card and brochure available.

Protests

ESTUARY PRESS

Suite 279, 408 13th Street, Oakland CA 94612, USA
© +1 510 763 8204
Ⓕ +1 510 763 8204

Contacts: Paul Richards
Subjects: Civil rights, protests, Vietnam War.
Research: By Paul Richards.
🕐 No office hours. Contact anytime.
Procedure: VHS viewing tapes on request. Access to masters varies.
Description: The collection contains the films of Harvey Wilson Richards including 1960s Bay Area peace and civil rights protests, anti Vietnam War protests, California farm workers, forestry and logging. Mississippi civil rights movement 1963 and 1964. Catalogue available. English and Spanish spoken.

Public domain

CHARLES CHAPLIN ENTERPRISES

318 Hillhurst Boulevard, Toronto, Ontario M6B 1N2, Canada
ⓒ +1 416 781 0131 / 2010
ⓕ +1 416 366 6503

Contacts: Charles S. Chaplin
Subjects: Russia, documentaries, feature films, public domain.

▦ Various film formats. Can supply any video format on request.

Research: Visits by appointment only. Requests by fax or mail.

☉ 7 days 09:00 to 18:00

Procedure: NTSC (some PAL) videocassettes for viewing. 2 weeks for access to masters.

Description: Wide range of documentary and feature film productions, specializing in Russia and USA.

EM GEE FILM LIBRARY

Suite 103, 6924 Canby Avenue, Reseda CA 91335, USA
ⓒ +1 818 881 8110
ⓕ +1 818 981 5506

Contacts: Murray Glass
Subjects: Public domain, classic films, feature films, comedy, documentaries, westerns, animation.

▦ All film formats; VHS, Umatic. NTSC.

Research: By both staff and outside researchers.

☉ Mon-Fri 08:30 to 17:00

Procedure: Viewing material on 16mm or VHS. 1 week for access to masters.

Description: Approximately 3000 titles in all genres - silent and sound, black and white and colour. Their speciality is in public domain material covering all subject areas including comedies, documentaries, westerns, animation and feature films. Partly computerized. Catalogue and rate card available.

FILM/AUDIO SERVICES

Suite 311, 430 West 14th Street, New York NY 10014, USA
ⓒ +1 212 645 2112
ⓕ +1 212 255 4220

Contacts: Bob Summers, Mike Cocchi, Dean Cady
Subjects: Historical archive, travelogues, culture, educational films, industry, public domain.

▥ Most film and video formats. NTSC.

Research: By staff preferably. Appointment to visit.

🕓 Mon-Fri 09:00 to 18:00 (or by appointment)

Procedure: Viewing material on VHS or 3/4" NTSC. 24 hours for access to masters.

Description: Worldwide travel footage dating from 1926 to 1980s; education and industrial films from the 1930s to 60s; historical actuality public domain material sourced from the National Archives and Library of Congress sold at less cost. Inexpensive and fast turnaround film to NTSC Beta SP and 1" tape in house. Partly computerized. Catalogue and rate card available. English and some Spanish spoken.

Religion

ARCTURUS MOTION PICTURES

65 Gray Cliff Road, Newton, MA 02159, USA
℅ +1 617 332 3802
Ⓕ +1 617 332 3310

Contacts: David Breashears
Subjects: Himalayas, mountaineering, culture, religion, aerial photography.
🎞 16mm; 1″ with matching 3/4″ and VHS.
Research: By both staff and outside researchers. Appointment to visit.
🕓 Mon–Fri 09:00 to 17:00
Procedure: All material on viewing cassettes. Copies from video masters.
Description: Collection specializes in the Himalayas with emphasis on the Mount Everest region. Extensive scenics and aerial shots of the area. Sherpa, Buddhist and Tibetan culture. Partly computerized. Rate card and catalogue available.

FILMS OF INDIA

P.O. Box 48303, Los Angeles, CA 90048, USA
℅ +1 213 383 9217

Contacts: Mr R.A. Bagai
Subjects: Asian cinema, dance, drama, documentaries, culture, religion.
🎞 Film.
Research: By staff. Appointment to visit.
🕓 Mon–Fri 09:30 to 17:30
Description: Feature films, shorts, drama, documentaries, religious films, etc. Ram Bagai also has extensive footage of Ghandi having acquired a large film library after his assassination. Brochure available.

MAURITIUS BROADCASTING CORPORATION

1 Louis Pasteur Street, Forest Side, Mauritius
© +230 675001/2/3 6743743
Ⓕ +230 6757332
𝒩 4230 MAUBROD IW

Contacts: Anne Marie Ginette Fabre
Subjects: National Archives, current affairs, religion, documentaries, childrens, music, personalities, sport.
🎞 16mm, 35mm; Beta/Beta SP, BVU, Umatic. PAL and SECAM.
Research: By staff. Outside researchers by appointment.
☉ 7 days 08:30 to 17:00
Procedure: Viewing on 16mm and video. 2 hours for access to masters.
Description: A wide range of programme material covering political, international and local events, religion, documentaries, television for children and teenagers, musicals, interviews and sports. English and French spoken.

NBC NEWS ARCHIVES

30 Rockefeller Plaza, Room 902, New York, NY 10112, USA
© +1 212 664 3797
Ⓕ +1 212 957 8917

Contacts: Nancy Cole, Yuien Chin
Subjects: Current affairs, culture, religion, environmental, natural history, personalities, social history.
🎞 16mm, 35mm; most video formats. NTSC.
Research: By both staff and outside researchers. Appointment to visit.
☉ Mon-Fri 09:00 to 18:00
Procedure: Time-coded viewing material. Fast turnaround service.
Description: Over four decades of news events worldwide. The library covers social commentary, interviews, cultural, historical and religious programming, the environment, wildlife and stock shots for almost any subject imaginable. Computerized. Rate card available. Chinese and Spanish spoken.

Skylines

BROAD STREET PRODUCTIONS

10 West 19th Street, New York, NY 10011, USA
Ⓒ +1 212 924 4700
Ⓕ +1 212 924 5085

Contacts: Jody Bergedick, David Fink
Subjects: Industry, skylines, business.
🎞 16mm. Most video formats. NTSC.
Research: By both staff and outside researchers.
Appointment to visit.
🕑 Mon–Fri 09:00 to 18:00 (other days and hours on request)
Procedure: Timecoded VHS or Umatic viewing copies.
Access to masters within 24 hours.
Description: The collection contains material relating to
business and finance with footage of financial markets,
industrial processes, city skylines, hi-tech communications
imagery and business people in various situations. Partly
computerized. Catalogue and rate card available.

PARAMOUNT PICTURES FILM LIBRARY

Hal Wallis Building, Room 108, 5555 Melrose Avenue,
Hollywood CA 90038, USA
Ⓒ +1 213 956 5510
Ⓕ +1 213 956 1833

Contacts: Pat Harris
Subjects: Stock shots, aerial photography, transport,
aviation, locations, building, skylines, out-takes.
🎞 35mm.
Research: By staff only (no charge made). Appointment to
visit.
🕑 Mon–Fri 09:00 to 18:00
Procedure: Film transferred to video at clients cost. 4–5
days for access to masters
Description: Out-takes and unused footage from
Paramount's features and television series spanning over 50
years. Over 9000 contemporary scenes catalogued in the
past year. Subjects vary from aerials of cities and
countrysides, stationary and moving process for cars, planes
and trains, buildings of every type, scenery to aviation,
amusements and skylines. Material is exclusively 35mm
including 3 strip technicolor. Rate card available.

Social history

DOKO VIDEO

33 Hayetzira Street, Ramat Gan 52521, Israel
© +972 3 5753555
Ⓕ +972 3 5753189

Contacts: Mrs Taly Kaufman
Subjects: Documentaries, war, Jewish history, travelogues, technology, educational films, social history, childrens'.
🎞 8mm; D2, BVU. All line standards available.
Research: By staff.
🕐 Sun-Thur 09:00 to 17:00
Procedure: VHS viewing copies supplied. 3-7 days for access to masters.
Description: Doko Video have a wide range of programmes available covering every aspect of Israel (history, religion, ethnic and social life, etc.). Titles available are listed in their catalogue under the following headings - battles for peace, holocaust and revival, follow the sun, biblical landscapes, innovative technology, Jerusalem, discovering the past, the social scene and children's program. Hebrew, English and French spoken.

NBC NEWS ARCHIVES

30 Rockefeller Plaza, Room 902, New York, NY 10112, USA
© +1 212 664 3797
Ⓕ +1 212 957 8917

Contacts: Nancy Cole, Yuien Chin
Subjects: Current affairs, culture, religion, environmental, natural history, personalities, social history.
🎞 16mm, 35mm; most video formats. NTSC.
Research: By both staff and outside researchers. Appointment to visit.
🕐 Mon-Fri 09:00 to 18:00
Procedure: Time-coded viewing material. Fast turnaround service.
Description: Over four decades of news events worldwide. The library covers social commentary, interviews, cultural, historical and religious programming, the environment, wildlife and stock shots for almost any subject imaginable. Computerized. Rate card available. Chinese and Spanish spoken.

SRI LANKA NATIONAL LIBRARY SERVICES BOARD

National Library of Sri Lanka, P.O. Box 1764, 14
Independence Avenue, Colombo 07, Sri Lanka
© +94 1 698847 / 685199 / 685201
Ⓕ +94 1 685201

Contacts: Mr M.S.U. Amarasiri (Director)
Subjects: National Archives, science, social history
Video.
Research: Researchers can visit.
🕓 Tues–Sat 09:00 to 17:00
Procedure: Material seen on site only, cannot be loaned.
Description: The library holds material relating to social
sciences, humanities, science and technology, library and
information science, mass communications. Materials
comprise of books, periodicals, newspapers, micro-fiches,
microfilms, manuscripts, maps, computer discs, recordings
and video cassettes. Partly computerized.

Space

A.R.I.Q. FOOTAGE

One Main Street, East Hampton, New York 11964, USA
© +1 516 329 9200
Ⓕ +1 516 329 9260

Contacts: Joe Lauro, Mart Heideman
Subjects: Historical archive, classic films, comedy, music, newsreels, industry, space.
🎞 Various film and video formats. All line standards available.
Research: By staff. Visits by appointment.
🕑 Mon–Fri 09:00 to 17:30
Procedure: Viewing material on VHS and Umatic. 24 hours for access to masters.
Description: Footage covers 1895 to 1990 with a very strong historical archive. Universal newsreel (1929 to 1967), musical performance footage including Jazz, Blues, Country, Rock and Roll, Pop from 1910 to 1990, silent films, industrial footage, space program, life styles and a range of general subject. Computerized. Rate card available.

FABULOUS FOOTAGE

4th Floor, 19 Mercer Street, Toronto, Ontario M5V 1H2, Canada
© +1 416 591 6955
⑤ +1 416 591 1666

Contacts: Steve Race, Patricia Harvey, Rhonda Olson, Julie Kovacs
Subjects: Stock shots, locations, culture, industry, medicine, military, music, environmental, leisure, transport, natural history, space, trailers.
Film; video (all film mastered onto tape).
Research: By both staff and outside researchers.
🕓 Mon-Fri 09:00 to 21:00
Description: Complete contemporary film and videotape library with a vast range of quality images. Subject headings include agriculture, buildings, cities, countries, cultural activities, industry and business, landmarks, landscapes, medical, military, music, natural phenomena, news, period recreations, professions, rain forests, recreation, space, special effects, spectacles, sports, transportation, underwater, water and wildlife. They also hold special collections of Nazi propaganda footage, Russian history, Russian space program, B-movies and trailers. Computerized. Rate card and catalogue available. NB: This is the head office, there is also an office in Vancouver, Canada Tel: (604) 684 8484, Fax: (604) 681 3299.
Foreign Offices: Argentina, Australia, Brazil, Canada, Chile, Germany, Indonesia, Japan, Malaysia, Philippines, Singapore, Mexico, Spain, USA.

FILM BANK STOCK FOOTAGE FILM & VIDEO LIBRARY

425 South Victory Boulevard, Burbank, CA 91502, USA
© +1 818 841 9176
Ⓕ +1 818 567 4235

Contacts: Paula Lumbard, Elizabeth Canelake
Subjects: News, space, special effects, science, sport, medicine, time-lapse, aerial photography, natural history, animation, locations, environmental.
🎞 16mm, 35mm; most video formats. NTSC masters.
Research: By staff only. Researchers occasionally visit for big projects.
🕐 Mon-Fri 09:00 to 17:00
Procedure: Umatics loaned or VHS assembled. 24 hours for access to masters.
Description: Diverse collection of broadcast quality film and video images aimed at supplying the full range of client productions. Most subjects are covered in the library, the latest new collections being world locations, children of the world, environmental images (destruction, scientific and beauty shots), History of Flight, more space and solar flares, aerials across the US, agriculture and animals. Partly computerized. Catalogue and rate card available.

FRONT LINE

Suite 3 Senyo Building, 5th Floor, 3-1-9 Nakameguro, Meguro-ku, Toyko 153, Japan
© +81 3 3760 6271
Ⓕ +81 3 3760 6012

Contacts: Seiichi Sugiura
Subjects: Stock shots, aviation, locations, natural history, industry, space, time-lapse, transport, environmental.
🕐 Mon-Fri 10:00 to 18:00
Procedure: Viewing tapes loaned. Masters copied after selection.
Description: Agents for UK company Index Stock Shots, USA company Opus Global and Canadian company Fabulous Footage in Japan.

HOLLYWOOD HOUSE VIDEO ARCHIVES / HOME ENTERTAINMENT HOLDINGS

Box 555, Bondi Beach, NSW 2026, Australia
ⓒ +61 2 365 1055
Ⓕ +61 2 365 1577

Contacts: Joe Shellim
Subjects: Classic films, documentaries, music, space, film industry, animation, war, personalities, circus, natural history.
▦ Film; Beta, 1", BVU, Umatic.
Research: By staff.
☉ Sun-Fri 10:00 to 19:00
Procedure: VHS viewing tape. Access to masters dependent on workload.
Description: Collection includes classic nostalgia movies complimented with interviews and rehearsals, behind-the-scenes, lost films, etc. Interviews with movie stars, candid films, footage of world leaders, space (NASA), music clips, nature and circus, cartoons, war and documentaries. Partly computerized. Rate card and catalogue available.

IMAGES OF THE EAST

19B Jalan 20/14, Petaling Jaya Selangor 46300, Malaysia
ⓒ +60 03 776 7199
Ⓕ +60 03 776 4560

Contacts: Theresa Khoo
Subjects: Stock shots, aviation, locations, natural history, industry, space, time-lapse, transport, environmental.
▦ Beta SP, 1", Umatic. PAL.
Research: By staff. Visits by appointment.
☉ Mon-Fri 08:30 to 17:45
Procedure: Viewing tapes loaned. Masters copied after selection, 3-4 days for access.
Description: Agents for UK company Index Stock Shots and German company Modern Video Library in Malaysia and Singapore. The library holds an A-Z of subject categories including landscape, destination and sports footage from Malaysia. Partly computerized. Rate card available. English spoken.

KESSER STOCK LIBRARY

21 SW 15 Road, Miami, Florida 33129, USA
ⓒ +1 305 358 7900
ⓕ +1 305 358 2209

Contacts: Emily Wilson, Charles Carrubba
Subjects: Stock shots, locations, space, agriculture, leisure, fishing, time-lapse, underwater photography, aviation.
Research: By staff.
🕓 Mon-Fri 09:00 to 17:00
Description: Range of archival and contemporary stock shot material. Subjects include world destinations, wildlife, sunsets, fireworks, horseracing, time-lapse and underwater photography, agriculture, space, fishing, etc. Partly computerized. Rate card and brochure available.

LARRY DORN ASSOCIATES / WORLD BACKGROUNDS

Suite 306, 5820 Wilshire Boulevard, Los Angeles CA 90036, USA
ⓒ +1 213 935 6266
ⓕ +1 213 935 9523

Contacts: Linda Dorn
Subjects: Stock shots, locations, Americana, aerial photography, underwater photography, aviation, transport, space.
🎞 35mm originals; 1" with matching 3/4" and VHS videotapes.
Research: By staff. Appointment to visit.
🕓 Mon-Fri 09:00 to 17:00
Procedure: Viewing tapes compiled. Masters copied on selection.
Description: Period and contemporary stock footage. European establishing shots, worldwide locations, Americana, scenics, aerials, various airlines and international airports, period wars, space, etc. Computerized. Rate card available.
Foreign Offices: France, Italy, UK.

STIMULUS / IMAGE RESEARCH

P.O. Box 170519, San Francisco, CA 94117, USA
© +1 415 558 8339
Ⓕ +1 415 864 3897

Contacts: Grant Johnson
Subjects: Computer imagery, special effects, space,
landscapes, science, educational films.
▦ Beta/Beta SP, Umatic. NTSC (also various formats of stills).
Research: By staff only.
☉ Mon-Fri 09:00 to 17:00
Procedure: VHS viewing cassettes, NTSC. 3 days for access
to masters.
Description: Stimulus are producers of scientific and
educational video programming. Their stock collection
includes Western US scenics, landscapes, geological and
computer generated terrain imagery. Also held is aerial,
satellite and computer terrain imagery of full US, some world
and planetary locations. Partly computerized.

Special effects

CASCOM INTERNATIONAL

806 4th Avenue South, Nashville, TN 37210, USA
© +1 615 242 8900
Ⓕ +1 615 256 7890

Contacts: Victor Rumore
Subjects: Special effects, computer imagery, time-lapse, animation.
▦ 16mm, 35mm; Beta SP. PAL.
Research: By outside researchers. Appointment to visit.
🕑 Mon-Fri 09:00 to 17:30
Procedure: VHS viewing tapes loaned. 1-2 hours for access to masters.
Description: Mainly computer generated effects but also time-lapse, animation and live action. Subjects covered include globes, fireworks, maps, grids, sport, health, entertainment, environment, music, space and hi-tech. Catalogue showing a freeze frame of each effect in the library is available.
Foreign Offices: Australia (Select Effects).

DARINO FILMS

222 Park Avenue South, New York, NY 10003, USA
© +1 212 228 4024
Ⓕ +1 212 473 7448

Contacts: Ed Darino
Subjects: Special effects, computer imagery, trailers, stock shots, environmental.
Research: By staff. Appointment to visit.
🕑 Mon-Fri 09:00 to 17:00
Description: Darino Films hold a library of special effects comprised of computer graphics and animated backgrounds. They also have The Producers Library of approximately 10 hours of stock footage, environmental, historic, nature, cities, etc. In addition they have the Hollywood Vaults collection of 2500 trailers. Computerized. Rate card and brochure available.

ENERGY PRODUCTIONS' TIMESCAPE IMAGE LIBRARY

4th Floor, 12700 Ventura Boulevard, Studio City, CA 91604 USA
© +1 818 508 1444
Ⓕ +1 818 508 1293

Contacts: Joan Sargent, Randy Gitsch
Subjects: Americana, sport, time-lapse, macro photography, natural history, locations, fashion, culture, landscapes, lifestyles, special effects.
16mm, 35mm, 70mm; most video formats.
Research: By staff. Visits by appointment.
Mon-Fri 09.00 to 18.00
Procedure: Viewing tapes assembled. Masters copied after selection.
Description: Energy Productions hold the Timescape Image Library, a huge library of stock material encompassing sports, wildlife, landmarks, cities, seascapes, macro/micro photography, fashion, underwater, botany, computer imagery and daily life from around the world. Also available via this office is The Playboy Fashion Collection, Namco Computer Imagery, Warren Miller Films and Sports Library, Windham Hills Video and Film Library and Bob Landis Wildlife. Computerized. Rate card and brochure available. NB: Energy also have a New York office, Tel: (212) 686 4900, Fax: (212) 686 4998.Mon-Fri 09:00 to 18:00
Foreign Offices: France, Germany, Italy, Japan, Spain, Sweden, Turkey, Israel, UK, USA.

FILM BANK STOCK FOOTAGE FILM & VIDEO LIBRARY

425 South Victory Boulevard, Burbank, CA 91502, USA
Ⓒ +1 818 841 9176
Ⓕ +1 818 567 4235

Contacts: Paula Lumbard, Elizabeth Canelake
Subjects: News, space, special effects, science, sport,
medicine, time-lapse, aerial photography, natural history,
animation, locations, environmental.
▦ 16mm, 35mm; most video formats. NTSC masters.
Research: By staff only. Researchers occasionally visit for big
projects.
🕐 Mon-Fri 09:00 to 17:00
Procedure: Umatics loaned or VHS assembled. 24 hours for
access to masters.
Description: Diverse collection of broadcast quality film and
video images aimed at supplying the full range of client
productions. Most subjects are covered in the library, the
latest new collections being world locations, children of the
world, environmental images (destruction, scientific and
beauty shots), History of Flight, more space and solar flares,
aerials across the US, agriculture and animals. Partly
computerized. Catalogue and rate card available.

SELECT EFFECTS – AUSTRALIA

11 Station Street, Naremburn, NSW 2065, Australia
Ⓒ +61 2 437 5620
Ⓕ +61 2 901 4505

Contacts: Jill Freestone
Subjects: Special effects, computer imagery, time-lapse,
animation.
▦ 16mm, 35mm; Beta SP. PAL.
Research: By outside researchers. Appointment to visit.
🕐 Mon-Fri 09:00 to 17:30
Procedure: VHS viewing tapes loaned. 1-2 hours for access
to masters.
Description: Mainly computer generated effects but also
time-lapse, animation and live action. Subjects covered
include globes, fireworks, maps, grids, sport, health,
entertainment, environment, music, space and hi-tech. This
company represents US company Cascom International.
Partly computerized. Catalogue showing a freeze frame of
each effect in the library is available.
Foreign Offices: USA (Cascom International).

STIMULUS / IMAGE RESEARCH

P.O. Box 170519, San Francisco, CA 94117, USA
ⓒ +1 415 558 8339
ⓕ +1 415 864 3897

Contacts: Grant Johnson
Subjects: Computer imagery, special effects, space, landscapes, science, educational films.
Beta/Beta SP, Umatic. NTSC (also various formats of stills).
Research: By staff only.
Mon-Fri 09:00 to 17:00
Procedure: VHS viewing cassettes, NTSC. 3 days for access to masters.
Description: Stimulus are producers of scientific and educational video programming. Their stock collection includes Western US scenics, landscapes, geological and computer generated terrain imagery. Also held is aerial, satellite and computer terrain imagery of full US, some world and planetary locations. Partly computerized.

Time-lapse

CASCOM INTERNATIONAL

806 4th Avenue South, Nashville, TN 37210, USA
© +1 615 242 8900
Ⓕ +1 615 256 7890

Contacts: Victor Rumore
Subjects: Special effects, computer imagery, time-lapse, animation.
▦ 16mm, 35mm; Beta SP. PAL.
Research: By outside researchers. Appointment to visit.
☉ Mon-Fri 09:00 to 17:30
Procedure: VHS viewing tapes loaned. 1-2 hours for access to masters.
Description: Mainly computer generated effects but also time-lapse, animation and live action. Subjects covered include globes, fireworks, maps, grids, sport, health, entertainment, environment, music, space and hi-tech. Catalogue showing a freeze frame of each effect in the library is available.
Foreign Offices: Australia (Select Effects).

CINEMA NETWORK (CINENET)

Suite 111, 2235 First Street, Simi Valley CA 93065, USA
© +1 805 527 0093
Ⓕ +1 805 527 0305

Contacts: Richard Spruiell, Jim Jarrard
Subjects: Stock shots, natural history, locations, sport, time-lapse, underwater photography.
▦ 35mm, 16mm; NTSC videotape.
Research: By staff. Appointment to visit.
Procedure: Viewing tapes compiled. Masters copied after payment received.
Description: Stock footage library with very comprehensive A-Z listing of subjects - almost every topic you can think of is covered in their brochure, they also undertake custom filming. Computerized on Cinemind software. Rate card and brochure available.

ENERGY PRODUCTIONS' TIMESCAPE IMAGE LIBRARY

4th Floor, 12700 Ventura Boulevard, Studio City, CA 91604 USA
ⓒ +1 818 508 1444
Ⓕ +1 818 508 1293

Contacts: Joan Sargent, Randy Gitsch
Subjects: Americana, sport, time-lapse, macro photography, natural history, locations, fashion, culture, landscapes, lifestyles, special effects.
16mm, 35mm, 70mm; most video formats.
Research: By staff. Visits by appointment.
🕐 Mon-Fri 09.00 to 18.00
Procedure: Viewing tapes assembled. Masters copied after selection.
Description: Energy Productions hold the Timescape Image Library, a huge library of stock material encompassing sports, wildlife, landmarks, cities, seascapes, macro/micro photography, fashion, underwater, botany, computer imagery and daily life from around the world. Also available via this office is The Playboy Fashion Collection, Namco Computer Imagery, Warren Miller Films and Sports Library, Windham Hills Video and Film Library and Bob Landis Wildlife. Computerized. Rate card and brochure available. NB: Energy also have a New York office, Tel: (212) 686 4900, Fax: (212) 686 4998.Mon-Fri 09:00 to 18:00
Foreign Offices: France, Germany, Italy, Japan, Spain, Sweden, Turkey, Israel, UK, USA.

FILM & VIDEO STOCK SHOTS

Suite E, 10700 Ventura Boulevard, Studio City CA 91604, USA
ⓒ +1 818 760 2098
Ⓕ +1 818 760 3294

Contacts: Stephanie Siebert, William Bolls
Subjects: Stock shots, current affairs, leisure, natural history, time-lapse, locations, macro photography, animation, culture, landscapes.
Film; videotape.
Research: By staff. Appointment to visit.
🕐 Mon-Fri 09:00 to 17:00
Description: Huge selection of both current and archival film and videotape original images. Subjects include news events, action sports, nature and wildlife, time-lapse cinematography, landscapes and cityscapes, microscopy, cartoons, lifestyles and travel footage. Next business day turnaround on master footage orders and competitive rates. Computerized. Brochure and rate card available.

FILM BANK STOCK FOOTAGE FILM & VIDEO LIBRARY

425 South Victory Boulevard, Burbank, CA 91502, USA
ⓒ +1 818 841 9176
ⓕ +1 818 567 4235

Contacts: Paula Lumbard, Elizabeth Canelake
Subjects: News, space, special effects, science, sport, medicine, time-lapse, aerial photography, natural history, animation, locations, environmental.

▦ 16mm, 35mm; most video formats. NTSC masters.

Research: By staff only. Researchers occasionally visit for big projects.

☉ Mon-Fri 09:00 to 17:00

Procedure: Umatics loaned or VHS assembled. 24 hours for access to masters.

Description: Diverse collection of broadcast quality film and video images aimed at supplying the full range of client productions. Most subjects are covered in the library, the latest new collections being world locations, children of the world, environmental images (destruction, scientific and beauty shots), History of Flight, more space and solar flares, aerials across the US, agriculture and animals. Partly computerized. Catalogue and rate card available.

FISH FILMS FOOTAGE WORLD

4548 Van Noord Avenue, Studio City, CA 91604-1013, USA
ⓒ +1 818 905 1071
ⓕ +1 818 905 0301

Contacts: David Fishbein
Subjects: Historical archive, stock shots, time-lapse, underwater photography, Americana, locations, leisure, comedy, transport, industrial.
Research: By staff. Appointment to visit.

☉ Mon-Fri 09:00 to 17:00

Description: Vintage and contemporary footage covering all subject areas. Time-lapse, underwater, scenics, aerials, sports, specializing in lifestyles, comedy, historic events, transportation, Americana, educational, travel, industrial, public domain. Partly computerized. Rate card and brochure available.

FRONT LINE

Suite 3 Senyo Building, 5th Floor, 3-1-9 Nakameguro,
Meguro-ku, Toyko 153, Japan
ⓒ +81 3 3760 6271
Ⓕ +81 3 3760 6012

Contacts: Seiichi Sugiura
Subjects: Stock shots, aviation, locations, natural history,
industry, space, time-lapse, transport, environmental.
☉ Mon–Fri 10:00 to 18:00
Procedure: Viewing tapes loaned. Masters copied after
selection.
Description: Agents for UK company Index Stock Shots, USA
company Opus Global and Canadian company Fabulous
Footage in Japan.

IMAGE BANK / FILM DIVISION

4th Floor, 111 Fifth Avenue, New York NY 10003, USA
ⓒ +1 212 529 6700
Ⓕ +1 212 529 8889

Contacts: Brian Mitchell
Subjects: Stock shots, aerial photography, time-lapse,
lifestyles, natural history, locations, sport.
▦ All film and video formats and line standards held.
Research: By both staff and outside researchers.
Appointment to visit.
☉ Mon–Fri 09:00 to 17:00
Procedure: 3/4"/VHS (any line standard) for viewing. 24
hours for access to masters.
Description: Vast collection of stock material, contemporary
and archival, acquired from Turner Broadcasting, Ocean
Images, I.R.E., Pigeon Productions, MacGillivray Freeman
Films, Dentsu Prox., McDonnell Douglas, Nature
Conservancy, etc. Offices worldwide and major cities of
North America – Chicago, Detroit, Mexico, Minneapolis,
Atlanta, Dallas and Los Angeles. Computerized. English,
French, Spanish, Italian, German and Greek spoken in the
NEW YORK HEADQUARTERS.
Foreign Offices: Argentina, Brazil, Chile, Colombia, Australia,
Canada, Hong Kong, Indonesia, Korea, Japan, Malaysia,
Philippines, Singapore, Taiwan, Thailand, South Africa, UK,
USA.

IMAGES OF THE EAST

19B Jalan 20/14, Petaling Jaya Selangor 46300, Malaysia
ⓒ +60 03 776 7199
Ⓕ +60 03 776 4560

Contacts: Theresa Khoo
Subjects: Stock shots, aviation, locations, natural history, industry, space, time-lapse, transport, environmental.
▦ Beta SP, 1″, Umatic. PAL.
Research: By staff. Visits by appointment.
🕓 Mon-Fri 08:30 to 17:45
Procedure: Viewing tapes loaned. Masters copied after selection, 3-4 days for access.
Description: Agents for UK company Index Stock Shots and German company Modern Video Library in Malaysia and Singapore. The library holds an A-Z of subject categories including landscape, destination and sports footage from Malaysia. Partly computerized. Rate card available. English spoken.

JACK CHISHOLM FILM PRODUCTIONS

Suite 50, 99 Atlantic Avenue, Toronto, Ontario M6K 3J8, Canada
ⓒ +1 416 588 5200
Ⓕ +1 416 588 5324

Contacts: Peter Robinson
Subjects: Stock shots, historical archive, locations, time-lapse, current affairs, newsreels, natural history, industry, science.
▦ 16mm, 35mm; Beta/Beta SP, 1″, Umatic, SVHS, some digital. NTSC.
Research: By staff only.
🕓 Mon-Fri 09:00 to 17:30
Procedure: Umatic or VHS viewing copies. 24 hours for access to masters.
Description: The stock footage library contains archive material dating from 1896 up to present day. Subjects cover major events around the world, wildlife, foreign locations, industry and science as well as quality shots of clouds, sunsets, time-lapse flowers, etc. The collection comprises of 10 000 hours of video footage and 4 million feet of film. They hold 35mm neg of across Canada scenics plus the Millenium television series. Computerized. Rate card available. English and Italian spoken.

KESSER STOCK LIBRARY

21 SW 15 Road, Miami, Florida 33129, USA
ⓒ +1 305 358 7900
Ⓕ +1 305 358 2209

Contacts: Emily Wilson, Charles Carrubba
Subjects: Stock shots, locations, space, agriculture, leisure, fishing, time-lapse, underwater photography, aviation.
Research: By staff.
🕐 Mon-Fri 09:00 to 17:00
Description: Range of archival and contemporary stock shot material. Subjects include world destinations, wildlife, sunsets, fireworks, horseracing, time-lapse and underwater photography, agriculture, space, fishing, etc. Partly computerized. Rate card and brochure available.

OPUS GLOBAL / THE ELECTRONIC LIBRARY

1133 N. Highland Avenue, Hollywood, CA 90038, USA
ⓒ +1 213 993 9888
Ⓕ +1 213 993 9899

Contacts: Todd Stubner, Masih Madani
Subjects: Stock shots, time-lapse, feature films, advertising, newsreels.
▦ Most film and video formats. NTSC.
Research: By staff and outside researchers. Appointment to visit.
🕐 7 days 24 hours
Procedure: Viewing on VHS, Umatic, CD-ROM. Less than 24 hours for access to masters.
Description: Contemporary and archival collection ranging from material specially shot for stock footage (real time and time altered) and out-takes from productions to vintage newsreels, feature films and commercials. The electronic library contains more than two million scenes catalogued by a unique object and relational database. Queries can be made on the content of image, the patterns, colours, texture and shapes of image objects, related layout and position information as well as keywords. Images are available in all formats including MPEG and JPEG for use in all mediums including CD-ROM. Stills, sound effects and music are also supplied. Fully computerized. Rate card and catalogue available electronically.
Foreign Offices: Represented by Front Line in Japan.

PLANET PICTURES

P.O. Box 65862, Los Angeles, CA 90065, USA
ⓒ +1 818 246 7700
Ⓕ +1 818 240 8391

Contacts: Jenny Hayden
Subjects: Documentaries, medicine, health, educational films, natural history, time-lapse.
▦ Time-lapse on film; mainly video.
Research: By both staff and outside researchers. Appointment to visit.
🕐 Mon-Fri 09:00 to 18:00
Description: Over 400 hours of footage and completed documentaries on a variety of subjects - medicine and health, high technology, workplace, nature, timelapse, wildlife, adventure, arts and entertainment and people. Computerized. Brochure available.

SECOND LINE SEARCH

1926 Broadway, New York, NY 10023, USA
ⓒ +1 212 787 7500
Ⓕ +1 212 787 7636

Contacts: Susan Luchars, George Bartko
Subjects: Locations, historical archive, sport, natural history, aerial photography, time-lapse, Americana, out-takes, industry, lifestyles.
▦ Variety of film and video formats.
Research: By staff.
🕐 Mon-Fri 09:30 to 18:00
Procedure: Umatic viewing cassettes (NTSC or PAL). 2-3 days for access to masters.
Description: A variety of material including scenics, archival footage, sports, wildlife, news, aerials, international locations, Americana, oddities/bloopers, industry, technology, lifestyle and time-lapse. Computerized. French, Spanish, Portuguese, Italian and German spoken.

SELECT EFFECTS – AUSTRALIA

11 Station Street, Naremburn, NSW 2065, Australia
© +61 2 437 5620
Ⓕ +61 2 901 4505

Contacts: Jill Freestone
Subjects: Special effects, computer imagery, time-lapse, animation.
🎞 16mm, 35mm; Beta SP. PAL.
Research: By outside researchers. Appointment to visit.
🕐 Mon-Fri 09:00 to 17:30
Procedure: VHS viewing tapes loaned. 1-2 hours for access to masters.
Description: Mainly computer generated effects but also time-lapse, animation and live action. Subjects covered include globes, fireworks, maps, grids, sport, health, entertainment, environment, music, space and hi-tech. This company represents US company Cascom International. Partly computerized. Catalogue showing a freeze frame of each effect in the library is available.
Foreign Offices: USA (Cascom International).

SOURCE STOCK FOOTAGE LIBRARY, THE

738 N. Constitution Drive, Tuscon, Arizona 85748, USA
© +1 602 298 4810
Ⓕ +1 602 290 8831

Contacts: John Willwater, Bill and Lynne Briggs
Subjects: Stock shots, natural history, industry, time-lapse, locations, mining.
Research: By staff.
🕐 Mon-Fri 08:00 to 17:00
Description: Scenics, time-lapse, clouds and suns, animals, petrochemical and mining industrial, US and international destinations, desert plants and animals, cowboys, Phoenix, Tuscson, Alaskan wilderness and animals. Computerized. Rate card and brochure available.

STUART JEWELL PRODUCTIONS

2040 Garden Lane, Costa Mesa, CA 92627, USA
© +1 714 548 7234
Ⓕ +1 818 508 1293 (agents fax)

Contacts: Agent Energy Productions
Subjects: Documentaries, natural history, culture, locations, time-lapse, aerial photography, steam trains.
▦ 16mm, 35mm; Beta SP, D2 1″, BVU. NTSC.
Description: Series of worldwide documentaries mostly natural history subjects - titles include Rolling to Guatemala, Following the Oregon Trail, Winter in Yellowstone, Teton and Mount. Rainer National Parks, The Great Aerial Odyssey, locations including Alaska, Hawaii, Borneo, Thailand, Africa, Egypt, India, Nepal plus steam trains in America, Canada, Australia and Guatemala. Partly computerized. NB: Represented by Energy Productions.
Foreign Offices: Contact local Energy Productions office.

TELECINE INTERNATIONAL PRODUCTIONS

P.O. Box 8426, Universal City, CA 91608, USA
© +1 818 889 8246
Ⓕ +1 818 889 5605

Contacts: Nick Archer
Subjects: Stock shots, locations, transport, aviation, time-lapse, landscapes.
▦ 35mm.
Research: By both staff and outside researchers.
🕐 Mon-Fri 09:00 to 18:00
Procedure: Film/cassette viewing reels. Minimum royalty due for masters.
Description: Worldwide establishing shots, cityscapes and traffic from 1957 to present day, transportation, jets, buildings, scenics, moons, sunrises, suns, time-lapse clouds. Rate card and brochure available.

Tourism

AUDIO VISUAL INSTITUTE, NATIONAL LIBRARY & ARCHIVE

P.O. Box 31519, Dar Es Salaam, Tanzania
© +255 51 72601/2/3/4

Contacts: M.I. Kange, Eva Sessoa
Subjects: National Archives, educational films, engineering, health, agriculture, tourism, current affairs.
🎞 16mm, 35mm.
Research: Permission and appointment needed prior to research.
🕐 Mon-Fri 07:30 to 15:30
Procedure: On request.
Description: Copyright to materials in the collection is owned by respective producers of films. The library is not computerized. A book catalogue is issued.

DELTA PRODUCTIONS

P.O. Box 4836, Darwin, NT 0801, Australia
© +61 89 817435 / 817568
Ⓕ +61 89 813213

Contacts: Bob West
Subjects: Historical archive, landscapes, tourism.
🎞 BVU, Beta/Beta SP, SVHS. PAL.
Research: By staff. Appointment to visit.
🕐 Mon-Fri 08:30 to 17:00
Procedure: Access to masters in 2-3 days.
Description: Main area covered is the Northern Territory of Australia with footage covering special events since 1982 and all major tourist locations and attractions. Delta also have some historical material dating from the 1920s to 1940s. Partly computerized.

FILM WORLD

2 Whiting Street, P.O. Box 313, Artarmon, NSW 2064, Australia
℃ +61 2 438 1888
Ⓕ +61 2 439 8541

Contacts: Naomi Saville
Subjects: Newsreels, locations, natural history, lifestyles, tourism, travelogues.
Film; Beta/Beta SP, 1″, D1. PAL and NTSC.
Research: By both staff and outside researchers.
Appointment to visit.
Mon-Fri 08:30 to 17:30
Procedure: VHS or Umatic viewing cassettes. 24 hours for access to masters.
Description: Over 3000 hours of footage covering archival news material, contemporary landscapes, wildlife and lifestyles. Film World are exclusive agents for the Cinesound and Movietone newsreel collection, Australian Tourist Commission, Queensland Tourist & Travel Corporation, Canadian company Fabulous Footage and many more. Computerized. Subject headings list and rate card available.

Trailers

AMAZING IMAGES

Suite 1581, 6671 Sunset Boulevard, Hollywood CA 90028, USA
ⓒ +1 213 962 1899
ⓕ +1 213 962 1898

Contacts: Michael Peter Yakaitis
Subjects: Historical archive, newsreels, classic films, trailers, out-takes, personalities.
▦ 16mm, 35mm; video.
Research: By staff only.
◷ Mon–Fri 09:30 to 18:00
Procedure: VHS or Umatic viewing copies. 24 hours for access to masters.
Description: The collection begins pre-1900 and includes old Hollywood stars of silent and sound motion pictures, locations around the globe, newsreels, historical events, world war, comedy, censorship, serial and weekly magazines, bloopers, Kodascopes, out-takes and film trailers. There is also a wide assortment of animal footage, celebrities and industrial material. Partly computerized. Rate card available.

DARINO FILMS

222 Park Avenue South, New York, NY 10003, USA
ⓒ +1 212 228 4024
ⓕ +1 212 473 7448

Contacts: Ed Darino
Subjects: Special effects, computer imagery, trailers, stock shots, environmental.
Research: By staff. Appointment to visit.
◷ Mon–Fri 09:00 to 17:00
Description: Darino Films hold a library of special effects comprised of computer graphics and animated backgrounds. They also have The Producers Library of approximately 10 hours of stock footage, environmental, historic, nature, cities, etc. In addition they have the Hollywood Vaults collection of 2500 trailers. Computerized. Rate card and brochure available.

FABULOUS FOOTAGE

4th Floor, 19 Mercer Street, Toronto, Ontario M5V 1H2,
Canada
℡ +1 416 591 6955
℻ +1 416 591 1666

Contacts: Steve Race, Patricia Harvey, Rhonda Olson, Julie
Kovacs
Subjects: Stock shots, locations, culture, industry, medicine,
military, music, environmental, leisure, transport, natural
history, space, trailers.
▦ Film; video (all film mastered onto tape).
Research: By both staff and outside researchers.
☺ Mon-Fri 09:00 to 21:00
Description: Complete contemporary film and videotape
library with a vast range of quality images. Subject headings
include agriculture, buildings, cities, countries, cultural
activities, industry and business, landmarks, landscapes,
medical, military, music, natural phenomena, news, period
recreations, professions, rain forests, recreation, space,
special effects, spectacles, sports, transportation,
underwater, water and wildlife. They also hold special
collections of Nazi propaganda footage, Russian history,
Russian space program, B-movies and trailers. Computerized.
Rate card and catalogue available. NB: This is the head
office, there is also an office in Vancouver, Canada Tel:
(604) 684 8484, Fax: (604) 681 3299.
Foreign Offices: Argentina, Australia, Brazil, Canada, Chile,
Germany, Indonesia, Japan, Malaysia, Philippines, Singapore,
Mexico, Spain, USA.

ORIGINAL FILMVIDEO LIBRARY

P.O. Box 3457, Anaheim, CA 92803, USA
© +1 714 526 4392
Ⓕ +1 714 526 4392

Contacts: Ronnie L. James
Subjects: Classic films, advertising, trailers, television,
animation.
▦ 16mm, 35mm.
Research: By staff only.
☉ Mon-Fri 10:00 to 16:00
Procedure: Viewing tapes available for small fee. All prints
on site.
Description: Over 10 000 original rare 16mm and 35mm
prints of vintage TV shows dating mainly from 1948 to 1970
and mostly produced by US companies. Many legendary
talents rediscovered in forgotten or undocumented
appearances on television, from Gloria Swanson to Richard
Burton. Also thousands of TV commercials, movie preview
trailers and other shorts. Transfers from prints can be made
on site to VHS and Umatic via the Elmo TRV-16G system.
Additionally there is an exhaustive reference library on TV
and movies. Selective catalogue available, collection
constantly being added to. Rates quoted based on title and
use.

TRAILERS ON TAPE

Suite 1, 1576 Fell Street, San Francisco CA 94117-2146,
USA
© +1 415 921 8273 / 5449
Ⓕ +1 415 921 8273

Contacts: Bill Longen, Stanton Schaffer
Subjects: Trailers.
▦ 16mm, 35mm; most video formats. NTSC.
Research: By staff only.
☉ Mon-Sat 10:00 to 14:00
Procedure: Timecoded VHS available for fee. 48 hours for
acess to masters.
Description: Over 6000 classic movie previews covering the
1920s through to the early 1970s. Partly computerized.
Catalogue and rate card available.

Transport

FABULOUS FOOTAGE

4th Floor, 19 Mercer Street, Toronto, Ontario M5V 1H2,
Canada
© +1 416 591 6955
Ⓕ +1 416 591 1666

Contacts: Steve Race, Patricia Harvey, Rhonda Olson, Julie
Kovacs
Subjects: Stock shots, locations, culture, industry, medicine,
military, music, environmental, leisure, transport, natural
history, space, trailers.
▦ Film; video (all film mastered onto tape).
Research: By both staff and outside researchers.
☾ Mon–Fri 09:00 to 21:00
Description: Complete contemporary film and videotape
library with a vast range of quality images. Subject headings
include agriculture, buildings, cities, countries, cultural
activities, industry and business, landmarks, landscapes,
medical, military, music, natural phenomena, news, period
recreations, professions, rain forests, recreation, space,
special effects, spectacles, sports, transportation,
underwater, water and wildlife. They also hold special
collections of Nazi propaganda footage, Russian history,
Russian space program, B-movies and trailers. Computerized.
Rate card and catalogue available. NB: This is the head
office, there is also an office in Vancouver, Canada Tel:
(604) 684 8484, Fax: (604) 681 3299.
Foreign Offices: Argentina, Australia, Brazil, Canada, Chile,
Germany, Indonesia, Japan, Malaysia, Philippines, Singapore,
Mexico, Spain, USA.

FISH FILMS FOOTAGE WORLD

4548 Van Noord Avenue, Studio City, CA 91604-1013, USA
© +1 818 905 1071
Ⓕ +1 818 905 0301

Contacts: David Fishbein
Subjects: Historical archive, stock shots, time-lapse,
underwater photography, Americana, locations, leisure,
comedy, transport, industrial.
Research: By staff. Appointment to visit.
☾ Mon–Fri 09:00 to 17:00
Description: Vintage and contemporary footage covering all
subject areas. Time-lapse, underwater, scenics, aerials,
sports, specializing in lifestyles, comedy, historic events,
transportation, Americana, educational, travel, industrial,
public domain. Partly computerized. Rate card and brochure
available.

FRONT LINE

Suite 3 Senyo Building, 5th Floor, 3-1-9 Nakameguro,
Meguro-ku, Toyko 153, Japan
© +81 3 3760 6271
Ⓕ +81 3 3760 6012

Contacts: Seiichi Sugiura
Subjects: Stock shots, aviation, locations, natural history,
industry, space, time-lapse, transport, environmental.
🕐 Mon-Fri 10:00 to 18:00
Procedure: Viewing tapes loaned. Masters copied after
selection.
Description: Agents for UK company Index Stock Shots, USA
company Opus Global and Canadian company Fabulous
Footage in Japan.

IMAGES OF THE EAST

19B Jalan 20/14, Petaling Jaya Selangor 46300, Malaysia
© +60 03 776 7199
Ⓕ +60 03 776 4560

Contacts: Theresa Khoo
Subjects: Stock shots, aviation, locations, natural history,
industry, space, time-lapse, transport, environmental.
🎞 Beta SP, 1", Umatic. PAL.
Research: By staff. Visits by appointment.
🕐 Mon-Fri 08:30 to 17:45
Procedure: Viewing tapes loaned. Masters copied after
selection, 3-4 days for access.
Description: Agents for UK company Index Stock Shots and
German company Modern Video Library in Malaysia and
Singapore. The library holds an A-Z of subject categories
including landscape, destination and sports footage from
Malaysia. Partly computerized. Rate card available. English
spoken.

JOHN E. ALLEN

116 North Avenue, Park Ridge, NJ 07656, USA
℡ +1 201 391 3299
℻ +1 201 391 6335

Contacts: John E. Allen, Beverley Allen
Subjects: Historical archive, newsreels, war, Russia, industry, transport, classic films, educational films, travelogues.
▦ Mainly film; some video.
Research: By both staff and outside researchers.
🕐 Mon-Fri 09:00 to 18:00
Description: Kinograms from 1915 to 1931. Telenews 1947 to 1953. World War I and II, Spanish American War, Mexican Revolution, Russian Revolution, Hungarian Revolution, Spanish Civil War, Korean War, etc. Industry 1910 to 1950s, transportation, educational, ethnographic, travel, nature, features 1905 to 1950s, stills, posters and lobby cards. Partly computerized. Rate card available.

LARRY DORN ASSOCIATES / WORLD BACKGROUNDS

Suite 306, 5820 Wilshire Boulevard, Los Angeles CA 90036, USA
℡ +1 213 935 6266
℻ +1 213 935 9523

Contacts: Linda Dorn
Subjects: Stock shots, locations, Americana, aerial photography, underwater photography, aviation, transport, space.
▦ 35mm originals; 1" with matching 3/4" and VHS videotapes.
Research: By staff. Appointment to visit.
🕐 Mon-Fri 09:00 to 17:00
Procedure: Viewing tapes compiled. Masters copied on selection.
Description: Period and contemporary stock footage. European establishing shots, worldwide locations, Americana, scenics, aerials, various airlines and international airports, period wars, space, etc. Computerized. Rate card available.
Foreign Offices: France, Italy, UK.

PARAMOUNT PICTURES FILM LIBRARY

Hal Wallis Building, Room 108, 5555 Melrose Avenue, Hollywood CA 90038, USA
ⓒ +1 213 956 5510
Ⓕ +1 213 956 1833

Contacts: Pat Harris
Subjects: Stock shots, aerial photography, transport, aviation, locations, building, skylines, out-takes.
35mm.
Research: By staff only (no charge made). Appointment to visit.
🕑 Mon–Fri 09:00 to 18:00
Procedure: Film transferred to video at clients cost. 4-5 days for access to masters
Description: Out-takes and unused footage from Paramount's features and television series spanning over 50 years. Over 9000 contemporary scenes catalogued in the past year. Subjects vary from aerials of cities and countrysides, stationary and moving process for cars, planes and trains, buildings of every type, scenery to aviation, amusements and skylines. Material is exclusively 35mm including 3 strip technicolor. Rate card available.

PETRIFIED FILMS / THE IMAGE BANK

Room 204, 430 West 14th Street, New York NY 10014, USA
ⓒ +1 212 242 5461
Ⓕ +1 212 691 8347

Contacts: Lori Cheatle, Rob Cates
Subjects: Historical archive, Hollywood, transport, consumerism, Americana, industry, war, aviation, feature film, out-takes.
35mm, 16mm; some on 1", D2, 3/4" with matching VHS.
Research: By staff. Visits by appointment.
🕑 Mon–Fri 09:30 to 18:00
Procedure: Viewing tapes assembled. Masters copied after selection.
Description: Historical collection including pre-1951 Warner Brothers stock and pre-1965 Columbia Pictures stock. A-Z of subjects including action sequences, period recreations, establishing shots, projection backgrounds, cityscapes and worldwide locations. Industrial, military and aviation collections. Car culture and 1950s daily life in the US. Majority dates from 1920s to 1960s. Partly computerized. Rate card and catalogue available.
Foreign Offices: Contact local Image Bank office.

STOCK SHOTS

1085 Louise Avenue, San Jose, CA 95125, USA
© +1 408 971 1325
Ⓕ +1 408 723 3846

Contacts: Tom Mertens
Subjects: Transport, agriculture, locations, medicine, health.
▦ 20 000 feet of film; 500 hours of videotape.
Research: By staff.
🕐 Mon–Fri 10:00 to 16:00
Description: Silicon Valley, San Francisco aerials, rail transit, agriculture, Europe, Asian, Africa collection filmed 1945 to 1975. Also incorporates The Justin Byers Film Collection. Partly computerized. Rate card available.

TELECINE INTERNATIONAL PRODUCTIONS

P.O. Box 8426, Universal City, CA 91608, USA
© +1 818 889 8246
Ⓕ +1 818 889 5605

Contacts: Nick Archer
Subjects: Stock shots, locations, transport, aviation, time-lapse, landscapes.
▦ 35mm.
Research: By both staff and outside researchers.
🕐 Mon–Fri 09:00 to 18:00
Procedure: Film/cassette viewing reels. Minimum royalty due for masters.
Description: Worldwide establishing shots, cityscapes and traffic from 1957 to present day, transportation, jets, buildings, scenics, moons, sunrises, suns, time-lapse clouds. Rate card and brochure available.

WPA FILM LIBRARY

5525 W. 159th Street, Oak Forest, IL 60452, USA
© +1 708 535 1540
Ⓕ +1 708 535 1541

Contacts: Michael Mertz
Subjects: Historical archive, newsreels, industry, Americana, music, transport, fashion, locations, natural history.
10 000 hours film; 2000 hours videotape.
Research: By both staff and outside researchers.
Mon-Fri 8:30 to 17:00
Description: Complete historical materials from 1896 to the present day. Specialities include newsreels, Americana from the 1940s and 50s, early rock and roll performances (Hullabaloo in 1964/5, The Music Scene in 1969/70), UFOs, automobiles, fashions, American Civil Rights, contemporary geographic materials, nature and wildlife, American industry collection from the 1940s to the present day. Also represent British Pathe News for North America only. Partly computerized. Rate card and brochure available.

Underwater photography

AL GIDDINGS – IMAGES UNLIMITED

8001 Capwell Drive, Oakland, CA 94621, USA
© +1 510 562 8000
Ⓕ +1 510 562 8001

Contacts: Terry Thompson
Subjects: Natural history, underwater photography, environmental.
▦ 16mm, 35mm; most video formats. NTSC.
Research: By staff. Appointment to visit.
🕐 Mon-Fri 09:00 to 17:00
Procedure: Umatic/VHS tapes compiled or view at studio. 1-3 days for access to masters.
Description: Library of material made up from Al Giddings undersea and nature adventure television specials. Images range in diversity from whales and sharks to minute creatures, and from polar regions to tropical islands. Scenics, wildlife, nature and marine life from ocean floor to mountain top, tropics, desert, north and south poles, kelp forests, redwood forests, rainforest, storms, moons, divers, shipwrecks, etc. New footage from an expedition to the shipwrecked Titanic. Computerized. Brochure available.

CINEMA NETWORK (CINENET)

Suite 111, 2235 First Street, Simi Valley CA 93065, USA
© +1 805 527 0093
Ⓕ +1 805 527 0305

Contacts: Richard Spruiell, Jim Jarrard
Subjects: Stock shots, natural history, locations, sport, time-lapse, underwater photography.
▦ 35mm, 16mm; NTSC videotape.
Research: By staff. Appointment to visit.
Procedure: Viewing tapes compiled. Masters copied after payment received.
Description: Stock footage library with very comprehensive A-Z listing of subjects - almost every topic you can think of is covered in their brochure, they also undertake custom filming. Computerized on Cinemind software. Rate card and brochure available.

FILMSEARCH AUSTRALASIA

P.O. Box 46, Lindfield, NSW 2070, Australia
ⓒ +61 2 4162633
ⓕ +61 2 4162554

Contacts: Chris Rowell
Subjects: Natural history, underwater photography, Asia.
16mm, 35mm; Beta SP, D2, 1". PAL.
Research: By both staff and outside researchers.
Appointment to visit.
🕐 Mon-Fri 09:00 to 17:00
Procedure: Timecoded PAL cassettes for viewing. 3 days for access to masters.
Description: Australian flora and fauna, underwater footage, some contemporary material and Asian footage.
Computerized. Rate card available.

FISH FILMS FOOTAGE WORLD

4548 Van Noord Avenue, Studio City, CA 91604-1013, USA
ⓒ +1 818 905 1071
ⓕ +1 818 905 0301

Contacts: David Fishbein
Subjects: Historical archive, stock shots, time-lapse, underwater photography, Americana, locations, leisure, comedy, transport, industrial.
Research: By staff. Appointment to visit.
🕐 Mon-Fri 09:00 to 17:00
Description: Vintage and contemporary footage covering all subject areas. Time-lapse, underwater, scenics, aerials, sports, specializing in lifestyles, comedy, historic events, transportation, Americana, educational, travel, industrial, public domain. Partly computerized. Rate card and brochure available.

KESSER STOCK LIBRARY

21 SW 15 Road, Miami, Florida 33129, USA
ⓒ +1 305 358 7900
Ⓕ +1 305 358 2209

Contacts: Emily Wilson, Charles Carrubba
Subjects: Stock shots, locations, space, agriculture, leisure, fishing, time-lapse, underwater photography, aviation.
Research: By staff.
☺ Mon-Fri 09:00 to 17:00
Description: Range of archival and contemporary stock shot material. Subjects include world destinations, wildlife, sunsets, fireworks, horseracing, time-lapse and underwater photography, agriculture, space, fishing, etc. Partly computerized. Rate card and brochure available.

LARRY DORN ASSOCIATES / WORLD BACKGROUNDS

Suite 306, 5820 Wilshire Boulevard, Los Angeles CA 90036, USA
ⓒ +1 213 935 6266
Ⓕ +1 213 935 9523

Contacts: Linda Dorn
Subjects: Stock shots, locations, Americana, aerial photography, underwater photography, aviation, transport, space.
▦ 35mm originals; 1" with matching 3/4" and VHS videotapes.
Research: By staff. Appointment to visit.
☺ Mon-Fri 09:00 to 17:00
Procedure: Viewing tapes compiled. Masters copied on selection.
Description: Period and contemporary stock footage. European establishing shots, worldwide locations, Americana, scenics, aerials, various airlines and international airports, period wars, space, etc. Computerized. Rate card available.
Foreign Offices: France, Italy, UK.

MARINE GRAFICS

Box 2242, Chapel Hill, NC 27515, USA
ⓒ +1 919 362 8867
Ⓕ +1 919 362 8861

Contacts: Bill Lovin
Subjects: Underwater photography, environmental.
▦ 16mm neg with matching 1", original Beta SP and M2 (video NTSC).
Research: By staff.
Description: Underwater stock footage. Unusual marine life, behaviour, marine mammals, divers, shipwrecks, sharks, manta rays, dangerous marine life, scenics of the Caribbean and Pacific, beaches, ships, environmental damage, rainforest, Mayan ruins, Red Sea/Caribbean/South Pacific/Atlantic/Great Lakes/rivers. Rate card and brochure available. NB: Also represented by Energy Productions.
Foreign Offices: See Energy Productions listings.

MOONLIGHT PRODUCTIONS

3361 Saint Michael Court, Palo Alto, CA 94306, USA
ⓒ +1 415 961 7440
Ⓕ +1 415 961 7440

Contacts: Dr Lee Tepley
Subjects: Underwater photography, environmental.
▦ 16mm transferred to 1" + timecoded cassettes; some original video.
Research: By staff. Appointment to visit.
☉ Mon-Fri 09:00 to 17:30
Description: Collected over the last 30 years, an extensive library of all types of undersea life, especially whales, dolphins and other large marine mammals. Also material of undersea lava flows and pollution. Partly computerized. Rates negotiable. Stock footage list available.

NATURAL SYMPHONIES

4 George Street, Redfern, NSW 2016, Australia
℃ +61 2 318 1577 / 46 55 1800
Ⓕ +61 2 318 1424 / 46 55 9434

Contacts: Neil O'Hare
Subjects: Underwater photography, natural history, culture, environmental.
▦ Beta SP, D2, 1". PAL.
Research: By staff mainly. Visits by appointment.
🕐 Mon-Fri 09:00 to 17:00 (often contactable outside these times)
Procedure: Timecoded VHS or other formats available. 24 hours for access to masters.
Description: Shot in Australia and The South Pacific, the library ranges from aerial sequences to microscopic subjects including flora, fauna, marine life, tourist and research activities. All material is recorded on Betacam SP using BTS LDK 90 and 91 CCD cameras. Many of the sequences available are of animals, birds and locations that are extremely difficult to access and film owing to seasonal variations and remoteness. Material includes coral reefs, coral spawning, whales, dolphins and sea lions, Australian birds, animals, insects and reptiles, Australian environments and Aboriginal and islander culture. Computerized with database list on disk accessible by most word processors. Summary print outs and rate card available.

NOMAD FILMS INTERNATIONAL

Perth Business Centre, Stirling Street (P.O. Box 8240), Perth 6849, Australia
℃ +61 9 3881177
Ⓕ +61 9 3811122

Contacts: Doug Stanley and Kate Faulkner
Subjects: Natural history, medicine, science, lifestyles, locations, environmental, China, Jewish history, underwater photography.
▦ 16mm; Beta/Beta SP, D2, 1", Umatic. PAL and NTSC.
Research: By staff only.
☉ Mon–Fri 08:30 to 18:30
Procedure: VHS or Umatic PAL/NTSC viewing copies. 3 days for access to masters.
Description: Enormous range of productions covering wildlife, medical and scientific topics with worldwide documentary series on people and places. Titles include The Intruders, A Walk in the Sea and Crocodiles – the deadly survivors (natural history), Land of the Dragon (Bhutan), Dream Merchants of Asia (Taiwan, India, Japan, Hong Kong), Journey to Hainan (China's most southerly province), Breakthroughs (science, medicine and technology), Eye in the Sky (satellite technology), Triumph of the Nomads (Aborigines) to name a few. Glossy brochures available for productions. Partly computerized.

QUALICUM FILM PRODUCTIONS

6340 Island Highway West, Qualicum Beach, BC V9K 2E5, Canada
℃ +1 604 757 8390
Ⓕ +1 604 757 8844

Contacts: Dick Harvey
Subjects: Natural history, underwater photography, fishing.
▦ 16mm; Beta/Beta SP. NTSC.
Research: By both staff and outside researchers. Appointment to visit.
☉ 7 days 08:00 to 18:00
Procedure: VHS or Umatic viewing cassettes. Same day for access to masters.
Description: Qualicum specialize in nature and wildlife photography, their particular interest over the last 30 years being rivers. Material includes extensive footage of salmon (migration, underwater, spawning, all species) also black bears, eagles on rivers, ocean, underwater herring etc.

REEFSCENES AUSTRALIA

P.O. Box 2427, Australia
🕾 +61 77 214819
🖷 +61 77 713341

Contacts: Steve Gardner
Subjects: Underwater photography, natural history.
▦ Beta SP, D2, Digital Beta, Hi 8. PAL.
Research: By staff only.
🕘 Mon–Fri 09:00 to 17:00
Procedure: Time coded VHS available. 48 hours for access to masters.
Description: Underwater, coral reef and marine related footage shot on Beta SP and Digital Betacam widescreen 16:9 format. Also natural history, underwater models and human related topics. Computerized. English, Pidgin and Norwegian spoken.

SPORTS CINEMATOGRAPHY GROUP

73 Market Street, Venice, CA 90291, USA
🕾 +1 310 785 9100
🖷 +1 310 396 7423

Contacts: David Stoltz
Subjects: Sport, leisure, underwater photography, motor racing.
▦ Mainly film; some videotape.
Research: By staff. Appointment to visit.
🕘 Mon–Fri 09:00 to 18:00
Description: Contemporary high action sports footage including extensive coverage of skydiving, summer and winter mountain sports, water sports, motor racing, beach sports, etc. The library also has underwater and nature footage. Partly computerized. Rate card and brochure available.

THOMAS HORTON ASSOCIATES

222 Sierra Road, Ojai, CA 93023, USA
℡ +1 805 646 7866

Contacts: Jean Garner
Subjects: Documentaries, adventure sports, exploration, natural history, underwater photography, Africa.
▦ 16mm, 35mm; most video formats. PAL and NTSC.
Research: By both staff and outside researchers. Appointment to visit.
☉ Mon–Fri 08:00 to 18:00
Procedure: Viewing on NTSC Umatic or VHS. 3 days for access to masters.
Description: Series of documentaries titled Search For Adventure (over 39 one-hour programmes) including adventure sports, exploration, nature and underwater footage. The collection also includes 18 hours of 16mm footage shot in Spring 1993 of African animals and people in South and Central Africa. Catalogue and rate card available. Spanish, French and German spoken.

ZIELINSKI PRODUCTIONS

Suite 80, 7850 Slater Avenue, Huntington Beach, CA 92647, USA
℡ +1 714 842 5050
℻ +1 714 842 5050

Contacts: Richard Zielinski
Subjects: Stock shots, sport, aerial photography, underwater photography.
▦ 8mm, 16mm; all video formats.
Research: By staff.
☉ 7 days, 24 hours
Procedure: Timecoded VHS (or as required) for viewing. Masters on-site.
Description: A collection of worldwide stock footage dating back 25 years including sports material (all levels), aerial and underwater photography, oldies, events, hi-tech, people, activities, equipment, etc. Will shoot original material if they don't have stock. Computerized. Rate card available.

Vietnam war

ESTUARY PRESS

Suite 279, 408 13th Street, Oakland CA 94612, USA
© +1 510 763 8204
Ⓕ +1 510 763 8204

Contacts: Paul Richards
Subjects: Civil rights, protests, Vietnam War.
Research: By Paul Richards.
🕒 No office hours. Contact anytime.
Procedure: VHS viewing tapes on request. Access to masters varies.
Description: The collection contains the films of Harvey Wilson Richards including 1960s Bay Area peace and civil rights protests, anti Vietnam War protests, California farm workers, forestry and logging. Mississippi civil rights movement 1963 and 1964. Catalogue available. English and Spanish spoken.

NHK INTERNATIONAL

Room 582, NHK Broadcasting Center, 2-2-1 Jinnan, Shibuya-ku, Tokyo 150-01, Japan
© +81 3 3481 1875
Ⓕ +81 3 3481 1877
✉ J34553 INTRENHK

Contacts: Akiko Numakami, Fumiko Chiba, Yoko Hagimoto
Subjects: Current affairs, documentaries, sport, Vietnam War, China, Nippon News.
🎞 Most film and video formats. NTSC.
Research: By staff only.
🕒 Mon-Fri 10:00 to 18:00
Procedure: Viewing on any format. Average of 4 days for access to masters.
Description: The NHK archives contain news, documentary, sports, etc. footage which has been broadcast on NHK over the past 40 years. Also included is exclusive footage of the Vietnam War and China from their respective governments. NHK owns the copyright for the vast majority of the available footage including the rights to Nippon News coverage of WWII and can assist with third party rights. Computerized. Rate card and catalogue available. English and Japanese spoken.

NORMELLA PICTURES

P.O. Box 562, Toowong, Brisbane Q4066, Australia
ⓒ +61 7 3665172
Ⓕ +61 7 3667661

Contacts: Evan Ham
Subjects: Vietnam War, travelogues, culture.
🎞 16mm, 35mm; VHS. PAL.
Research: By staff and outside researchers under supervision.
🕑 Mon-Sat 08:00 to 17:00
Procedure: Viewing of workprints on premises or VHS. 48 hours for access to masters.
Description: 80 000 16mm feet of Vietnam and Cambodia footage dating from 1985 to 1993 covering a wide range of subjects (all on 16mm negative). 50 000 35mm feet of Vietnamese archive film of Indochina wars including Cambodia. 80 000 16mm feet of Northern Australia footage. Computerized. Rates negotiated on application. English and Vietnamese spoken.

War

DOKO VIDEO

33 Hayetzira Street, Ramat Gan 52521, Israel
℡ +972 3 5753555
℻ +972 3 5753189

Contacts: Mrs Taly Kaufman
Subjects: Documentaries, war, Jewish history, travelogues, technology, educational films, social history, childrens'.
🎞 8mm; D2, BVU. All line standards available.
Research: By staff.
🕐 Sun-Thur 09:00 to 17:00
Procedure: VHS viewing copies supplied. 3-7 days for access to masters.
Description: Doko Video have a wide range of programmes available covering every aspect of Israel (history, religion, ethnic and social life, etc.). Titles available are listed in their catalogue under the following headings - battles for peace, holocaust and revival, follow the sun, biblical landscapes, innovative technology, Jerusalem, discovering the past, the social scene and children's program. Hebrew, English and French spoken.

HOLLYWOOD HOUSE VIDEO ARCHIVES / HOME ENTERTAINMENT HOLDINGS

Box 555, Bondi Beach, NSW 2026, Australia
℡ +61 2 365 1055
℻ +61 2 365 1577

Contacts: Joe Shellim
Subjects: Classic films, documentaries, music, space, film industry, animation, war, personalities, circus, natural history.
🎞 Film; Beta, 1", BVU, Umatic.
Research: By staff.
🕐 Sun-Fri 10:00 to 19:00
Procedure: VHS viewing tape. Access to masters dependent on workload.
Description: Collection includes classic nostalgia movies complimented with interviews and rehearsals, behind-the-scenes, lost films, etc. Interviews with movie stars, candid films, footage of world leaders, space (NASA), music clips, nature and circus, cartoons, war and documentaries. Partly computerized. Rate card and catalogue available.

JOHN E. ALLEN

116 North Avenue, Park Ridge, NJ 07656, USA
© +1 201 391 3299
Ⓕ +1 201 391 6335

Contacts: John E. Allen, Beverley Allen
Subjects: Historical archive, newsreels, war, Russia, industry, transport, classic films, educational films, travelogues.
Mainly film; some video.
Research: By both staff and outside researchers.
Mon-Fri 09:00 to 18:00
Description: Kinograms from 1915 to 1931. Telenews 1947 to 1953. World War I and II, Spanish American War, Mexican Revolution, Russian Revolution, Hungarian Revolution, Spanish Civil War, Korean War, etc. Industry 1910 to 1950s, transportation, educational, ethnographic, travel, nature, features 1905 to 1950s, stills, posters and lobby cards. Partly computerized. Rate card available.

NORTHSTAR PRODUCTIONS

3003 "O" Street NW, Washington DC 20007, USA
© +1 202 338 7337
Ⓕ +1 202 337 4387

Contacts: Don North
Subjects: War, locations, industry, leisure.
Videotape.
Research: By both staff and outside researchers.
Appointment to visit.
7 days
Description: Footage of various international war zones including Afghanistan (1987 combat), El Salvador (Guerilla war 1983 to 1990), Nicaragua, Middle East (Beirut siege 1982), Gulf War and rebuilding of Kuwait, Vietnam (1967 to 1990), Sarajevo. Also footage from Hong Kong, Austria, Prague, Washington DC, Estonia (Balkans independence movement), Finland (modern and World War II) etc. Partly computerized. Brochure available.

PETRIFIED FILMS / THE IMAGE BANK

Room 204, 430 West 14th Street, New York NY 10014, USA
℡ +1 212 242 5461
🖷 +1 212 691 8347

Contacts: Lori Cheatle, Rob Cates
Subjects: Historical archive, Hollywood, transport, consumerism, Americana, industry, war, aviation, feature film, out-takes.
🎞 35mm, 16mm; some on 1", D2, 3/4" with matching VHS.
Research: By staff. Visits by appointment.
🕐 Mon–Fri 09:30 to 18:00
Procedure: Viewing tapes assembled. Masters copied after selection.
Description: Historical collection including pre-1951 Warner Brothers stock and pre-1965 Columbia Pictures stock. A-Z of subjects including action sequences, period recreations, establishing shots, projection backgrounds, cityscapes and worldwide locations. Industrial, military and aviation collections. Car culture and 1950s daily life in the US. Majority dates from 1920s to 1960s. Partly computerized. Rate card and catalogue available.
Foreign Offices: Contact local Image Bank office.

SHOVAL FILM PRODUCTION

32 Alenby Street, Tel Aviv 63325, Israel
℡ +972 3 5179288
🖷 +972 3 5179289

Contacts: Benni Shvily
Subjects: Documentaries, feature films, war.
🎞 16mm, 35mm; all video formats.
Research: By staff and outside researchers. Appointment to visit.
🕐 Sun–Thur 09:30 to 16:00
Procedure: Viewing material on any video format. 24 hours for access to masters.
Description: Documentary film of Israeli history and wars. 20 feature films containing well known Israeli songs as well as World War II footage, Nazis fighting against British troops, etc. English and Hebrew spoken.

UNITED STUDIOS OF ISRAEL

Kesem St. 8, Herzlia 46100, Israel
ⓒ +972 52 550 151-7
ⓕ +972 52 550 334

Contacts: Mirjana Gross
Subjects: Newsreels, documentaries, educational films, war, current affairs, culture.
🎞 35mm; BVU.
🕐 Sun-Thur 08:00 to 17:00
Description: Newsreels made in Israel from 1951 to 1971 covering events, wars, emigrations, new settlements and political life in the state. Documentary films on education, the army, water problems, Arab and Jewish life, etc. Brochure available. NB: Collections are also at the Spielberg Archive (Jerusalem) and the Harvard Judaica Department (Boston USA).

VILLON FILMS

77 W 28 Avenue, Vancouver, BC V5Y 2K7, Canada
ⓒ +1 604 879 6042
ⓕ +1 604 879 6042

Contacts: Peter Davis
Subjects: Historical archive, documentaries, advertising, Africa, AIDS, apartheid, Cuba, culture, espionage, war.
🎞 Majority of material is 16mm. Some original video.
Research: Visits by appointment.
🕐 7 days, 24 hours
Procedure: Viewing of VHS and 16mm on premises, some video elsewhere.
Description: The collection comprises films made and collected by Peter including out-takes, commercials from the 1950s and 60s and valuable historical material. Subjects covered include Africa, AIDS, Rhodesia and Zimbabwe and especially South Africa 1900 to 1990; Catskills (Borscht Belt) 1900 to 1990; US covert activities, spies, the Cold War; D.H. Lawrence; Middle East late 1960s, 70s, 80s; US anti-war movement and counter culture 1960s and 70s; Britain early 1960s; World War II China; Native Americans (Crow and Navajo) 70s and 80s; Cuba 1960s. Partly computerized. Rates negotiable. English, French, Swedish and some Italian spoken.

Westerns

EM GEE FILM LIBRARY

Suite 103, 6924 Canby Avenue, Reseda CA 91335, USA
ℂ +1 818 881 8110
Ⓕ +1 818 981 5506

Contacts: Murray Glass
Subjects: Public domain, classic films, feature films, comedy, documentaries, westerns, animation.
▦ All film formats; VHS, Umatic. NTSC.
Research: By both staff and outside researchers.
☉ Mon-Fri 08:30 to 17:00
Procedure: Viewing material on 16mm or VHS. 1 week for access to masters.
Description: Approximately 3000 titles in all genres - silent and sound, black and white and colour. Their speciality is in public domain material covering all subject areas including comedies, documentaries, westerns, animation and feature films. Partly computerized. Catalogue and rate card available.

National
archives

Abu Dhabi

NATIONAL LIBRARY - CULTURAL FOUNDATION

Zaid the Second Street, Abu Dhabi 2380, Abu Dhabi

Albania

ARCHIVES D'ETAT DU FILM DE LA REPUBLIQUE D'ALBANIE

Rue Aleksander Moisiu 76, Tirana, Albania
© +355 42 327 33
Ⓕ +355 42 327 33

Algeria

CENTRE DES ARCHIVES NATIONALES

B.P. 38 Birkhadem, Alger, Algeria
© +213 2 56 61 62
✐ 62524

Angola

CINEMATECA NACIONAL DE ANGOLA

Place Luther King 4, Luanda 3512, Angola
© +244 330918
✐ 3398 EDECINE AN

Argentina

FUNDACION CINEMATECA ARGENTINA

2nd Floor, Corrientes 2092, Buenos Aires 1045, Argentina
© +54 1 953 3755 / 7163
Ⓕ +54 1 951 8558

Contacts: Guillermo or Paulina Fernandez Jurade
Subjects: National Archives, feature films, documentaries, newsreels.
▦ 35mm, 16mm; video.
Research: Appointment necessary.
☽ Mon-Fri 10:00 to 17:00
Procedure: Problems at present with duplication of material.
Description: The library holds feature films, documentaries and newsreels. Not all copyrights are held.

Australia

NATIONAL FILM AND SOUND ARCHIVE

G.P.O. Box 2002, McCoy Circuit, Acton, Canberra, ACT
2600, Australia
ⓒ +61 6 267 1711
Ⓕ +61 6 247 4651
↗ AA 61930

NATIONAL LIBRARY OF AUSTRALIA

Film & Video Lending Service, Parkes Place, Canberra 2600,
Australia
ⓒ +61 6 262 1361
Ⓕ +61 6 262 1634

Contacts: Reference Officer
Subjects: National Archives, educational films,
documentaries, feature films, animation.
▦ 16mm; Umatic, VHS. PAL, some NTSC.
Research: Researchers can visit, appointments
recommended not essential.
☉ Mon-Fri 09:00 to 16:30
Procedure: Free loan to institutes, businesses and groups.
No masters held.
Description: Over 23 500 instructional and educational
documentary titles held covering most subject areas. Also a
film and TV study collection with feature films, short fiction,
animation and experimental film and video. Computerized.
Full catalogue available on microfiche and screen studies
catalogue in print form.

Bangladesh

BANGLADESH FILM ARCHIVE

Block No. 3, Ganabhaban, Sher-e-Bangla Nagar, Dhaka
1207, Bangladesh
ⓒ +880 2 814816 / 323727

Bermuda

BERMUDA GOVERNMENT ARCHIVES

30 Parliament Street, Hamilton HM12, Bermuda
ⓒ +1 809 297 7833
Ⓕ +1 809 292 2349

Bolivia

CINEMATECA BOLIVIANA

P.O. Box 9933, Pichincha Esq. Indaburo s/n, La Paz, Bolivia
℡ +591 1 325346
⚡ 3288 CORMESA BV

Botswana

BOTSWANA NATIONAL ARCHIVES AND RECORDS SERVICES

P.O. Box 239, Government Enclave - Khama Crescent/State Drive, Gaborone, Botswana
℡ +267 3601000
Ⓕ +267 313584
⚡ 2994BD

Brazil

ARQUIVO NACIONAL (AUDIOVISUAL AND CARTOGRAPHIC DIVISION)

Rua Azeredo Coutinho, 77/6 andar, Rio De Janeiro, RJ 20230, Brazil
℡ +55 21 252 2766
Ⓕ +55 21 232 8430
⚡ 21 34103

Brunei Darussalam

BRUNEI NATIONAL ARCHIVES

Brunei Museums, Ministry of Culture Youth and Sports, , Darussalam, Brunei Darussalam
℡ +673 2 244545/6
Ⓕ +673 2 44047
⚡ BRUART 2655

Canada

NATIONAL ARCHIVES OF CANADA

395 Wellington Street, Ottawa, Ontario K1A 0N3, Canada
ⓒ +1 613 995 5138
ⓕ +1 613 995 6274

Subjects: National Archives, Canadian history.
▦ Most film formats including 28mm. All video formats. NTSC.
Research: Visits by appointment, consultation prior to
viewing needed.
☉ Mon-Fri 08:30 to 16:45
Procedure: Viewing on premises only, SVHS, VHS and
Umatic available.
Description: The Archives hold materials on a large variety of
subjects related to Canadian history. Copyright or donor
restrictions may apply, information is supplied if known but
researchers have ultimate responsibility to search for
copyrights. Partly computerized. French and English spoken.

Chile

BIBLIOTECA NACIONAL DE CHILE

Seccion Musica Y Medios Multiples, Avenida Libertador
Bernardo O'Higgins, Clasificador 1400, Santiago 651, Chile
ⓕ +56 2 381975

China, People's Republic of

CHINA RECORD CORPORATION

2 Fuxingmewai St., Beijing 100866, People's Republic of
China
ⓒ +86 1 6092867
ⓕ +86 1 3262693
⬈ 222309CRC CN

Colombia

FUNDACION PATRIMONIO FILMICO COLOMBIANO

Carrera 13 # 13-24, Piso 9, audiorio, Sante Fe De Bogota,
Colombia
℡ +57 1 2815241 / 2836496
℻ +57 1 3421485

Contacts: Claudia Triana de Vargas, Jorge Nieto
🎞 Film; video. Original material.
Research: By outside researchers. Appointment necessary.
🕑 Mon–Fri 08:30 to 17:30
Procedure: Copyright needs to be checked prior to
duplication.
Description: The archive holds 120 000 reels of Colombian
newsreels, film and video productions. It also has 12 000
stills, press clippings and documents relating to Colombian
films and cinematography.

UNIVERSIDAD DE ANTIOQUIA

Escuela Interamericanan de Bibliotecologia - Biblioteca, Clle
67 No 53-108, Medellin A.A. 1307, Colombia
℡ +57 4 2630011 Ext.358 / 2634436
℻ +57 4 263 82 82

Congo

BIBLIOTHEQUE NATIONALE DU CONGO

B.P. 1489, Brazzaville, Congo

Costa Rica

DIRECCION GENERAL DEL ARCHIVO NATIONAL DE COSTA RICA

P.O. Box 10217-1000, Calle 7, avdas 4 y 6, San Jose, Costa
Rica
℡ +506 335754
℻ +506 219129

Cuba

CINEMATECA DE CUBA

Calle 23 No 155, 10300 La Habana 4, Cuba
✆ +53 7 3 4719 / 30 5041 to 45

Ecuador

CINEMATECA NACIONAL DEL ECUADOR

P.O. Box 17 01 3520, Av 6 Diciembre 794 y Patria, Quito,
Ecuador
✆ +593 2 230 505

Fiji

LIBRARY SERVICE OF FIJI

P.O. Box 2526, 162 Ratu Sukuna Road, Suva, Fiji
✆ +679 315344 / 315303
⊕ +679 303511

Guinea, Republic of

ARCHIVES DE LA RADIO TELEVISION GUINEENNE

BP 391, Conakry, Guinea, Republic of
✆ +210 224 44 22 01 / 22 06
✍ 22341 RTG

Guinea-Bissau

INSTITUTO NACIONAL DE ESTUDOS E PESQUISAS (INEP)

Institut National des Etudes et des Recherches (INER),
Complexo Escolar, 14 de Novembre Cobornel, P.O. Box 112,
Bissau, Guinea-Bissau
✆ +245 252 21 13 01
⊕ +245 28 20

Hong Kong

TELEVISION BROADCASTS LTD. (TVB)

Videotape library / archive, Clearwater Bay Road, Kowloon,
Hong Kong
© +852 719 4828
Ⓕ +852 358 1337

India

NATIONAL FILM ARCHIVE OF INDIA

Law College Road, Pune 411004, India
© +91 212 331559/338516/333649
↗ 145 7759 NFAI IN

Indonesia

NATIONAL ARCHIVES OF THE REPUBLIC OF INDONESIA

Jalan Ampera Raya, Cilandak Timur, Jakarta Selatan 12560,
Indonesia
© +62 21 7805851 to 5853
Ⓕ +62 21 7805812

Contacts: Mr. A.A.G. Putra
▦ 16mm, 35mm. Negatives of photographs.
Research: Researchers can visit with an appointment.
☺ Mon-Fri 09:00 to 15:00
Procedure: Written request, copyright clearance and relevant
fees paid.
Description: The audio-visual collection was started in 1980
and comprises films, photographs and sound recordings the
majority of the collection being photographs. The archive is a
division of the Indonesian National Archives, the copyright
holders being the state or individual creators of the material.
Catalogue computerized.

Iran

NATIONAL FILM ARCHIVE OF IRAN

P.O. Box 5158, Baharestan Sq., Teheran 11365, Iran
© +98 21 3291583
Ⓕ +98 21 3117734
⟋⟋ 215642 RECU IR

Contacts: Fereydoun Khameneipour
Film.
Research: Researchers welcome with an appointment.
⊙ Sat-Tues 08:00 to 16:00, Wed 08:00 to 15:00
Procedure: Limited access to master copies.

Israel

JEWISH NATIONAL AND UNIVERSITY LIBRARY

National Sound Archives, P.O. Box 34165, Jerusalem 91
341, Israel
© +972 2 584 651
Ⓕ +972 2 511 771
⟋⟋ +972 2 25367

Subjects: National Archives, Jewish history
⊙ Sun-Thurs 09:00 to 16:00

STEVEN SPIELBERG JEWISH FILM ARCHIVE

Law Building, The Hebrew University of Jerusalem, Mount
Scopus, Jerusalem 91905, Israel
© +972 2 882513
Ⓕ +972 2 322545

Contacts: Marilyn Koolik
Subjects: National Archives, Jewish history, newsreels.
Film; videocassettes.
Research: By both staff and outside researchers. Visits by
appointment.
⊙ Sun-Thur 09:00 to 17:00
Description: Founded in 1969 the Spielberg archive
maintains and acquires film and video material relating to
Jewish and Israeli subjects. Newsreels include the Agadati
Collection (1932 to 1956), the Carmel newsreels shot by
Natan Axelrod (1905 to 1987), the Carmel-Herzliya and Geva
newsreels. Computerized. Rate card available.

Jamaica

NATIONAL LIBRARY OF JAMAICA

Audio Visual Archive Department, Box 823, 12 East Street,
Kingston, Jamaica
© +1 809 9220620
Ⓕ +1 809 9225567
⟋ Cable NALIBJAM

Japan

NATIONAL FILM CENTER, NATIONAL MUSEUM OF MODERN ART

Tokyo Film Center - Archive, 3-1-4 Takane, Sagamihara-Shi,
Kanagawa, Ken 229, Japan
© +81 3 427580128
Ⓕ +81 3 427574449

Jordan

UNIVERSITY OF JORDAN LIBRARY

Amman, Jordan
© +962 6 843555 Ext. 3135
Ⓕ +962 6 832318
⟋ UNVJ. JO 21629

Kenya

KENYA NATIONAL ARCHIVES

P.O. Box 49210, Moi Avenue, Nairobi, Kenya
℡ +254 2 228959/228020/226007

Contacts: Mr Musila Musembi, Mrs A. Akhaabi, Mr Koo Ombati
Subjects: National Archives, current affairs, culture
▦ Film; video.
Research: Researchers need to purchase a permit to gain access.
☉ Mon–Fri 08:00 to 16:30, Sat 08:00 to 14:00
Procedure: Permission needed from the Director, fees for labour and copies.
Description: This is a public archive – the department being under the control of the Ministry of Home Affairs and National Heritage. All manner of records from public offices are held including files, reports, microfilms, maps, books, films, video and audio tapes plus a few cultural items. It also holds material from private individuals and publishes guides of these. Copyright is held by the owners, not the archive. Partly computerized.
Foreign Offices: Kenyan missions in other countries represent them, particularly the Kenya High Commission in London.

Kiribati

KIRIBATI NATIONAL ARCHIVES

P.O. Box 6, , Bairiki, Tarawa, Kiribati
℡ +686 21337
Ⓕ +686 28222

Korea, Democratic People's Republic of

NATIONAL FILM ARCHIVE - DEMOCRATIC PEOPLE'S REPUBLIC OF KOREA

15 Sochangdong, Central District, Pyongyang, Democratic People's Republic of Korea
℡ +850 2 3 45 51
✍ 5345 NFA KP

KOREAN FILM ARCHIVE

Seocho P.O. Box 91,
700 Seocho-dong, Seocho-gu, , Seoul 137-070, Korea
© +82 2 521 3147/9 521 2102/2
Ⓕ +82 2 582 6213
⋀⋀ ARTCNTR K29150

Contacts: Mr. Sul Gee-hwan, Mr. Park Jin-Seok, Mr. Yang Jae-young
Subjects: National Archives, feature films, documentaries
Film; video.
Research: Restricted access to public.
🕓 Mon-Fri 09:00 to 18:00, Sat 09:00 to 13:00
Procedure: Copyright permission required prior to duplication.
Description: The archive holds feature films, documentaries, screenplays, posters, photographs, slides and books. Copyright is held by outside producers who need to be contacted prior to duplication. The library is in the process of being computerized, a catalogue only being published occasionally.

Lesotho

LESOTHO GOVERNMENT ARCHIVES

Ministry of Tourism, Sports & Culture, P.O. Box 52, Maseru, Lesotho
© +266 323034

Malawi

NATIONAL ARCHIVES OF MALAWI

P.O. Box 62, McLeod Road, Zomba, Malawi
© +265 522 922 / 184
Ⓕ +265 522 148-33

Contacts: C.B. Malunga, Mrs. L.C. Chiotha, D.D. Najira
Film.
Research: Researchers welcomed.
🕓 Mon-Fri 07:30 to 12:00, 13:00 to 17:00
Procedure: Not yet established.
Description: The film collection was inherited from the Department of Information, the archives being a legal deposit and research facility enforcing the Printed Publications Act. Material relating to the country available elsewhere has also been purchased or given. A card catalogue, periodical registers and lists exist but as yet the library is not computerized.

Malaysia

NATIONAL ARCHIVES OF MALAYSIA

Jalan Duta, Kuala Lumpur 50568, Malaysia
© +60 3 2562688
Ⓕ +60 3 2555679

Marshall Islands

MUSEUM OF THE MARSHALL ISLANDS

Alele Museum Library, P.O. Box 629, Majuro MH 96960,
Marshall Islands
© +692 625 3372
Ⓕ +692 625 3226

Contacts: Alfred Capella
▦ Video.
Research: Appointment required in advance.
🕓 Mon-Fri 10:00 to 12:00, 15:00 to 17:00
Procedure: Master copies available for a fee, notice required.
Description: The library holds computerized and microfilm
records relating to government archives including court
records. Video films are also held on Marshall Islands oral
traditions.

Mauritius

MAURITIUS BROADCASTING CORPORATION

1 Louis Pasteur Street, Forest Side, Mauritius
© +230 675001/2/3 6743743
Ⓕ +230 6757332
〰 4230 MAUBROD IW

Contacts: Anne Marie Ginette Fabre
Subjects: National Archives, current affairs, religion,
documentaries, children's, music, personalities, sport.
▦ 16mm, 35mm; Beta/Beta SP, BVU, Umatic. PAL and
SECAM.
Research: By staff. Outside researchers by appointment.
🕓 7 days 08:30 to 17:00
Procedure: Viewing on 16mm and video. 2 hours for access
to masters.
Description: A wide range of programme material covering
political, international and local events, religion,
documentaries, television for children and teenagers,
musicals, interviews and sports. English and French spoken.

Mexico

ARCHIVO GENERAL DE LA NACION

Eduardo Molina y Albaniles, Col. Penitenciaria Ampliacion,
Apartado Postal 1999, Mexico 1, D.F., Mexico D.F. 15350,
Mexico
ℂ +52 5 7895915
Ⓕ +52 5 7895915

Namibia

NATIONAL ARCHIVES OF NAMIBIA

Private Bag 13250, 4 Luderitz Street, Windhoek 9000,
Namibia
ℂ +264 61 293387

New Zealand

NEW ZEALAND FILM ARCHIVE

P.O. Box 11-449, First Floor, The Film Centre, Cnr. Cable
Street & Jervois Quay, Wellington, New Zealand
ℂ +64 4 3847647
Ⓕ +64 4 3829595

Contacts: Bronwyn Taylor (public programmes), Diane Pivac
(documentation)
Subjects: National Archives, newsreels, documentaries,
feature films, animation.
▦ Film; video.
Research: By appointment only.
🕓 Mon-Fri 09:00 to 17:00
Procedure: Access to view is available. Master material not
available.
Description: Held in the archive's collection are New Zealand
and overseas films from 1897 to the present day, comprising
fiction and feature films, shorts animated films,
documentaries, newsreels, video and television programmes.
A wide variety of promotional, critical and historical
documentation and information is also held for New Zealand
and overseas films. Copyright is not held by NZFA.
Computerized. Rate card available.

Nigeria

FEDERAL UNIVERSITY OF TECHNOLOGY, AKURE LIBRARY

P.M.B 704, Akure, Nigeria

Papua New Guinea

NATIONAL LIBRARY OF PAPUA NEW GUINEA

Film Library, P.O. Box 5770, Boroko, Papua New Guinea
✆ +675 256200
🖷 +675 25 1331
✉ NE 22234

Contacts: Neil Nicholls (National Librarian), Mary Warus (Film Librarian)
🎞 16mm; VHS, Umatic.
Research: Written request required prior to access.
🕓 Mon-Fri 09:00 to 12:00, 13:00 to 16:00
Procedure: Copies not normally available, may be considered on request.
Description: The collection consists of materials relating to Papua New Guinea dating from the 1920s to the present day. It also keeps footage passed on from the Office of Information (established in August 1953 and abolished in December 1983). Two catalogues are presently available, one for the 16mm collection and another for the VHS collection.

Peru

NATIONAL ARCHIVES OF PERU

P.O. Box 3124, Manuel Cuadros s/n, Lima 100, Peru
✆ +51 14 275930

Philippines

UNIVERSITY OF THE PHILIPPINES FILM CENTER ARCHIVES

P.O. Box 214, Magsaysay Avenue, Quezon City 1101, Philippines
✆ +63 2 962722
🖷 +63 2 992863 / 986780
✉ 63199 ETPIMO PN

Saudi Arabia

KING SAUD UNIVERSITY LIBRARIES

P.O. Box 22480, Dhiriyya, Riyadh 11495, Saudi Arabia
© +966 1 4676152
Ⓕ +966 1 4676162
✎ 401019 KSU SJ

Seychelles, Republic of

NATIONAL ARCHIVES AND MUSEUMS - SEYCHELLES

P.O. Box 720, Victoria, Mahe, Republic of Seychelles

Solomon Islands

NATIONAL ARCHIVES OF SOLOMON ISLANDS

P.O. Box 780, Hibiscus Avenue, Honiara, Solomon Islands
© +677 21426
Ⓕ +677 21397
✎ HQ 66311

South Africa

SOUTH AFRICAN NATIONAL FILM, VIDEO AND SOUND ARCHIVES

Private Bag X236, 698 Churchstreet East, Arcadia Pretoria
0002, Pretoria 0001, South Africa
© +27 12 343 9767/8
Ⓕ +27 12 344 5143/9

Sri Lanka

SRI LANKA NATIONAL LIBRARY SERVICES BOARD

National Library of Sri Lanka, P.O. Box 1764, 14
Independence Avenue, Colombo 07, Sri Lanka
© +94 1 698847 / 685199 / 685201
Ⓕ +94 1 685201

Contacts: Mr M.S.U. Amarasiri (Director)
Subjects: National Archives, science, social history
▦ Video.
Research: Researchers can visit.
☺ Tues–Sat 09:00 to 17:00
Procedure: Material seen on site only, cannot be loaned.
Description: The library holds material relating to social
sciences, humanities, science and technology, library and
information science, mass communications. Materials
comprise of books, periodicals, newspapers, micro-fiches,
microfilms, manuscripts, maps, computer discs, recordings
and video cassettes. Partly computerized.

Sudan

NATIONAL RECORDS OFFICE, THE

P.O. Box 1914 Khartoum, Al-Jumhuryyia Street, Khartoum,
Sudan
© +249 11 81995 / 84255
◢ Watjaiq - Khartoum

Syria

ASSAD NATIONAL LIBRARY

Omayyad Square, Damascas, Syria
© +963 11 3332883
Ⓕ +963 11 3320804
◢ 419134

Contacts: Ghassan Lahham (Director)
☺ Open 6 days (12 hours)
Procedure: Access to masters not yet permitted.
Description: The library holds copyright material from 1984
and is in the process of computerization.

Tanzania

AUDIO VISUAL INSTITUTE, NATIONAL LIBRARY & ARCHIVE

P.O. Box 31519, Dar Es Salaam, Tanzania
© +255 51 72601/2/3/4

Contacts: M.I. Kange, Eva Sessoa
Subjects: National Archives, educational films, engineering, health, agriculture, tourism, current affairs.
🎞 16mm, 35mm.
Research: Permission and appointment needed prior to research.
🕑 Mon-Fri 07:30 to 15:30
Procedure: On request.
Description: Copyright to materials in the collection is owned by respective producers of films. The library is not computerized. A book catalogue is issued.

Thailand

NATIONAL ARCHIVES OF THAILAND

Samsen Road, Bangkok 10300, Thailand
© +66 2 2823829
Ⓕ +66 2 2816947

Tunisia

CENTRE DE DOCUMENTATION NATIONALE (CDN)

4 Rue Ibn Nadim, Cite Montplaisir - BP 350, Tunis 1002, Tunisia
© +216 1 894 266
Ⓕ +266 1 792 241

Contacts: Abdelbaki Daly, Director General
Research: By staff only.
🕑 Mon-Thurs 08:00 to 18:00, Fri and Sat 08:00 to 13:30
Description: The centre holds databases (biographies, politics, French culture), 8000 monographs, 10 000 newspaper articles, 50 000 photographs, microfiche and journals.

Turkey

TURKISH FILM AND TV INSTITUTE

80700 Kislaonu-Besiktas, Istanbul, Turkey
© +90 1 166 10 96
Ⓕ +90 1 167 65 99

Uruguay

ARCHIVO NACIONAL DE LA IMAGEN - SODRE

Sarandi 430 1er piso, Casilla de Correo 1412, Montevideo
11.000, Uruguay
© +598 2 955493
Ⓕ +598 2 963240
⋏⋏ UY 6553

Contacts: Juan Jose Mugni (Director), Graciela Dacosta
(Librarian)
Film; video
Research: Research by appointment only.
🕐 Mon-Fri 10:00 to 16:00
Procedure: Access to masters not possible.
Description: The archive collects materials relating to cinema
including books, serials, brochures, press books and cuttings,
photographs, slides, films and videos. The collection is
available for study purposes only.

USA

LIBRARY OF CONGRESS - MOTION PICTURE &
BROADCASTING DIVISION

10 First Street, S.E., Washington, DC, USA
© +1 202 707 5840
Ⓕ +1 202 707 2371

NATIONAL ARCHIVES AND RECORDS ADMINISTRATION

Motion Picture, Sound and Video Branch, , Washington, DC
20408, USA
© +1 202 501 5446
Ⓕ +1 202 501 5778

NATIONAL CENTER FOR FILM AND VIDEO PRESERVATION

The American Film Institute, P.O. Box 27999, 2021 North
Western Avenue, Los Angeles, California 90027, USA
ⓒ +1 213 856 7637
Ⓕ +1 213 467 4578

Vietnam

VIETNAM FILM INSTITUTE

115 Ngoc Khanh Street, Hanoi, Vietnam
ⓒ +844 2 43451

Zambia

MULTIMEDIA ZAMBIA AUDIO VISUALS ARCHIVE

P.O. Box 320199, Bishops Road, Kabulonga, Lusaka
101001, Zambia
ⓒ +260 1 264117
Ⓕ +260 1 264117
↗ ZA 40340

Zimbabwe

NATIONAL ARCHIVES OF ZIMBABWE

Private Bag 7729 Causeway, Borrowdale Road, Gun Hill,
Harare, Zimbabwe
ⓒ +263 4 792741

Indexes

SUBJECT INDEX

USA: FILMS OF INDIA 192
Aviation
  Japan: FRONT LINE 98
  Malaysia: IMAGES OF THE EAST 114
  USA: AIRLINE FILM & TV PROMOTIONS 161, CAE-LINK
  CORPORATION 174, CAMEO FILM LIBRARY 175, HOT SHOTS
  COOL CUTS 199, KESSER STOCK LIBRARY 209, LARRY DORN
  ASSOCIATES / WORLD BACKGROUNDS 213, PARAMOUNT
  PICTURES FILM LIBRARY 229, PETRIFIED FILMS / THE IMAGE
  BANK 230, TELECINE INTERNATIONAL PRODUCTIONS 247,
  WGBH FILM & VIDEO RESOURCE CENTER 257
Beauty
  USA: VIDEO TAPE LIBRARY 255
Biology
  USA: NEW YORK ZOOLOGICAL SOCIETY 223
Boxing
  USA: BIG FIGHTS, THE 170
Building
  USA: PARAMOUNT PICTURES FILM LIBRARY 229
Buildings
  USA: PORT AUTHORITY OF NEW YORK AND NEW JERSEY 233
Business
  USA: BROAD STREET PRODUCTIONS 171
Canadian history
  Canada: NATIONAL ARCHIVES OF CANADA 54
Childrens
  Australia: M.C. STUART & ASSOCIATES (MSCAA) 21
  Brunei: RADIO TELEVISION BRUNEI 42
  Israel: ARGO FILMS 86
Children's
  Israel: DOKO VIDEO 87
Childrens
  Mauritius: MAURITIUS BROADCASTING CORPORATION 120
  New Zealand: KIDS TV 124
Children's
  USA: AMERICAN MOTION PICTURES 166
China
  Australia: NOMAD FILMS INTERNATIONAL 26
  Japan: NHK INTERNATIONAL 101
Circus
  Australia: HOLLYWOOD HOUSE VIDEO ARCHIVES / HOME
  ENTERTAINMENT HOLDINGS 19
Civil rights
  USA: DOWNTOWN COMMUNITY TELEVISION 184, ESTUARY
  PRESS 187
Classic films
  Australia: HOLLYWOOD HOUSE VIDEO ARCHIVES / HOME
  ENTERTAINMENT HOLDINGS 19
  Japan: ARCHIVE FILMS JAPAN 96

Canada: CANADIAN BROADCASTING CORPORATION (CBC) 44, FABULOUS FOOTAGE 49, IMAGES PIXART 52, OASIS PICTURES 55, SOCIETE RADIO-CANADA 59
Chile: FOTOBANCO INTERNATIONAL / FABULOUS FOOTAGE 62
India: TIMES TELEVISION LIBRARY 81
Indonesia: P.T. KREASIVIDEO HEDKWARTER MAS / FABULOUS FOOTAGE 84
Japan: AD HOC / FABULOUS FOOTAGE 95, FRONT LINE 98
Malaysia: IMAGES OF THE EAST 114, VIDEO HEADQUARTERS (KL) / FABULOUS FOOTAGE 117
Mexico: BANCO INTERNATIONAL DE FOTOGRAFIA (BIF) / FABULOUS FOOTAGE 122
Philippines: VHQ DIMENSIONS / FABULOUS FOOTAGE 133
Singapore: VIDEO HEADQUARTERS / FABULOUS FOOTAGE 138
USA: AL GIDDINGS - IMAGES UNLIMITED 162, DARINO FILMS 182, FABULOUS FOOTAGE BOSTON 188, FILM BANK STOCK FOOTAGE FILM & VIDEO LIBRARY 190, MARINE GRAFICS 215, MOONLIGHT PRODUCTIONS 217, NBC NEWS ARCHIVES 221, NEW YORK ZOOLOGICAL SOCIETY 223, RICHTER PRODUCTIONS 236, VIDEO TAPE LIBRARY 255, WORLDWIDE TELEVISION NEWS (WTN) 260
Espionage
  Canada: VILLON FILMS 60
Exploration
  Canada: OASIS PICTURES 55
  USA: THOMAS HORTON ASSOCIATES 248
Farming
  USA: DOWNTOWN COMMUNITY TELEVISION 184
Fashion
  India: TIMES TELEVISION LIBRARY 81
  Israel: ENERGY PRODUCTIONS ISRAEL / VISUAL ENERGY 88
  Japan: ENERGY PRODUCTIONS TOKYO / IMAGICA CORP. 97
  Turkey: ENERGY PRODUCTIONS ISTANBUL 154
  USA: ENERGY PRODUCTIONS' TIMESCAPE IMAGE LIBRARY 186, WPA FILM LIBRARY 261
Feature film
  USA: PETRIFIED FILMS / THE IMAGE BANK 230
Feature films
  Argentina: FUNDACION CINEMATECA ARGENTINA 6
  Australia: M.C. STUART & ASSOCIATES (MSCAA) 21, NATIONAL LIBRARY OF AUSTRALIA 24, PARAMOUNT PICTURES / AUSTRALIA 29, RONIN FILMS 31
  Canada: CHARLES CHAPLIN ENTERPRISES 46, DOOMSDAY STUDIOS 48, PARAMOUNT PICTURES / CANADA 56
  Cuba: ICAIC 72
  India: RAJSHRI PRODUCTIONS 80
  Israel: ARGO FILMS 86, SHOVAL FILM PRODUCTION 91
  Korea: KOREAN FILM ARCHIVE 108
  New Zealand: NEW ZEALAND FILM ARCHIVE 125, NEW ZEALAND FILM COMMISSION 126
  Turkey: BARLIK FILM 153, KILIC FILM 156

Locations

Argentina: FOCUS STOCK FOTOGRAFICO / FABULOUS FOOTAGE 5, IMAGE BANK / ARGENTINA 7

Australia: AUSTRALIAN BROADCASTING CORPORATION (ABC) 8, FILM WORLD 16, IMAGE BANK / AUSTRALIA 20, NOMAD FILMS INTERNATIONAL 26

Brazil: IMAGE BANK / BRAZIL 40, NOVA IMAGENS / FABULOUS FOOTAGE 41

Canada: CANADIAN BROADCASTING CORPORATION (CBC) 44, CARLETON PRODUCTIONS 45, FABULOUS FOOTAGE 49, IMAGE BANK / CANADA 51, IMAGES PIXART 52, JACK CHISHOLM FILM PRODUCTIONS 53, ROBERT BOCKING PRODUCTIONS 58

Chile: FOTOBANCO INTERNATIONAL / FABULOUS FOOTAGE 62, IMAGE BANK / CHILE 63

Colombia: IMAGE BANK / COLOMBIA (ARCHIVO FOTOGRAFICO LTDA.) 66

Hong Kong: IMAGE BANK / HONG KONG 77

Indonesia: IMAGE BANK / INDONESIA (CREATIVE RESOURCES) 82, P.T. KREASIVIDEO HEDKWARTER MAS / FABULOUS FOOTAGE 84

Israel: ENERGY PRODUCTIONS ISRAEL / VISUAL ENERGY 88, IMAGE BANK / ISRAEL (IMAGE MAR'OT LTD.) 89

Japan: AD HOC / FABULOUS FOOTAGE 95, ENERGY PRODUCTIONS TOKYO / IMAGICA CORP. 97, FRONT LINE 98, IMAGE BANK / JAPAN 99

Korea: IMAGE BANK / KOREA 107

Malaysia: IMAGE BANK / MALAYSIA 113, IMAGES OF THE EAST 114, VIDEO HEADQUARTERS (KL) / FABULOUS FOOTAGE 117

Mexico: BANCO INTERNATIONAL DE FOTOGRAFIA (BIF) / FABULOUS FOOTAGE 122

Philippines: IMAGE BANK / PHILIPPINES 131, VHQ DIMENSIONS / FABULOUS FOOTAGE 133

Singapore: IMAGE BANK / SINGAPORE (ASIA CREATIVE RESOURCES) 137, VIDEO HEADQUARTERS / FABULOUS FOOTAGE 138

South Africa: IMAGE BANK / SOUTH AFRICA 140, PAUL ZWICK PRODUCTIONS 141, STOCK OPTIONS 143

Taiwan, Republic of China: IMAGE BANK / TAIWAN (HARVARD MANAGEMENT SERVICES) 148

Thailand: IMAGE BANK / THAILAND 150

Turkey: ENERGY PRODUCTIONS ISTANBUL 154, IMAGE BANK / TURKEY (TRANSIMAJ MAR'OT LTD) 155

Peru: NATIONAL ARCHIVES OF PERU 130
Philippines: UNIVERSITY OF THE PHILIPPINES FILM CENTER ARCHIVES 132
Saudi Arabia: KING SAUD UNIVERSITY LIBRARIES 134
Seychelles, Republic of: NATIONAL ARCHIVES AND MUSEUMS - SEYCHELLES 135
Solomon Islands: NATIONAL ARCHIVES OF SOLOMON ISLANDS 139
South Africa: SOUTH AFRICAN NATIONAL FILM VIDEO & SOUND ARCHIVES 142
Sri Lanka: SRI LANKA NATIONAL LIBRARY SERVICES BOARD 144
Sudan: NATIONAL RECORDS OFFICE, THE 145
Syria: ASSAD NATIONAL LIBRARY 146
Tanzania: AUDIO VISUAL INSTITUTE, NATIONAL LIBRARY & ARCHIVE 149
Thailand: NATIONAL ARCHIVES OF THAILAND 151
Tunisia: CENTRE DE DOCUMENTATION NATIONALE (CDN) 152
Turkey: TURKISH FILM AND TV INSTITUTE 157
Uruguay: ARCHIVO NACIONAL DE LA IMAGEN - SODRE 158
USA: LIBRARY OF CONGRESS - MOTION PICTURE & BROADCASTING DIVISION 214, NATIONAL ARCHIVES AND RECORDS ADMINISTRATION 219, NATIONAL CENTER FOR FILM AND VIDEO PRESERVATION 220
Vietnam: VIETNAM FILM INSTITUTE 263
Zambia: MULTIMEDIA ZAMBIA AUDIO VISUALS ARCHIVE 264
Zimbabwe: NATIONAL ARCHIVES OF ZIMBABWE 266
Natural history
Argentina: FOCUS STOCK FOTOGRAFICO / FABULOUS FOOTAGE 5, IMAGE BANK / ARGENTINA 7
Australia: AUSTRALIAN BROADCASTING CORPORATION (ABC) 8, CENTRAL COAST MEDIA HOLDINGS (CCM GROUP) 10, FILM WORLD 16, FILMSEARCH AUSTRALASIA 17, HOLLYWOOD HOUSE VIDEO ARCHIVES / HOME ENTERTAINMENT HOLDINGS 19, IMAGE BANK / AUSTRALIA 20, M.C. STUART & ASSOCIATES (MSCAA) 21, NATURAL SYMPHONIES 25, NOMAD FILMS INTERNATIONAL 26, OLIVER FILMS 28, REEFSCENES AUSTRALIA 30, STORYTELLER PRODUCTIONS 34
Brazil: IMAGE BANK / BRAZIL 40, NOVA IMAGENS / FABULOUS FOOTAGE 41
Canada: CANADIAN BROADCASTING CORPORATION (CBC) 44, FABULOUS FOOTAGE 49, IMAGE BANK / CANADA 51, JACK CHISHOLM FILM PRODUCTIONS 53, QUALICUM FILM PRODUCTIONS 57, ROBERT BOCKING PRODUCTIONS 58
Chile: FOTOBANCO INTERNATIONAL / FABULOUS FOOTAGE 62, IMAGE BANK / CHILE 63
Colombia: IMAGE BANK / COLOMBIA (ARCHIVO FOTOGRAFICO LTDA.) 66
Hong Kong: IMAGE BANK / HONG KONG 77
Indonesia: IMAGE BANK / INDONESIA (CREATIVE RESOURCES) 82, P.T. KREASIVIDEO HEDKWARTER MAS / FABULOUS FOOTAGE 84
Israel: ENERGY PRODUCTIONS ISRAEL / VISUAL ENERGY 88, IMAGE BANK / ISRAEL (IMAGE MAR'OT LTD.) 89

Japan: AD HOC / FABULOUS FOOTAGE 95, ENERGY PRODUCTIONS TOKYO / IMAGICA CORP. 97, FRONT LINE 98, IMAGE BANK / JAPAN 99

Kenya: CAMERAPIX 104

Korea: IMAGE BANK / KOREA 107

Malaysia: IMAGE BANK / MALAYSIA 113, IMAGES OF THE EAST 114, VIDEO HEADQUARTERS (KL) / FABULOUS FOOTAGE 117

Mexico: BANCO INTERNATIONAL DE FOTOGRAFIA (BIF) / FABULOUS FOOTAGE 122

New Zealand: NEW ZEALAND TELEVISION ARCHIVE 127

Philippines: IMAGE BANK / PHILIPPINES 131, VHQ DIMENSIONS / FABULOUS FOOTAGE 133

Singapore: IMAGE BANK / SINGAPORE (ASIA CREATIVE RESOURCES) 137, VIDEO HEADQUARTERS / FABULOUS FOOTAGE 138

South Africa: IMAGE BANK / SOUTH AFRICA 140, PAUL ZWICK PRODUCTIONS 141, STOCK OPTIONS 143

Taiwan, Republic of China: IMAGE BANK / TAIWAN (HARVARD MANAGEMENT SERVICES) 148

Thailand: IMAGE BANK / THAILAND 150

Turkey: ENERGY PRODUCTIONS ISTANBUL 154, IMAGE BANK / TURKEY (TRANSIMAJ MAR'OT LTD) 155

USA: ACTION SPORTS ADVENTURE (ASA) 160, AL GIDDINGS – IMAGES UNLIMITED 162, CINEMA NETWORK (CINENET) 178, COE FILM ASSOCIATES 180, ENERGY PRODUCTIONS' TIMESCAPE IMAGE LIBRARY 186, FABULOUS FOOTAGE BOSTON 188, FILM & VIDEO STOCK SHOTS 189, FILM BANK STOCK FOOTAGE FILM & VIDEO LIBRARY 190, IMAGE BANK / FILM DIVISION 201, NBC NEWS ARCHIVES 221, NEW YORK ZOOLOGICAL SOCIETY 223, PLANET PICTURES 232, PYRAMID FILM & VIDEO 235, SECOND LINE SEARCH 238, SOURCE STOCK FOOTAGE LIBRARY, THE 240, STUART JEWELL PRODUCTIONS 246, THOMAS HORTON ASSOCIATES 248, WGBH FILM & VIDEO RESOURCE CENTER 257, WPA FILM LIBRARY 261

New York
  USA: PORT AUTHORITY OF NEW YORK AND NEW JERSEY 233
News
  USA: FILM BANK STOCK FOOTAGE FILM & VIDEO LIBRARY 190
Newsreels
  Argentina: FUNDACION CINEMATECA ARGENTINA 6
  Australia: FILM WORLD 16
  Canada: JACK CHISHOLM FILM PRODUCTIONS 53
  Israel: STEVEN SPIELBERG JEWISH FILM ARCHIVE 92, UNITED STUDIOS OF ISRAEL 93
  Japan: ARCHIVE FILMS JAPAN 96
  New Zealand: NEW ZEALAND FILM ARCHIVE 125, NEW ZEALAND TELEVISION ARCHIVE 127

USA: AMAZING IMAGES 165, ARCHIVE FILMS 167, A.R.I.Q. FOOTAGE 169, BUDGET FILMS STOCK FOOTAGE 172, FRANKLIN D. ROOSEVELT LIBRARY 194, IMAGEWAYS 202, JOHN E. ALLEN 207, NEWSREEL VIDEO SERVICE 224, OPUS GLOBAL / THE ELECTRONIC LIBRARY 226, SHERMAN GRINBERG FILM LIBRARIES 239, STREAMLINE ARCHIVES 245, UCLA FILM & TELEVISION ARCHIVE RESEARCH & STUDY CENTER 252, UNIVERSITY OF SOUTH CAROLINA NEWSFILM LIBRARY 253, VIDEO TAPE LIBRARY 255, WORLDVIEW ENTERTAINMENT 259, WORLDWIDE TELEVISION NEWS (WTN) 260, WPA FILM LIBRARY 261

Nippon News
  Japan: NHK INTERNATIONAL 101
Olympics
  USA: ACTION SPORTS ADVENTURE (ASA) 160, BIG FIGHTS, THE 170
Out-takes
  USA: AMAZING IMAGES 165, PARAMOUNT PICTURES FILM LIBRARY 229, PETRIFIED FILMS / THE IMAGE BANK 230, SECOND LINE SEARCH 238, UNIVERSITY OF SOUTH CAROLINA NEWSFILM LIBRARY 253, VIDEO TAPE LIBRARY 255
Personalities
  Australia: HOLLYWOOD HOUSE VIDEO ARCHIVES / HOME ENTERTAINMENT HOLDINGS 19
  India: TIMES TELEVISION LIBRARY 81
  Mauritius: MAURITIUS BROADCASTING CORPORATION 120
  USA: AMAZING IMAGES 165, HOLLYWOOD FILM REGISTRY 198, NBC NEWS ARCHIVES 221, SPECTRAL COMMUNICATIONS 241
Protests
  USA: ESTUARY PRESS 187
Public domain
  Canada: CHARLES CHAPLIN ENTERPRISES 46
  USA: EM GEE FILM LIBRARY 185, FILM/AUDIO SERVICES 191
Racism
  Australia: SPECIAL BROADCASTING SERVICE 33
Religion
  Mauritius: MAURITIUS BROADCASTING CORPORATION 120
  USA: ARCTURUS MOTION PICTURES 168, FILMS OF INDIA 192, NBC NEWS ARCHIVES 221
Russia
  Canada: CHARLES CHAPLIN ENTERPRISES 46
  USA: JOHN E. ALLEN 207
Sailing
  USA: MERKEL FILMS ACTION SPORTS LIBRARY 216, MYSTIC SEAPORT MUSEUM 218, WILLIAM G. BEAL 258
Science
  Australia: BEYOND INFORMATION SERVICES 9, NOMAD FILMS INTERNATIONAL 26
  Canada: GREAT NORTH RELEASING 50, JACK CHISHOLM FILM PRODUCTIONS 53, OASIS PICTURES 55
  India: TIMES TELEVISION LIBRARY 81
  Sri Lanka: SRI LANKA NATIONAL LIBRARY SERVICES BOARD 144

USA: FILM BANK STOCK FOOTAGE FILM & VIDEO LIBRARY 190, STIMULUS / IMAGE RESEARCH 243, WGBH FILM & VIDEO RESOURCE CENTER 257

Skylines
USA: BROAD STREET PRODUCTIONS 171, PARAMOUNT PICTURES FILM LIBRARY 229

Social history
Israel: DOKO VIDEO 87
Sri Lanka: SRI LANKA NATIONAL LIBRARY SERVICES BOARD 144
USA: NBC NEWS ARCHIVES 221

South Africa
South Africa: SOUTH AFRICAN NATIONAL FILM VIDEO & SOUND ARCHIVES 142

Space
Argentina: FOCUS STOCK FOTOGRAFICO / FABULOUS FOOTAGE 5
Australia: HOLLYWOOD HOUSE VIDEO ARCHIVES / HOME ENTERTAINMENT HOLDINGS 19
Brazil: NOVA IMAGENS / FABULOUS FOOTAGE 41
Canada: FABULOUS FOOTAGE 49
Chile: FOTOBANCO INTERNATIONAL / FABULOUS FOOTAGE 62
Indonesia: P.T. KREASIVIDEO HEDKWARTER MAS / FABULOUS FOOTAGE 84
Japan: AD HOC / FABULOUS FOOTAGE 95, FRONT LINE 98
Malaysia: IMAGES OF THE EAST 114, VIDEO HEADQUARTERS (KL) / FABULOUS FOOTAGE 117
Mexico: BANCO INTERNATIONAL DE FOTOGRAFIA (BIF) / FABULOUS FOOTAGE 122
Philippines: VHQ DIMENSIONS / FABULOUS FOOTAGE 133
Singapore: VIDEO HEADQUARTERS / FABULOUS FOOTAGE 138
USA: A.R.I.Q. FOOTAGE 169, FABULOUS FOOTAGE BOSTON 188, FILM BANK STOCK FOOTAGE FILM & VIDEO LIBRARY 190, KESSER STOCK LIBRARY 209, LARRY DORN ASSOCIATES / WORLD BACKGROUNDS 213, STIMULUS / IMAGE RESEARCH 243

Special effects
Australia: SELECT EFFECTS - AUSTRALIA 32
Israel: ENERGY PRODUCTIONS ISRAEL / VISUAL ENERGY 88
Japan: ENERGY PRODUCTIONS TOKYO / IMAGICA CORP. 97
Turkey: ENERGY PRODUCTIONS ISTANBUL 154
USA: CASCOM INTERNATIONAL 176, DARINO FILMS 182, ENERGY PRODUCTIONS' TIMESCAPE IMAGE LIBRARY 186, FILM BANK STOCK FOOTAGE FILM & VIDEO LIBRARY 190, STIMULUS / IMAGE RESEARCH 243

Sport
Argentina: IMAGE BANK / ARGENTINA 7
Australia: AUSTRALIAN BROADCASTING CORPORATION (ABC) 8, IMAGE BANK / AUSTRALIA 20, M.C. STUART & ASSOCIATES (MSCAA) 21, SPECIAL BROADCASTING SERVICE 33
Brazil: IMAGE BANK / BRAZIL 40
Canada: GREAT NORTH RELEASING 50, IMAGE BANK / CANADA 51
Chile: IMAGE BANK / CHILE 63

Colombia: IMAGE BANK / COLOMBIA (ARCHIVO FOTOGRAFICO LTDA.) 66

Hong Kong: IMAGE BANK / HONG KONG 77

India: TIMES TELEVISION LIBRARY 81

Indonesia: IMAGE BANK / INDONESIA (CREATIVE RESOURCES) 82

Israel: ENERGY PRODUCTIONS ISRAEL / VISUAL ENERGY 88, IMAGE BANK / ISRAEL (IMAGE MAR'OT LTD.) 89

Japan: ENERGY PRODUCTIONS TOKYO / IMAGICA CORP. 97, IMAGE BANK / JAPAN 99, NHK INTERNATIONAL 101

Korea: IMAGE BANK / KOREA 107

Malaysia: IMAGE BANK / MALAYSIA 113

Mauritius: MAURITIUS BROADCASTING CORPORATION 120

Philippines: IMAGE BANK / PHILIPPINES 131

Singapore: IMAGE BANK / SINGAPORE (ASIA CREATIVE RESOURCES) 137

South Africa: IMAGE BANK / SOUTH AFRICA 140

Taiwan, Republic of China: IMAGE BANK / TAIWAN (HARVARD MANAGEMENT SERVICES) 148

Thailand: IMAGE BANK / THAILAND 150

Turkey: ENERGY PRODUCTIONS ISTANBUL 154, IMAGE BANK / TURKEY (TRANSIMAJ MAR'OT LTD) 155

USA: ACTION SPORTS ADVENTURE (ASA) 160, AMATEUR ATHLETIC FOUNDATION LIBRARY 164, CINEMA NETWORK (CINENET) 178, ENERGY PRODUCTIONS' TIMESCAPE IMAGE LIBRARY 186, FILM BANK STOCK FOOTAGE FILM & VIDEO LIBRARY 190, IMAGE BANK / FILM DIVISION 201, PYRAMID FILM & VIDEO 235, SECOND LINE SEARCH 238, SPORTS CINEMATOGRAPHY GROUP 242, STREAMLINE ARCHIVES 245, VIDEO TAPE LIBRARY 255, WORLDWIDE TELEVISION NEWS (WTN) 260, ZIELINSKI PRODUCTIONS 262

Zambia: ZAMBIA NATIONAL BROADCASTING CORPORATION 265

Sports

Canada: CARLETON PRODUCTIONS 45

Steam trains

USA: STUART JEWELL PRODUCTIONS 246

Stock shots

Argentina: FOCUS STOCK FOTOGRAFICO / FABULOUS FOOTAGE 5, IMAGE BANK / ARGENTINA 7

Australia: AUSTRALIAN BROADCASTING CORPORATION (ABC) 8, IMAGE BANK / AUSTRALIA 20, OLIVER FILMS 28

Brazil: IMAGE BANK / BRAZIL 40, NOVA IMAGENS / FABULOUS FOOTAGE 41

Canada: CANADIAN BROADCASTING CORPORATION (CBC) 44, FABULOUS FOOTAGE 49, IMAGE BANK / CANADA 51, IMAGES PIXART 52, JACK CHISHOLM FILM PRODUCTIONS 53, SOCIETE RADIO-CANADA 59

Chile: FOTOBANCO INTERNATIONAL / FABULOUS FOOTAGE 62, IMAGE BANK / CHILE 63

Colombia: IMAGE BANK / COLOMBIA (ARCHIVO FOTOGRAFICO LTDA.) 66

Hong Kong: IMAGE BANK / HONG KONG 77

Time-lapse
   Argentina: IMAGE BANK / ARGENTINA 7
   Australia: IMAGE BANK / AUSTRALIA 20, SELECT EFFECTS - AUSTRALIA 32
   Brazil: IMAGE BANK / BRAZIL 40
   Canada: IMAGE BANK / CANADA 51, JACK CHISHOLM FILM PRODUCTIONS 53
   Chile: IMAGE BANK / CHILE 63
   Colombia: IMAGE BANK / COLOMBIA (ARCHIVO FOTOGRAFICO LTDA.) 66
   Hong Kong: IMAGE BANK / HONG KONG 77
   Indonesia: IMAGE BANK / INDONESIA (CREATIVE RESOURCES) 82
   Israel: ENERGY PRODUCTIONS ISRAEL / VISUAL ENERGY 88, IMAGE BANK / ISRAEL (IMAGE MAR'OT LTD.) 89
   Japan: ENERGY PRODUCTIONS TOKYO / IMAGICA CORP. 97, FRONT LINE 98, IMAGE BANK / JAPAN 99
   Korea: IMAGE BANK / KOREA 107
   Malaysia: IMAGE BANK / MALAYSIA 113, IMAGES OF THE EAST 114
   Philippines: IMAGE BANK / PHILIPPINES 131
   Singapore: IMAGE BANK / SINGAPORE (ASIA CREATIVE RESOURCES) 137
   South Africa: IMAGE BANK / SOUTH AFRICA 140
   Taiwan, Republic of China: IMAGE BANK / TAIWAN (HARVARD MANAGEMENT SERVICES) 148
   Thailand: IMAGE BANK / THAILAND 150
   Turkey: ENERGY PRODUCTIONS ISTANBUL 154, IMAGE BANK / TURKEY (TRANSIMAJ MAR'OT LTD) 155
   USA: CASCOM INTERNATIONAL 176, CINEMA NETWORK (CINENET) 178, ENERGY PRODUCTIONS' TIMESCAPE IMAGE LIBRARY 186, FILM & VIDEO STOCK SHOTS 189, FILM BANK STOCK FOOTAGE FILM & VIDEO LIBRARY 190, FISH FILMS FOOTAGE WORLD 193, IMAGE BANK / FILM DIVISION 201, KESSER STOCK LIBRARY 209, OPUS GLOBAL / THE ELECTRONIC LIBRARY 226, PLANET PICTURES 232, SECOND LINE SEARCH 238, SOURCE STOCK FOOTAGE LIBRARY, THE 240, STUART JEWELL PRODUCTIONS 246, TELECINE INTERNATIONAL PRODUCTIONS 247
Tourism
   Australia: DELTA PRODUCTIONS 13, FILM WORLD 16
   Tanzania: AUDIO VISUAL INSTITUTE, NATIONAL LIBRARY & ARCHIVE 149
Trailers
   Argentina: FOCUS STOCK FOTOGRAFICO / FABULOUS FOOTAGE 5
   Brazil: NOVA IMAGENS / FABULOUS FOOTAGE 41
   Canada: FABULOUS FOOTAGE 49
   Chile: FOTOBANCO INTERNATIONAL / FABULOUS FOOTAGE 62
   Indonesia: P.T. KREASIVIDEO HEDKWARTER MAS / FABULOUS FOOTAGE 84
   Japan: AD HOC / FABULOUS FOOTAGE 95

Vietnam War
  USA: ESTUARY PRESS 187
War
  Australia: HOLLYWOOD HOUSE VIDEO ARCHIVES / HOME
  ENTERTAINMENT HOLDINGS 19
  Canada: VILLON FILMS 60
  Israel: DOKO VIDEO 87, SHOVAL FILM PRODUCTION 91, UNITED
  STUDIOS OF ISRAEL 93
  USA: JOHN E. ALLEN 207, NORTHSTAR PRODUCTIONS 225,
  PETRIFIED FILMS / THE IMAGE BANK 230
Westerns
  USA: EM GEE FILM LIBRARY 185

SOURCE INDEX

CENTRE DES ARCHIVES NATIONALES (Algeria) 3
CHANNEL 10 NEWS LIBRARY (Australia) 11
CHARLES CHAPLIN ENTERPRISES (Canada) 46
CHINA RECORD CORPORATION (China, People's Republic of) 64
CINAR (Canada) 47
CINEMA NETWORK (CINENET) (USA) 178
CINEMATECA BOLIVIANA (Bolivia) 37
CINEMATECA DE CUBA (Cuba) 71
CINEMATECA NACIONAL DE ANGOLA (Angola) 4
CINEMATECA NACIONAL DEL ECUADOR (Ecuador) 73
CNN LIBRARY TAPE SALES (USA) 179
COE FILM ASSOCIATES (USA) 180
COLUMBIA PICTURES / COLUMBIA TRISTAR INTERNATIONAL (USA)
181
CVA FILM & TELEVISION (Australia) 12
DARINO FILMS (USA) 182
DELTA PRODUCTIONS (Australia) 13
DICK WALLEN PRODUCTIONS (USA) 183
DIRECCION GENERAL DEL ARCHIVO NATIONAL DE COSTA RICA
(Costa Rica) 70
DOKO VIDEO (Israel) 87
DOOMSDAY STUDIOS (Canada) 48
DOWNTOWN COMMUNITY TELEVISION (USA) 184
EM GEE FILM LIBRARY (USA) 185
ENERGY PRODUCTIONS ISRAEL / VISUAL ENERGY (Israel) 88
ENERGY PRODUCTIONS ISTANBUL (Turkey) 154
ENERGY PRODUCTIONS' TIMESCAPE IMAGE LIBRARY (USA) 186
ENERGY PRODUCTIONS TOKYO / IMAGICA CORP. (Japan) 97
ESTUARY PRESS (USA) 187
FABULOUS FOOTAGE (Canada) 49
FABULOUS FOOTAGE BOSTON (USA) 188
FEDERAL UNIVERSITY OF TECHNOLOGY, AKURE LIBRARY (Nigeria)
128
FILM & TELEVISION INSTITUTE (WA) (Australia) 14
FILM & VIDEO STOCK SHOTS (USA) 189
FILM BANK STOCK FOOTAGE FILM & VIDEO LIBRARY (USA) 190
FILM STOCK RESEARCH AUSTRALIA (Australia) 15
FILM WORLD (Australia) 16
FILM/AUDIO SERVICES (USA) 191
FILMS OF INDIA (USA) 192
FILMSEARCH AUSTRALASIA (Australia) 17
FISH FILMS FOOTAGE WORLD (USA) 193
FOCUS STOCK FOTOGRAFICO / FABULOUS FOOTAGE (Argentina) 5
FOTOBANCO INTERNATIONAL / FABULOUS FOOTAGE (Chile) 62
FRANKLIN D. ROOSEVELT LIBRARY (USA) 194
FRONT LINE (Japan) 98
FRONTLINE VIDEO & FILM (USA) 195
FUNDACION CINEMATECA ARGENTINA (Argentina) 6
FUNDACION PATRIMONIO FILMICO COLOMBIANO (Colombia) 65
GLOBAL VILLAGE STOCK FOOTAGE LIBRARY (USA) 196
GREAT NORTH RELEASING (Canada) 50
HIPS FILM & VIDEO PRODUCTIONS (Australia) 18
HISTORIC THOROUGHBRED COLLECTIONS (USA) 197

PLACES INDEX

Rio De Janeiro: ARQUIVO NACIONAL (AUDIOVISUAL AND CARTOGRAPHIC DIVISION) 39
Sao Paulo: NOVA IMAGENS / FABULOUS FOOTAGE 41
Brunei
Bandar Seri Begawan: RADIO TELEVISION BRUNEI 42
Brunei Darussalam
Darussalam: BRUNEI NATIONAL ARCHIVES 43
Canada
11523-100 Avenue: GREAT NORTH RELEASING 50
19 Mercer Street: FABULOUS FOOTAGE 49
40 Eglinton East: IMAGE BANK / CANADA 51
99 Atlantic Avenue: JACK CHISHOLM FILM PRODUCTIONS 53
Downsview: ROBERT BOCKING PRODUCTIONS 58
Montreal: CINAR 47, IMAGES PIXART 52, SOCIETE RADIO-CANADA 59
Ottawa: CARLETON PRODUCTIONS 45, DOOMSDAY STUDIOS 48, NATIONAL ARCHIVES OF CANADA 54
Qualicum Beach: QUALICUM FILM PRODUCTIONS 57
Station A: CANADIAN BROADCASTING CORPORATION (CBC) 44
Toronto: CHARLES CHAPLIN ENTERPRISES 46, OASIS PICTURES 55, PARAMOUNT PICTURES / CANADA 56
Vancouver, BC: VILLON FILMS 60
Chile
Clasificador 1400, Santiago: BIBLIOTECA NACIONAL DE CHILE 61
Off 1103, Providencia: FOTOBANCO INTERNATIONAL / FABULOUS FOOTAGE 62
Providencia: IMAGE BANK / CHILE 63
China, People's Republic of
Beijing: CHINA RECORD CORPORATION 64
Colombia
Medellin: UNIVERSIDAD DE ANTIOQUIA 68
No. 11-37 Of. 213: IMAGE BANK / COLOMBIA (ARCHIVO FOTOGRAFICO LTDA.) 66
Santafe de Bogota DC: RCN TELEVISION DE COLOMBIA 67
Sante Fe De Bogota: FUNDACION PATRIMONIO FILMICO COLOMBIANO 65
Congo
Brazzaville: BIBLIOTHEQUE NATIONALE DU CONGO 69
Costa Rica
San Jose: DIRECCION GENERAL DEL ARCHIVO NATIONAL DE COSTA RICA 70
Cuba
10300 La Habana 4: CINEMATECA DE CUBA 71
1155 Vedado: ICAIC 72
Ecuador
Quito: CINEMATECA NACIONAL DEL ECUADOR 73
Fiji
Suva: LIBRARY SERVICE OF FIJI 74
Guinea, Republic of
Conakry: ARCHIVES DE LA RADIO TELEVISION GUINEENNE 75
Guinea-Bissau
P.O. Box 112, Bissau: INSTITUTO NACIONAL DE ESTUDOS E PESQUISAS (INEP) 76

Lesotho
  Maseru: LESOTHO GOVERNMENT ARCHIVES 111
Malawi
  Zomba: NATIONAL ARCHIVES OF MALAWI 112
Malaysia
  11A Jalan Tandang: SISTEM TELEVISYEN MALAYSIA BERHAD 116
  Bukit Damansara, Kuala Lumpur: VIDEO HEADQUARTERS (KL) /
  FABULOUS FOOTAGE 117
  Damansara Heights: IMAGE BANK / MALAYSIA 113
  Kuala Lumpur: NATIONAL ARCHIVES OF MALAYSIA 115
  Petaling Jaya Selangor: IMAGES OF THE EAST 114
Malta
  Valletta: PUBLIC BROADCASTING SERVICES 118
Marshall Islands
  Majuro: MUSEUM OF THE MARSHALL ISLANDS 119
Mauritius
  Forest Side: MAURITIUS BROADCASTING CORPORATION 120
Mexico
  24 esq. Calle 1: BANCO INTERNATIONAL DE FOTOGRAFIA (BIF) /
  FABULOUS FOOTAGE 122
  Mexico 1, D.F.: ARCHIVO GENERAL DE LA NACION 121
Namibia
  Windhoek: NATIONAL ARCHIVES OF NAMIBIA 123
New Zealand
  Auckland: KIDS TV 124, NEW ZEALAND TELEVISION ARCHIVE
  127
  Wellington: NEW ZEALAND FILM ARCHIVE 125, NEW ZEALAND
  FILM COMMISSION 126
Nigeria
  Akure: FEDERAL UNIVERSITY OF TECHNOLOGY, AKURE LIBRARY
  128
Papua New Guinea
  Boroko: NATIONAL LIBRARY OF PAPUA NEW GUINEA 129
Peru
  Lima: NATIONAL ARCHIVES OF PERU 130
Philippines
  One Corporate Plaza: VHQ DIMENSIONS / FABULOUS FOOTAGE
  133
  Quezon City: UNIVERSITY OF THE PHILIPPINES FILM CENTER
  ARCHIVES 132
  Velero Street, Cor HV dela Costa Street: IMAGE BANK /
  PHILIPPINES 131
Saudi Arabia
  Riyadh: KING SAUD UNIVERSITY LIBRARIES 134
Seychelles, Republic of
  Hermitage: SEYCHELLES BROADCASTING CORPORATION (SBC)
  136
  Mahe: NATIONAL ARCHIVES AND MUSEUMS - SEYCHELLES 135
Singapore, VIDEO HEADQUARTERS / FABULOUS FOOTAGE 138
  15 Beach Road, : IMAGE BANK / SINGAPORE (ASIA CREATIVE
  RESOURCES) 137
Solomon Islands
  Honiara: NATIONAL ARCHIVES OF SOLOMON ISLANDS 139

6924 Canby Avenue: EM GEE FILM LIBRARY 185
7850 Slater Avenue: ZIELINSKI PRODUCTIONS 262
86th North: PORT AUTHORITY OF NEW YORK AND NEW JERSEY 233
Anaheim: ORIGINAL FILMVIDEO LIBRARY 227
Binghamton: CAE-LINK CORPORATION 174
Boston: WGBH FILM & VIDEO RESOURCE CENTER 257
Bronx: NEW YORK ZOOLOGICAL SOCIETY 223
Burbank: FILM BANK STOCK FOOTAGE FILM & VIDEO LIBRARY 190
Carpinteria: MERKEL FILMS ACTION SPORTS LIBRARY 216
Chapel Hill: MARINE GRAFICS 215
Charlotte: IVY CLASSICS 206
Columbia: UNIVERSITY OF SOUTH CAROLINA NEWSFILM LIBRARY 253
Costa Mesa: STUART JEWELL PRODUCTIONS 246
Culver City: COLUMBIA PICTURES / COLUMBIA TRISTAR INTERNATIONAL 181
Del Mar: FRONTLINE VIDEO & FILM 195
East Hampton: A.R.I.Q. FOOTAGE 169
Escondido: DICK WALLEN PRODUCTIONS 183
Hawthorne: PHOTO-CHUTING ENTERPRISES 231
Hollywood: HOLLYWOOD FILM REGISTRY 198, OPUS GLOBAL / THE ELECTRONIC LIBRARY 226, PARAMOUNT PICTURES 228, PRODUCERS LIBRARY SERVICE 234
Hyde Park: FRANKLIN D. ROOSEVELT LIBRARY 194
Kansas City: CABLE FILMS & VIDEO 173
Los Angeles: AMATEUR ATHLETIC FOUNDATION LIBRARY 164, BUDGET FILMS STOCK FOOTAGE 172, FILMS OF INDIA 192, NATIONAL CENTER FOR FILM AND VIDEO PRESERVATION 220, PLANET PICTURES 232, TWENTIETH CENTURY FOX 251
Malibu: ACTION SPORTS / SCOTT DITTRICH FILMS 159
Miami: KESSER STOCK LIBRARY 209
Mystic: MYSTIC SEAPORT MUSEUM 218
N. Hollywood: CAMEO FILM LIBRARY 175
Nashville: CASCOM INTERNATIONAL 176
New York: ACTION SPORTS ADVENTURE (ASA) 160, ARCHIVE FILMS 167, BIG FIGHTS, THE 170, BROAD STREET PRODUCTIONS 171, CBS NEWS ARCHIVES 177, COE FILM ASSOCIATES 180, DARINO FILMS 182, DOWNTOWN COMMUNITY TELEVISION 184, HOT SHOTS COOL CUTS 199, ICARUS FILMS INTERNATIONAL 200, INTERNATIONAL MEDIA RESOURCE EXCHANGE 204, JUDSON ROSEBUSH COMPANY 208, NBC NEWS ARCHIVES 221, RICHTER PRODUCTIONS 236, SECOND LINE SEARCH 238, SHERMAN GRINBERG FILM LIBRARIES 239, WORLDVIEW ENTERTAINMENT 259, WORLDWIDE TELEVISION NEWS (WTN) 260
Newton: ARCTURUS MOTION PICTURES 168
Oak Forest: WPA FILM LIBRARY 261
Oakland: AL GIDDINGS - IMAGES UNLIMITED 162
Ojai: THOMAS HORTON ASSOCIATES 248
One CNN Center: CNN LIBRARY TAPE SALES 179
Pacoima: AIRLINE FILM & TV PROMOTIONS 161